LYNN STEPHEN

WOMEN AND
SOCIAL MOVEMENTS
IN LATIN AMERICA
POWER FROM BELOW

University of Texas Press
Austin

First edition, 1997

Requests for permission to reproduce material
from this work should be sent to:
Permissions
University of Texas Press
Box 7819
Austin, TX 78713-7819

Permission to reprint previously published materials is gratefully acknowledged:
  Approximately 3 pages from *Neoliberalism Revisited: Economic Restructuring and Mexico's Political Future* by Gerardo Otero. Copyright © 1996 by Westview Press. Reprinted by permission of Westview Press.
  "Women's Rights Are Human Rights: The Merging of Feminine and Feminist Interests among El Salvador's Mothers of the Disappeared (CO-MADRES)" by Lynn Stephen. Reprinted by permission of the American Anthropological Association from *American Ethnologist* 22:4, November 1995. Not for further reproduction.
  "Challenging Gender Inequality and Grassroots Organizing among Women Rural Workers in Brazil and Chile" by Lynn Stephen. Reprinted by permission of Sage Publications from *Critique of Anthropology* 13, No. 1, pp. 33–35.

♾ The paper used in this publication meets the minimum requirements of American National Standard for Information Sciences—Permanence of Paper for Printed Library Materials, ANSI Z 39.48–1984.

Library of Congress Cataloging-in-Publication Data

Stephen, Lynn.
    Women and social movements in Latin America : power from below /
by Lynn Stephen. — 1st ed.
        p.   cm.
    Includes bibliographical references and index.
    ISBN 0-292-77715-9 (alk. paper). — ISBN 0-292-77716-7 (pbk. : alk. paper)
    1. Women in development—Latin America—Case studies. 2. Social
movements—Latin America—Case studies. 3. Feminism—Latin America—
Case studies. 4. Women's rights—Latin America—Case studies.
5. Women—Latin America—Interviews. I. Title.
HQ1240.5.L29S74 1997
305.42'098—dc20   96-45788

This book is dedicated to Guadalupe Musalem M. (1955–1995) in memory of her activism and dedication to improving the lives of women in Mexico, to Lucina Cárdenas (1945–1995) who fought to empower indigenous women, and to my son Gabriel Stephen-Herman who will grow up to be a man in the better world Guadalupe and Lucina helped to create.

CONTENTS

ILLUSTRATIONS

PREFACE

Most of the fieldwork this book is based on comes out of collaborative research with grassroots activists and with other researchers. Most of these people are specifically named in the acknowledgments that follow this preface.

From 1990 until 1992 I worked with the political scientist Jonathan Fox on an interdisciplinary and team-based research project concerning issues of democratization in grassroots movements. We collaborated with anthropologists, sociologists, and political scientists in Mexico, Brazil, and Chile to study rural grassroots movements, focusing on political culture, the internal relationships and divisions of movements, issues of accountability between leadership and base, and the ways in which movement participants related to other movements, nongovernmental organizations, and state-based institutions. Gender was one of the pivotal categories of difference we looked at within and between movements.

During 1990 and 1991 I made two trips to Brazil and one to Chile, spending time with members of the Rural Women Workers' Movement (MMTR) in Brazil, and the Interindustry Union of Seasonal and Permanent Workers of Santa María, Chile. Data gathered during these trips included interviews, life histories, observations of meetings, and collection of organizational documents. In Brazil, movement activists participated in all aspects of the research, including selection of initial questions for investigation, gathering of data, review of the results, and putting together the final products. The results were presented in a variety of forms—brochures, photographs, videos, movement histories, and an edited book in Portuguese.

In December of 1990 I gathered data in Nayarit, Mexico, on the Women's Council of the Lázaro Cárdenas Ejidos Union (UELC). The chapter on the Women's Regional Council of the National Council of the Urban Popular Movement (CONAMUP) in central Mexico derives from research carried out in the late 1980s and was updated after a brief field trip in late 1994.

The two chapters on Salvadoran women's organizations, including CO-MADRES (Mothers and Relatives of the Political Prisoners, Disappeared, and Assassinated of El Salvador "Monseñor Romero") and DIGNAS (Women for Dignity and Life), came out of a research trip to El Salvador in 1991 to interview women in seven grassroots movements. I collected extensive testimony from CO-MADRES members and met with women from DIGNAS. I continued to interview and work with women from both organizations when they visited the United States.

One of the products from my research in El Salvador—a testimonial book done with María Teresa Tula and titled *Hear My Testimony: María Teresa Tula, Human Rights Activist of El Salvador*, first published in English (Stephen 1994a)—has now been published in Spanish and is being distributed in El Salvador and elsewhere in Latin America. The translation was done by a team of Salvadorans. María worked with her children to review every word of the translated manuscript. In this case, it was clear from the beginning that the product of María's collaboration with my research could not be directed solely toward a North American market, but also had to be packaged in an accessible form for Salvadorans. The work of Sheila Kraybill and Maria Morelli in transcribing the original Spanish-language interview is gratefully acknowledged.

In Mexico, the work done with the Agro-Industrial Units for Woman (UAIM) in Nayarit was part of a larger research project on the history of the Unión de Ejidos "Lázaro Cárdenas" which involved the creation of a wide range of research products including comic books and pamphlets. In Mexico as well as in El Salvador and Brazil, many of the written transcripts from interviews conducted with women were returned to them as organizational resources.

Working with grassroots activists from Latin America, I have learned that the elements of my experience and skills which are of most interest to the women I worked with are, first, my experience as a political activist in the United States and, second, the range of resources and information I have been able to utilize in my research on women's organizations in diverse parts of Latin America. In fact, my access to women activists in El Salvador and, more recently, in Mexico has been made possible largely because of my political activism.

For the past five years I have belonged to a women's solidarity organization in Boston called Mujeres sin Fronteras/Women across Borders. We have engaged in educational, technical, and political exchanges with other women's organizations. We have also organized conferences and meetings between North American and (for the most part) Central American and Mexican women, sending delegations to Latin America and sponsoring visits of Latin American women to the United States. Finally, we have provided small amounts of financial support for women's organizations in Latin America.

In the process of carrying out educational and political work, I have developed important relationships with women activists, some of whom are featured in this book. Mutual concerns (though experienced in different ways) about capitalist development and U.S. foreign policy, domestic battering and rape as well as the experiences we shared as activists on the left shaped our encounters and exchanges and continue to do so. This exchange of experience has proven to be quite valuable.

In my work with the women discussed in this book, the questioning of unequal relations of power has been central. While issues of inequality linked through gender informed the research, our different experiences of doing political work to contest inequality and marginality were equally important. Their work is well documented. Mine has focused on anti-intervention, divestiture in South Africa, gay and lesbian rights, building coalitions that link feminism and the fight against racism, and solidarity work in Central America and Mexico, both generally and specifically with women. Our mutual interest in contesting some of the relations of power that bind us together in a global political economy provides an important answer as to why we worked together with different results, expectations, and consequences.

cardo was also a wonderful tour guide. Cândido Grzybowski and his wife, Lourdes, were gracious hosts in Rio, and Cândido provided background information, contacts, and constant encouragement. Fatima Vianna Mello also provided helpful background and interesting discussions in Rio. Many women in the MMTR were extremely helpful to me as well as to others who worked with the movement. Gessi Bonês and Marlene Pasquali, leaders of the MMTR, were outstanding in their efforts to include me in discussions and meetings. Our relationship and exchanges have meant a great deal to me.

My work in El Salvador grew out of the testimonial project I developed with María Teresa Tula. In the fall of 1991 I traveled to El Salvador to understand María's life and to get to know the CO-MADRES. I want particularly to thank Alicia Panameño de García and Sofía Escamillas of the CO-MADRES for the long hours they spent talking with me. In El Salvador I worked with the anthropologist Kelley Ready, who was a wonderful coworker and taught me much of what I know about women's movements in that country. She also provided tremendous help in establishing contact with many different women's organizations in El Salvador. During that trip I also met Serena Cosgrove, who later came to work with me at Northeastern University. Serena has been a terrific friend and colleague. She has transcribed tapes for this book and has also given generous amounts of her time discussing the state of women's organizing in El Salvador and supplying me with a never-ending stream of popular publications from women's groups. Morena Herrera and Gloria Castañeda of DIGNAS (Women for Dignity and Life) have been intellectual guideposts in my understanding of Salvadoran feminism and have given freely of their time and thoughts. We also share the organizing experience of bringing two women to Boston from the central planning committee of the Sexto Encuentro Feminista which took place in El Salvador in 1993. I also acknowledge the collaboration of Gudelia Abrego, Cecilia Masín, Pacita Rosales, Susana Rodríguez, Margarita Jiménez, Alba América Guirola Zelaya, Oralia de Rivas, and Mercedes Cañas in El Salvador. Finally, my friendship with María Teresa Tula has been critical not only to my understanding of women's organizing in El Salvador, but also to my awareness of how, why, and with what vision women everywhere engage in grassroots organizing. Our work in El Salvador and on the testimonial we produced together was generously supported by Genevieve Vaughn and the Foundation for a Compassionate Society.

In Nayarit, Mexico, I benefited from previous work carried out there by Luis Hernández, Pilar López, Milagros Camarena, and Jonathan Fox on the Unión de Ejidos "Lázaro Cárdenas" (UELC). Milagros Camarena provided useful, up-to-date information as well as introductions to many women. Pilar López was a fantastic partner in the field in Nayarit and has been the source of many important exchanges and insights. Esmeralda Avalos, a leader in the Women's Council of the UELC, gave unselfishly of her time and provided us with an introduction to the region and to many of the UAIMs participating in the Women's Council. Many members of the Women's Council as well as men from the UELC also provided valuable information and insights. Emiterio Silva Valerio was an excellent guide to the region. His interest and generosity in providing transportation were a tremendous help. In 1995, Horacia Fajardo and Magdalena Villarreal made a quick visit to the Women's Council of the UELC to provide an update. Their insightful field notes and discussions have proven to be very important.

In Mexico City, Gloria Tello, Carmen Martínez Flores, Irene Soto, and Eugenia Flores Hernández facilitated connections and provided valuable insights and information about the Women's Regional Organization of the CONAMUP. Norma Mogrovejo Aquiese, whom I met while giving a talk at CIESAS, Occidente (Centro de Investigación y Estudios Superiores en Antropología Social), Guadalajara, wrote a wonderful master's thesis on popular feminism in Mexico. Her unique work provided data and analyses of the relationship between feminist groups and grassroots organizations in Mexico City. It is an outstanding piece of research and proved essential to my conceptualization of the chapter on the CONAMUP.

The initial research support for fieldwork carried out in Mexico, Brazil, and Chile came from the Learning and Dissemination Office of the Inter-American Foundation. I received additional support for field research and writing from the Research and Scholarship Development Fund of Northeastern University (1991–1993), a Young Faculty Fellowship from the Project on Governance of Nonprofit Organizations at the Indiana University Center on Philanthropy (1991–1992), and a research award from The Whiting Foundation (1990–1991). The writing of the final draft of this book was supported by a sabbatical leave from Northeastern University in 1994–1995 and in part by a postdoctoral research fellowship from the Center for U.S.-Mexican Studies at the University of California–San Diego in 1995. Without the generous support of all these foundations and institutions I would not have been able to conduct the fieldwork or find the time to write this book.

Throughout the six years I have been researching and writing this book, exchanges with many friends and colleagues in the United States have been invaluable. Jeffrey Rubin, Christine Gailey, Deborah Kaufman, Michael Blim, David Myhre, Helga Baitenmann, Jane Hindley, Cynthia Peters, Mike Prokosh, Matthew Gutmann, Vivienne Bennett, Karen Sacks, and Norma Chinchilla all read portions of what was to become this book and gave me honest and valuable suggestions for how to improve it. Sonia Alvarez, Temma Kaplan, Arturo Escobar, and Neil Harvey provided important comments on oral presentations of this material and provided me with important insights into social movements theory. Anonymous reviewers for *American Ethnologist* provided useful suggestions for revision of the chapter on the CO-MADRES. June Nash, Fran Rothstein, and Florence Babb, who reviewed the manuscript for the University of Texas Press, proved invaluable in helping to make this a better book. My editor, Theresa May, supported this project from the beginning, and her enthusiasm and confidence in my work inspired me to complete it through a difficult time.

My close circle of friends in Oaxaca, Mexico, including Margarita Dalton, Julia Barco, Guadalupe Musalem, and the González family, nourished me and this book during my continued visits to Oaxaca and despite my distractions with research elsewhere. Kate Raisz, Lynn Tibbetts, Kate Dobroth, Janet Randall, Steve Birnbaum, Jenny Purnell, Petri Flint, and Eric Flint are all close friends in Boston who provided a lot of support and good times while I was working on this project. My parents, Suzanne Brown and Jim Stephen, stood by me while I wrote this book and our relationships and friendships deepened even further as I too became a parent. My brother Bruce, his wife Rachel, and my nephews Ben and Jordan were a source of joy on weekends and holidays. Rebecca Herman, Bill Mack, and my niece Sara Mack Herman also shared in the spirit of activism embodied in this book.

Alejandro de Avila has shared so much with me and opened up our family to so many new people over the past five years that he may never know all the wonderful ways he has changed my life. Alice, Alejandro Sr., Lisa, and Marco de Avila, as well as Brian Bennett and my nephew Adrian, have all enriched my life.

Finally, Ellen Herman and Gabriel Stephen-Herman, my immediate family and soul mates, make each day special. We have grown together in the time of this book, and its completion reminds me of what a wonderful life we have together.

Women and
Social Movements
in Latin America

CHAPTER 1

Introduction
Gender and Politics,
Experience and Structure

Committing spoken words to paper is a translation of many dimensions. A primary aim of this book is to communicate by means of the written word the thoughts, ideas, experiences, and perceptions of women who have chosen to participate in collective action in four countries: Brazil, Chile, El Salvador, and Mexico. A second major goal is to provide readers with an understanding of the structural conditions and ideological discourses that set the context within which women act and interpret their experience. The cases of women's activism studied here include groups with an explicitly self-labeled feminist agenda as well as those that are struggling to improve the material circumstances under which they and their families live, but without explicitly declaring feminist loyalties. They include (1) the Committee of Mothers and Relatives of the Political Prisoners, Disappeared, and Assassinated of El Salvador "Monseñor Romero" (CO-MADRES), (2) Women for Dignity and Life (DIGNAS) in El Salvador, (3) The Women's Regional Council of the National Council of the Urban Popular Movement (CONAMUP) in central Mexico, (4) the Women's Council of the Lázaro Cárdenas Ejido Union (UELC) in Nayarit, Mexico, (5) the Rural Women Workers' Movement (MMTR) of southern Brazil, and (6) the Interindustry Union of Seasonal and Permanent Workers of Santa María, Chile (which hereafter is usually referred to as the Seasonal and Permanent Workers' Union or simply the Seasonal Workers' Union).

The six movements included here were not chosen to represent particular countries or even particular sectors such as "peasants," "the urban poor," or "the urban middle class." Many of these movements are heterogeneous in their composition and cannot be said to exclusively represent any particular constituency. They were chosen because the type of activism they represent, articulated by increasing numbers of

Nayarit
Women's Council of the UELC

Mexico City
Women's Regional Council
of the CONAMUP

San Salvador
CO-MADRES and DIGNAS

Santa María
Interindustry Union of Seasonal
and Permanent Workers

Rio Grande do Sul
MMTR

Map of Latin America showing locations of case studies.

women's organizations in Latin America, integrates a commitment to basic survival for women and their children with a challenge to the subordination of women to men. Their work challenges the assumption that the issues of sexual assault, violence against women, and reproductive control (for example) are divorced from women's concerns about housing, food, land, and medical care. In part, the integrated nature of the demands of the movements highlighted here is a result of their historical location. As discussed below, the emergence and strengthening of a clearly articulated feminist movement in Latin America during the 1980s was an important ideological influence on how women's demands were framed by the movements highlighted in this book.[1] Feminism as well as dominant cultural ideologies about women's proper place in the home and family influenced the public discourses and individual interpretations of the goals, strategies, and results of these movements.

This book is an attempt to compare the common elements found within the movements, rather than to provide a comparison of the totality of women's organizing in the vast region known as Latin America. While the case studies are taken from four countries, they are not equally weighted in this book because I did not carry out research for the same amount of time in each country. The heavier emphasis on Mexico and El Salvador is a reflection of my longer-term knowledge and experience in those countries. The cases included from Brazil and Chile are perhaps best seen as contrasting material for the more in-depth chapters on Mexico and El Salvador.

Common elements explored include

1 *Political and economic conditions that contributed to the building of a grassroots organization.*

2 *The relationship of organizations to different agencies and actors of the state.*

3 *The influence of the traditional and liberation theology Catholic church.*

4 *The limits placed on women's political activity by dominant cultural ideologies which specify that their proper place is at home and within the family.*

5 *Conflicts experienced by women in their homes, communities, and in larger mixed organizations as they became more active.*

6 *The merging of gender and class-based issues (e.g., working conditions and domestic violence) in organizational agendas.*

7 *The relationship of different strands of feminism to organizing efforts.*

8 *The relationship of the organizations studied to other social movements, particularly of the left.*

9 *Differences in identity, perspective, and experience found among women participating in the same organization.*

10 *The creation of new forms of political culture by women in the organizations studied.*

The movements chosen were also included because of their relative success in achieving some of their self-defined goals. While is it equally important to study movements that fail and why, relatively little is written about successful women's organizing. As is maintained repeatedly by the women whose voices permeate this book, their efforts remain invisible and unrecognized all too often, even when they succeed. The CO-MADRES of El Salvador were not only one of the few grassroots movements to continue operating openly throughout the horrific repression of any form of opposition which characterized the Salvadoran civil war, but they also achieved international recognition for their work in human rights. The DIGNAS of El Salvador have been pathbreakers in challenging the authoritarianism of the left and in building popular feminism nationally while also examining critically their own political culture and practice. Within southern Brazil, the MMTR is one of the fastest growing women's movements in the country and has not only organized impressive numbers of women locally, but has participated in several national campaigns to win legal rights for rural women and, in 1995, worked with rural women's organizations from all seventeen states in Brazil to form a national coordinating body. In Chile, the Seasonal and Permanent Workers' Union of Santa María was one of the first successful efforts by rural laborers, primarily women, to control the conditions of their work after seventeen years of dictatorship under Augusto Pinochet. In Mexico, the Women's Council of the Lázaro Cárdenas Ejido Union represents one the few instances in which rural women successfully organized to gain a political voice in their communities (until 1994 when indigenous and peasant women formed the statewide Women's Assembly in Chiapas). And in urban Mexico, the Women's Regional Council of the CONAMUP has one of the most strongly sustained and creative records of organizing women through several presidential regimes, surviving where most other organizations have fallen by the wayside.

The primary vehicle I have chosen for representing the ideas and experiences of women activists is that of edited transcripts of the conversations I had with women from each of the organizations featured here. This form seems to best capture the context in which they spoke and allows them to speak from the page as "translated women" (Behar 1993: 275–276). While such a format clearly does not allow the women to speak for themselves, it may make the dialectic between my feminism and women's answers to my questions and their representations about the meaning of their activism more transparent.[2]

In writing this book, I made a decision to examine a wide range of women's organizing experiences, rather than simply focus on one organization or one country. Obviously this entails sacrificing the richness of a thorough case study for the advantage of comparison. I have attempted to recover some of the depth found in individual case studies by focusing on the detailed conversations, narratives, and self-histories of women who participate in each organization from a variety of perspectives—leaders as well as those who might be called "the base" by political scientists or "everyday informants" by empirically oriented anthropologists. My belief is that by concentrating on a smaller number of in-depth exchanges, I am better able to translate the meaning and depth of women's varied experiences onto the page.

The research for this book took place between 1989 and 1995 when much of Latin America was completing processes of economic restructuring. In all four countries included here, continued and accelerated economic inequality was the result of policies aimed at promoting foreign investment, production for export, and overall economic growth. Brazil and Chile were taking the first steps away from regimes run by military dictatorships; El Salvador was caught in the final throes and initial stages of recovery from a long civil war. Mexico continued its tradition of single-party rule with a slight loosening of the ruling party's hegemony. All four countries saw the emergence or continued existence of significant social movements including human rights efforts, rural and urban movements for improved living conditions, organized land reclamation, a clamor for indigenous rights and autonomy, student movements, groups representing relatives of the disappeared, labor union activism, feminist movements, struggles for abortion and reproductive rights, the democratization of political systems, and more. Women were a major presence in these movements; in each country, moreover, women calling themselves "feminists" emerged to add their vision to the wide range of political groups calling for change. Democratization of the political process and the extension of active citizenship to women is a common theme in Latin America during the late 1980s and during the 1990s (Jaquette 1994, 1995).

Trying to mesh the two goals of this book is not easy, because experience and structure have traditionally been seen as alternative (not complementary) topics of study. I was trained in a traditional anthropology graduate program, and my initial work therefore focused on carrying out participant observation and interviews, administering questionnaires, and reading and interpreting documents in archives. Later on I began recording life histories and testimonials. I found that the life histories and testimonials illuminated the often stark picture painted by political economics and gave such abstract processes and categories as "relations of production," "migration," and even "gender hierarchy" concrete meaning—not only for those who experienced structures of inequality and hierarchy, but for me and my readers. Since conceptual categories are created in specific cultural and historical contexts, each time they are used they must be given meaning in relation to a specific cultural and historical location. The use of narratives, life histories, testimonials, and conversations helps to give specific meaning to the categories used in social science.

One of the positive contributions of a poststructural perspective has been to reconceptualize the individual subject as "more fragmented and incomplete, composed of multiple 'selves' or identities in relation to the different social worlds we inhabit, something with a history, 'produced' in process" (Hall 1989:121). The idea of the multiple aspects of each person's identity and experience in life is one that, of course, predates poststructuralism and can be found in feminist studies and writings of people of color whose multiple identities were often overlooked until they became fashionable when cited by the elite of the academy. In the quest to make room for all these voices, however, we must not make the mistake of ignoring structures, relations, and networks of power.

The activism that women in this book have chosen to undertake emerges from daily life situations in which all voices are not equal. Historical, political, cultural, and economic systems of inequality have combined to produce positions in the relations of power that can be characterized by exploitation, pain, suffering, struggle, and marginality. These abstract subject positions are, of course, inhabited by real people—in the instances studied here, by women. In many cases women who inhabit these positions have found ways of coping, of redefining marginality, of struggling and resisting, of encountering joy and happiness in human relations. In some instances, they have also built strong organizations and have moved slowly but steadily to confront the systems of inequality that push them to the margins. Since we are not the women featured here and cannot become them, we need information about the conditions they live under if we are to begin to understand their experience and to use it to reflect upon our own. While economic statistics and descriptions of political and economic circumstances fall far short of a lived experience and are not culturally neutral, a nuanced reading of them can provide some basis for understanding how, why, and from what positions women decide to engage in collective action. For this reason, each chapter contains general background information on economics, politics, and the gendered division of labor.

Nevertheless, while the constraints of political and economic factors are very real in people's lives, such factors are not fixed structures and are not all-determining. The analytical categories we use to talk about political economy—"mode of production," "class system," etc.—are inadequate to convey either the political economy as a dialectical process or people's experience in that process. People's responses to politics and economics also affect history and culture as their identities change through time. Thus it is necessary both to understand what the political, economic, and cultural restraints on women's political mobilization are, and yet be equally committed to unraveling how women see themselves, how they experience and give meaning to structural context, how they interpret what happens to them on a daily basis, and how they come together through the process of political activity to form movements that push back on structural conditions of inequality.

Bridging Dichotomies, Validating Experience   A major challenge in writing this book has been how to theorize women's involvement in collective action without framing their experience with dualist concepts that are not only found in local and national culture but are also embedded as the "hidden transcripts" of social analysis. This is, of course, a reference to James Scott's notion of covert ideas contained in popular forms of culture as signs of resistance (Scott 1990). I believe that social science paradigms also contain "hidden transcripts" which are signs of resistance to change and challenges to the socialization of those who write and use the paradigms. Many of these hidden transcripts are universal unstated assumptions about how the world is gendered. Many of these hidden transcripts are found in feminism as well.[3]

The most important of these dichotomies is the division of social, political, cultural, and economic life into a private-female sphere and a male-public sphere. While first forged and later discarded by many feminist anthropologists, this dichotomy has been adopted by other disciplines and incorporated into government development policy. Here I will briefly discuss its emergence and rejection in anthropology and its subsequent incorporation into analyses of women's economic and political participation. I do this in order to lay the groundwork for how the case studies presented here suggest an alternative analysis which links individual women's social, political, economic, and cultural worlds through a unity of experience, not a public/private dichotomy.

The second wave of feminist theory in anthropology was marked by the emergence of several important books, including *Woman, Culture, and Society* (1974), edited by Michelle Rosaldo and Louise Lamphere.[4] The book was a landmark effort to explain what the authors perceived as the universal subordination of women. In that book, Rosaldo proposed the existence of a universal public/private dichotomy in which women were affiliated with the private or domestic sphere because of their involvement in child rearing and men were associated with the public sphere of politics and culture.[5]

While Rosaldo and others argued that it was not inevitable that women were associated with the domestic sphere, they almost always appeared to be. The influence of mainstream American gender ideology on their theorizing was, of course, not evident to Rosaldo and other feminist theorists until they began to take apart their unified concept of women. As other work stressing the intersection of gender with class, race, ethnicity, and sexuality emerged, the notion of explaining the status of all women in all places with the same theory was shown to be too simplistic (see Sacks 1989 and Zavella 1991 for summaries of some of the relevant literature). Rosaldo and others reformed their own theories.

Rosaldo noted (1980:401) that a focus on universal dichotomies makes us "victims of a conceptual tradition that discovers 'essence' in the natural characteristics that distinguish the sexes and then declares that women's present lot derives from what, 'in essence,' women are." Later, Yanagisako and Collier (1987) sought to avoid analytical dualisms by studying gender institutions as social wholes, asking how all social inequalities are culturally constituted, and not taking sex or gender differences as a universal given.

While Yanagisako and Collier's suggestions are important for avoiding the naturalization of gender, we need to ask additional questions in order to understand how structural inequalities limit women's actions in specific historical and geographical locations. In Latin America, dominant cultural ideologies proposing that women's proper place is in the domestic sphere are still powerful obstacles to women's political mobilization. The emergence of Latin American feminism, as discussed below, has provided an important counterbalance to "women in the home" ideas and has created a complex ideological terrain for women's organizations.

One of the clearest policy areas where adoption of the public/private dichotomy has resulted in major obstacles for women's organizing is in the field of economic development. Many "women's development projects" have reproduced a biologized version of gender which held that women did better in small-scale projects focused on domestically linked productive and reproductive activities and which did nothing to challenge most women's subordinate position in the economy. As structural adjustment clearly resulted in less income and fewer resources for the majority poor as well as increased levels of formal unemployment, the boom in the so-called informal economy was seen by such development agencies as the World Bank to be an important source of income and economic activity, not only for the poor but particularly for women.

The arbitrary division of the economy into "formal" and "informal" sectors does not reflect the reality of most people's working lives. As pointed out by Hans and Judith-Maria Buechler (1992:13), the concept of the "informal sector" comes from dualistic concepts of the economy which previously associated smaller-scale production and commerce with traditionalism as opposed to a "modern" sector. They cite Redclift and Mingione (1985:2–3), who state that the informal and formal sectors "proved to have shifting parameters that varied according to context. . . . [H]ouseholds themselves were difficult to characterize along sectoral lines making use [as they do] of multiple strategies to ensure their survival" (cited in Buechler and Buechler 1992:14–15). As pointed out by many, the "informal sector" is heterogeneous and includes people who are so poor that they cannot produce commodities for exchange or participate in commercial activities along with those who have higher levels of income, but who still work without state regulation (see Cosgrove 1995:6; Portes and Sassen Koob 1987; Castells and Portes 1989; Portes, Castells, and Benton 1989). And as a result of structural adjustment, many people who are supposed to be in the "formal" sector (i.e., where there is a clear separation of capital and labor, a contractual relationship between capital and labor, and conditions of work that are legally regulated) now have a ten- to twenty-year history of also working in various kinds of unregulated commerce.[6] The formal and informal sectors are thus largely fictional in terms of actual people. The invocation of the word "informal" to label part of the economy, however, does have an important political function.

The readjustment of the labor market into what some have called "more flexible patterns of work" has resulted in an ever-growing periphery including part-timers, subcontract labor, temporary workers, and casuals which fit in with the notion of "informal" workers as a sort of haphazard and unimportant part of the economy (Harvey 1989:150). Such "flexible" patterns of work in the "informal" sector are often deemed appropriate for women because they allow women to combine the unsalaried tasks of childcare and food preparation with part-time paid labor.[7] The "informal" economy serves primarily as a symbolic (rather than actual) counterpoint to the "formal" economy which is read as male, public, and legitimate.[8]

In addition, the scale of an enterprise or activity is often confused with "formality" or "informality." As discussed by Buechler and Buechler

(1992:15), smallness of scale is often regarded as a means of competing with "legitimate" and "economically sound" larger enterprises and thereby "receives a connotation of illegality and residualness." Both the terms "small scale" and "informal" suggest illegitimacy and marginality, in addition to dividing economic life into false and separate spheres.

Despite the insistence on the labels of "formal" and "informal," women's economic participation includes a wide range of activities that crosscut unpaid domestic labor, salaried work (regulated as well as unregulated), and small and large business ownership and management. This diversity is seen in the work experience of many of the women in the present book. For example, many Chilean women who are seasonal fruit packers spend six to eight hours in the morning and early afternoon cooking, cleaning, tending animals, and feeding people while perhaps intermittently tending to a small business such as sewing clothes; then they leave their homes at two or three in the afternoon to work a ten-hour shift in a packing plant.

Development projects for women which remain focused on small-scale economic activity that generates minimal amounts of income—whether these projects are government- or nongovernment-sponsored—reproduce a false dichotomy that relegates women to the margins of the economy. Such projects also do little or nothing to economically empower women. Positive outcomes from such projects are more likely to come from the unintended political and cultural consequences of women attempting to change the gendered division of labor in their homes and organizations in order to carry out their small economic development projects. Often, however, women's challenges to gender subordination that occur in the context of very conventional projects (as in Nayarit, where women's demands for direct access to government funds to set up tortilla factories and bakeries upset the gendered power structure of a regional peasant organization) are overlooked in an attempt to categorize the content of their demands.

Until recently many attempts to explain women's grassroots mobilization have closely followed the work of Temma Kaplan (1982, 1990) and Maxine Molyneux (1986).[9] In an analysis of women's collective action in early twentieth-century Barcelona, Kaplan (1982) elaborates a theory of "female consciousness." She states that when women who have internalized their designated roles as domestic providers and caretakers are unable to carry out their duties, they will be moved to take action in order to fulfill their social roles as females. This may even include taking on the state when it impedes their day-to-day activities. Kaplan has extended this analysis to women's participation in grassroots movements within contemporary Latin America (1990).

Many authors have used Kaplan's paradigm to explain the rise of groups of "mothers of the disappeared"—whose legitimacy, they believe, is based on women's roles within the family. Discussing the emergence of the Mothers of the Plaza de Mayo in Argentina, for example, María del Carmen Feijoo writes:

The creation of certain rules of the game incorporated a feminine logic based on respect for the traditional role of women, who are thought to be altruistic and vicarious. . . . In practice, the Madres became another movement of women who, without trying to change patriarchal ideology or abandon their femininity, produced a transformation of the traditional feminine conscience and its political role. . . .The task of defending life itself was forced out of the private sphere of the household and into the autonomous space of public and political discussion. (1989:77–78)

How the Mothers think is explained by reference to their "traditional feminine conscience" and their femininity. In this discussion, the homogenization of a group of women is based on the fact that they identify themselves as mothers. How they may vary individually or through time or what the public aspects of mothering may be are not a part of their ascribed collective identity as "traditional" mothers.

Kaplan's "female consciousness" is similar to what Molyneux (1986) terms "practical gender interests"—interests that emerge from an acceptance of cultural gender roles, including female subordination and the assertion of rights based on those roles. Against these "practical gender interests," Molyneux contrasts "strategic gender interests," which are derived deductively and focus on strategic objectives to overcome women's subordination, such as alleviation of the burden of domestic labor and childcare and the removal of institutionalized forms of discrimination (1986:284). Molyneux did not try to characterize the agendas of whole movements or organizations according to either strategic or practical demands; rather, she considered how different sets of strategic and practical interests were met by the Sandinistas in Nicaragua. The typology she presented, however, did set up opposing types of demands.

The implication of practical-feminine movements such as movements that focus on organizing collective kitchens or movements of mothers of the disappeared is that they reinforce women's place in the domestic-private side of society. Feminist movements with strategic interests, such as movements that demand abortion rights, are seen as allowing women to break into the public side of life and to gain access to arenas previously dominated by men. By breaking into the traditionally "male" sphere of public power, feminist movements thus are seen to challenge oppressive gender hierarchies and to carve out a new place for women. While such a progression may sound very desirable and convincing to Western feminists, it is built on the old assumption of a gendered public/private dichotomy and in fact indirectly reinforces the structural position that many women, particularly in organizations of the left, found themselves in during the 1970s and 1980s. If women's work is labeled as "practical" and as outside the center of organizational politics, then their political work remains at the margins. In addition, the equivalence of "practical" demands with women's participation in the "private" sphere begs the question of how practical demands can be asserted, if not in the public sphere—a point avidly made by those who point out how "practical" demands become public.

While I was conducting fieldwork for this book, I found again and again in the actions and words of the women I worked with, whether or not they linked their political activism to feminism, that the feminine/feminist dichotomy did not hold. With hindsight it is not hard to see why. In part, it had to do with the historical period of the movements I studied. Most of these movements solidified in the 1980s when the second wave of Latin American feminism included a variety of currents and, ultimately, came to embrace the integration of "feminine" and "feminist" movements under the rubric of *feminismo popular*, or "grassroots feminism."[10] Before going on to discuss alternatives to the feminine/feminist dichotomy for theorizing women's political mobilization, we shall look at the content and influence of contemporary feminism in Latin America.

The Second Wave of Latin American Feminism   In countries such as Brazil, Chile, Argentina, Venezuela, and Mexico, the second wave of feminism began as a primarily middle-class and intellectual movement. In Cuba, where socialist feminism emerged as part of the revolutionary process, gender concerns have often remained subordinated to class. In Peru, second-wave feminism had its beginnings almost simultaneously in the middle class and in the rise of social movements where women were a majority of the participants. Somewhat later, organizations such as the Municipal Milk Program organized a hundred thousand women to distribute milk in 1986, and by 1988 it was estimated that six hundred communal dining halls had been organized by poor women in Peru (Barrig 1989:134).

Francesca Miller argues that the multiple origins of Peruvian feminism ultimately resulted in a more flexible and open feminism which provided a critical bridge to making feminism appealing to a wide range of Latin American women:

Feminism in Peru is a multiplicity of expressions that reflect the broader political spectrum and the divisions that exist in every Latin American country — and in countries across the globe — but are especially stark in the Peruvian polity. . . . It is also an indicator of the direction Latin American feminist thinking took after 1983, which is an acceptance and pride in multiplicity and a rejection of the only-one-right-way-to-think politics of the early and mid-1970s. (1991: 222–223)

Central American feminisms, particularly those of El Salvador and Nicaragua, represent another model of development—distinct from both the Peruvian model and that of Mexico and the Southern Cone. As discussed in Chapter 3, most Salvadoran and Nicaraguan women's organizations were created as part of the clandestine political-military organizations and parties that made up the FMLN (Farabundo Martí National Liberation Front) and the FSLN (Sandinista National Liberation Front). Unlike national women's organizations in Cuba and Nicaragua which remained linked to revolutionary parties that came to head governments, though, some of El Salvador's women's organizations declared their autonomy from the parties that founded them, either before or shortly after these revolutionary parties entered into the formal political process.

In an article titled "Marxism, Feminism, and the Struggle for Democracy," Norma Chinchilla carefully outlines some of the convergences between democratic Marxists and Latin American feminists. She points out that the tendency on the part of some Marxist theorists "to elaborate a Marxist understanding of democracy and daily life" was an important step in the possible convergence of feminism with Marxism (1992:44). Within the Central American revolutionary left, the recognition of plural social subjects, the delinking of "the working class" as the vanguard of socialist movements, and discussions of the importance of organizational autonomy from the state and from political parties were important steps toward creating more space for feminism within revolutionary movements.

In Mexico, the Zapatista Army of National Liberation (EZLN), which publicly emerged in January of 1994, provided a different model of women's organizing from that associated with the revolutionary left of Latin America. For one thing, the fact that 30 percent of the Zapatista rank-and-file insurgents were indigenous women from the Tzeltal, Tzotzil, Chol, Zoque, Mam, and Tojolobal ethnic groups provided immediate visibility for women as part of the rebellion launched by the EZLN. On the first day of their rebellion, moreover, the Zapatistas publicized their Revolutionary Law of Women, which resonated with women throughout Mexico. Although it was released on the first day of the Zapatista rebellion, the women's law was not picked up by the press for sixteen days.

The law stated:

First, *women have the right to participate in the revolutionary struggle in the place and at the level that their capacity and will dictates without any discrimination based on race, creed, color, or political affiliation.*

Second, *women have the right to work and to receive a just salary.*

Third, *women have the right to decide on the number of children they have and take care of.*

Fourth, *women have the right to participate in community affairs and to hold leadership positions if they are freely and democratically elected.*

Fifth, *women have the right to primary care with respect to their health and nutrition.*

Sixth, *women have the right to education.*

Seventh, *women have the right to choose who they are with [i.e., choose their romantic/sexual partners] and should not be obligated to marry by force.*

Eighth, *no woman should be beaten or physically mistreated either by family members or by strangers. Rape and attempted rape should be severely punished.*

Ninth, *women can hold leadership positions in the organization and hold military rank in the revolutionary armed forces.*

Tenth, *women have all the rights and obligations set out by the revolutionary laws and regulations.* (*Doble Jornada* 1994:8)

The Zapatista Revolutionary Law of Women was widely discussed in Mexico outside of Chiapas and served as a way to bring indigenous women together with working-class, middle-class, and urban intellectual women in new ways. Several well-known and charismatic women leaders of the EZLN, such as Comandante Ramona, also provided revolutionary role models for women throughout Mexico. The moral authority with which the Zapatistas brought forward their overall case for indigenous rights, a democratic transition, economic justice, and the important role of women as participants and leaders in these processes provided a unique platform and crucial political opening as well as a larger discussion of women's rights (see Stephen 1996b). Instead of waiting for disenfranchised women to demand the inclusion of women's rights and issues, the Zapatistas brought women into their demands, discussion, and leadership in a more self-conscious manner than had previous revolutionary movements in Central America and Cuba.

The most concrete evidence of a second wave of international Latin American feminism can be found in the establishment of a series of regional Latin American and Caribbean Feminist Encuentros (meetings, encounters, happenings) beginning in 1981 (see Saporta Sternbach et al. 1992 and Miller 1991).[11] By following the advances and difficulties (*avances y nudos*) of the six Latin American and Caribbean Feminist Encuentros that were held between 1981 and 1993 we put ourselves in a good position to monitor some of the important discussion that took place among Latin American feminists during the 1980s and 1990s. While the *encuentros* by no means represent all of the work being done in the name of feminism in Latin America, they became increasingly diverse with time and raised some of the major issues being debated in many countries.

The first *encuentro* (held in Bogotá, Colombia, in 1981) attracted over two hundred feminists from fifty different organizations from Mexico, the Dominican Republic, Puerto Rico, Panama, Curaçao, Venezuela, Ecuador, Peru, Chile, Brazil, Argentina, and Colombia. The *encuentro* marked the first time that women from so many countries met to share perspectives and experiences. The primary debate at the first *encuentro*—one that continued to haunt future *encuentros*—was about whether and how feminism and socialism could be integrated. This debate has been fundamental in Latin American feminism.

As described by Saporta Sternbach and colleagues, there were two primary positions at the Bogotá *encuentro*:

The first position held that neither capitalism nor socialism alone could eliminate women's oppression and that, consequently, women's specific demands must be articulated in a movement outside of and independent of all existing political parties. . . .

Those who held the second position . . . insisted that feminism in and of itself could not be a revolutionary project. Because of their primary commitment to socialism, they argued that feminism should not be separated from the party, but that it should have an organic autonomy within that structure. Feminists' objectives, in this view, could not be separated from those of the working class and its struggle to end class oppression. (1992:217)

These two positions staked out one of the major arenas of conflict at future encuentros.

The second *encuentro*, held in Lima in 1983, attracted over six hundred women. At this *encuentro*, disagreements focused on the overly intellectual nature of the analysis (all workshops were titled "Patriarchy and . . .") and on the lack of participation from women in organizations focused on economic survival and human rights. At the subsequent *encuentro* (Bertioga, Brazil, in 1985), the arrival of a busload of women from a Rio de Janeiro shantytown who were denied admission generated a flurry of activity and some incipient discussion about the race and class implications of the *encuentros*—issues that did not go away (Saporta Sternbach et al. 1992:223).

The fourth *encuentro*, held in 1987 in Taxco, Mexico, marked the first widespread participation of Central American women (forty-two from Nicaragua, nine from El Salvador, ten from Honduras, and fifteen from Guatemala according to Miller 1991:235). Many of the Central American women who attended did not consider themselves feminists at the time, with the exception of a few Nicaraguans who were militating for more feminist themes in AMNLAE (Association of Nicaraguan Women "Luisa Amanda Espinoza") (see Comité Nacional Feminista 1994a). Records from the fourth *encuentro* document the presence of Salvadoran women from the Mothers and Relatives of the Political Prisoners, Disappeared, and Assassinated of El Salvador "Monseñor Romero" (CO-MADRES, Comité de Madres y Familiares de Presos, Desaparecidos y Asesinados de el Salvador "Monseñor Romero") and from the Mélida Anaya Montes Union of Salvadoran Women for Liberation (UMSL, Unión de Mujeres Salvadoreñas por la Liberación "Mélida Anaya Montes") formed by Salvadoran women exiled in Mexico. These last were presumably militants for the Popular Forces of Liberation "Farabundo Martí" (FPL–FM, Fuerzas Populares de Liberación "Farabundo Martí"), one of five military-political organizations in the FMLN.[12]

The meeting at Taxco was characterized by widespread participation of women from a variety of grassroots movements including textile workers, union members, human rights activists, peasants, and urban activists. Besides marking the first appearance of organized Salvadoran women at an international feminist meeting, the fourth *encuentro* featured a three-day workshop on Central American feminism. The workshop provided the first opportunity for Central American activist women to talk with one another and compare perspectives, particularly about their roles as women within revolutionary movements, political parties, unions, and peasant and human rights organizations. The Guatemalan women and the CO-MADRES of El Salvador were particularly concerned with generalized violence and the forms that it took against women (Miller 1991:235–236). While Central American women still had many questions about feminism and how to integrate it with their other political work, many left with *new* ideas and questions. At the final plenary, the Central American women as well as others who had not identified themselves as feminists when they arrived were all shouting "Todos somos feministas" (We are all feminists) (Saporta Sternbach et al. 1992:226).

Owing to the location of the fifth *encuentro*—in San Bernardo, Chile, in 1990—the number of Central American women who attended was low. The Fifth Feminist Encuentro was attended by up to three thousand women and represented the diversity of Latin American and Caribbean feminism. Separate meetings for indigenous women and newly formed networks such as the Latin American and Caribbean Black Women's Network reflected the integration of racial concerns. The presence of legislators from several countries as well as a large number of regional and topical networks spoke to the maturity of the movement. As Saporta Sternbach and colleagues conclude about the conference (1992:236), "Though the tensions between *militantes* and *feministas* remain in evidence, they are mostly in the background. Many women of both groups now insist that they must organize around issues of class and race insofar as these shape the way gender oppression is manifest in the lives of women of varied classes and racial ethnic groups."

At the fifth *encuentro* it was decided that the sixth would take place "somewhere in Central America." After a two-year regional planning process carried out by Central American women, El Salvador was designated the site for the sixth *encuentro*.[13]

Bringing an international feminist meeting to El Salvador also brought women's issues into the news media—though not always with desirable publicity. In October 1993, weeks before the *encuentro* was to begin, the Salvadoran right began a systematic campaign to shut down the *encuentro*. The Mexican newspaper *La Jornada* reported that "conservative forces in El Salvador are trying to cancel the Latin American and Caribbean Feminist Encuentro scheduled for October 30th, arguing that all of the women who have come together every two or three years since 1980

RARA

LA LABOR DE CISPES

CISPES son las iniciales de Committee In Solidarity with the People of El Salvador, una formidable organización montada en Estados Unidos durante el conflicto bélico, para apoyar financieramente al FMLN, realizar actividades de sabotaje a la economía salvadoreña y combatir la ayuda militar norteamericana a la FAES.

Recoger dinero para fines no lucrativos (Fund Raising) es, en Estados Unidos una profesión bastante bien remunerada y -cosa importante en momentos de recesión- una fuente de buenos empleos. En THE NEW YORK TIMES de los domingos, en la sección de trabajos, se publican varias páginas dedicadas a los "recogedores de fondos". Sus fines van desde los culturales y religiosos hasta la protección de las ballenas, la guerrilla nacionalista de Azerbaiján, la protección de los lobos en Alaska y, desde luego, los temas de moda: la libertad sexual, el SIDA, Michael Jackson...

En cuanto al sabotaje, CISPES ejecutó una campaña entre los estibadores de California para que no desembarcaran las mercaderías provenientes de El Salvador, en verdad con poco éxito. En cambio lo tuvieron   con

Opening page of an article titled "Are the Lesbians Coming?" Published in Gente *magazine before the Sixth Feminist Encuentro, Costa del Sol, El Salvador, 1993.*

from different countries are linked to the FMLN and are trying to create forums for the expression of lesbianism and homosexuality" (Lovera 1993:15).[14] A right-wing magazine called *Gente* featured the banner headline "¿Vienen las lesbianas?" (Are the Lesbians Coming?) on its front cover and a four-page story supposedly exposing the links of

CISPES (Committee in Solidarity with the People of El Salvador) with the FMLN and its promotion of homosexuality. The magazine published the names and phone numbers of CISPES offices and organizers in the United States and in San Salvador.

The *Gente* article was based on a flyer distributed by CISPES in the United States calling for a "Lesbian, Gay, Bisexual/Queer Delegation to El Salvador in November, 1993." The flyer suggested participants could "attend the Feminist Encuentro, lend support to a newly formed Lesbian organization in El Salvador and meet with members of the Salvadoran opposition including representatives of the FMLN." *Gente* implied that hundreds of lesbians and gay men, possibly infected with AIDS, would be invading one of El Salvador's most important development poles, the Costa del Sol: "[W]e know that male and female homosexuals are a high-risk population, so that the minimum our government should require is that everyone who is a part of the [CISPES] delegation should be given an AIDS test" (*Gente* 1993:42).

Articles such as that published in *Gente* not only threatened members of CISPES and other conference participants but created a climate of impunity with respect to violence directed against the women who organized and supported the conference. Hotel and restaurant owners who were going to serve *encuentro* participants on the Costa del Sol were threatened by phone that their establishments would be bombed and their property destroyed if they served any of the women attending the conference. Five Salvadoran women who were part of the local organizing committee, including two members of DIGNAS, received repeated death threats in the weeks leading up to the *encuentro*. Feminist organizations and women's studies departments in the United States and Europe were asked by E-mail and fax to send letters of protest to then-president of El Salvador Alfredo Cristiani. In the end, the *encuentro* took place without incident and was attended by over fifteen hundred women.

The Sixth Feminist Encuentro achieved an even higher level of racial, ethnic, and class diversity than previous ones, enjoying first-time participation by black women from the Caribbean, indigenous women from Andean countries and Guatemala, and many poor women from the cities and rural areas of Central America. Workshops held by participants covered a wide range of topics—"Violation of Women's Human Rights," "What the Catholic Hierarchy Never Says," "Feminists in Political Parties," "Maternal Health," "Feminisms in Central America," "Heterosexual Women Wanting to Stop Homophobia," "Feminist Power in Municipios," "Lesbian Visibility," "Women and the Foreign Debt," "Health and Refugee Women," and more. Broad plenaries at the *encuentro* focused on how to build the movement while incorporating its rich diversity as well as how to work inside of and outside of patriarchy.

Indeed, the wide range of topics included under the rubric of a "feminist" *encuentro*, together with the greater diversity of participants in terms of class, race, ethnicity, sexuality, and region, served to position Latin American feminisms for the next century. The *encuentro* itself made the feminine/feminist dichotomy obsolete through the lived experiences of the women who attended and planned it.

The way in which the women who planned the *encuentro* narrate their own political lives—such as Morena Herrera, an urban working-class Salvadoran who was a guerrilla commander and who then went on to help found one of El Salvador's first feminist organizations—weaves together commentaries on gender, class, race, location, and politics through a web of experience. The lens through which Morena and other women in this book view their past and present political experience reveals the whole person they have become through the process of political activism. That whole person includes their childhood socialization and ways of acting within the family as well as their various political formations. For example, Morena will bring her father anything he wants, on demand and without question, yet during the same afternoon she will publicly denounce revolutionary ex-guerrilla commanders for their sexism in a large meeting. As whole people, Morena and others integrate their own lived experience with everything they speak and think about. As political activists, the women highlighted here vary tremendously in what they bring to their movements, how they participate in them, and how they interpret what those movements mean.

Unfixed Boundaries and the Dangers of Assumed Collective Identities

What is it that binds women together in collective action? Resource mobilization theory tries to explain collective action in terms of structural opportunities, leadership, and ideological and organizational networks (see McClurg Mueller 1992:12–16; Morris and McClurg Mueller 1992). Theorists of new social movements offer the concept of "collective identities" as a way of explaining how people act in concert, often with the object of achieving a new, distinct, or semiautonomous kind of presence and cultural recognition. People writing from a "new social movements" perspective are interested in the construction, contestation, and negotiation of collective identities in the process of political activity. Collective identity refers to "the (often implicitly) agreed upon definition of membership, boundaries, and activities for the group"

(Johnston, Laraña, and Gusfield 1994:15). As pointed out by Johnston, Laraña, and Gusfield (1994), and by Escobar (1992:72) following Alberto Melucci, some theorists assume the constitution of identity rather than explaining how it is built through interactions, negotiation, and relationships with the environment. If collective identity is perceived as constructed in action, then it is a very difficult concept to pin down empirically.

The existence of collective identity, just like the notion of "collective consciousness" or "false consciousness," is difficult to substantiate. "First, it is predicated on a continual interpenetration of—and mutual influence between—the individual identity of the participant and the collective identity of the group. Second, by the very nature of the phenomena we study, the collective identity of social movements is a 'moving target,' with different definitions predominating at different points in a movement career. Third, distinct processes in identity creation and maintenance are operative in different phases of the movement" (Johnston, Laraña, and Gusfield 1994:16).

The cases of women's organizing included here suggest that, rather than assuming the natural existence of collective identities, we have to look contextually at how mobilization arises and how its meaning and interpretation may vary between individuals and over time. Groups of women who act together are often quite heterogeneous, and their ability to act comes from respecting difference while also forging a common argument through a shared set of questions. In his essay "The Production of Culture in Local Rebellion," Gavin Smith suggests that it makes little sense to talk about heterogeneous groups forging a common identity or even being in a dialogue. Instead, he maintains that they argue. The participants in a rebellion "are committed both to the importance of the differences among themselves and simultaneously to the ongoing production of an image of themselves internally homogeneous and externally distinctive" (Smith 1991:181).[15]

For some, the rejection of typologies and clearly demarcated units of social identity and interaction may simply herald the return of an evangelical relativism often associated with Boasian anthropology. However, while early American anthropology was built on a colonial model of university-trained experts salvaging the last remnants of culture from disappearing tribes and ethnic groups, the proposition of "letting the natives speak for themselves" has a very different meaning and result. The "natives" of Chicana feminism tell us that unitary subjects and typologies do not work since they defy Chicana experience and reality and homogenize difference (Alarcón 1989, 1990; Anzaldúa and Moraga 1981;

Anzaldúa 1987, 1990). Boundaries and borders are not fixed: they are sites of "historicized struggles" (C. Kaplan 1994:149–150).

The point is well stated by Gloria Anzaldúa in relation to the unified racial/ethnic concept of the *mestiza*:

These numerous possibilities leave la mestiza floundering in uncharted seas. . . . [S]he has discovered that she can't hold concepts or ideas in rigid boundaries. . . . La mestiza constantly has to shift out of habitual formations; from convergent thinking, analytical reasoning that tends to use rationality to move toward a single goal (a Western mode), to divergent thinking, characterized by movement away from set patterns and goals and toward a more whole perspective, one that includes rather than excludes. The new mestiza copes by developing a tolerance for contradictions, a tolerance for ambiguity. She learns to be an Indian in Mexican cultures, to be Mexican from an Anglo point of view. She learns to juggle culture. She has a plural personality, she operates in a pluralistic mode — nothing is thrust out, the good, the bad, and the ugly, nothing rejected, nothing abandoned. Not only does she sustain contradictions, she turns the ambivalence into something else. (Anzaldúa 1987:79)

Chicana "natives" such as Anzaldúa also tell us that they are their own experts. They are constructing their own theories and inscribing them in ways that defy academic convention. Anzaldúa writes poetry, stream-of-consciousness prose, and theory all in one textual form. Poetry and short stories are included in anthologies that speak to "hardcore" theoretical categories such as race, ethnicity, class, sexuality, and gender. Theory becomes performance rather than abstraction—words in action, actively engaging and challenging the reader.

If we truly want to understand what the experience of collective action means to women, then we have much to learn from Chicana women who are theorizing themselves in action. Theories of collective action cannot be abstracted from the context within which they appear. They have to grow out of historically and specifically grounded instances of mobilization and must be mediated by the voices and interpretations of those who are doing the acting.

Elsewhere (Stephen 1994a) I have proposed that testimonial and life history genres discourage either/or typologies by revealing in detail the politicizing process that people go through. The blending of personal identity with political activism underscores how different and conflicting pieces of individual identity interact with structural conditions to influence the evolution of political commitment and strategy. Claudia Salazar also points out how oral histories directly and indirectly address and transgress "socially coded binary oppositions such as text/context, personal/political, public/private, knower/known, orality/literacy, and high culture/low culture" (1991:93).[16]

The Structure of This Book   Part I focuses on El Salvador. Chapter 2 uses a detailed ethnographic analysis of El Salvador's "mothers of the disappeared" (CO-MADRES) to suggest that looking at multiple facets of women's identities and at the ways in which they both accommodate and resist the dominant ideologies of gender hierarchy and national security best explains their political activity. Personal narratives and testimonies document how the CO-MADRES have incorporated issues of state repression, domestic inequality, and women's sexuality into a new discourse on human rights.

Chapter 3 has to do with the emergence of feminisms from the revolutionary left in El Salvador. Women for Dignity and Life, or DIGNAS, was originally created as an arm of the National Resistance (RN), one of the five political-military organizations that made up the Farabundo Martí National Liberation Front. Soon after DIGNAS was founded, however, women acted from within to make the organization autonomous. Chapter 3 focuses on that process, highlighting the development of the organization, its relationship to emerging feminist movements in other countries, its internal differences, and the new types of identities forged by its participants with respect to class, gender, and political affiliation and ideology.

The activist testimonial/interview featured in Part I is with Morena Herrera. Growing up in an urban working-class family, she became a student activist within the AES (Association of High School Students) at age fourteen. Morena later joined another high school student organization, and eventually she became an urban guerrilla for one of the parties and military organizations of the Farabundo Martí National Liberation Front. She became an FMLN commander and went on to found and work within DIGNAS, one of El Salvador's first openly feminist organizations.

Part II of this book sheds light on two activists and two different types of women's organizations in Mexico, both emerging from larger mixed (i.e., male and female) movements and organizations. This is the most common pathway for women's organizing in Mexico. In Chapter 4, the example of the Women's Regional Council of CONAMUP is presented in the context of background information that illustrates the marginal conditions Mexican women lived under during the 1980s and the relationship of those conditions to structural adjustment policies. I outline women's grassroots responses to poverty, joblessness, and increased workloads. In addition, I explore the ways in which class and gender issues are integrated in the organization as well as the different relationships, ranging from antagonism to adamant support, that women in the organization have with feminism. Chapter 4 details how poor urban women have met the ongoing Mexican economic crisis with a strategy of collective action—how they have learned that they do not need to adopt the same identity or share identical interpretations of their experience in order to act together. What they do share is an overlapping set of questions regarding the various dimensions of inequality they experience as women. This, rather than a unitary collective identity, is what holds them together.

Chapter 5 focuses on a rural women's organization, the Women's Council of the Lázaro Cárdenas Ejido Union in the state of Nayarit. This chapter explores how the agenda of women's grassroots organizing is strongly influenced by structural constraints built into the larger political economy, yet how it also responds to the creative abilities of women to challenge political and economic systems that have left them on the outside. In this case, it is the unintended consequences of women's attempts to carry out seemingly nonthreatening projects (e.g., the establishment of bakeries, collective farming, and chicken raising) that have offered the strongest challenge to entrenched gender roles in local politics and economics. Also emphasized is how women of different ages and family groups interpret their gains differently.

The first activist interviewed in Part II is Irene Soto, an urban working-class woman who was an organizer in the Women's Regional Council of the CONAMUP. Irene has worked with poor and low-income women in Mexico City's marginal neighborhoods; she began working as a teenager in neighborhood organizing. In contrast, Doña Kata Moreno is a seventy-year-old peasant organizer who was one of the first women to become involved in organizing in rural Nayarit, having done so during the 1940s.[17] She was a key actor in the formation of an *ejido* union which brought together fourteen agrarian communities, and she participated in the formation of the Women's Council of the Lázaro Cárdenas Ejido Union. This second interview also includes Doña Aurora Cruz, who worked with Doña Kata in establishing the Women's Union of the UELC.

Part III is dedicated to a single rural movement in Brazil. Chapter 6 documents how rural women workers in southern Brazil have used consciousness-raising and an alternative political structure to build a new political culture countering that found in male-run labor unions. Many of the women in this Rural Women Workers' Movement had experience mobilizing in other contexts, such as in Christian base communities, the landless movement, antidam activism, or rural labor unions. Others had no prior experience in political action. Their varied backgrounds and talents, combined with organizing methods learned in feminist-leaning NGO workshops, have resulted in the rich new political culture of the MMTR.

The activist highlighted in Part III is Gessi Bonês, one of the founders of the MMTR. Gessi began organizing when she was sixteen. She had worked in conjunction with the liberation theology branch of the Brazilian Catholic church, organizing rural workers, as well as in antidam activism. Then, in 1987, she went on to form what would be one of the largest autonomous organizations of rural women in Brazil. The Gessi Bonês interview also includes Marlene Pasquali, another founder of MMTR.

Part IV of this book concentrates on women who are seasonal workers in Chile's huge fruit-exporting sector. Chapter 7 documents the evolution of Chile's first seasonal workers' union, an organization which has many women in leadership positions. Women's engagement in Santa María's labor force and their active participation in the union has fundamentally changed traditional gender roles among working families. Women are out on the streets at night, aim to control their own sexuality, and have a strong hand in union politics. This experience suggests that while some of the conditions of commercial agriculture and global capitalism have placed clear cultural, political, and economic constraints on women, these same conditions of work can allow women increased autonomy if they develop an independent base of power and acquire confidence through grassroots organizing.

The activist portrayed here is Antonia Gómez, a Mapuche Indian. Antonia was the wife of a miner who was imprisoned under the Pinochet regime. She fled to the north, where she began to work in commercial-export agriculture and became a leader in the largely female Seasonal and Permanent Workers' Union of Santa María.

The conclusion to this book, Chapter 8, comparatively analyzes the case studies in relation to themes that recur in feminist conversations about gender relations, economic development, political mobilization, identity, and power relations between researchers and "the researched."

Through their actions, words, and deeds, Latin American women such as those highlighted in the pages that follow are blazing a brave path into the future. Their creative integration of spheres and issues that have been deemed separate by social scientists, by politicians, and even by feminists redefines women's activism from the bottom up. Regardless of the label that is applied to this work, by crossing boundaries, breaking schemata, and questioning assumptions about who they are and what their actions mean, grassroots women's organizations in Latin America have provided an exemplary model for others.

PART I   EL SALVADOR

CHAPTER 2

Women's Rights Are Human Rights
The Merging of Feminine and Feminist Interests among El Salvador's Mothers of the Disappeared (CO-MADRES)

This chapter highlights the case of the CO-MADRES (Committee of Mothers and Relatives of the Political Prisoners, Disappeared, and Assassinated of El Salvador "Monseñor Romero"), an organization that has attracted members by appealing to the concept of the rights and responsibilities of women as mothers and wives. CO-MADRES includes rural as well as urban women from a mix of poor, working, and middle classes.[1] The historical trajectory of the publicly stated demands and goals of the CO-MADRES as well as my interviews with members suggest that women's lives were certainly changed through their political activism but that such changes were not experienced uniformly. Beginning with demands that the Salvadoran government and various military and security forces provide information about disappeared, incarcerated, and assassinated family members, the CO-MADRES moved into a political sphere from which they had previously been marginalized as women. They are now demanding women's inclusion in formal political decision making bodies as a fundamental part of the democratization process in El Salvador. They have also brought issues of domestic violence, rape, and women's lack of control over their own sexuality into their political analysis and work, with the encouragement of self-identified feminists. In the process they have clearly been transformed—but again not in a uniform manner, nor with the same experience and interpretation of events. They have been able to act together in contingent moments of unity. Their experience of that unity remains, like them, diverse. Here I argue that labeling their movement as either "feminine" or "feminist," with corresponding "private" and "public" claims, makes little sense and does not capture the richness and complexity of the political ideologies and agendas they have developed.

The Ideology of National Security and El Salvador's Civil War   El Salvador was in a civil war from 1979 until January 1992, when formal peace accords were signed by the Alfredo Cristiani government and the FMLN (Farabundo Martí National Liberation Front) in Mexico City. In the spring of 1994, El Salvador held national, state, and local elections in which the FMLN participated as an open political party within the Democratic Convergence headed by presidential candidate Rubén Zamora. While the FMLN did not fare well in the elections, its emergence as a legitimate political force has changed the political culture of El Salvador.

It is estimated that one out of every one hundred Salvadorans was murdered or "disappeared" during the civil war. As of late 1991, a total of eighty thousand had died and seven thousand more had disappeared. Human rights organizations such as Amnesty International have linked the Salvadoran military to tens of thousands of cases of assassination, torture, rape, and imprisonment of peasants, union leaders, students, and others. The final report of the U.N. Truth Commission (Comisión de la Verdad), published in March 1993, found that the military and far-right death squads with ties to the army were responsible for 85 percent of twenty-five thousand civilian deaths the commission investigated (Naciones Unidas 1993). In life, the thousands of disappeared, tortured, and assassinated were men and women—sons and daughters, husbands and wives, brothers and sisters, aunts, uncles, and cousins. They were *comadres* and *compadres*, *ahijados* and *ahijadas* (godmothers and godfathers, godsons and goddaughters). They lived in the social world of family and kinship relations. They also had occupational and class identities as workers, peasants, intellectuals, lawyers, artists, musicians, priests, businessmen and women, nuns, doctors, nurses, librarians, shopkeepers, market vendors, and more. They had cultural and ethnic identities as Indians, part Indians, and *mestizos*. Some of them had political identities as well, belonging to political organizations, political parties, and grassroots organizations such as peasant cooperatives, human rights organizations, labor unions, student groups, consumer organizations, teachers' unions, and other groups.

For the military, for various security and police units, and for many branches of the Salvadoran state, these people had one identity—that of subversives who were a threat to national security and to the capitalist modernization process under way in El Salvador. In death, they were at best faceless numbers and, at worst, nonexistent and invisible as the disappeared. For their relatives, these thousands of people remained whole human beings, vibrant in all the aspects of their identity and social relations. And the fact of kinship was never severed from the other aspects of the dead and disappeared's identity in terms of class, occupation, politics, and culture. To understand how thousands of people came to be victims of the Salvadoran civil war, we must look at the emergence of doctrines of national security in Latin America and their relationship to state ideologies promoting gender hierarchy.

A watershed event in the political history of El Salvador is known as the *Matanza* (massacre). In 1931, Arturo Araujo was elected president of El Salvador in what many called the country's only free elections. He was overthrown by the military at the end of the year and replaced by General Maximiliano Hernández Martínez. During 1932, Communist Party members who had expected to make significant electoral gains became dismayed when Hernández Martínez called off the elections. Party members, headed by Augustín Farabundo Martí, responded by trying to harness widespread insurrectionary actions for a full-scale revolution. They were planning to build on widespread discontent in the countryside caused by a drastic drop in world coffee prices and by widespread layoffs and pay cuts instituted throughout El Salvador. A large trade-union federation influenced by the clandestine Communist Party also figured importantly in their sources of support.

The planned insurrection went awry when Martí and others were arrested and could not provide coordination. The revolt happened anyway. Peasants armed with machetes attacked government offices and coffee warehouses, and took over several towns in the heart of El Salvador's coffee district of Sonsonate. Government troops took the offensive and forced most of the rebels into the town of Sonzacate. The military quickly regained control of the country and unleashed a campaign of terror that killed between ten thousand and thirty thousand mostly indigenous peasants (Anderson 1971).

The cultural and political effects of the Matanza were enduring. Because the majority of those killed were perceived as being Indian, outward manifestations of Indian identity (language, dress, religious customs) were quickly abandoned. The region of Sonsonate has also remained one of the few areas in El Salvador where grassroots organizations have found only mediocre support. The Matanza set a precedent in which the military established itself as the client of El Salvador's ruling class, primarily invested in the coffee and export sector. A political culture was established in which the defense of Salvadoran national security focused on protecting the interests of El Salvador's agro-export elite. The involvement of the clandestine Salvadoran Communist Party in the revolt also provided fertile ground for anticommunist ideology. An exception was the anti-fascist movement during World War II that succeeded in ousting Hernández Martínez in 1944 (Ready 1994), but the military regained control of the Salvadoran government within a year and continued to serve the interests of the country's elite.

The emerging post-Matanza culture of national security was reinforced and cultivated by the U.S. anticommunism campaigns which solidified after the Cuban Revolution. After 1959, U.S. foreign policymakers became very worried about the "spread of communism" throughout Latin America. In 1961, the nationalist revolution in Cuba was attacked by counterrevolutionaries trained by U.S. Special Forces and flown in U.S. planes to the Bay of Pigs. That same year, President John F. Kennedy proposed the opening of a new stage of U.S.–Latin American relations by forging the Alliance for Progress. The Alliance preached that certain reforms were necessary if Castro-like revolutions were to be contained. Tax, land, and labor reforms could help bridge the gap between rich and poor. Electoral contests could provide channels for discontent.

While the Alliance for Progress had many socioeconomic proposals, it also had a military strategy. The armies and police forces of Latin America were trained in the latest techniques of counterinsurgency warfare to be used against current and expected guerrilla threats. Local police forces took courses in interrogation methods to be used for extracting information from potential subversives. They were also schooled in how to use kinship and social networks to retrieve more information, getting torture victims to reveal the names and addresses of others they were close to. While national governments in Central America eagerly signed up for military training and assistance, the economic and political reforms proposed in the Alliance did not fare so well.

Land reform was proposed but never realized in El Salvador. Oligarchs and right-wing forces in the country did not accept the argument that agrarian reform was needed to prevent agrarian revolutions. What was needed, they argued, were more national security measures (Barry 1987:109). Since the 1960s, a majority of El Salvador's top military officers have been trained at Fort Benning and elsewhere in the United States, in Panama, and in Honduras. In El Salvador, the U.S. commitment went from training officers to helping the Salvadoran military grow.

The increasing amounts of U.S. dollars poured into the Salvadoran military corresponded to the 1979 victory of the Sandinistas in neighboring Nicaragua. The troop strength of the Salvadoran armed forces mushroomed from fewer than ten thousand in 1979 to close to seventy thousand in 1991. During the same period, the United States sent close to $6 billion to the Salvadoran government. Most of this money was military aid. All of El Salvador's top-ranking officers received extensive U.S. training. U.S. advisors created the Salvadoran army's elite counter-insurgency units, including the Atlacatl Battalion, whose soldiers were responsible for the brutal killing of six university Jesuits in 1989 and for an earlier massacre of up to seven hundred people at El Mozote in 1981 (Danner 1994).

In El Salvador, as elsewhere, the doctrine of national security assigned to the armed forces and their allies "the role of safeguarding internal security and waging war against 'subversive elements' within their borders" (Fisher 1993:10). Threats to national security could include any type of idea, event, project, or organization that threatened the status quo politically, economically, or culturally.

A basic look at economic, health, and land distribution statistics compiled in the 1980s reveals the grave social and economic situation that most Salvadorans lived in. In 1980, the richest 20 percent of the Salvadoran population received 66 percent of the income; the poorest 20 percent received 2 percent of the income. Per capita gross domestic product was $900 in 1987.

Land distribution mirrored the distribution of wealth. In 1987, 1 percent of the farms used 71 percent of the total farmland, and 41 percent of the farms used only 10 percent of the total farmland. Life expectancy at birth in 1988 was 58.8 years, and the infant mortality rate was 86 per 1,000 live births. Finally, in 1988 urban unemployment was 50 percent while rural unemployment was 71 percent.[2]

While these figures from the late 1980s clearly represent the extended crisis of the civil war, they also demonstrate the consistent patterns of extreme disparity in wealth distribution, widespread under- and unemployment, landlessness, and poor health found throughout this century in El Salvador. These marginal living conditions for the majority are linked to a consistent dependency on export agriculture, with coffee as the major export, and a growing external public debt which went from $88 million in 1970 to 1.825 billion in 1989 (Barry 1990:177). This debt has grown despite major infusions of aid from the United States and remittances sent by Salvadorans living in the United States to their families. These remittances are estimated to total from $500 million to over $1.3 billion annually (Barry 1990:79).

Any group of people perceived to be challenging the economic status quo represented in the preceding statistics was a threat to national security. Anyone questioning the political system that held the economic system in place was even more suspect. Many political analysts believe that the widespread electoral fraud, extreme repression, and violation of human rights during the 1970s marked a total breakdown of El Salvador's political order (Central America Information Office 1982:15; Arnson 1982:15). The decade of the 1970s was also characterized by a resurgence of popular organizations (community-based, peasant, urban poor) and labor unions which responded to a faltering economy and to army repression by increasing their demands and public presence. The obvious electoral fraud of 1972, in which José Napoleón Duarte and Guillermo Ungo were robbed of a clear victory, physically beaten, and exiled, called into question the process for achieving democracy in El Salvador (Arnson 1982:27).

The popular Catholic church, following liberation theology, was an important political actor during this period. In response to the Latin American Episcopal Conference at Medellín in 1968, the progressive Salvadoran Catholic church began to define poverty and oppression of the masses as a sin, as the most profound contradiction to Christian faith (Berryman 1986). The organization of hundreds of Christian base communities that discussed and organized around the problems of poverty in relation to biblical teaching politicized both the rural and the urban poor.

The late 1970s were marked by a campaign of terror by death squads and the military against grassroots organizations and the liberation theology sectors of the church. Priests—along with peasant leaders, union leaders, and others who were labeled "subversives"—were arrested, tortured, and made to disappear. Every morning, the people of San Salvador and other urban areas were greeted by the sight of bodies dumped on the streets and bearing visible signs of torture. On the outskirts of the capital, areas known as body dumps would carry further evidence of the previous night's slaughter. Some of the people who were detained, the "disappeared," were simply never seen again.

During the 1970s, the armed left also began to emerge in El Salvador. Three important guerrilla groups, dedicated to achieving profound socioeconomic and political transformations, were formed in the first half of the decade. They included the Popular Forces of Liberation "Farabundo Martí" (FPL–FM), formed in 1970 from a radical wing of the Salvadoran Communist Party (PCS); the People's Revolutionary Army (ERP), formed in 1971 by dissident Christian Democrats and other leftists; and the Armed Forces of National Resistance (FARN or RN), formed in 1975 from a faction of the ERP (Central America Information Office 1982:124). The Salvadoran Communist Party, founded in 1930 and banned in 1932, did not support armed resistance until 1980. Another small armed group, the Revolutionary Party of Central American

Workers (PRTC–El Salvador), was formed in 1979. In 1980, a coalition of four guerrilla groups and the Salvadoran Communist Party formed the Farabundo Martí National Liberation Front. They became legalized as a political party as part of the peace accords in January 1992.

The Gendered Aspects of National Security Doctrine   The Salvadoran status quo, which is projected as necessary to protect national security, has gendered as well as political, cultural, and economic aspects. Writers who have analyzed the "motherist" movements (Fisher 1989, 1993; M. Navarro 1989; Schirmer 1993a, 1993b) have all pointed out the links between Catholic images of femininity and their use by repressive states to control women. Images of the various incarnations of the Virgin Mary portray an idealized woman who is an obedient, self-sacrificing mother, subordinating her needs to those of her children. The Virgin Mary obeyed the wishes of her son, Christ, and of other men including the disciples and God himself. As summarized by María Pilar Aquino, a feminist and advocate of liberation theology:

First, there is the image of Mary as obedient and passive, resigned and suffering, humbly dedicated to domestic tasks in accordance with the role that is naturally hers in the private sphere. This figure of weakness and submission, of all the "typically feminine" virtues, becomes a symbol of the subordinate position women should occupy in the church and society. Second, there is the exalted and idealized image of Mary as the supreme symbol of purity and virginity, which neutralizes her human integrity and her sexuality as a woman. (1993:173)

The counterpart to the image of the Virgin Mary is that of the Whore, as manifested in the story of Mary Magdalene, the prostitute who is counseled by Christ. As a Virgin Mary opposite, the Whore is seen as aggressive, impure, disconnected from motherhood, and a male sexual object. Her sexuality is constructed to service men, and her personhood (if she is granted any) is focused through this role.[3] Women as citizens are projected as being under the care and supervision of the state, consistent with their dependence on males, first their fathers and then their husbands and sons. In this extension of Catholic imagery, the various offices of the state—whether they are heads of state, generals, or police authorities—are extensions of male family members. Women who deviate from the characteristics associated with the Virgin Mary by disobeying state authority and assuming an active role in society can be cast into the opposite role of symbolic whore. As discussed by

Schirmer, another aspect of the traditional Catholic view of women is that "women are naturally culpable for men's transgressions and those of their children" (1993a:54). As family caretakers and citizens, Salvadoran women—like women in Argentina, Chile, Paraguay, Guatemala, and elsewhere in Latin America—were responsible for ensuring that their family members did not become a threat to national security.

When the Salvadoran government installed an ideology of "national security" and left its interpretation up to various military and police units, an ideological contradiction was created in the state's discourse on gender. When large numbers of Salvadoran women began to move into the streets in the 1970s in order to take part in grassroots movements and actively confront state authorities, often as mothers, they invoked the images of mother, virgin, and whore simultaneously. The predominant imagery of women as sacrificial mothers and wives was shattered. After women established the street as their territory through their participation in marches, sit-ins, hunger strikes, and public meetings, the members of El Salvador's security forces began to view all women in public places with suspicion and treated them accordingly.

The following incident illustrates this phenomenon. Sofía Aves Escamillas, a fifty-eight-year-old member of CO-MADRES, describes what it was like to go shopping at the central market in San Salvador during the late 1970s and early 1980s:

When we went to the market, we would have to use see-through shopping bags so that the soldiers posted around the market could see what we had bought. If not, they would tell us that we had bombs in our shopping bags. One day I had bought a ball of soap wrapped in dark paper and they detained me for an entire day. The soldiers who detained me were little boys. They were only sixteen years old, if that. They kept telling me I had a bomb in my shopping bag. I just kept telling them that it wasn't a bomb and finally they let me go at the end of the day. Imagine, boys making an old woman stand in the hot sun for hours and hours.

If Sofía had met a sixteen-year-old boy in her neighborhood out of uniform, he would have been expected to help carry her bag of groceries. Gender and age conventions would have required this young man to show deference and respect to Sofía because of her age and her clear parallel position to his mother and grandmother in kinship relations. If the identities of older woman, wife, mother, and poor female shopper are reread and collapsed into a frame of "potential subversive" by a sixteen-year-old soldier with a gun, power relations change instantly. Sofía can be lumped into the homogeneous category of "subversive" and treated accordingly, losing her humanity and all her rights and privileges as a human being, citizen, and protected woman in a patriarchal state. Later, in 1989, Sofía was kidnapped and detained for fifteen days during the FMLN's "final offensive." She was literally transformed into a guerrilla-subversive when a combined force of the National Police and the Treasury Police broke into the CO-MADRES office, destroyed its contents, photographed Sofía and others in front of an FMLN banner the police had brought, and forced some of them to pose in Che Guevara T-shirts.

As Schirmer points out, once a woman is perceived as a subversive or as having become political, regardless of whether or not she in fact is, another standard of gendered behavior is applied to her by her captors. If a woman has been reclassified by a male in the military or police from "wife, mother, daughter" to "subversive," then her femaleness is read as " 'tainted,' soiled, and by definition sexually aggressive and active— she becomes a whore" (Schirmer 1993a: 55). Women prisoners are then punished uniformly with rape, sexual brutality, and often death. If released, they are told not to discuss their tainted condition and are urged to return to their homes. Not only do ideologies of national security fracture and redefine gender and kinship roles for women, but they do so for men as well. While this subject is not pursued here, men who are read in the category of subversive assume a position of feminine equivalence with their captors; they are often called feminine names and treated as women, including sexually.

This discussion of the origins of national security ideology and its gendered implications has been provided in order to show the hegemonic ideological environment within which the CO-MADRES began operating during the 1970s. What follows is a description of the birth and development of the CO-MADRES as an organization.

The CO-MADRES Story   Founded in 1977 by a group of mothers, CO-MADRES was one of the first groups in El Salvador to denounce the atrocities of the Salvadoran government and military. The group was formally constituted as a committee on Christmas Eve, 1977, under the auspices of the Archdiocese of Monseñor Romero (Schirmer 1993b: 32). The initial group of mothers numbered approximately nine, but grew to between twenty-five and thirty by early 1978 (Schirmer 1993b: 32; interviews). The first group of women (and a few men) who constituted CO-MADRES was quite heterogeneous with respect to class and occupation.

This has been consistently true throughout the life of the organization. The initial group included teachers, workers, peasants, students, lawyers, market women, housewives, and small shopkeepers.

The group contained significant numbers of people who resided in Christian base communities and whose families had suffered severe repression because of their church activism (Schirmer 1993b). Following liberation theology, a philosophy that regarded poverty and exploitation as a sin, these women worked with priests and nuns to begin confronting the Salvadoran military and oligarchy in order to change the gross inequities that had characterized El Salvador by the late 1960s. They brought this philosophy with them into CO-MADRES.

Slowly the CO-MADRES removed the shroud of silence surrounding the repression that had become normal in El Salvador during the 1970s. Armed with a short list of missing relatives, they demanded to know who was in the jails, forced the excavation of clandestine cemeteries, and made the repression tactics of the government known to an international audience. Their first actions in 1978 included taking over the Salvadoran Red Cross Building and organizing a hunger strike and a peaceful occupation of the United Nations building in San Salvador. They then moved on to occupying Catholic churches and holding public demonstrations in the parks and plazas.

For the first two years of their existence the CO-MADRES did not have an office. They held their meetings in various locations and did not leave any of their materials in a permanent location. The three committees of the group focused on finances, publicity, and organizing.

The year 1979 was a turning point for the organization in two significant ways. First of all, the CO-MADRES chose a permanent location and set up an office. This gave the organization a more stable structure and allowed them to set up archives and files. Second, they made their first trip abroad and began to receive international recognition. Once they were settled in their new office, the CO-MADRES set up a governance structure of four committees: Publicity; Finances; Organizing; and Exterior Political Relations, which related to foreign governments, the foreign press, and international solidarity organizations. Each committee had five full-time members. The organization as a whole holds assemblies as often as once a week, or as needed, and makes policy decisions in those assemblies. During the early 1980s, an additional layer of organizational structure was added: a director and five representatives elected by the larger assembly. The director and representatives are responsible for the day-to-day planning and running of the organization.

Alicia Panameño de García receiving the Robert F. Kennedy Human Rights Award on behalf of CO-MADRES in 1984. Photo courtesy of CO-MADRES, El Salvador.

After their first invitation abroad (Costa Rica in 1979), the CO-MADRES began an extremely effective campaign to build international solidarity for their work. In the 1980s the CO-MADRES traveled around the world to Europe, Australia, Canada, the United States, and other Latin American countries, bringing their demands for justice with them. They became one of the leading voices of FEDEFAM, the Federation of the Relatives of the Disappeared and Detained in Latin American, which includes organizations from seventeen Latin American and Caribbean countries.

In 1984, the CO-MADRES were the first recipients of the Robert F. Kennedy Human Rights Award. The Kennedy family along with the musician Bonnie Raitt have been long-standing supporters of CO-MADRES. "Friends of CO-MADRES" solidarity organizations were established in the United States, Australia, Switzerland, Germany, Mexico, and Canada beginning in the mid-1980s. They carried out fund-raising and acted as political watchdogs for human rights abuses in El Salva-

Sofía Aves Escamillas (left) and another member of CO-MADRES assess the damage to their office building after a bombing in October 1989. Photo courtesy of CO-MADRES, El Salvador.

dor. Nine chapters of Friends of CO-MADRES were established in the United States. During the 1980s, solidarity delegations from the United States, Europe, Australia, and New Zealand also came to visit the CO-MADRES in El Salvador.

Soon after the CO-MADRES began organizing in the late 1970s, they themselves became victims of government repression. Their first office was bombed in 1980, and since then their offices have been bombed four additional times (most recently in 1989, shortly before the FMLN's November offensive). Each time, they regrouped and continued working. In 1989, the women's section of the Norwegian Social Democratic Party donated money that was used to purchase a permanent office site.

A majority of the most active CO-MADRES have been detained, tortured, and raped. Since 1977, forty-eight members of CO-MADRES have been detained, five have been assassinated for their activism, and three have disappeared (Stephen 1994a; Schirmer 1993b). Even after the peace accords were signed in December 1991, harassment and disappearances continued. In February 1993, the son and the nephew of one of the founders of CO-MADRES were assassinated in Usulután. This woman had already lived through the experience of her own detention, the detention and gang rape of her daughter, and the disappearance and assassination of other family members. For many women, the kinds of human rights abuses they have suffered have fortified their determination and have resulted in a painful self-awareness and acknowledgment of their treatment as women at the hands of national security forces.

While the formal agenda of the CO-MADRES remained focused on confronting the sources of human rights abuse in El Salvador, in their private conversations and experience these women also began a serious questioning of female gender roles. Many women activists were not supported by their husbands at best and were beaten by them at worst. When CO-MADRES members were raped as a routine part of their torture, they would be rejected by their husbands and families as damaged goods. Private internal discussions about what kinds of rights they had as women, as workers, and as mothers slowly became part of their public agenda during the late 1980s. Support for a questioning of oppressive gender roles for women came in part from a small feminist movement emerging in El Salvador at that time. As women's sections of other popular organizations began to question their subordinate position within their own organizations and homes, other Salvadoran women were beginning to take a public stand on issues often identified with feminism: rape, unequal work burdens in the home, the political marginalization of women, and women's lack of control over their own sexuality and bodies.

Methods of Analysis and Presentation The growth and change of the organizational agenda of the CO-MADRES are the focus of the ethnographic analysis which follows. Rather than using tidbits of interviews from many different women, I have chosen to focus on three activists within the CO-MADRES and to use their histories and experiences to represent the diversity within the organization. Sofía Aves Escamillas and Alicia Panameño de García were interviewed at length during a field trip to El Salvador in 1991. During that time seven members of CO-MADRES were interviewed in-depth, and meetings were observed. María Teresa Tula was interviewed periodically over a two-year period from 1991 to 1993 for forty hours. Some of the material from those interviews has been published as her testimonial (see Stephen 1994a). Other sources of information were documents from the CO-MADRES offices in San Salvador and Washington, D.C. In 1991 I also interviewed women activists from seven other organizations and discussed the CO-MADRES with them.

I chose to focus on María Teresa, Sofía, and Alicia because they represent the range of experience, political perspectives, and age cohorts found within the CO-MADRES. While María and Sofía come from poor peasant and rural worker backgrounds, Alicia was reared in a lower-middle-class urban family in San Salvador. María grew up in the town of Izalco, and Sofía in a small community in the district of Guazapa. Alicia grew up in a neighborhood of San Salvador known as Santa Lucía. María and Sofía attended only the first two years of primary school, but Alicia finished high school. María made a living taking in people's laundry. Sofía worked in the countryside in subsistence agriculture and later made leather wallets and suitcases. Alicia was a maternity nurse in a large hospital. All three were married and had children.

While María came into CO-MADRES without prior political experience, Alicia had been active in a Christian base community[4] in one of San Salvador's shantytowns for some time before joining CO-MADRES. Sofía, like María, had little previous political experience, but had children who were heavily involved in labor and peasant movements. Alicia has been working with the CO-MADRES since the organization's inception and continues to live in San Salvador. María began working full-time for the CO-MADRES during the mid-1980s. She received political asylum and now lives in Minneapolis. Sofía continues to work making leather goods and still attends CO-MADRES meetings. In the analysis that follows, wherever the comments from Alicia, Sofía, or María are in direct response to an interview question, I have included that question.

On the Diverse Experiences and Meanings of Motherhood   A majority of the women in CO-MADRES are mothers. While these women share the biological experience of giving birth to and/or adopting children as well as a general socialization in what it means to be a Salvadoran mother, this by no means ensures that they joined CO-MADRES with identical interpretations of what motherhood means. The diversity of class and occupational sectors represented as well as the varied political experiences of women when they joined CO-MADRES virtually guaranteed a variety of perspectives on motherhood. Once in the organization, the various paths of political work which put CO-MADRES women into contact with everyone from lesbian feminists in Europe to the archbishop of San Salvador ensured a variety of political experiences within the group.

A significant number of women in CO-MADRES came into the organization after having suffered repression within their own families for participating in Christian base communities. Alicia Panameño de García, one of the founding members of CO-MADRES, was one such member. She recalls of herself and several other founding members that they came into CO-MADRES having already done some critical thinking about the relationships between mothers and children, husbands and wives. Alicia is forty-nine years old and has been a CO-MADRES member since 1977; she became director in 1993. Alicia started participating in Christian base communities in 1972, and she began to work in the area of human rights in 1975. Of her participation in Christian base communities, she says:

A lot of work was done in this time to change family relations. A lot of families had very bad relations between people. We learned about how to divide the housework. We taught that everyone had to share in the housework — husbands, wives, and children. Everyone was supposed to participate, not just mothers. We also talked about what went on between couples. So we had already started to discuss these issues. A lot of the original mothers were mothers of catechists. These were people who were active in the base communities and the cooperatives. A lot of them were captured or assassinated so it was logical that the mothers of these young people were part of the committee.

While leaders such as Alicia came into the organization already questioning their roles as wives and mothers supposedly responsible for all housework, childcare, and general reproductive maintenance, other members such as María Teresa Tula and Sofía Aves Escamillas did not. María Teresa Tula became a part of the CO-MADRES after her husband was incarcerated as a political prisoner for his role in leading a sugar mill strike in Izalco during 1978. María was unaware of his union activism and had never attended any kind of political meeting or belonged to any grassroots organization. Her original reason for joining was to help get her husband out of jail and back home so that he could help support the children. At the time of his arrest, she was ironing other people's clothing to earn a living. She was forty-one years old at the time of the interview. She comments on her life at the time of the arrest:

During that time I didn't really have an occupation that would allow me to work. I had no idea what Rafael was doing at the time. He never told me. What I did was to keep house. He would go to work and I would iron for other people. I couldn't do washing for money because it was hard to go down to the river with my kids. So I ironed for working people who didn't have time to press their clothes. They would bring me clothes to iron at home. I would iron with a steam iron and received ten cents for each piece of clothing. Sometimes I would be ironing from two o'clock in the afternoon until eleven o'clock at night just to earn about eight colones, *about two dollars. It was hard work. I always had calluses on my hands from where I had grabbed the iron in the wrong place.*

When María first began coming to CO-MADRES meetings, at the suggestion of her husband, she was quite intimidated. Alicia recalls María's first visits in 1978:

> **Lynn:** How did you get to know María?
>
> **Alicia:** I got to know María after her husband was arrested in the sugar strike and she started to work with us. She attended some of our meetings and courses on how to help political prisoners, but she had never had any experience with self-development before. She was very nervous.
>
> **Lynn:** So CO-MADRES was the first political work she participated in?
>
> **Alicia:** Yes.
>
> **Lynn:** So she had to learn everything?
>
> **Alicia:** Yes. It is where she started to discover herself as María Teresa Tula. It was where she started to feel important as a human being.

María went on to become one of the best known and most vocal leaders of CO-MADRES internationally. Her integration into the group raised issues for her that had never surfaced before. As discussed below, her struggle to legitimize her work with CO-MADRES later conflicted with her husband's expectations of her as wife, mother, and homemaker, once he got out of jail.

Sofía Aves Escamillas came into CO-MADRES from the countryside, where her son and husband were killed because of their participation in peasant and labor organizing. When I interviewed her and asked what she thought about CO-MADRES being a group of women, the question did not seem particularly meaningful to her. I repeated it several times. What did seem to be meaningful to her was the role of suffering mother that they all shared, mourning their lost husbands and children:

> **Lynn:** So why do you think that people identified themselves so strongly as mothers when CO-MADRES started?
>
> **Sofía:** We started out as a group of mothers who were asking for our children. I was trying to find out about my son. My husband had already died. . . . Before, you see, there were cooperatives where the people

who were poor got together to plant rice, beans, and other food. The army thought that these co-ops were bad. So they threw everyone in the co-ops out of their houses, detained them, and then disappeared them. This caused us to join CO-MADRES. The reason we are all women is that we were looking for our children because we are mothers.

Sofía came into CO-MADRES identifying as a mother who has a legitimate right to know the whereabouts of her children. As she stayed with CO-MADRES over a fifteen-year period, she began to explore other issues, such as female sexuality and the overall oppression of women. Her thinking on these issues, however, remained distinct from that of María and Alicia, as is discussed below.

Redefining Human Rights to Include Women's Rights   The trajectory of CO-MADRES' programmatic activities between 1977 and 1994 is a reflection of the personal and political experiences of the women in the organization. Rather than shifting from an initial focus on human rights abuses to issues more directly related to the oppression of women, CO-MADRES has expanded to embrace a much wider definition of human rights—one that incorporates the rights of women. This change has not been a sudden move from a "motherist" agenda to a feminist agenda, but a nuanced process in which women's detention, rape, and torture at the hands of police and military authorities, their domestic conflicts with their husbands and children, and their contacts with other human rights organizations and with self-identified feminists have combined to give "human rights" a new meaning for the women in CO-MADRES. While most women in CO-MADRES have shared many common experiences over the past fifteen years, their interpretations of the relationship between women's rights and human rights remain varied, as discussed below.

Rape is a well-documented method of terrorizing and torturing women in the name of maintaining national security (Bunster-Burotto 1986; Schirmer 1993a). Salvadoran men and boys have been victims of rape as well. The Salvadoran army, National Police, National Guard, and Treasury Police have all been implicated in the use of rape as a systematic method of torture. All of the women who were active participants in CO-MADRES have been detained, raped, and tortured. Rape as a routine part of torture was a common experience not only for the women in CO-MADRES but for many other Salvadoran women during the course of the civil war, especially in rural areas. María Teresa Tula describes women she met in the women's prison while recovering from

her own torture and rape. The horror of what she was telling was evident
by the tears welling up in her eyes as she spoke and remembered:

*We women would talk to each other about all of the horrible things
that had happened to us. We had been tortured and raped by as many
as eight or ten men, and some women got pregnant when they were
raped. That is where some of the children in the prison came from.
Some of the women were refugees who had been captured by the army.
I still remember one who was over sixty years old. They raped her with
a flashlight over and over again. "Shove the flashlight in her vagina, in
her vagina. See what she is hiding in there." That's what they shouted
to her. We women suffered horrible things. It was terrible. Almost
everyone had signs of torture. People had received electric shock on
their breasts, in their ears, and in their private parts. They were treated
like animals, not respected like human beings. I will never forget it.*

María has been an organizer for CO-MADRES in the United States
since 1987. As part of her work, she has traveled to most of the fifty
states and recounted her story. Every time she tells it, however, she says
that discussing her own rape is always the most difficult aspect. What is
most painful for her is the fact that some people seem to doubt her story:

*We have to make people understand how men of power in El Salvador
have turned into beasts who don't respect women of any age. Women
from thirteen to seventy have been systematically raped as part of their
torture. This is the hardest thing to deal with. I feel deeply ashamed
telling people that I was raped during my torture. The reality is that the
majority of women who are detained are raped. They always think that
rape is something that happens to someone else. Even in El Salvador.
It's difficult to bring up. When other women would come to the office in
El Salvador and talk about what happened to them in their torture, I
would want to tell them, "It didn't just happen to you." Many women
have been raped.*

While the use of rape as an instrument of torture has been common
knowledge among activists for the past ten years, the issue has only recently been openly discussed in a systematic manner. Says Alicia Panameño de García, who was herself raped:

Here in El Salvador there isn't one woman who has been captured
and detained who hasn't been raped. This is psychologically very diffi-

cult for women. And our own culture here still requires women to be virgins when they are married.

Rape was one of those things we didn't really think about. We weren't really prepared for it happening to us. We didn't think that the military would systematically be using these practices. So the first few women were detained and they were raped, and because we are taught that women are supposed to be pure, they didn't talk about that. They didn't say, "They did this to me . . ."

Lynn: They didn't talk about it?

Alicia: That's right. But little by little we discovered it. The women started talking about it. They had to because it had consequences for their health. They needed medical assistance, and when we would give people medical aid we started to learn that every one of the women had been raped.

With time, the CO-MADRES discovered that rape was not only used as a form of torture against women, but against men as well. Men were even more reluctant to talk about their rape than women. Alicia began to realize men were raped because of her work as a nurse who provided people with medical assistance after their release from detention:

We began to realize that it wasn't just women who were raped by the military. It was happening to men, too. First we saw it with one boy who had been badly beaten. Then I worked in the hospital where a lot of boys came after their detention. Many of them had been raped. It was happening to men, too. It was a form of torture used to lower people's morale, men and women. . . . The men would never talk about it. We knew because we were nurses. I had to take care of them.

The sexual brutalization of all women detainees helped to bring the issue of sexuality forward in CO-MADRES, as women found that they needed a place to talk about their experiences. They also needed to face their fear that if they told anyone, their husbands in particular, they would be abandoned. Through their discussions and denunciations of torture and detention, CO-MADRES and other human rights groups composed primarily of women raised the issue of rape for public discussion. This has benefited women, who are now beginning to question the legal codes that give rape victims no rights.

During 1991, the CO-MADRES were discussing problems that are specific to women, with rape and sexuality at the top of the list. Many group members reported that they had never felt sexual pleasure, had never discussed sexual relationships or their own rapes. This discussion program, however, was not received equally well by all women. Some older women like Sofía, despite their own rape in detention, were very uncomfortable talking about the subject. Alicia continues on this topic:

At first when we tried to talk about rape and sexual relations between couples, it was rejected by various women. They would say, "Oh, that is disgusting. How can we talk about this?" . . . There are a lot of women who have many children and who have never felt satisfied in a sexual relationship. They have never felt sexual pleasure. The man just arrived, did what he wanted, and then left. . . . We have discussed this here and how couples can be happy.

Eventually many women did join discussions on sexuality, and these went on until all hours of the morning; everyone was interested in the topic. In my interviews in 1991, however, some CO-MADRES members were still uneasy about the subject.

Another common experience women shared was the reluctance of their husbands, if they were still alive, to let them be active in CO-MADRES. Such activism was often perceived as taking away from women's time to do domestic chores and to take care of the children. After María's husband was released from jail, he pushed very hard to stop her from working with the CO-MADRES. He got her to stay away from the organization until members of CO-MADRES came looking for her. María describes what happened, leading up to her husband's confrontation by a older woman known as *la abuela*, or grandmother. The sequence begins with her husband, Rafael, talking. María relates what happened in the form of a conversation:

"The truth is that I don't want you to keep working with CO-MADRES. I need you here at home. Sometimes I want to talk to you and you aren't here. Sometimes I get tired of taking care of the kids, and they need you to be here more than I do. And sometimes I really ask myself, What is she doing with them? What is she doing fooling around in San Salvador?"

"Really?" I sighed, surprised. "You really think I go to San Salvador to fool around?" I was crying, embracing him and kissing him. "You really think that I'm just wasting my time?"

"Yes," he said.

"Ok, then," I replied. "I will obey the man of the house. If he wants me to stay home, then I will. But if they come from CO-MADRES and ask what happened to me, then you will have to answer to them."

"No, they won't come here looking for you," he said. "They won't even remember you."

I felt very conflicted. I had an appointment that day and people were counting on me. But at the same time, I was still ruled by my love for my compañero *[spouse] more than by my love for my work. Two days went by, and he was very happy because I stayed at home the whole time. Then, at five o'clock in the morning on the third day, there was a loud knock on the door.*

"It is the abuela. *That's what they call her," I responded.*

"They came looking for you," he said.

"No, they are looking for you," I answered, and opened the door.

"What's going on? How come you haven't come to the CO-MADRES office?" she asked, staring at me.

"Well," I said, shouting so Rafael could hear: "You see, it seems that when I go I don't really do anything at all. I don't do anything in the office and I'm just going into San Salvador to hang around on the streets. My beloved husband doesn't want me to leave anymore. He wants me to stay here to take care of him and the kids, to clean the house."

The abuela *turned toward the bed where Rafael was lying down and raised her voice. "Mmmm. Compañero, I had you pegged for a more intelligent person. But look at the foolishness that has come out of your mouth."*

Rafael got up. "Good morning, abuela," he said sleepily.

"Good morning," she said to him. "So now, answer my question."

"Look abuela, it isn't like it seems. This woman is just fickle. I was just kidding when I said those things to her, and she took me seriously. I don't keep her from going out."

"Listen," the abuela *told him. "This woman has responsibility. People are counting on her. When she isn't there, it is a problem."*

"Why didn't you tell me that?" Rafael asked.

That day I got a change of clothes and left with the abuela *to go off and do some work. But it was the beginning of a long struggle with Rafael about my work.*

Sofía describes similar episodes that have occurred often in the fifteen years she has worked with CO-MADRES.

We often would have women in the group who would say, "Look, my husband is beating me because he doesn't want me to come here." So what we would do is go to talk with the man and tell him, "Look, she is coming here to work with us." The problem is that the men misunderstand. They don't believe the women are coming here with us. My husband was already dead when I joined CO-MADRES, so I didn't have this problem.

Sofía also noted that some women had to leave CO-MADRES because of pressure from their husbands, often combined with economic pressure.

The CO-MADRES explained the necessity of their work—both to men who were questioning it and to each other—in terms of the need to struggle for the human rights of all Salvadorans, the importance of women doing some domestic work, and the right of women to work outside the home and control their own lives. Alicia, who had been part of another visit to Rafael when he was questioning María's participation, found his resistance difficult to understand:

Alicia: When I went there he told me that he didn't want her to participate. He said that she was away from the house too much. . . . So I told him that taking care of the house was as important as the work she was doing with us for human rights. I said that what she needed to learn was how to organize her time. She needed some time with us and some time at home. That would make them both feel better.

Lynn: So you gave him a little marriage counseling? Talked with him about how couples could get along?

Alicia: Yes. He wasn't paying much attention to her, and she would come home and feel bad. He would accuse her of doing all kinds of things. So I told him that he was mistaken about what she was doing. I was really surprised by his attitude because of his education and involvement with the union.

When María described the treatment she got from her husband after returning to work with CO-MADRES, she focused primarily on the kinds of rights she had as a woman. Sofía and several other women interviewed also followed up their discussions about women's repression by their husbands with remarks about the general oppression of women. Sofía commented:

Here in El Salvador we are exploited by the government. They behave as if they are our bosses. And women have been the most exploited.

*Because even when a woman goes to work in the countryside, she is
paid less than a man for the same work. She gets this same kind of
exploitation from her husband. You know, we have to do the wash and
everything else for our husbands. We are beginning to realize that we
are exploited by them as well.*

The rationale that different women in CO-MADRES use to justify
their work is reflective of the different political and ideological spheres
that they have been working in. Several leaders of the CO-MADRES, like
María and Alicia, have had wide experience within the international human rights community as well as exposure to various forms of feminism.
Others, such as Sofía, have not done as much traveling or been to feminist meetings and workshops. They hear reports about what went on
from those who attended and then integrate what they hear with their
own experience.

Most CO-MADRES have met with women from other organizations
formed by relatives of the disappeared. In 1981, Alicia and several other
CO-MADRES went to the first meeting of the Federation of the Relatives of the Disappeared and Detained in Latin America. There they met
women from the Mothers of the Plaza de Mayo, an Argentine group
formed in the early 1970s:

> **Lynn:** Was it important for you to meet the Mothers of the Plaza
> de Mayo?
> **Alicia:** Yes, because their work was very similar to ours and they
> had the same problems. The same methods are used by the military all
> over Latin America. The same repressive scheme is applied to all the
> countries.

In 1985, Alicia traveled to the United Nations Conference on Women
in Nairobi, Kenya. She has been to three international meetings, or *encuentros*, of Latin American feminists as well as to meetings of European
feminists. María went to Europe twice on tours organized by feminist
women, and she has met with a wide variety of women's groups in the
United States and Europe. Alicia and María both seem quite comfortable
discussing feminism:

> **Lynn:** How did you feel at the Latin American feminist *encuentros*
> you attended?
> **Alicia:** Well, maybe it is because of the work that we do, but we have
> already been taking some courses on human rights work that incorpo-

rate the problems raised by feminists. This includes the problems of feminist women as well as lesbian women. From our point of view we understand perfectly well the problems of feminist women and lesbian women. They are all discriminated against.

Lynn: Do you see any of the struggles of feminists as struggles that are connected with what you are doing?

Alicia: Well, I already mentioned that women have been the victims of men's machismo for centuries, right? So in this sense there is a need for women to create a movement which has women's rights as its principal struggle. I don't feel like a feminist, because I need to learn more about it. But the general struggle for women, I understand that. I have to learn some more about the concept of feminism. That isn't entirely clear to me.

María's discussion of her first contact with feminists in Germany was laced with frustration about the difficulty she had in getting women to understand her need to talk with the Salvadoran men she met. It was also her first contact with openly lesbian women. Since that trip, and other trips, she has refined her discussion of feminism and reflects in it, as does Alicia, a mixture of influences. The following passage, quoted from María's testimonial, captures the unique sort of Salvadoran feminism she has developed. While it cannot be construed as representative of the position of all women in CO-MADRES, it does contain many elements which have influenced the thinking of the women in that organization:

In El Salvador we don't run around calling ourselves feminists, but we are feminists because we are fighting for our rights. The difference for us in El Salvador is that our struggle as women comes together with our struggle for change in El Salvador. Our feminism doesn't just involve fighting for ourselves, but for a change for all of us. We can't forget about the system that oppresses all of us. So we are doing two things at once. We are fighting for our rights as women and we are also fighting for social change in our country. If there isn't drastic social change in our country, then we will always be oppressed even though we are fighting for our rights as women. For us, our struggle as women includes many things. I think it's fine for the women in the groups we met to be talking about feminism and discussing the oppression that women have suffered for centuries, and to be working for change through a women's movement. Everyone has the right to wage their struggle as they see fit. I have heard a lot about the abortion debate. I

*believe that I or any woman should have the right to decide what she
wants to do. I am a mother of six children and I'm not going to criticize
anyone's choice.*

*Women do share some common history. We are all different colors,
but I think that we share some common sentiments and our blood is all
the same color. We all have red blood, not yellow or orange. We all
share the same blood and some commonalities as women that make us
identify with one another. I think the suffering that women have gone
through everywhere helps to build international solidarity among us.*

*But the system that we live under in El Salvador gives feminism a
different meaning. We see all women as feminists, whether they are
workers, peasants, or professionals. In El Salvador and other Latin
American countries, there are big differences between bourgeois women
who call themselves feminists and other women. Sometimes we see
these women who call themselves feminists, but all they do is talk, roar-
ing like lions, but not doing anything. They go on marches, but they
don't really do anything, just march around in the name of feminism.
To be that kind of feminist in El Salvador means that you are a member
of the bourgeoisie, not an ordinary woman like a peasant or a house-
wife, who have always been oppressed for years and years. These
women don't call themselves feminists, but they are more oppressed
than someone who is the wife of the president or a businessman. These
humble women have demonstrated that they have the political, ideological, and military capacity to help make changes in El Salvador. Being united for women's rights won't do us any good unless we change
the government.*

*You know, being women doesn't necessarily make for change. There
are women in positions of power, even presidents or prime ministers,
who have the bodies of women, but the minds and hearts of oppressive men. It's a shame. It just goes to show that it isn't enough to have
women in power, we have to change the whole system — in El Salvador, the United States, and Europe. If we don't, then we could die and
another generation of feminists would be born with more ideas, but
they would all continue to be repressed. (Stephen 1994a: 125–126)*

The work of the CO-MADRES in the 1990s has focused on holding
the state accountable for human rights violations committed during the
war and, most recently, on making sure that the recommendations of the
U.N. Truth Commission are followed. In addition, the CO-MADRES
are (1) confronting the legal system to provide better protection for political prisoners as well as assurances that human rights abuses will not

be committed in the future; (2) working against domestic violence, and to some extent, against unequal gender relations in the home; (3) educating women about political participation and how to take part in elections; and (4) sponsoring small economic projects such as sewing co-ops to help women support themselves. They formed part of a coalition of women's groups called "Mujeres '94" (Women in 1994) which worked on a unified platform for women and delivered it to all the political parties who participated in the 1994 elections. The platform called for an end to incest, rape, and sexual harassment; free and voluntary motherhood; sex education for women; land, credit, and technical assistance for women; adequate housing with ownership for women; economic development programs and job training for women; more education for women and girls; better medical attention for women; and an end to the rising cost of wage goods. During 1993 the coalition held debates on the following topics for incorporation into the platform: domestic violence, women and the land reform process, the legal system, education, the environment, health, reproductive rights, sexuality, and political participation. As seen from the above description, then, the political trajectory of CO-MADRES is not a unilateral move from the private-domestic-feminine sphere into the public-political-feminist sphere.

Conclusions   The case of the CO-MADRES highlights the need to approach the analysis of women's organizations and movements with a model that allows for both accommodation and resistance to so-called traditional gender roles and for a multiplicity of interpretations and truth claims within the same movement. If we want to understand how and why people act, we must carefully consider the synthetic results of people's own experience on their behavior. This prevents us from portraying women activists as flattened, uniform caricatures who fall on either one side or another of some universal feminist continuum. The CO-MADRES' understanding of their gendered position in the world did not emerge suddenly or in a uniform manner. This was not a transition from "traditional" ideas about women to a model of total liberation. Members' awareness of the gendered meanings of national security ideology and of women's unequal treatment under the law and at home came in spurts and was integrated with other kinds of political experience. Existing gender and kinship relations were politicized through government repression which made more visible the integration of public and private spheres that already existed in women's lives and which pointed to the contradictions of women's treatment within those spheres. In many ways, the women of CO-MADRES retained some of their original and varied ideas about motherhood and added to them, incorporating ideas about women's rights within a discourse on human rights. Although identifying motherhood simultaneously with child rearing, personal sacrifice for one's children, persistent confrontation with military authorities, and campaigns to end rape and promote sex education may appear contradictory to people outside the movement, the experience of the women in CO-MADRES has made these ideas consistent. The way they have framed their ideas is now part of the rich variety of discourse found within El Salvador's feminisms and women's movements.

CHAPTER 3

Women for Dignity and Life
The Emergence of Feminisms from El Salvador's Revolutionary Left

Women for Dignity and Life (DIGNAS, Mujeres por la Dignidad y la Vida) was born in 1990 after the final offensive carried out by the FMLN in 1989. Originally created as an arm of the National Resistance (RN, Resistencia Nacional), a member of the FMLN, the DIGNAS engaged in a struggle for autonomy to determine their own agenda. By late 1993 they had largely succeeded in doing that, having achieved elected representation on their central coordinating committee from three other parties of the FMLN as well as several from other political tendencies on the left. Their work has included small income-generating projects such as chicken farming, bakeries, and craft production. They have also provided public domestic services such as collective kitchens, communal stores, and day-care centers for women in resettlement populations located in zones of conflict during the war. In addition, they have conducted consciousness-raising workshops on a wide range of topics including sexuality, maternity, domestic work and wage labor, domestic violence, power, and the women's movement. They have provided a unique model in El Salvador by combining work focused on creating gender consciousness with more traditional work, such as organizing productive projects and socialized domestic services.

The DIGNAS have also been key figures in networking among women's organizations within El Salvador, doing so through a number of coalitions which culminated in a women's political platform and coalition for the 1993 and 1994 elections. The content of the platform is diverse, demanding everything from land, credit, and technical assistance for women to the expression of women's sexuality without prejudice (Stephen 1994a:218). The diversity of the demands provides the clearest indication that the DIGNAS and other women who created the platform are clearly in the process of building a women's movement that refuses to be pigeonholed as "feminine" or "feminist." Since 1991, the DIGNAS began working with other Central American women's groups—first to organize a regional meeting, then to form an ongoing regional council, and finally to sponsor the Sixth Latin American and Caribbean Feminist Encuentro (El Salvador, 1993).

This chapter follows the birth and growth of the DIGNAS in the midst of great economic and political turmoil in El Salvador as the thirteen-year-long civil war wound down and the clandestine parties of the FMLN came above ground to participate in the national electoral process. In order to set the scene for the emergence of the DIGNAS, the rise of the Association of Women Confronting the National Problem (AMPRONAC), which became the Luisa Amanda Espinoza Association of Nicaraguan Women (AMNLAE), is discussed along with the role of U.S. citizens and feminist women in the movement for solidarity with El Salvador. This is followed by a section outlining the emergence of the revolutionary left in El Salvador and the types of women's organizations that were created to support the political and social programs of the parties within the FMLN. The civil war and the political situation in El Salvador will be briefly discussed, but readers are encouraged to refer to the previous chapter on the CO-MADRES for a fuller discussion.

Lessons from Nicaragua   Women's organizing in El Salvador has undergone a long and diverse history, particularly in relation to the trajectory of its thirteen-year civil war waged between 1979 and 1992. In El Salvador, as in Cuba, Nicaragua, and elsewhere, the emergence of parties on the revolutionary left included the formation of mass organizations for women that were initially created to develop an additional social base of support. The experience most familiar to many women in El Salvador who now call themselves feminists is that of Nicaragua. Many of them spent time in Nicaragua during the Salvadoran civil war, and it was in that country that some gained their first knowledge of the joys and pitfalls of trying to construct women's organizations and movements.

As described by Chinchilla (1990), Maier (1985), and Randall (1981), the creation of AMPRONAC (Asociación de Mujeres frente a la Problemática Nacional) by the Sandinista National Liberation Front (FSLN, Frente Sandinista de Liberación Nacional) in 1977 was premised on a basic demand of respect for human rights that by 1978 called for the overthrow of the Somoza dictatorship. Maier (1985:70–71) writes that AMPRONAC went from a small group of petit bourgeois and bourgeois women to a mass organization of over ten thousand members that came to represent a wide range of classes, but particularly women from the urban margins and the countryside. As pointed out by Chinchilla, while the organization had no vision of what would happen to women after the dictatorship was overthrown, their founding document did contain a section titled "Women's Struggles for Their Own Emancipation," which makes reference to "a double burden of discrimination on the basis of sex . . . dependence and submission to men" (AMPRONAC program: cited in Maier 1980:155–156; trans. in Chinchilla 1990: 374 375).[1]

Participating in the Sandinista revolution to oust Anastasio Somoza greatly transformed women's lives, as documented in the works of Maier (1980, 1985) and Randall (1981). Daily household routines were turned upside down: women left on long trips, were training in militias, were preparing food to take to clandestine safe houses and guerrilla camps, kept late hours attending meetings, and confronted Somoza officials and the National Guard in their searches for disappeared and imprisoned relatives. Most of those who have studied the women who entered AMPRONAC note that they entered the organization "more out of a strong identification with their roles as mothers, grandmothers, and spouses than out of any critique of the gendered division of labor or their circumstances as women" (Chinchilla 1990:375). Nevertheless, the potentially transforming experiences of women provided an opening for them to begin rethinking their position. This has happened in all situations of war. What is critical, however, is the ideological context that women in organizations such as AMPRONAC encountered after 1979 when the Sandinistas came to power.

As pointed out by Maier (1985:82), there is a major difference between being an opposition organization and then coming to form a women's organization within the structures of power. Once the Sandinistas came to power, they created seven sectoral organizations within the FSLN, including AMNLAE (Asociación de Mujeres Nicaragüenses "Luisa Amanda Espinoza"). Luisa Amanda Espinoza was the first female to die in the struggle to overthrow Somoza. Other sectoral organizations were created for urban workers, rural workers, farmers and cattle ranchers, youth, and children. The original charge of AMNLAE was to create a program which would simultaneously take care of women's needs, develop women as an organized sector, and support the overall demands of the FSLN revolutionary government. From the beginning, AMNLAE's development was confined within the priorities of the FSLN.

Many discussions of AMNLAE divide its existence into several different phases. Most agree that in its initial stage, while declaring itself dedicated to the emancipation of women ("No Revolution without Women's

Emancipation, No Emancipation without Revolution"), the organization was primarily dedicated to integrating women into the reconstruction of the country and defense of the revolution (see Chinchilla 1990; Molyneux 1985; Comité Nacional Feminista 1994a). There were also a variety of positions within the FSLN regarding the appropriateness of feminism as a form of struggle within a revolutionary society. In 1982, AMNLAE became actively involved in recruiting women into the military and the militia as the Sandinistas struggled to defend their revolution against the U.S.-backed Contras. Earlier gains that had benefited women (particularly poor women) in important ways—such as reducing the illiteracy rate from over 50 percent to 13 percent, eradicating many deadly diseases, and providing basic healthcare and housing—gave way to a focus on military defense (Molyneux 1985:248; Chinchilla 1990:382–383).

During its second phase, AMNLAE became focused on defense of the country. More traditional ways of incorporating women into the struggle, such as those fostered in an earlier organization called the Committee of Mothers of Martyrs and Heroes (Comité de Madres de Héroes y Mártires) began to appear. Support for mothers of combatants, logistical support for the war, and getting women involved in the economy were priority areas. With many women, however, this did not sit well, and criticism of AMNLAE began to emanate from urban neighborhoods and the countryside.

According to Chinchilla (1990), facing the first national elections in 1984 and fearful of a conservative backlash from women such as that seen in Chile, the FSLN called for a critical reevaluation of AMNLAE—in its structure, decisionmaking process, and agenda. It was already apparent by this time that there was considerable ideological diversity among the women who participated in AMNLAE. While some were strict adherents to FSLN doctrine, others had begun to undertake more radical work with respect to changing gender roles in mixed organizations such as labor unions and peasant organizations. In the Association of Agricultural Workers (ATC, Asociación de Trabajadores Agrícolas) women's demands were integrated with the overall agenda of the organization (Comité Nacional Feminista 1994a:8; Chinchilla 1990:384).

Chinchilla describes how in the mid-1980s AMNLAE's structure was modified so that groups of women with similar interests meeting at the base level could send proposals to AMNLAE for action instead of receiving orders from the AMNLAE leadership. In 1985, AMNLAE called a national assembly that promoted campaigns organized around sexuality, workplace discrimination, and domestic violence (Chinchilla 1990:385).

In the mid-1980s, about eighty women from AMNLAE who worked in mixed organizations began an informal discussion group with the amusing name "Party of the Erotic Left" (PIE, Partido de la Izquierda Erótica). They devoted themselves to analyzing the situation of women in different types of organizations and the treatment of women by the leadership of mixed organizations. They also had discussions on such themes as violence against women, voluntary maternity and abortion, sexuality, respect for different sexual preferences, valorizing domestic work, women's right to political participation, and gendered inequality in general (Comité Nacional Feminista 1994a). In short, they devoted themselves to themes that were often left out of the agenda of AMNLAE. Women who participated in this discussion group went on to lead a campaign to democratize AMNLAE and to broaden its agenda to include the previously mentioned themes, which they saw as explicitly feminist. These same women later formed an autonomous national women's committee and began to work closely with several women from DIGNAS in El Salvador. One of them eventually went to El Salvador to work permanently with the DIGNAS.

Women lobbying for AMNLAE to become an autonomous women's organization began to discuss their dilemma with a wide range of other Latin American feminists during the Fourth Latin American and Caribbean Feminist Encuentro, held in Taxco, Mexico, in 1987. Forty-two women from Nicaragua attended. A primary debate at the conference was over the issue of whether women's movements should be autonomous or whether feminism should be integrated into the revolution. A workshop with Cuban women brought this question into clearer focus (Miller 1991:236–237).

While AMNLAE seemed to be moving toward democratization, setting up a National Council made up of regional leaders and representatives from a collection of women's centers spread throughout the country, in 1989 a movement to elect the general secretary of AMNLAE was defeated. The process was aborted when the FSLN said that it was going to name the head of the organization. For many women within AMNLAE who had worked to democratize the organization, this was a devastating move on the part of the FSLN.

In February 1990 the FSLN lost at the polls and Violeta Barrios de Chamorro, the candidate of a loose coalition of fourteen parties, won the vote for president. After their surprise electoral defeat, the Sandinistas decided to consult with their bases of support and called for reexamination of all their sectoral organizations. In 1990 they carried out a series of workshops that brought together women from different sectors and also included autonomous organizations. The process was to culminate in a National Women's Meeting that would result in public recognition of the women's movement as autonomous, diverse, and with its own forms of communication. The final proposal for the meeting was rejected by the AMNLAE leadership. When AMNLAE rejected the proposal prepared for the national meeting, many women's organizations left AMNLAE.

In January 1992, a group of eight hundred women met for the First Women's Encuentro ("Unity in Diversity"). Instead of creating a new organization, the meeting ended with the establishment of a variety of networks focused on specific themes such as health, sexuality, and violence (Comité Nacional Feminista 1994a:10). The lack of consensus around creating a new national women's organization was because of strong differences of approach among those present at the *encuentro*. In May of that same year, the National Feminist Committee was created by women who were not satisfied with the outcome of the First Women's Encuentro. The committee included twenty-five collectives and women's organizations that wanted to build an autonomous feminist movement. They were committed to participatory democracy and consensus decision-making, and they endorsed the following agenda: fighting violence against women, insisting on respect for different sexual preferences, defending voluntary motherhood, and fighting against all forms of oppression, including those based on race, sex, ethnicity, and age. During 1993 the group held a series of seminars, debates, and exchanges that focused on understanding "the origins of the patriarchal system, its historical development, the role played by women in patriarchy, and the kind of new knowledge that can be learned from women's individual and collective experience" (Comité Nacional Feminista 1994a:11).

In October 1993 the committee held the First National Feminist Encuentro. The key outcome of this meeting was a proposal for the creation of a national coordinating organization of women that would be autonomous and based on feminist principles. Unfortunately, this "Concertación" was never realized and, one year after Nicaragua's first-ever explicitly feminist national meeting of women, the National Feminist Committee dissolved itself. Their letter of dissolution cited ten months of conflict and contradictions that had led them to conclude it was best to disband (Comité Nacional Feminista 1994b).

Besides bringing about national networking among feminist and women's organizations in Nicaragua, the Comité Nacional Feminista and other organizations mounted the first Central American Feminist Encuentro (Managua, 1992), which was attended by women from Honduras, El Salvador, Costa Rica, and Guatemala. This meeting and the subsequent creation of a loose regional organization called the "Corriente Feminista Centroamericana" (Central American Feminist Current) provided important forums for the dissemination of the Nicaraguan experience to other women's organizations. The "Corriente" was quite active in the planning of the Sixth Latin American and Caribbean Feminist Encuentro, which took place in El Salvador in October 1993. "Corriente" affiliates worked together within their individual countries and regionally to prepare platforms and to send representatives to the World Conference on Population and Development (Cairo, Egypt) in 1994 and to the Fourth United Nations World Conference on Women (Beijing, China) in 1995.[2]

The struggle of some Nicaraguan women within AMNLAE to achieve organizational autonomy from the FSLN and to bring a wide range of women's concerns, including those that challenged traditional gender roles, to the agenda of their organization was closely watched by women from DIGNAS. As is discussed below, some of the key elements of the DIGNAS organizational plan, as well as their own efforts to create a national body for coordinating women's organizations and to devise a women's political platform, can be traced to the Nicaraguan experience.

The Structure of the Salvadoran Left and Its Impact on Women's Organizing Before going on to discuss the trajectory of women's organizing in El Salvador and the specific case of the DIGNAS, it is necessary to briefly explicate the nature of Salvadoran left-wing politics during the civil war. Severe conditions of political repression in El Salvador during the 1970s required that opposition parties and organizations carry out their activities in secret. During the late 1960s and 1970s a broad range of grassroots movements flourished among peasants, urban workers, students, teachers, professionals, and the urban poor.[3] People participating in these mass organizations were responding to increasingly severe economic conditions and political repression.[4] The number of rural cooperatives rose from 246 to 543 between 1973 and 1980. In the urban sector, labor-union membership increased steadily beginning in the late 1960s, reaching 71,000 by 1977 (Booth and Walker 1989: 77). The spread of liberation theology through Christian base communities was also prevalent in the 1970s. Christian base communities became increasingly involved in making economic and political demands for the poor. They also supported the strikes called by urban workers, teachers, and others.

The government's response to an increasingly militant civil population was increased repression. By 1974, death squads and various branches of the national security forces were operating with impunity. Not only were people directly attacked while engaging in civil protests, but those who organized in Christian base communities—with peasants, urban workers, students, workers for human rights, and other sectors—were increasingly targeted for assassination, capture, and torture. The government's own statistics on violent deaths rose from 1,837 in 1977 to 11,471 in 1980. Until the late 1960s, the average number of violent deaths per year was about 864 (Booth and Walker 1989:79). A more complete description of the conditions of the war, repression, and daily life is found in Chapter 2 above.

Before the Salvadoran peace negotiations in late 1991, the links between mass sectoral organizations and the political-military organizations that made up the FMLN were seldom discussed because of the severe consequences faced by anyone believed to be associated with the FMLN. Since 1992, many members of the five parties that made up the FMLN have now become open about their organizational affiliations. In order to accurately describe the emergence of feminism in El Salvador, an understanding of the revolutionary left is vital. Most women's organizations, including those that in the 1990s self-identified as feminist, emerged from one of the parties in the FMLN. This point has now been made publicly by women discussing their struggle to form autonomous organizations (Mujeres por la Dignidad y la Vida 1993a; Ueltzen 1993). As seen below, separating themselves from the party that founded them was a long and bitter struggle for the DIGNAS.

The guerrilla organizations that came to make up the FMLN were formed between 1970 and 1979. During the same period, in response to government repression, four large opposition coalitions were formed that linked labor, peasant, student and, eventually, women's groups to one or another of the guerrilla organizations.[5] In 1970, the Popular Forces of Liberation "Farabundo Martí" (FPL–FM) was formed and would remain the largest of the guerrilla forces. It was headed by the former secretary general of the Salvadoran Communist Party. The largest of the left-wing coalitions (including peasants, workers, students, teachers, and slum dwellers) was the Popular Revolutionary Bloc (BPR), formed in 1975. The BPR included two major peasant federations, the Federation of Christian Peasants (FECCAS) and the Union of Rural Workers (UTC), as well as the national teachers organization (ANDES). It also included the Union of Urban Dwellers (UTP) and three university and secondary-school federations (MERS, FUR, and UR-19). The BPR was linked to the FPL–FM.

In 1971, the second guerrilla organization was formed: the People's Revolutionary Army (ERP). In 1977 the Popular Leagues "28th of February" (LP-28) was founded; it was dominated by student organizations but had one union affiliate, one peasant league, and an association of market workers (ASUTRAMES). The LP-28 was linked to the ERP.

In 1975, the third guerrilla force, the Armed Forces of National Resistance (FARN, also known as RN) emerged out of an ERP split following the assassination of the poet Roque Dalton by ERP members. The United Popular Action Front (FAPU), the oldest of the leftist coalitions, was founded in 1974. It included two student unions (FUERSA and ARDES), one peasant union (MRC), one labor union, and one teachers' organization. It later came to include organizations in support of human rights, prisoners, and other causes. FAPU had links to the RN.

In 1979, the Revolutionary Party of Central American Workers (PRTC–El Salvador) was formed, with a small guerrilla contingent. That same year, the smallest of the leftist coalitions, the Popular Liberation Movement (MLP) was also formed.

In October 1980, the four guerrilla organizations just enumerated—the FPL–FM, the ERP, the RN, and the PRTC–El Salvador—plus the preexisting Salvadoran Communist Party joined together to form the FMLN. That same year, the Democratic Revolutionary Front (FDR) was created, uniting popular organizations and coalitions associated with the five FMLN organizations as well as several others. The FDR and the FMLN allied to form a joint political-military opposition. Together the popular organizations could mobilize large numbers of people in demonstrations, raise funds, and serve as a source of recruits for the guerrillas. As a coordinated opposition, the FMLN-FDR also adopted a platform for a revolutionary government, established government structures, and organized the civil population in zones they controlled. They also prepared plans to take over with a revolutionary government (Booth and Walker 1989:81).

By 1984, FMLN troop strength had reached almost ten thousand, and the FMLN held a significant part of the country. Government troop strength grew from fifteen thousand in 1980 to fifty-two thousand in 1986 (Booth and Walker 1989:85). The major source of funds supporting this vast increase in the Salvadoran military was the U.S. government. By fiscal year 1989, the United States had provided a total of $3.55 billion in military and civilian aid to El Salvador. The money prolonged the war and rescued several tottering Salvadoran regimes. Without U.S. aid, the Salvadoran government would most likely have fallen quickly in

1981. Ironically, U.S. military aid provided an opening for the creation of a broad solidarity movement in the United States that provided financial and material aid to organizations in the FDR, pressured the U.S. Congress to stop funding military aid, and provided political platforms in the United States for people from the FMLN and from Salvadoran popular organizations.

The Role of Women in U.S. Solidarity with the People of El Salvador   From 1980 until the Salvadoran elections in April of 1994, approximately five thousand to six thousand North Americans went to El Salvador as part of solidarity delegations.[6] Sister cities, sister parishes, the Committee in Solidarity with the People of El Salvador (CISPES), and Christians for Peace in El Salvador (CRISPAZ) were the major conveners of these tours. Several of the political-military organizations of the FMLN worked to create solidarity support in the United States. Some solidarity organizations in the United States directed their tours, material, and financial aid toward popular organizations supported by a particular party. CISPES and several affiliated programs and foundations directed most of their support to organizations and communities aligned with the Popular Forces for Liberation (FPL). The People's Revolutionary Army (ERP) had a somewhat different strategy, focusing most of its support efforts on setting up sister city relationships with two towns in Morazán.[7] The National Resistance (RN) created companion communities, linking up several U.S. communities at a time to one community in El Salvador. Most companion communities were in the area of Santa Marta. The RN also carried out solidarity work through labor unions, human rights groups, and U.S. celebrities.[8] The Salvadoran Communist Party (PCS) and the Revolutionary Party of Central American Workers (PRTC–El Salvador) organized similar U.S. solidarity work on a smaller scale (owing to their smaller size). Besides the thousands of people sent to El Salvador through formally organized solidarity tours, U.S. organizations sent a total of at least $10 million (perhaps $20 million) in direct cash transfers to Salvadoran grassroots organizations and movements.[9] In addition to support from U.S. solidarity organizations, grassroots opposition organizations also received aid from European countries.

At the same time that the U.S. government was funneling millions of dollars in military aid to the Salvadoran army and security forces, a wide range of North American organizations were forging long-lasting links with grassroots organizations in El Salvador. Even after the war had officially ended, with the signing of the peace accords on New Year's Eve,

1991, the enduring ties between U.S. and Salvadoran activists remained. In March and April of 1994, the three biggest solidarity-tour organizers sent seven hundred U.S. citizens as election observers.

While the continued presence of U.S. activists was not a major ideological influence on those in the guerrilla organizations, the case of women may be slightly different. At the height of the Salvadoran war in the mid-1980s, it was estimated that at least 30 percent of all FMLN combatants were women. In the rear guard and among the organized civilian population, women were a majority. By 1989, 51 percent of Salvadoran households were headed by women as men left to fight in the war, escape persecution, or look for work in the United States or elsewhere (García and Gomariz 1989:115; Ready 1994:196–197). Many men had also abandoned their families. Outside the military core of the FMLN, as just noted, a majority of participants in organized civil society were women. And these were the people most often charged with coordinating U.S.-sponsored solidarity tours.

It also appears that most of the participants in the U.S. solidarity tours were women. While no systematic study has been carried out on the politics of women involved in solidarity organizing, it appears that a significant number of them self-identified as feminists. One of the most frequent complaints made by women within the U.S. solidarity organizations was about "machismo" and women's invisibility (Meyer 1994:12–13). Some organizations, such as CISPES, organized tours specifically for women. CISPES began running annual tours for women focused on International Women's Day (March 8) in 1989. Each tour would bring ten to fifteen women to El Salvador and put them in contact primarily with women's organizations. Other solidarity groups have also sponsored women's tours. Between the large number of women who went on mixed solidarity tours as well as those who went specifically on women's tours it is probably safe to say that at least a thousand women who identified with feminist politics came into sustained contact with Salvadoran women and men. In many cases, tours that brought women together resulted in U.S. or European women inviting Salvadoran women abroad for extended tours of from one week up to two months. In this way, the ideas of a range of U.S. feminisms were disseminated to Salvadoran women, and the ideas of Salvadoran women were introduced into Europe and the United States. Some Salvadoran women's organizations are now strongly encouraging a continued exchange of ideas and experiences with U.S. and European women. Before moving on to discuss the particular history of the DIGNAS, the emergence of women's organizations in El Salvador will be briefly discussed.

Women's Organizations in El Salvador   Like other Central American countries, El Salvador had some history of women's organizations prior to the 1970s. Women participated in the 1932 insurrection which led to the Matanza as well as in a 1944 strike to overthrow General Hernández Martínez. Between 1957 and 1969 the first Salvadoran women's organization, the Women's Fraternity, organized more than fifteen hundred market vendors, professionals, teachers, and nurses. In the 1960s and early 1970s several other women's organizations emerged, associated with labor and professional sectors (Mujeres por la Dignidad y la Vida 1993a:86–87).

Contemporary observers of and participants in the second wave of the Salvadoran women's movement often divide women's organizing into three distinct phases (Stephen 1994a; Mujeres por la Dignidad y la Vida 1993a; Ueltzen 1993).[10] The first phase, roughly from 1975 to 1985, includes women's organizations that emerged as part of grassroots movements and in response to high levels of repression. CO-MADRES, founded in 1977 in defense of human rights, was one such organization. The Association of Salvadoran Women (AMES, Asociación de Mujeres de El Salvador), founded in 1979, directed its work toward market vendors, maids, and urban slum dwellers. In the early 1980s the Unitary Women's Committee (CUMS, Comité Unitario de Mujeres) was founded by Salvadorans exiled in Costa Rica. In 1983 the Salvadoran Women's Association (ASMUSA) was founded; in 1984 the Federation of Salvadoran Women (FMS, Federación de Mujeres Salvadoreñas) emerged; and in 1985 the Organization of Salvadoran Women (ORMUSA, Organización de Mujeres Salvadoreñas) arrived on the scene.

Most of these organizations mobilized women around economic issues, survival in the war, and human rights. Their programs had to do with teaching women how to read and write, the promotion of health and nutrition, and housing. In addition, large numbers of women were mobilized to support the revolutionary process. The military-political organizations of the FMLN were active promoters of these women's organizations and benefited from the energy and resources that women put into the war effort. All but two of these organizations (CO-MADRES and ORMUSA) disappeared in the 1990s owing to severe repression by the state and tactical changes in the sectoral organizing carried out by the FMLN.

Phase two of the second wave of women's movements was from 1985 to 1989 and coincided with a general restructuring of El Salvador's popular movements. Pressure on President José Napoleón Duarte to look like a tolerant "centrist" also probably contributed to the explosion of women's organizations that took place in this period. At least ten new organizations were founded. In 1986, the National Coordinating Committee of Salvadoran Women (CONAMUS, Coordinadora Nacional de Mujeres Salvadoreñas) appeared. Although CONAMUS originally served as an educational and informational clearinghouse for other organizations, it later pioneered work with battered women in El Salvador, opening the country's first battered women's shelter in 1989. Like other women's organizations that emerged during this period, CONAMUS began to focus on more specifically gendered demands and to begin questioning women's legal, political, and domestic subordination. The year 1986 also saw the founding of the Institute for Research, Training, and Development of Women (IMU, Instituto para la Investigación, Capacitación, y Desarrollo de la Mujer). IMU provided support to grassroots women's organizations in the areas of communications, legal rights, and education. Its founder, the well-known feminist Norma Virginia Guirola de Herrera, was assassinated in 1989.

El Salvador's first indigenous women's organization was also founded during this period: the Association of Salvadoran Indigenous Women (AMIS, Asociación de Mujeres Indígenas Salvadoreñas).[11] In 1989, the first national coordinating committee of women's organizations, called the COM (Coordinación de Organismos de Mujeres), was formed. It included five women's organizations.[12]

Most of the women's organizations formed from 1985 to 1989 had strong ties to one of the political-military organizations of the FMLN. Some women within these organizations, however, began to participate in international meetings such as the United Nations Conference on Women in Nairobi (1985) and the Fourth Latin American and Caribbean Feminist Encuentro in Taxco, Mexico (1987). In addition, exiled Salvadoran women who had spent time working with feminist movements in Costa Rica, Mexico, Nicaragua, and the United States also began to return to El Salvador (Mujeres por la Dignidad y la Vida 1993a: 90). This time period also represents a peak in visits by U.S. solidarity delegations that included a significant number of feminist women.

As described by women in these movements (Mujeres por la Dignidad y la Vida 1993a:90–91; Stephen 1994a:210–213), although such specifically women's concerns as sexual violence, domestic battering, legal discrimination, women's reproductive health, and the unequal division of domestic labor became organizing foci of many groups, few of these women's organizations (with the notable exception of CONAMUS and perhaps IMU), were willing to embrace the concept of feminism. Says Mercedes Cañas, who worked with CONAMUS in the late 1980s:

"Within CONAMUS, we didn't just have problems with the right . . . but also with the popular movement. Because we were talking about feminism they told us that we were wrong, that we were influenced by the foreign ideas of the petite bourgeoisie. There was no feminist movement inside of El Salvador then" (Ueltzen 1993: 155–156). The winding down of the Salvadoran war in the early 1990s and the signing of the peace accords changed the context of Salvadoran politics significantly and paved the way for the emergence of a budding feminist movement.

The years 1990 and 1991 saw the creation of more women's organizations and of women's committees or secretariats within a wide range of grassroots groups. By the 1990s, feminism was slowly being incorporated into the identities of more and more women's organizations. In 1990 the Center for Feminist Studies (CEF, Centro de Estudios Feministas) opened and was dedicated to the dissemination of feminist materials and organizing techniques. DIGNAS was also founded that year. In 1991 the Norma Virginia Guirola de Herrera Center for Women's Studies (CEMUJER, Centro de Estudios de la Mujer "Norma Virginia Guirola de Herrera") was founded with a feminist agenda that focused on technical assistance, legal aid, and training for grassroots organizations. The Christian Women's Initiative (IMC, Iniciativa de Mujeres Cristianas) and Salvadoran University Women (MUES, Mujeres Universitarias de El Salvador) emerged in 1991 with a strongly feminist agenda as well. That same year, a new national women's coordinating committee, the Concertación de Mujeres por la Paz, la Dignidad y la Igualdad (Women's Coalition for Peace, Dignity, and Equality) was also formed, embracing twenty-four organizations. While originally formed of women's organizations aligned primarily with the RN, the Concertación became a space where groups concerned with establishing an identity independent from political parties came together. Efforts to increase national coalition building were also helped by the sponsorship of the First National Women's Meeting in El Salvador in late 1991 and attendance of fifty Salvadoran women at the First Central American Feminist Encuentro in Nicaragua in 1992.

Nineteen ninety-two marked the beginning of important national coalition building and cooperation among diverse women's groups that originally had been tied to competing parties within the FMLN. Unlike the primarily male-led parties of the FMLN, which had considerable trouble remaining unified through the 1994 elections and which finally tore apart the original FMLN in late 1994, women began forging a more coordinated political front before, during, and after the elections. In 1992, another national women's organization was formed, the Mélida

Anaya Montes Women's Movement (MAM, Movimiento de Mujeres "Mélida Anaya Montes"), which also adopted a stance of "feminist autonomy." While many people believe that MAM was created by the FPL, the founders of MAM are firm in stating that MAM has maintained a position of autonomy since its foundation, even though it has many members who also participate in the FPL (Ueltzen 1993: 200–201). The year 1992 also marked the emergence of El Salvador's first self-proclaimed lesbian organization, called the Half-Moon Salvadoran Lesbian Feminist Collective (Colectivo Lésbico Feminista Salvadoreña de la Media Luna).

On November 25, 1992, the International Day against Violence against Women, the two national coordinators of women's organizations—i.e., the Coordinator of Women's Organizations (COM, created in 1988) and the Women's Coalition for Peace, Dignity, and Equality (the Concertación)—marched together with MAM. The three groups wrote a platform together calling for the newly created National Civil Police to eradicate violence against women. This marked the first time that women associated with the full range of FMLN parties had joined together.

This event was the basis for the creation of "Mujeres '94" (Women in 1994), a broad-based coalition that brought together COM, MAM, the Concertación, and a variety of other groups to create a women's platform for the 1994 elections. They held a series of open debates in 1993 on a wide range of topics including violence against women, women in the informal sector, women's place in land reform, women and ecology, sexuality, education, legal issues, and political participation. In August 1993 they published a platform that included the following goals:

• *An end to incest, rape, and sexual harassment.*
• *Land, credit, and technical assistance for women.*
• *Adequate housing with ownership for women.*
• *Worker training, more places in the workforce, and salaries equal to those of men.*
• *An end to the rising costs of basic wage goods.*
• *Equal opportunity for girls in schools.*
• *Coordinated medical attention for women in more and better hospitals.*
• *Consistent sex education and the expression of women's sexuality without prejudice.*
• *Freely chosen motherhood.*
• *Responsible fatherhood and an increase in food rations.*

- *Respect for the environment and a better quality of life for women.*
- *Development policies that take care of women's needs.*
- *Laws that do not discriminate against women.*
- *Occupation by women of 50 percent of the positions of power.*

(Stephen 1994a:218)

Mujeres '94 sent their platform to political parties of the left, center, and right for discussion. At the same time, Mujeres '94 analyzed the political platforms of each party in terms of what they did for women. The FMLN partially recognized some of the points of the platform at its national convention in 1993. While Mujeres '94 did raise women's issues to the national level, the coalition did not have the organizational power to truly negotiate with El Salvador's major political parties.

With the history and context for women's organizing in El Salvador now in place, the evolution of the DIGNAS is detailed below. DIGNAS serves as an example of the kind of feminist organizing that emerged in El Salvador during the 1990s and of the kind of new agenda that the future may hold.

From the Revolutionary Left to Feminism   According to their self-history, Women for Dignity and Life was created as a result of a decision by the RN as well as a sense of many women within the RN that women needed to start focusing on their own needs. The original organizers of the DIGNAS came from a variety of class backgrounds, ranging from urban marginal to working class and middle class. Despite this class disparity, which was often a source of conflict within the RN, the DIGNAS were determined to unify as women:

After the final offensive of 1989, the National Resistance needed to make inroads into new sectors of the civilian population because the possibility for working among the traditional sectors of the population had diminished considerably. The RN decided to carry out political work in the area of feminine organizations, which at the time were seen as a new means for carrying out party work. Such work would also allow the RN to obtain financial resources from international sources of solidarity. And it also made it possible for several of its leaders to begin engaging in open and legal work. . . . These elements, in addition to the conviction of women that we needed to organize ourselves to work on our own struggles, were determinant in the formation of Women for Dignity and Life by the RN. (Mujeres por la Dignidad y la Vida 1993a:116)

The struggle to extricate themselves from the RN is a central thread running throughout the historical accounts of the DIGNAS, both as spoken by their leaders and as articulated in their own literature. Writing and telling their history in the mid-1990s makes it possible for the DIGNAS to speak openly about their origins, something which would not have been possible five or ten years earlier. There is also a tone of bitterness in the DIGNAS' self-history as they recount their exploitation within guerrilla organizations and grassroots movements.

The original call to form the DIGNAS came in July 1990. Before that time, women who were active in RN-linked grassroots movements met to discuss the possibility of a national women's organization. The DIGNAS activist Gloria Castañeda remembers this first meeting as being full of emotion. Gloria was a forty-one-year-old woman in 1991 when I interviewed her. She had worked on a variety of fronts for the RN. She left her three children with her husband's parents for six years, while working in the countryside, and later separated from her husband. For Gloria, the birth of the DIGNAS was an important time:

At this first meeting we all started talking about our experiences as women, in the war, at home, everywhere. It was very sad because a lot of women started to cry. They talked about how they had to resort to prostitution to live, how they were experiencing motherhood . . . eternal motherhood because they had one child after another. Many had ten children. No one had ever talked with them about how to make a living. After this meeting we knew we had to go ahead with our work.

According to the DIGNAS' self-history, while the RN had wanted their founding meeting to be a high-profile and very public event with a lot of media coverage, the women charged with organizing the meeting developed a more intimate plan that called for plenty of discussion and focused on the specific needs of women. The RN pulled its financial support for the event after they learned of its altered structure, and the first meeting was delayed for a month. Finally, in July 1990, six hundred women came to the meeting. They included women working in human rights (CO-MADRES), in labor (Feminine Committee of the National Federation of Salvadoran Workers, or CO-FENASTRAS), in urban marginal sectors (Feminine Committee of the National Union for Social and Economic Development, or COFE-UNADES), and in the resettled populations controlled by the RN in Cuscatlán, Cabañas, La Libertad, Santa Ana, and San Miguel.

During 1990, the small group of ten to twelve women who were the organizing force behind the DIGNAS spent a lot of time in different parts of the country trying to consolidate women's groups which existed in the conflict zones as well as among poor women in urban areas. At first they worked primarily through structures that had been created by the RN in their areas of support.

During 1990 and 1991, as the Salvadoran peace negotiations advanced and it became clear that the FMLN was likely to become a legal political force, relations within the RN became difficult. This occurred within all the guerrilla organizations as the strain of more than a decade of war took its toll. Several women activists from the DIGNAS, as well as other men and women in the RN, began to read and study and meet for discussions about the vertical structure of the larger organization and its lack of true participatory democracy.[13] They complained about how popular movements were given orders by the party, and they demanded that internal leaders be selected through elections. This new thinking—prompted by a questioning of sectarian, vertically organized politics and by the introduction of feminist ideas—began to foment a rebellious tendency among the DIGNAS which caused them big problems with the RN and led them to seriously question the way that most women's organizations had been initiated and structured.

Late in 1990, one of the DIGNAS attended the Fifth Latin American and Caribbean Feminist Encuentro, in Argentina. In 1991, following the Argentine *encuentro*, the DIGNAS began a period of intense self-reflection on the causes of female subordination. They worked with women from feminist nongovernmental organizations, such as the Human Development Collective of Latin America (CIDHAL) in Mexico and Puntos de Encuentro (Points of Encounter) in Nicaragua, to put together workshops on sexuality, domestic work, violence against women, power, and the experience of Nicaraguan women in AMNLAE. The workshops were extremely popular and drew up to eighty-five people.

During 1991 the DIGNAS also began to participate in regional meetings of Central American feminists, in preparation for a major regional women's event in Nicaragua in 1992. In their self-history the DIGNAS say of this period:

Analyzing our own experiences in light of feminist theory allowed us to understand the unequal and hierarchical relationships that exist between men and women, be they on the right or on the left. We discovered the political background of female subordination and the power relations that maintain our situation. With this discovery, we started to develop our own way of thinking. (Mujeres por la Dignidad y la Vida 1993a: 122)

One DIGNAS activist, who prefers not to be named, remembers of that time:

All of these experiences gave us a whole new set of elements to work with . . . the meeting in Argentina, the meetings in Nicaragua, a workshop in Guatemala, all the workshops we did here. It brought us to another level of identification that was very important. We knew that we had to focus on what was important to women and not take on other people's platforms, like that of labor. We had our own work to do.

During 1991 the DIGNAS continued to question the political models according to which the RN had socialized them. Their questioning was not appreciated by the party; indeed, according to DIGNAS activists, the RN acted as if DIGNAS had declared war on them. The DIGNAS were forbidden access to the zones of the country that the RN controlled; financial resources were cut; and, according to some, the party forbade RN women from associating with the DIGNAS. Nonetheless, the DIGNAS visited those parts of the country controlled by the RN in order to assure the women they worked with that they were not there to divide the revolutionary organization. Some women continued to work with them, others were afraid to.

In March of 1992, the DIGNAS were the primary organizers of the Concertación de Mujeres por la Paz, la Dignidad y la Igualdad which brought together twenty-four women's organizations on International Women's Day and continued as a coalition. One of the primary purposes of the Concertación, from the DIGNAS' perspective, was to prepare for the First Central American Feminist Encuentro in Nicaragua.

That same year, the DIGNAS began to have increased contact with feminist women from the United States. They met with several specifically women's delegations and began to exchange some ideas. According to several DIGNAS members interviewed who spent time with North American women in the delegations, in some cases the North American women openly espoused feminist viewpoints, but in other cases they hid their politics, unsure of what would be thought. Some of these exchanges were the first time that the topic of lesbianism was brought up before the DIGNAS as an organization. Gloria Castañeda recalled a workshop in

1992, attended by eight North American women and some two dozen women from DIGNAS:

At this workshop, some women openly declared that they were lesbians. This didn't result in their total rejection, but at the same time not all of the DIGNAS were comfortable with it. Nevertheless, these types of exchanges opened people's eyes and brought this issue out into the open. It had also come up at other kinds of meetings.

Also in 1992, the DIGNAS formally broke with the RN after a long and tortuous process. They found that they were spending increasing amounts of their own meeting time discussing harassment by the party and trying to figure out how to get around the obstacles the RN put in their way. They drew up a declaration of autonomy, outlining in a positive sense what kind of organization they wanted to be, and they delivered it to the RN:

We told them that the DIGNAS were an autonomous organization and that we didn't belong to any political party. We said that women in DIGNAS can participate in whatever political party they choose, but that their participation is individual and should not compromise the work of our organization. We also asked that when they referred to "women in DIGNAS who also participate in the RN" that they identify them with their own names because the DIGNAS are not the property of the RN. The party never answered our communiqué. (Mujeres por la Dignidad y la Vida 1993a: 127)

Once they had formally broken with the RN, the DIGNAS set out to carve out their own political identity and to integrate their ideas about democracy into their own organization and political agenda.

Democracy, Difference, and Forging a New Identity In 1992 the DIGNAS began to elect their central coordinating committee from a national assembly that included delegates from all the areas they worked in. Local leaders were chosen by local women's committees who were organized into six regional committees. In 1991 the DIGNAS had been working with eighty-one local women's groups and organizations. This number decreased somewhat in 1992 when they formally split with the RN.

A major factor in the DIGNAS structure inherited from the RN was a split between the urban, better-educated women, who as party leaders had originally formed the organization, and the largely rural, poor, and uneducated constituency they worked with. While the original organizers of the DIGNAS came from a variety of class backgrounds, many had completed high school or received additional practical education during the war and some had university education. All had more than a decade of organizing experience within the RN, and many had left their children with other relatives to actively participate in the war effort. Most were accustomed to operating as autonomous women, though within the framework of RN directives. They shared with the women in the countryside the loss of lovers, husbands, and family members in the war. And they shared the harsh living conditions experienced by those who had to survive in rural areas during the war.

The core of the women participating in the rural work of the DIGNAS are between the ages of nineteen and sixty-six, with an average age of forty. The majority cannot read or write. Those who are exceptional finished the fourth grade. Almost all are mothers and most are female heads of households, either because of abandonment or being widowed.

Dedicated to subsistence farming and wage work before the war, most spent from ten to twelve years of their lives in refugee camps. Later they returned to defend their resettled communities. Most had survived miserable economic conditions, living on international aid and from whatever they could eke out from attempts at subsistence agriculture while on the run. Formal unemployment for Salvadoran women had reached 54 percent by 1989. Underemployment statistics are not available, but most Salvadorans were underemployed during the war (Ready 1994: 195). The lack of electricity and running water, particularly in areas of conflict during the war, prolonged a woman's workday by several hours. Basic healthcare was also not usually available in the countryside. Almost three-quarters of the maternal deaths in El Salvador between 1983 and 1987 were in rural areas (Ready 1994: 194). By 1989, 80 percent of Salvadoran families were living in poverty (García and Gomariz 1989: 108).

All of the women having a hand in DIGNAS projects were organized during the war, signifying that they participated in community women's groups and also participated in other kinds of organizations. Most are vocal about their support of the FMLN during the war and are proud of their revolutionary legacy. Many of the core activists who formed DIGNAS had worked with these women in a variety of venues during the war and were familiar to them as RN leaders.

The differences among women in DIGNAS resulted in varying interpretations concerning not only the organization's priorities, but also how the organization should be run. While democracy looked good on paper, activists state that it was not easy to carry out: they had little experience, and there were major differences between the DIGNAS founders and the rural women they served. One thirty-year-old DIGNAS activist who worked in the countryside with the RN stated:

Some of us who were also working in political parties decided that, first, we have to figure out how democracy works within our own organizations because we don't know. We didn't really learn about democracy in the work we did. Also the question of power is key. That is why we had all these workshops on power. The idea is to see the relationship between power and democracy and see how power can be dispersed so that it isn't centralized in one person.

Trying to get women in local-level committees to take on an agenda of democratization and autonomy was complex. Many DIGNAS activists found that women who had settled in repopulated areas controlled by the RN had become accustomed to receiving aid during the time that they were refugees (before returning to resettlements) and had no control over money that was spent in their name. They received little technical training and had no experience administering what were supposed to be their own projects. In addition, their models of political organization were decidedly vertical. One DIGNAS publication on economic projects notes, concerning projects in resettlement areas, that

*the first thing a group develops is usually the "junta directiva" [loosely translated, the "committee in charge"]. They tend to be dependent on "those who are responsible" [*los responsables: *in this case, the coordinating committee of the DIGNAS], and it is difficult for them to establish ways of functioning that involve collective and horizontal decision-making. (Mujeres por la Dignidad y la Vida 1993b:9)*

In response to the intense poverty of women and their sense that no one had trained them to earn a basic living, the DIGNAS focused their first three years of work in the countryside on income-producing projects and services for rural women. Agricultural projects included soybean production, fruit orchards, and chicken, goat, and cattle raising. Small rural industries included bakeries and different forms of craft production such as embroidery and sewing. Services set up for women included communal stores, corn mills, childcare centers, and communal kitchens. Service projects were intended both to decrease the amount of time women had to spend on domestic chores and to create public valuation of their domestic work.

While the DIGNAS were successful in channeling some money to the projects—between $6,000 and $18,000 per project—very few of the projects had become commercially viable by 1993, with the notable exception of a bakery in Santa Marta, Cabañas. Some of the agricultural projects increased family food consumption and decreased what families had to buy in the market. The DIGNAS believe that the income-generating projects helped some women raise cash, but on a very limited basis (Mujeres por la Dignidad y la Vida 1993b:1–3). Although the service projects did provide some relief to women, the DIGNAS found that they had not provided women with enough technical assistance to develop the projects beyond a rudimentary level.

In late 1993 the DIGNAS concluded that there were some significant problems with their rural projects. These problems had to do not only with the technical functioning of the projects, but also with important ideological differences between DIGNAS organizers and the rural women who formed the base of the organization. The following quotes from their evaluation indicate these differences:

1. *Feminist organizations, including our own, have a tendency to only consider work that develops the so-called strategic interests of gender—violence, control over one's own body, maternity, and autonomy—as truly feminist. . . . We also have to consider women's practical interests as feminist. We have to admit that we didn't spend as much time training women in aspects of project administration, accounting, and other technical aspects of economic projects as we did on consciousness-raising about women's subordination.*
2. *In the second place, we have to admit that the fact that we were busy discovering our own subordination . . . meant that we fell into the temptation of considering women whose daily life hadn't been turned upside down by questioning their gendered condition as "not very feminist." . . . The result of all this is a lack of consistency between our feminist objectives and the urgent daily-life necessities of the women we work with. We have to learn how to put together the practical, daily necessities of women with strategic issues of gender. . . .*
3. *This leads us to conclude that we haven't valued simple survival as an important line of organizing for feminism. . . . If we don't pay*

attention to the struggles of survival we will lose rural women, poor women, resettled women, and illiterate women who are also fighters, firm in their struggles. (Mujeres por la Dignidad y la Vida 1993b: 10–11)

The document reveals class, experiential, and educationally based differences in what urban leaders and rural women in DIGNAS thought the core issues of the organization should be. It also hints at the influence that intellectual distinctions found within Latin American feminism (e.g., "strategic" versus "practical" gender interests) had on the DIGNAS leadership. The most optimistic reading of the document suggests that the DIGNAS had squarely faced the divisions within their organization and had made a commitment to redefine what feminism meant for them in order to accommodate the needs of the rural women they were supposed to be serving. Constraints on fieldwork during the war did not permit widespread interviewing of rural women in order to collect their contrasting points of view. That will be an important research objective for further investigation of organizations like the DIGNAS.

By the end of 1993, the DIGNAS had begun to discard the distinction between "practical" and "strategic" gender interests and to work on creating a national women's political platform that truly integrated a wide range of demands usually segmented by the strategic/practical dualism. The experience of founding and participating in Mujeres '94, described above, gave the DIGNAS a way to combine their national coalition-building work with an integrated platform of women's demands that took into consideration a range of issues affecting a majority of women in El Salvador. In addition to offering a wide-ranging platform for women, Mujeres '94 also provided a succinct analysis of the situation of women in El Salvador. The DIGNAS were a major force in disseminating this information, which featured the following:

- *More than 50 percent of women are physically or emotionally mistreated.*
- *Thirty-two percent of women are illiterate.*
- *The agrarian reform that was never completed nonetheless showed major discrimination: 56,651 men were beneficiaries but only 6,731 women were.*
- *Basic health services don't exist for Salvadoran women.*

- *There isn't one maternity hospital for women in the country.*
- *Clandestine abortion is the fourth leading cause of women's death among women.*
- *A lot of us don't know how or why we reproduce, but we keep having large numbers of children.*
- *We are now 57 percent of the heads of household in El Salvador, but our civil law still says we should obey our husbands.*
- *We have no political representation. There are no women on the Supreme Court; and in the legislative assembly, with 84 representatives, only 7 are women.*
  (Edición Mujeres 1994:8–9)

Participating in the Mujeres '94 coalition proved to be a major testing ground of the DIGNAS' tolerance for a wide range of political perspectives, primarily within the left. The newly found language of democracy and autonomy was put to the test as women who had left the parties of the FMLN and those who still participated joined together to work out a platform that eventually incorporated a hundred different points distilled into fourteen areas. The coalition also incorporated a broad range of women's organizations which had varying relationships with feminism.

More than anything, the DIGNAS felt that participating in Mujeres '94 made the Salvadoran women's movement visible in mainstream politics and gave the movement its own voice. The ability of the coalition to actually negotiate with political parties was limited. Morena Herrera, a thirty-five-year-old DIGNAS activist who was a long-time RN organizer and guerrilla leader, stated:

After the experience of the elections, we believe that we have to build strength at the local level. We can't just have faith that the political parties are open to our ideas. . . . We believe that we have to return to civil society and strengthen the women's movement at the base. Right now we are giving ourselves three years to evaluate our experience in trying to promote women's platforms at the municipal level, but without abandoning our national plan of actions. . . . In three years we hope that there will be women as municipal-level candidates for mayor and city councillors who are part of the women's movement.

As a result of their experience in the elections, the DIGNAS have reoriented their work in important ways. First of all, instead of continuing with their income-generating and service projects for women, they turned them over to two or three women in each locale where they had been working. They found that the projects were only capable of supporting a few women and that the local women were capable of running them alone. Three of the projects—a bakery, a communal store, and a cattle-raising project—have proven to be commercially viable. Rather than continuing their rural domestic-service projects such as corn mills, the DIGNAS are instead creating a series of women's reproductive health centers at the municipal level. In general, the DIGNAS have abandoned extremely localized methods of organizing and are working at the municipal level.

Perhaps most important is their new focus on getting women to create local political platforms at the municipal level and training women as potential political candidates for upcoming elections. In 1994, the DIGNAS had teams of rural trainers set up in six *municipios* and were preparing for work in another four. In the municipality of Victoria, for example, local women created a political platform that includes demands for electricity, potable drinking water, education, responsible fa-

Drawing from a DIGNAS educational pamphlet showing their nine basic demands for municipal governments: electricity, potable water, education, an end to crime, health, cleaning up the streets, work, an end to violence against women, and housing.

therhood, healthcare, housing, and an end to violence against women (Mujeres por la Dignidad y la Vida 1994). In their scope, the demands are reminiscent of those represented in the Mujeres '94 coalition. They also suggest a fusion between practical and strategic gender interests.

The DIGNAS were also major participants in the regional planning committee which prepared for the Sixth Latin American and Caribbean Feminist Encuentro (El Salvador, October 1993). The sixth *encuentro* is described in detail in Chapter 1 above. While smaller than some of the previous feminist *encuentros*, the sixth one, held on the Costa del Sol, helped to consolidate the influence that the DIGNAS had as a feminist organization both in El Salvador and internationally. Although an intensive right-wing media campaign in September and October of 1993 labeled the *encuentro* as a meeting of homosexuals and lesbians who were going to degrade Salvadoran morality and culture and bring on an AIDS epidemic, the international campaign organized by the DIGNAS and others resulted in more than 100 letters of protest from organizations in more than twenty-five countries (Comité Centroamericano Organizador del VI Encuentro Feminista Latinoamericano y del Caribe 1994:15–22). The effort to shut down the *encuentro* backfired, and the DIGNAS and others involved in the regional organizing committee gained far more legitimation and publicity than they would have if the Salvadoran government had simply allowed the *encuentro* to take place unimpeded.

In the space of four short years (1990–1994), the DIGNAS had come full circle in their quest for autonomy from the RN and for an organizing agenda that would meet the needs of a wide range of women. The DIGNAS and other women in the Mujeres '94 coalition continued meeting and were perhaps the most successful segment of the left with respect to remaining united behind a common set of demands. Their successful organization of a large international feminist meeting in El Salvador brought the DIGNAS and other participants into the limelight of Latin American feminism. It also moved Central American women from the margins into the center of a new ideology which refused to split women's organizing into "practical" or "strategic" or to calculate just how feminist it was.

Conclusions   The emergence of the DIGNAS and their struggle for autonomy, primarily as women who were members of clandestine revolutionary political-military organizations, signals a new chapter in the history of Latin American feminism as well as of the left. The notions of diversity, autonomy, and participatory democracy which have been at the heart of the DIGNAS struggle have created a challenge not only for the Salvadoran left but for the larger national political process as well. While the DIGNAS come from a revolutionary-left perspective and will never abandon their economic concerns, their insistence on being able to deal with the multiple dimensions of women's oppression places them on a new plane.

Ironically, the way in which the FMLN came to be a legitimate political force in El Salvador and was immediately forced to compete in national elections probably favored the possibilities for construction of an autonomous women's movement. In Nicaragua, where the FSLN took power through armed victory and ousted Somoza, the fact that elections were delayed for five years until 1984 probably allowed hierarchical tendencies within the FSLN to solidify rather than be challenged. The FSLN did face continual external opposition from the U.S. government and from the U.S.-funded Contras, but this external threat initially served to dampen internal opposition until the overall economic, ecological, and human costs of the war were felt by everyone at the end of the 1980s. For women in AMNLAE who wanted to challenge the Sandinstas, their only choice for independence was to remove themselves from AMNLAE and therefore disassociate themselves from the FSLN. Feminists in Nicaragua were not really able to create an autonomous organization until the Sandinistas were defeated at the polls in 1990 and had lost their grip on AMNLAE and other sectoral organizations.

In El Salvador, the peace negotiation process forced all of the parties of the FMLN to begin broadening their constituency and allowed those within the FMLN parties who wanted to incorporate more democratic practices an opening for doing so. The declarations of autonomy by groups like DIGNAS were possible in part because of what appeared to be a political opening in larger Salvadoran society linked to the peace process. For the DIGNAS, this opening came at a time when their organization was just coming into its own.

In addition to the political opening created by the peace negotiations, Salvadoran women in the DIGNAS and in other self-declared feminist organizations were able to benefit from more than a decade of international feminist organizing in Latin America. By the time Salvadoran women began attending the larger Latin American and Caribbean Feminist *encuentros*, as well as the regional women's meetings in Central America, the fundamental issues of Latin American feminism had been debated and worked on for quite some time. Salvadoran women were able to participate in meetings where the pressure to make a choice between class revolution and gender equality was receding. By and large, Latin American feminists had begun to conclude that feminist organizing would benefit from the broadest definition possible, including issues of survival, employment, health, violence against women, sexuality, human rights, and women's political participation. Salvadoran women also entered the discourse on Latin American feminism at a time when middle-class and intellectual feminists focused on women's subordination had a history of working with women concerned with issues that were not always gender-specific. When Salvadoran women such as the DIGNAS began to realize their own subordination and marginalization within the Salvadoran revolutionary left, they had alternative models in other countries readily available. Most important, they had the close-to-home experience of AMNLAE in Nicaragua to draw on as a lesson not to be repeated. The lessons they learned from other Latin American feminists could also be compared with work being done by women in the United States. Of particular interest to the DIGNAS and other Salvadoran women were the establishment of battered women's shelters across the United States, legal abortion and discussions of birth control, the experience of U.S. women in the New Left during the 1960s, and women's health clinics and publications.

The DIGNAS' own experience also revealed internal contradictions in their organizational agenda and ideology rooted in class, educational, and urban/rural differences between women. The challenge from within the DIGNAS' own ranks is to fashion a structure, style of leadership, and agenda which can incorporate the interests of poor, rural women with those of more educated, urban activists. To meet this challenge, the DIGNAS have had to redefine what feminism means for them and to agree to disagree on its meaning, leaving that up to each particular woman. Rather than insisting on a unified line of interpretation which led to their own marginalization within the left, the DIGNAS are struggling to allow the multiple points of view found in their organization not only to coexist, but to codefine the breadth of what they hope to accomplish.

The trajectory of the DIGNAS lends credence to analyses of social movements which point to the multiple identities represented within movements and away from the idea of a vanguard coming from the urban working class. By being marginalized within the opposition and then realizing their own tendency to marginalize the rural women they were supposed to be helping, DIGNAS activists came to recognize the necessity of incorporating a variety of perspectives into what constitutes feminism.

Morena Herrera
Women for Dignity and Life

Political activist, mother, ex-guerrilla commander, and architecture student—Morena Herrera has had a full life for her thirty-four years. Coming from a politically oriented family, Morena first began organizing her urban classmates in junior high school, where she led student strikes. Later recruited into one of the parties of the FMLN, Morena became a top military strategist and commander, holding a pivotal position in the FMLN's final offensive on San Salvador in 1989. Within the FMLN she faced discrimination for being female, and through her experiences with other women during the war she began to explore Latin American feminism. With several other women she founded Women for Dignity and Life (known as the DIGNAS), one of El Salvador's first autonomous and explicitly feminist organizations. She also participates in the Corriente Feminista Centroamericana (Central American Feminist Current), which includes women from organizations in Guatemala, El Salvador, Nicaragua, and Costa Rica.

I first met Morena briefly in San Salvador, where I spent time in 1991 carrying out fieldwork for a book on El Salvador's mothers of the disappeared: namely, CO-MADRES (Committee of Mothers and Relatives of the Political Prisoners, Disappeared, and Assassinated of El Salvador "Monseñor Romero"). As part of this work, I spent several weeks talking with women from a wide range of organizations including DIGNAS. In 1994, a political organization I work with in Boston (Women across Borders) organized an East Coast tour for Morena and a Nicaraguan feminist. I spent several days with Morena and we talked in cars, in classrooms, over coffee, and in a friend's kitchen. On the day of our longest talk, transcribed and edited here, Morena and I were both dressed casually in jeans and T-shirts. We drank several cups of coffee to waken our-

Recorded April 11, 1994,
in Boston, Massachusetts.

Morena Herrera, an activist in the DIGNAS of El Salvador. Photo courtesy of Robin Braverman.

selves from an early morning stupor caused by lack of sleep. We began talking about the multiple meanings of feminism.

Lynn: What do you think people mean when they talk about some organizations being feminist and others being part of the women's movement?

Morena: We had a discussion about this several months ago in El Salvador, when women we work with wanted us to make a clear distinction between the feminist movement and the women's movement. I told them that you can't take a group of organizations and classify them into being either exclusively feminist or just women's organizations. Everyone has a lot of different aspects to who they are. Here's how I feel about myself. On the one hand, I am a feminist and I intend to live my life more and more as a feminist, but at the same time I am part of the women's movement in El Salvador that is also concerned with economic relations and class. I have both identities. When I go out to talk to people I say, "I am a woman and because of that I feel oppressed. At the same time, I am poor and I also feel it is necessary to struggle to change unjust social and economic relationships that affect all the people in our country, not just women." I also say, even though I don't have a specific ethnicity—like, say an Indian—in my own country, that we also are discriminated against when we come here to the North. All of this fits together. . . .

Lynn: How did you start to bring all these ideas together? How did you enter into politics?

Morena: Even though my mother was not a revolutionary activist, she was a woman who knew what was going on. She was an urban artisan, but she grew up in the countryside. She made clothing for people in our neighborhood. She always knew about the workers' strikes going on, and I remember that in 1967 I went downtown to a strike to take her some food and a little bit of money. I was seven years old. Then in 1968 she took me to the teachers' strikes and to some of the marches that went on. . . . I remember teasing other kids using the slogans of the teacher's union that was called ANDES.[1] In our poor little neighborhood of San Jacinto I used to turn my back to other kids and wiggle my buns back and forth and shout "ANDES, ANDES, ANDES, ANDES" to insult them. I wasn't participating in politics, but I used the slogans as a way to make my place in the neighborhood.

Lynn: What was your family situation then? Were your parents living together?

Morena: No. They were separated. They separated when I was really little. My mother was always working, and even though she worked all the time there was never enough money. I had a younger sister. I also had two older brothers and a sister who lived with my father. . . . My mother always told us that we should study so that we would be able to support ourselves. She told us that because she was never able to do it. I didn't get any messages about how I should learn how to wash and iron in order to serve my husband. Instead, my mother taught me how to do things really well and told me I had to have a profession so that I could take care of myself and not depend on anyone else.

My father was always pressuring my mother for sexual favors in exchange for money to support us. I grew up watching my mother in a constant struggle. She was always going to an attorney's office to get my father to give her money for food. This would infuriate him and he would say, "You don't have to throw me in jail to get child support." Their relationship was very difficult. Watching all of this made me quite rebellious in spite of the fact that I got along well with my father.

I put myself in competition with the siblings I had who lived with him. I decided that despite the difficult conditions I lived under, I was going to show them and my father that I could be a better student than any of them, despite the material advantages they had. They were in the most expensive schools in San Salvador.

I opted for a Catholic school that had both boys and girls in it. But I left after the sixth grade because of all the problems in my family. I decided to enroll in public school and to stop taking the money my father gave me to study in the private school. I told my mother and she supported my decision.

I wanted to be the top-ranked high school graduate in the country that year. (But) a lot of things happened, and I had to leave my studies. I started to learn that politics was more important than my personal ambition.

Lynn: Did going to public school put you into contact with very different kinds of people?

Morena: The Catholic school was right in my neighborhood. I knew most of the people who went there. I had always studied there. All my teachers knew me and my family as well. So my whole life was within four blocks of my house. When I went to the public school, I had to travel to downtown San Salvador. I got to know a lot of other girls. It was a girls' school and a lot of them had very different backgrounds from me. During my second year at the public school, in eighth grade, I started to participate in a group of students from other schools who provided support for strikes and marches. Later on I started participating in a student group called the Association of Secondary Students (AES, Asociación de Estudiantes de Secundaria). At the time, I didn't know that it was run by the Communist Party of El Salvador.

When I was fifteen years old, there was a huge massacre of students. I had been at the demonstration awhile and then left to go and find a boyfriend I had at the time. It was in 1975. The boyfriend I had went to a very exclusive high school. He said, "Why are you participating in this kind of thing?" After that, I ended our relationship. He had no idea what was going on in our country.

Lynn: So your personal desires began to conflict with your political goals?

Morena: Yes, they did at age fifteen. That year I started to get really bad citizenship grades in school. I had excellent academic grades, but very bad grades on my "conduct," as they called it. I also had to face my conflict with my father again. Even though I didn't want to depend on him, no public school would let me in with my terrible citizenship grades. I wanted to get a high school degree. But I had to take an entrance exam. I did nothing but study for two months. I studied twelve hours a day and then took entrance exams from all the national schools. I had the fifth-highest score in San Salvador. I was really surprised by this. I was offered admission to five high schools. You have to understand that most people in El Salvador don't go to high school.

I thought that if I scored high enough on the entrance exam that I would be able to keep going to a public high school and my bad citizenship grades wouldn't matter. I decided to pursue an academic degree in the mornings at a very prestigious school called the Instituto Nacional de Francisco Meléndez and, in the afternoons and evenings, to pursue another degree in fine arts. I really liked the arts and enjoyed painting and graphic arts, but I knew that if I was going to stop being economically dependent on my father, I would have to study for a career that would allow me to be independent. I decided to major in architectural drawing because this was a well-paying career at the time. This degree would also allow me to start working fairly soon and begin earning money to pay for my education. I was a good student and got good grades.

Around this same time I also participated in a Catholic youth group in my neighborhood. More than anything it was a group of friends from the church who got together to sing. Some of the songs had revolutionary content. We also went for walks and on short trips. It was a space that gave us a certain amount of freedom. The girls in the group needed this even more than the boys.

Lynn: Do you think that if you hadn't participated in this group, then . . .

Morena: . . . I wouldn't have had this space. Precisely. Because of this group, for example, I was able to go on short outings. My mother never would have let me go out on my own. I also started to participate in another organization, called the Movement of Revolutionary Secondary Students (MERS, Movimiento de Estudiantes Revolucionarios de Secundaria), which depended on the FPL (Popular Forces of Liberation "Farabundo Martí").[2] After I had participated in this group for about six months, a friend of mine who I was in school with and who was also in the church group persuaded me to join a different organization. He is the one who got me to join ARDES (Revolutionary Action of Secondary Students, Acción Revolucionaria de Estudiantes de Secundaria), which was linked up to another group, FAPU (United Popular Action Front, Frente de Acción Popular Unificada), which was the civil and political front for the RN.[3] There was a lot of competition between organizations then. I didn't know about all of the political links the groups had at the time. . . .

There was something else that happened that made me aware of the repression going on in my country. When I was about twelve years old, my mother rented a room in our house to a man named Don Julián, who lived there with his family. He had an unusual personality for our neighborhood. He didn't drink or have any vices. He did yell at his wife, but that was typical of everyone.

One day they came and captured him outside our house. He had fought with a police lieutenant who lived in front of us. They arrived and said that they had found two LSD pills in his car. They came into our house with their guns and started to carry out a search. My mother walked with them through the house.

I am telling you this long story to explain how I came to know about repression in my country at an early age. The next day, Don Julián's body showed up at the morgue. The police came to our house to ask my mother questions. They asked, "Is everything that man had in his room? Did he have anything else?" "Yes" (that was all), she said. So they didn't search the rest of the house.

Before Don Julián was buried, we could see that his body was covered with signs of torture. The National Police said he died because he hung himself. After Don Julián was buried we went back to the house. There I heard my mother talking to his wife. My mother said, "Here are some other boxes that belong to Don Julián, but I didn't tell the police they were his. Let's see what's inside." They opened the boxes and they were full of literature for the ERP (People's Revolutionary Army, Ejército Revolucionario del Pueblo). My mother and Don Julián's wife burned all of this literature.

Something else happened around this same time that I remember very vividly. My mother had a Costa Rican friend (a woman) who lived in the neighborhood. A Guatemalan man named Raúl was her friend and they were always after them. One day they ran after them and cornered them and Raúl was shot. There he was, shot dead, his body on the street, and we couldn't say he was our friend. I didn't know exactly what was going on, but after seeing things like this I began to see the repression clearly.

In 1976 it became increasingly difficult for people to participate politically. I kept on studying and was very active in school on a committee that offered academic support for those who were having a hard time in school. Being on this committee was very prestigious, and I enjoyed it. I was still into studying because I wanted to be the top-ranked high school graduate.

I also spent a lot of time in political discussions with my group ARDES and read a lot of documents. In 1977 we had elections that were extremely fraudulent. We went down to the plaza to support our presidential candidate. It was the 28th of February. I remember because it was the night there was a huge massacre in the Plaza de la Libertad. We had been there earlier in the evening with my mother. The next day when we got to school, we told our professors that we couldn't have classes because of the massacre. Many of us had heard the shots and we couldn't imagine having classes after such a horrible event.[4]

Lynn: Who decided to close the school?

Morena: Mostly it was those of us who were in ARDES. It wasn't a coordinated action, just a group of students who were outraged by what happened. We closed down the school and other students followed our lead. I think they also followed us because some of the most respected students in school were with us.

After we closed the school, we went to downtown San Salvador to see what was going on. When we got to the plaza they were cleaning up the blood. We started yelling at the police about what they had done, and they threw tear gas at us. They ran after us with sticks. They didn't fire on us that day, but just chased us. That was the first time I felt physical repression. They pursued us all over the center of San Salvador. We finally had to take refuge in someone's house.

When I finally arrived home my mother said to me, "What are you doing? Why are you getting involved in politics? Someday we are going to find you in the street all beaten up or dead."

After this experience I began to dedicate more and more time to politics. My interest in academics was waning. I went to speak with my father and I told him that I was part of the movement and that I had a lot of commitment to the people of El Salvador. I told him about all of the injustice in El Salvador. He smiled at me and asked if I was with MERS, another student organization I was in. I said, "No. I am working with ARDES." He said to me, "Okay. Look, just don't stop studying." I had already planned to stop studying fine arts in the afternoons and evenings because it was too much. "Listen," I said, "I can't keep studying because I have too many commitments to the organization I am with." He said, "No, you can't stop studying. You can participate in your organization, but you have to keep up with your studies." I accepted his deal.

Then I went to speak with my mother, and she put up a lot of resistance. Obviously she didn't want me involved because she was afraid of what could happen to me. She put a lot of pressure on my friends so that they would convince me to quit.

When I was having a lot of problems with my family, I left home for two weeks. When I came back home I got to know a guy named "Alberto," that was his pseudonym, who was also participating in the movement. I had my first sexual relations with him during a group outing. We didn't use anything to prevent pregnancy or even talk about it. I got pregnant.

At this point I was finishing my third out of four years to get my high school degree, and I wasn't even eighteen years old. I was really frightened. I was pregnant and I didn't even think about the possibility of abortion. Nobody even mentioned it. My work in school was important and the pregnancy was going to make it very difficult for me to finish.

Alberto and I went to speak with my father. He said, "I can't do anything. You live with your mother. You will have to talk with her." When we went to see my mother she said, "You don't have my permission to get married." After that, Alberto went to his organization and asked them for permission to get married. He was very tight with the organization, the RN. He had been an urban guerrilla since 1975. People in the organization got angry and said, "How could you do that? You are going to ruin the work we have been doing. It's a really bad example for young people. . . ." They punished us both. They gave him permission to get married, but we were both forbidden from participating in the movement. I was banned from the student organization I was in, and he was banned from the activities he was participating in.

I moved out of my house and into his house with his mother. She was a retired urban worker and a widow. He was her oldest child. We lived with her for some months and began to be active in the Christian base movement of liberation theology. I started working in several Christian base communities.[5] After three months, the *compañeros* from our political organization realized they had made a mistake and they invited us to work with them again.

My mother came to talk with me and said, "I know you are going to have this baby. At least finish your high school degree. Here is some money to pay for your final exams."

After her visit I went to speak with my teachers, and they let me take the final exams without having finished all of my classwork. This was a big concession from them. I think they let me do it because I had been very active in school and supportive of a lot of things.

Lynn: They let you back in school when you were pregnant?

Morena: Only for the exams. I went in with my uniform stretched to the max. I only had to put it on for the exams and I hardly was able to wear it through the exams, it was so tight. A few days after I took the exams, some friends of ours said, "Why don't you go and live some-place else?" I couldn't stand living with (Alberto's) mother any longer. She wanted me to wash his socks and everything, and I wasn't used to doing that. Sometimes I didn't even wash my own clothes.

Lynn: Who washed your clothes then?

Morena: Sometimes my mother did, and sometimes we had some-one who helped out with the wash. And sometimes I washed my own clothes. This guy's mother started to get on my case, saying "My son is walking around with dirty socks. Why don't you wash them?"

"I didn't move in here to wash his socks," I told her. It was fine with him. He was used to washing his own socks. I just couldn't put up with his mother any more. So we moved in with some *compañeros* from the organization.

Lynn: When you say "organization" what do you mean? Were you aware of the links to the party?

Morena: Yes. I knew that I was working with the party (RN), and I was a collaborator in urban guerrilla activities. I helped out with security measures that were required of us. . . . I first found out about all of the connections because I had a friend whose father was an old activist in the Communist Party. She knew how all the organizations were linked to parties, so she told me that ARDES was part of the RN. . . .

In 1979 the situation became very difficult in El Salvador. There was terrible repression and I learned about more and more things. I was very active with the urban guerrillas when I was pregnant. Then on April 4, 1979, my *compañero* (Alberto) died in an urban action. He was killed in combat with another close friend of ours from where I went to school. They died in a place called the Plaza de la Alianza. I was eight months pregnant. He died eighteen days before my daughter was born.

This was a great blow to me. The night before he died he came home to sleep and didn't say anything to me. He left me all his personal docu-ments. The next morning I didn't know that he had died. I first knew something was up when another *compañero* who lived with us told me that he had heard something on the radio. "What are you going to do now?" he asked. "I am going to go to the university because I have a meeting there. I'm going to take a shower. Go ahead and I'll meet you there." "Maybe I'll wait for you," he said. It seemed so strange to me that this person who I had a hard time getting along with was suddenly being nice and waiting for me. "I'll go with you to the university," he said.

We went out together to take the bus. He bought a newspaper and we sat down on the bus. I opened up the paper and there on the front page it said, "Combat. Shoot-out in the Plaza de la Alianza Where Two Young Men Died." Below the headline was a photograph of my *compañero's* body sprawled on the ground.[6] I just stared at it. I had started to cry when the guy who came with me said, "No. Don't cry. Not here. Not now."

I had to wipe my tears away. I didn't cry again for the whole forty-five minutes it took us to get from Soyapango to the university.

When we got off the bus at the university, I said to the guy who was with me, "Was it really him? Go and find out." I walked over to an abandoned construction site at the university and waited for him a long time. I saw some *compañeros* stick their heads out the door of the Medical School and look at me. Then they went back inside. After they did this I knew it was true but that they didn't want to come over and tell me. Later, everyone was very nice to me and they told me that I had to go and tell his mother that he was dead.

I found his mother and said, "Someone will have to go and pick up the body. I can't go because it is too dangerous for me. You will have to go and do it." She went and got the body. He was full of bullet holes. It turns out that several policemen were also wounded, so he died in combat. We didn't have anywhere to hold a wake for him because of how he died. No one wanted to give us a place to put the body. Finally we decided to take over the cathedral. We took the bodies of both men who died there.

I remember there was a priest inside the cathedral who said, "I'll say a mass for your dead, but then you will have to take them home for the wake." We stood there with the bodies in the coffins and said, "This is the people's cathedral and we are going to have our wake here." We stayed up all night with them in the cathedral.

My mother came to see me the next morning before the burial and told me, "I am going to bring you some clothing because you are all dirty." She came back with a black maternity mourning dress. I remember that the only one who walked with me in the funeral march was an aunt of mine. Everyone else was afraid.

After the funeral my aunt told me, "Come on. Let's go. You are about to give birth." I was very close to labor, but there was a problem. Some of the *compañeros* told me that I couldn't go to a hospital because they couldn't find one where they could guarantee my security. The week before, a woman had been kidnapped out of the maternity ward. So we set up a clandestine clinic in my aunt's house, and I gave birth to my daughter there. I remember that we pretended there was a party going on. They put on party music and brought bread and turkey in. They told me not to scream so that the neighbors wouldn't hear.

After my daughter was born, my family put a lot of pressure on me to quit the organization. I completely broke off my relationship with my father. I never spoke to him again before he died. One of the things I want to do this year is to go and talk to him at his grave.

I left my aunt's house when my daughter was a few weeks old and moved into a safe house with *compañeros* from the organization. I was the only one in the house with a child. They gave me the responsibility of organizing neighborhood committees in the city.

I was living with several men and another woman. Here I established a second relationship with another guy who was really great.

We got into a debate in this house that he started. He said to the others, "I don't think it's fair that Morena has to shoulder all the responsibilities of having a child by herself. We should all help out with washing clothes, preparing formula, and taking care of her daughter because she is the only child who lives here with us."

Lynn: What was his name?

Morena: His pseudonym was "Guillermo." His name was Dolores Antonio Aragón. In 1980, when I was with him, I didn't think about having any more children. We started having a sexual relationship. They sent him off to the countryside to expand one of the guerrilla fronts. He would go for two or three weeks and then return. During one of these times when he returned I got pregnant. I wasn't really being very careful. I tried not to have sexual relations with him on the days that I could get pregnant by using the rhythm method. But it was stupid of me not to use something else. He came back on a regular basis and I got pregnant.

By then I knew about abortion and I told him, "I am not going to have this child. I can't. I already have a daughter." I was about six weeks along when I realized I was pregnant. He asked me to think about it, saying "I don't have any children." He told me that he loved my daughter Natalia and that the decision was up to me.

After that, I didn't see him for fifteen days. By that time I was living alone with my daughter and he would come home once in a while. He left me a message on tape, part of which was later published in an independent newspaper. On the tape he said, "Look, if you decide that you want this child to be born, take care of it. I hope that it is born healthy and strong. If I don't come back, I have left you a few things." It was a beautiful declaration of love with a lot of ideology mixed in. He left me some vitamins because I wasn't feeling well and some cloth for making baby clothes in case I decided to keep the child. He said he would be back in fifteen days.

I still thought that I didn't want to keep this baby, but I still hadn't got an abortion. The fifteen days hadn't completely gone by when a friend of mine called out to me at a bus stop. "Hi. What do you hear from Guillermo?" she asked. "Nothing," I said. "He said that he would be back in about two weeks. He'll probably be home in a day or two."

"Did you know he just died? He was killed in combat in an ambush?"

"What?" I said. "It can't be."

"Yes," she answered. "Didn't the *compañeros* tell you?"

"No," I told her. "They haven't said anything to me."

"He just died. He got caught in an ambush in Santa Marta. He was one of the first to die."

There I was with my second pregnancy, in shock. I went to see my mother. My mother asked me why I got pregnant. "But, why did you get pregnant?" she said.

"It's not just that I'm pregnant," I answered. Then I told her about Guillermo and that he had died. My mother had gotten to know him and she liked him, but she didn't want me to keep the baby.

After all of that, I decided I was going to keep the baby. And during that pregnancy I began one of the hardest periods of my life. It was toward the end of 1980 and the repression was terrible. I had a lot of responsibility. I was the citywide director of the party in San Salvador.

I had a lot of security problems because one of the safe houses we maintained in the city was discovered and raided. Inside this house were a bunch of passports we were going to use to get people out of the country to a party congress. Most of them were under false names, but there were two passports with real names on them — mine and the person who was the vice-rector of the national university. The names on all the passports were published in the newspaper, so I couldn't use my legal name anymore. I was even afraid to go to the neighborhood where I grew up.

But I still had to go there because my mother took care of my daughter. She began to take care of her more and more because of the difficult circumstances I lived under. I would come to leave her and to pick her up. Sometimes my mother would bring her to the center of the city. Even though my mother kept pressuring me to leave the party, she always supported me.

In 1981 when I was seven months pregnant, we mounted our first major offensive. We had a big discussion with everyone and one of them said, "I think that you should stay in the rear guard getting supplies for us."

"Do you think I am going to stay in the rear after I have done so much to prepare for this? I am going to be on the front lines," I said. And I fought with them. I felt this intense need to be in the middle of things, participating. I didn't even think about my own life. That's how I think about it now with a little bit of hindsight.

So I made damn sure that I participated in this offensive with my huge belly. It was a big joke among the *compañeros*. "Hey, we will have to dig you an extra big ditch with lots of room in front," they would say, holding their hands out in front of them as if they were pregnant.

Well, we had our offensive. It didn't have the results that we wanted. We called it the "final offensive." But it didn't turn out to be final at all. It was just the beginning.

I remember going to tell my mother, "I'm off to the final offensive."

"How long are you going to be there?" she asked me.

"Two or three months," I answered.

"Well, take this bag with you," she said. "This baby is going to be born there." Inside the bag were diapers, a pacifier, some bottles. I took this little bag with me all over.

But I came home after two days and said, "No. It didn't happen. It's a big mess." There were curfews all over and a lot of people were getting killed. Some of my girlfriends died during that time. On the 2nd of March my second daughter was born in a private clinic in the center of San Salvador. It was a clinic where we had an agreement with the doctors to take care of some of our wounded. They also took care of me. My daughter Alma, who is thirteen years old now, was born. I went home to my mother's house — which was taking a big chance. But I couldn't take care of my two daughters alone.

Lynn: In the 1980s, did you feel discriminated against as a woman?

Morena: I think I started to feel more discrimination as a woman when I went to work in the countryside in 1981. A few months after my second daughter was born, I became a member of the Central Committee of the party. They sent me to a guerrilla front. There I found my third love, who was a *comandante* (guerrilla commander and military strategist). At first, I asked him not to make our relationship public because I didn't want people to see me as his. We have an expression. I didn't want to be seen as his "key chain" — that is, something that he takes on and off. I said, "If they know that I have a relationship with you, they will think that the only reason I am here is because of you. I am here because I want to be here and because of the responsibilities I have. I want people to respect me for who I am." He accepted my condition for the relationship.

He was a peasant from Guazapa, the same region we were working in. He had left the countryside to study in the seminary and had also spent some time studying at the university. He wasn't a typical peasant, but he *was* very conservative about some things. His name was Misael, and he respected my decisions. But there was a lot of machismo on the rural guerrilla front. The women had to prove themselves, and so did the people from urban areas. I was an urban woman so they were suspicious of me.

Lynn: How did you have to prove yourself?

Morena: I had to be able to grind corn, to find and haul large loads of firewood. Grinding corn was women's work. I always refused to wash my *compañero*'s clothes. I only washed mine. Later, when people knew about us, they would always say to me, "Misael is such a good person and he has so much responsibility, but you don't wash his clothes. And you don't even warm up his tortillas? Why not? . . ." Things like that.

They put me in charge of the political education program in the countryside. I was always especially concerned about getting girls into the school and getting them educated. Then they put me in charge of all of the work with the civilian population for the entire front. Then they also put me in charge of local militias and coordinating military actions with the civilian population.

While I was there I had my third pregnancy. I was using contraception—I injected myself. But I didn't know that you had to do the injections on exactly the same day every month. I injected myself when I remembered, and I didn't always have the contraceptive drug I needed.[7]

Lynn: Did many women in the guerrilla forces use this form of birth control?

Morena: Not very many. There were only a few of us who used any form of birth control. The injections were a way to prevent pregnancy, but we didn't have any control over the process because I wasn't aware of what the drug in the injections did to my body.

When I realized I was pregnant, I said to my *compañero*: "Look, I can't have this child. I already have two daughters. If I have another child, I will have to stop participating. I don't just want to collaborate. I want to be really involved. I'm going to have an abortion."

Getting an abortion on the front was very complicated. We spoke with a friend who was a Mexican doctor. "I'll help you," she said, "but this pregnancy is pretty far along."

She put me on an intravenous fluid that was supposed to cause me to abort. Right there in the countryside. Misael went with me, in spite of all his religiosity. The fluid didn't work. We went back the next day and it didn't work again. The doctor said, "We are going to have to take you to a hospital and do a surgical scraping to remove the fetus."

The three of us sneaked into a field hospital where she began the abortion. Then I began to hemorrhage. I have always bled really easily. I have a problem with my blood coagulating. She said to me, "I'm not going through with this because you could die and that will make things really difficult."

So I didn't get an abortion. I went through this third pregnancy with a lot of internal conflict. The final deal I made with my *compañero* was that I was not going to be responsible for this child. He was going to take on all the responsibility, and we were going to leave the child with his family.

Finally, when we were at a meeting in Managua, the other *compañeros* saw that I was pregnant. They told me to have the baby there in Nicaragua and forbade me to go back to the mountains in El Salvador. So I had a little girl who is technically Nicaraguan. Misael went back to the countryside, and I stayed in Managua taking care of her for two months.

Because of my past experience, I had convinced Misael that he was going to die before she was born. He started to believe me. When he made it back to meet his child, he said he was always thinking, "I just survived a bombing attack. I just survived a mortar attack. I just escaped capture. The plane I was in didn't crash. The car I rode in didn't burst into flames." He was convinced that he had lived to see his daughter because of his constant fear.

After that, I went back to the countryside and our daughter went to live with his family. . . . A little bit later, they sent me to work on another front, away from my *compañero*. I was the second in command and had a lot of political and military responsibility. After I had worked there for about eight months, we had an evaluation meeting. The whole time I was there, I worked much harder than my superior. So at the meeting I said, "Why don't you put me in charge? He hardly does anything. Anytime there is a difficult situation he passes it along to me."

They didn't like this. Their response was, "He has a lot more experience working in this area. Don't try to take over for him." . . . Around that time, I found out about something else that was going on that infuriated me. It concerned a rape case and how it was dealt with.

I went to another evaluation meeting, and when I got there Misael and two other *compañeros* told me about a decision they had made.

They thought they had done a terrific job in resolving this problem. They told me that there were three men from the party, guerrilla soldiers, who had raped a woman. One of the rapists was the woman's husband. Then they said: "This was a very difficult case to judge because the three men accused the woman of provoking the rape. So we sentenced all four of them — the three men for being rapists and her for provoking it. We symbolically shot the three men with blanks, but at the time they didn't know that they were being shot with blanks. They thought they were really going to be shot. Then they received two other punishments. First they had to walk from camp to camp acknowledging in public that they had committed a major wrong. The men who were rapists had to do this as well as the woman who was accused of provoking the rape. The final punishment was that all four of them had to build an air raid tunnel in the mountains. The tunnel will remind future generations of how they shouldn't behave."

After they finished telling me this story, they looked really pleased with themselves. I got furious and said, "Why did you punish the woman? You didn't have any right to. She didn't do anything wrong." I really yelled at my *compañero* and I told the other two that they were sons of bitches who didn't deserve anything.

Of course they got angry with me and shouted, "You don't belong in this camp. You are from the eastern front and you don't have any right to meddle in our business here. Get out."

This episode really bothered me, and that is when I started to think about how women were treated within the guerrillas. Then something else happened that also upset me. I was resting on leave for a few days with my *compañero* when another friend of his arrived who was part of the leadership. They started to have a discussion in front of me.

"Guess what," this other guy said to Misael. "So and so is a homosexual. He is a fairy. A fag. A cocksucker. Imagine. One of our superiors is queer. How can we respect a leader like that? How can the other men look up to a fairy?" He goes on and on and Misael lights up and starts talking about this *compañero* as well. Then they start saying that he should be kicked out of the leadership because he is homosexual. The other guy who was talking had also been a homosexual before. I knew him years ago.

I got really upset, and it was the first time that I started fighting with people over sexual preference. I said, "Haven't you always told me that this *compañero* is someone whose political and ideological presence has a lot of impact? Who people respect? Haven't you told me that he is one of the best leaders we have? That he really knows how to work with

people? That he inspires people to work really hard? Why are you talking about kicking him out of the leadership? Because he is so good at
all this? It isn't right. I really disagree with you." Finally they paid attention to me and they didn't take him out of the leadership, but they sent
me off to the eastern front.

There is also a third event which I think of as pivotal in helping me to
realize the unequal position of women. In 1987, the leadership of the
party decided to open another battlefront just south of San Salvador.
They sent Misael there and then told me to go there too. It bothered me.
I said, "Why should I go just because he goes there? I'll go to another
front." "No," they told me. "We didn't send you there because you are a
couple. We sent you both because you know the urban area well and he
knows how to work in the countryside. We need you there because of
your urban experience. The mission of this front is to link up the countryside with the city. This area is going to be the rear guard for the city." I
finally gave in and went to this new front, but still resenting the fact that
they sent me there because I was with Misael.

After we had been there awhile, something happened that made me
realize I was invisible. Misael was absent from the area and I prepared
an ambush. It was on the road called La Libertad in 1988. It was the first
big ambush we had set up that close to the city. I prepared it together
with other *compañeros* who were in the zone, but I was in charge of it.
Misael sent me a letter that said I should meet him in the city on December 23rd and that we would spend Christmas together with my daughter. I wrote back to him and said I couldn't because I was getting ready
for this action. That night, we had the ambush and it was a success.
The next day on Radio Venceremos (the radio station of the FMLN) they
announced, "And our troops have established a presence in the southern part of the city where they just had a successful ambush led by
Comandante Misael."

I had gotten everything ready and carried it out, but I didn't get any of
the credit. I was really angry.

Now I want to take you to 1989 and the final offensive we carried
out there. I was sent to the city in 1989 to prepare the urban part of
the offensive. My job was to make preparations for the arrival of other
troops. Well, once again they put me in the same zone as my *compañero* Misael. He was the *comandante* and I was second in command.
We pulled off some really good occupations. I remember that when we
were preparing for the arrival of other troops I was working exclusively
with women and we did everything really carefully.

We were working in Santa Marta and San Jacinto. When I think back now, I can see that the care with which we prepared everything was something that only women could have done. We got this area ready without any confrontations because we planned things so carefully.

For example, in order to bring in lots of extra people, we pretended that we were having a wedding. We dressed up a man and woman as the bride and groom. We even had gifts and maids of honor. We had smuggled in arms several days before. So we threw this fake wedding with all these people arriving who were really with our military front. After three days of combat, my *compañero* died. We couldn't remove any of the wounded from there. He was wounded for an hour and we desperately tried to get him out, but it was a very intense battle. We were surrounded by soldiers.

Before we started the action, we had a military meeting in which he made the lines of command very clear. He said, "If I die, then "Lucía" becomes the boss." Lucía was my pseudonym in those days.

You can imagine the internal conflict I must have felt when he died. My *compañero* had just died. I had been with him for many years and had a daughter with him. And even though we were having trouble at that time as a couple, for the most part we had shared a wonderful relationship. And he was gone. I couldn't stop to mourn him. I had to take over the unit and assume leadership.

When I started to cry, one of the *compañeros* came over and said, "*Compañera*, you can't cry now. You have to keep on going. The fucking army is getting really close and you have to take over."

Nobody questioned my authority. They did what I said and followed my orders. They really supported me. . . . I remember thinking after we had been there for a week, engaged in intense combat, "Why did Misael have to die so that they would really put me in a position of leadership and respect me?" I really resented what happened and the personal cost to me.

Lynn: When did you first begin to carry out work specifically with women?

Morena: After that offensive in 1989 some of us started reading things by other Latin American women such as Marta Harnecker, and we came up with an analysis that was different from that of some of the men. There also was a segment of the party leadership that wanted to create a women's organization in order to gain access to more economic resources and to have a feminine presence in the party. They wanted women, but as a women's auxiliary. They wanted a female branch to the party that would participate in the political debates we were having and promote the party's viewpoint. . . .

They wanted to fill the vacuum that had been left by a grassroots female leader who died in 1989. They decided to create a new organization. The guy they assigned to do this wasn't able to carry it out. . . . He came to me and said, "Why don't you help me get the women organized. They can't seem to come to an agreement with one another. There are some women from CO-MADRES, there are other women in FENASTRAS (National Federation of Salvadoran Workers), and there are women in a lot of communities. They can't seem to work together. You built a women's organization that supported the front in 1982. Come and help me."

"Okay," I said. "I'll give you a hand." It wasn't my responsibility to do. I was just helping him out.

I invited another woman I knew from before to help me build the women's organization. We had some differences between us about how to approach the work. I said, "I think the work with women transcends the revolution. It is not the same thing. Look at what happened in the Soviet Union and in Cuba. The party told them that their problems would be solved after the revolution. They still haven't resolved women's problems there."

She said, "No, women have to work for the revolution first."

It turned out that we both changed some of our thinking. A lot of the women we worked with thought that we were just going to promote the party's agenda and that we would be very hierarchical in our approach to the work. It turned out to be just the opposite. We forgot about what the party wanted us to do, and we started to work on the issues that concerned the women. . . .

The first thing we talked about was what we understood about being women. What kind of experiences did we have? What had gone wrong for us? What were we afraid of as women? Once we asked these questions, there was no stopping us. For many of us, the kind of space we were creating was the first time we could ever talk about our experiences of rape, of having children. A lot of us had worked side by side, but we had never talked about our children, about our *compañeros* and the problems we had with them.

This was an amazing period for me. I was getting really close to these women, and at the same time I started having major conflicts with the *compañeros* in the party. I was starting to see things in a very different way. Not only with respect to women, but with respect to everything. They started to pressure me to stop directing the work with the women.

I told them, "Actually, the women don't need to be directed. They know what to do." "So," they replied, "If they don't need to be directed, then why are you there?"

I told them that I wasn't there because I wanted to be in charge, but because I personally needed to be there. *I* needed what was happening there. They didn't understand the personal enrichment I was getting from being there. After they had originally pushed for us to form this group, they started putting a lot of pressure on us. They withdrew all their economic and political support. The group was born in 1990 in the midst of some very strong contradictions.

From the very beginning, we said we wanted an organization that was independent. We wanted to create an organization that was not directed by a party and that did not just support the war or popular grassroots struggles. We wanted an organization of our own that supported women's particular struggles.

When we decided to call ourselves "Women for Dignity and Life" the *compañeros* from the party didn't like it. "Why are you using the word 'dignity'? It is so abstract." It didn't go along with their ideas about what a group should be called.

In the middle of all this, I began living with the terrible tension of having all this responsibility for party work but really wanting to spend my time working with the women.

Lynn: How did you resolve this contradiction?

Morena: I decided to keep working with the women. For me this meant that I had to renounce my place in the party leadership. I left the party in 1991. Things were very complicated for me. I also had to leave the country because I had been captured in 1990.

Lynn: When were you captured?

Morena: I was captured in April of 1990, but I was released quickly.

Lynn: How many days did they hold you?

Morena: They had me for four days and then they let me go. . . . At the time, one of my daughters was in Cuba. It was my third daughter, the one I had with Misael. I told the *compañeros* from the party that I wanted to go and visit her and bring her back to El Salvador.

They said, "No. You can go and visit her, but don't bring her back here. It's going to cause us a lot of security problems if you bring back this girl who speaks Cuban Spanish."

In the end I went to Nicaragua and to Cuba. I told them I was going to bring my daughter Laura back to El Salvador. I knew that if I didn't reunite with her then, that I would never have a real relationship with her. I had to wait a month to get her from Cuba to Nicaragua and then into El Salvador. They captured me when I was coming back with my daughter. They didn't realize that she had come back from Cuba. They knew we were coming from Nicaragua, but I told them a good story so they didn't realize what was up.

I was in El Salvador for four months and the *compañeros* kept telling me to leave the country and I kept refusing. By this time, I had a new love as well. Finally I left, and I went to Mexico in October of 1990.

I brought some materials from Women for Dignity and Life with me. We were still a small group. We had just completed our first women's congress, and six hundred women had come to it. That was a lot of women, but the core group of activists was only about twelve to sixteen people.

Around this time I decided that I wanted to have a child. I told the *compañeros* in the party, "I am going to get pregnant. I have never decided on my own to have a child. I'm not asking your permission, but just informing you that I am going to get pregnant."

I got pregnant and then went to Mexico. I told them I was going on a strategic mission for the party, but (such a mission) didn't really exist. I spent twenty-six days going from place to place, gathering all the material I could possibly find on women to take back for my work. I spoke with CIDHAL (Human Development Collective of Latin America), EMAS (Women's Team for Action in Solidarity), and other groups.[8] CIDHAL has come to El Salvador and done a number of workshops for us.

I ran around Mexico City and met with all these women's organizations. I came back to El Salvador with two big boxes of written material. I had also seen an ad in the newspaper in Mexico for an international feminist meeting in Argentina.[9] When I was in Mexico, I told a friend that I wanted to go (to the meeting). First I asked her, "What is this? What are they going to do at this meeting?" She said, "It's a big meeting of women who are doing work with women."

"I really want to go," I said. My friend set me up with someone who gave me some money toward a plane ticket, and we also met with someone from Oxfam England in Mexico City.[10] I explained to her what we were doing in El Salvador with our group, the DIGNAS. She saw me holding the newspaper ad for the international meeting in Argentina and she said, "I can help you out. I will help your organization participate in this event. I will pay for a ticket."

When I returned to El Salvador, I met with all the women in DIGNAS. I was very excited. I said, "Look at all the things I brought back." I unloaded my boxes. "Look at this. If I showed all of this stuff to the *compañeros*, nothing would happen. I have books, posters, pamphlets, all kinds of things. And this letter says that one of us can go to a large women's meeting in Argentina. I am going to be honest with you. I really want to go. The plane ticket is for us as an organization. We can choose whomever we want to go, but I hope you consider how much I want to go."

"That's fine," they said. "Go ahead. Let's see if we can get support for some other women to go as well. If we can't get more support, then you go ahead."

We weren't able to get support for anyone else to go, so I went alone. This was the end of October, and the *encuentro* was November 10th. I had to leave right away, so I went to tell the *compañeros* that I was going. I said, "There is a big meeting of women in Argentina and the women from DIGNAS have chosen me to go." I just went and told them. I didn't ask their permission.

By the time I got to Argentina I was about four or five months pregnant. What can I tell you about that *encuentro*? I fell in love with feminism in Argentina. It was wonderful to be able to speak so freely with so many women. I went to all kinds of workshops. I heard what many different kinds of women had to say.

I went back to El Salvador very inspired by what I had seen. I told them that I had seen lesbians there and that people hadn't rejected them. I told them that I still couldn't look at a female couple with the same indifference that I could with a man and a woman. It was a new experience. Everyone wanted to talk about these women. Another woman told me she had seen lesbians at a previous *encuentro* she had gone to in Taxco, Mexico. She had been surprised, too, she said, but we talked about it.[11]

In 1991, right before my daughter was born, the tension really started to mount with the party. In March of 1991 I told the *compañeros* from the party that I was going to quit my position in the leadership because I didn't agree with what they were doing. They got really upset when I told them this, and they did something terrible. They created a document that highlighted all the examples of my insubordination to the party. They mentioned my "unsanctioned" trip to Argentina as the last occurrence.

I quit my position in the party leadership, and my fourth daughter was born. DIGNAS really began to take off and there was a lot of work to do. Personally, though, I was having a financial crisis. I had a new baby and I also had charge of my daughter who had returned from Cuba. I was living with my *compañero*, the father of my newest daughter.

After a few months, the DIGNAS decided that we needed a long-term work plan and that we were going to raise some money to pay for a permanent staff. I was one of three people who began to get paid. It was very little money, but it was wonderful and very important work. I was really able to combine what I did before with my focus on working with women. We already had strong relationships with women from the war, in the conflict zones where the RN had been in charge. So we decided to keep working in these regions where we knew women and they trusted us. We did a lot of work focused on education, training women to organize themselves in different ways. After my daughter was born, something very important also happened for me. She was the first child I wanted to have, and so I wanted to really experience motherhood. I spent more time with my family and thought about ways to get close to my other daughters. Maybe I was coming full circle back to a different beginning from when I was eighteen.

PART II   MEXICO

CHAPTER 4

The Politics of Urban Survival
The Women's Regional Council
of the CONAMUP, Mexico

The end of 1994 marked a major devaluation of the Mexican peso, recalling the widespread panic associated with "la Crisis" of 1982 when the peso had also undergone a major devaluation. In the twelve-year interim between the two devaluations, urban survival had become more difficult, particularly for Mexican women and their families. During the 1980s, a wide range of urban movements flourished, focused on land reclamations, obtaining basic services, and pressuring the government to meet minimal obligations with respect to social welfare. Many of these urban movements were headed by men but sustained by women.

In Mexico City, the Women's Regional Council of the National Council of the Urban Popular Movement (CONAMUP) has emerged as the most successful long-term regional coordinating organization for poor women in the country. The CONAMUP was formally organized in 1981 and embraced over sixty organizations. Initial demands focused on improving urban living conditions, but also on democratizing Mexican society. Two years later, the Women's Regional Council was formed within the CONAMUP to further demands particular to women who were marginalized within the larger organization and to promote local women's councils. The Women's Regional Council combined issues of urban survival with programs to combat domestic violence and rape and to improve women's health and nutrition and provide them with leadership skills for political organizing.

The present chapter begins with a description of Mexico's economic crisis in the 1980s and its impact on the majority of Mexicans, particularly in terms of increasing economic inequality. This opening section provides important background information for understanding some of the conditions which led to the formation of the CONAMUP and the Women's Council. Next is a discussion of antipoverty programs sponsored by the Mexican government in the 1980s and the ways in which the government worked to get organizations such as the CONAMUP and the Women's Council to participate in government food-subsidy, milk, breakfast, and collective-kitchen programs. Women in the Regional Council participated in some government programs to procure much-needed resources for their members, to hold the government accountable for meeting the needs of the urban poor, and to have an entrée into the formal political arena without the mediation of a political party.

With this larger background in place, we then move on to concretely explore the difficult living conditions in Mexico City in the 1980s and the individual coping mechanisms that women developed for dealing with the economic crisis. The rest of the chapter focuses first on the rise of grassroots urban movements in Mexico City, then on the particular story of the CONAMUP and the Women's Regional Council of the CONAMUP from 1983 through 1994.

While many researchers have documented a trend toward the individualization of Mexico's economic crisis by urban women in the 1980s—that is, as wives and mothers assumed greater loads of domestic work in order to increase consumption of self-produced goods and as they increased the number of hours they spent in paid employment (Benería 1992; González de la Rocha 1991)—the Women's Regional Council of the CONAMUP suggests a different strategy. Women from the twenty-four or so neighborhood groups affiliated with the council have found ways to collectively share the costs of the crisis, to pressure the government for increased resource allocation to the poor, and to try to change some of the oppressive social conditions women encounter (e.g., domestic violence). While their actions do not reflect the strategy of the majority, they occupy an important political position by suggesting an alternative model for how to confront the conditions of economic adjustment experienced by many Mexican women. Women from the CONAMUP provide an important counterimage of nonpassivity as they regularly confront government officials, businessmen, and even members of their own organization to demand their rights. Massolo (1988, 1994) and her coauthors also document responses to the Mexican economic crisis based on collective action.

More specifically, this chapter seeks to highlight the context in which the Women's Regional Council of the CONAMUP was organized, the process that led to its inception, and the tensions that arose out of its existence. Most notable are the ways in which the organization successfully synthesized demands for urban survival with campaigns against domestic violence. The integration of these two types of demands, the former often seen as "traditional" and the latter as challenging women's oppression, suggests the futility of trying to pigeonhole the organization as "feminine" or "feminist" and its demands as "strategic" or "practical." While the term "popular feminism" (indicating the integration of class and gender concerns) has been problematic within the Women's Regional Council, the actual agenda of the organization suggests a new synthetic type of vision for women's organizing—what some would call "grassroots feminism."

The Women's Regional Council also defies attempts to classify social movement organizations as either "autonomous" or "assimilationist." The council both carried out independent actions with other organizations and utilized selective government programs to redistribute resources to its members—collaborating with the DIF (Family Services Agency), for example, in developing a neighborhood kitchen that distributes free breakfasts to children. The continued struggle for autonomy within the CONAMUP as well as the ability to work with a wide range of outside organizations were both important to the successes realized by women in the council.

Structural Adjustment and Economic Inequality in Mexico   A key factor in understanding the emergence and continued strength of the Women's Regional Council of the CONAMUP is the increasing socioeconomic inequality that has characterized Mexico since the 1970s. According to a 1992 survey, the wealthiest 20 percent of the population of Mexico has enjoyed 50 percent of the national income since 1982, while the poorest 20 percent has access to only 5 percent (González Amador 1994:60). In 1994, *Forbes* magazine reported that Mexico, with at least twenty-four billionaires, now ranks fourth in the world; in 1987, Forbes could name only one billionaire in Mexico (D. Bennett 1994).

The situation of economic hardship that many Mexican families find themselves in during the 1990s is linked to Mexican development policy in the 1970s and 1980s and to subsequent economic restructuring. Important sectors within the Mexican government pushed for measures related to structural adjustment beginning in the 1970s. In the 1980s, spurred on by the devaluation of the peso, decisionmakers in Mexico's government and business community were more successful in promoting economic policies that resulted in increasing economic disparities and the availability of fewer resources for the majority. These policies were combined with social welfare policies that in the 1980s became increasingly targeted and limited in what they offered.

Mexico's economic crisis of the 1980s is clearly linked to huge spending programs funded by international lending agencies in the 1970s which banked on Mexican oil production to pay the growing foreign debt. By 1980, oil had become Mexico's largest generator of export earnings (Chant 1991:37). The foreign debt leapt from $29 billion in 1977 to $75 billion in 1981 (Chant 1991:38). In 1981, slumping oil prices caused a panic among creditors and gave way to capital flight.

In 1982, the official beginning of the 1980s "crisis" was marked with a 50 percent devaluation of the peso. By August of that year Mexico's reserves of foreign exchange were almost exhausted. In September, President José López Portillo announced the nationalization of private banks in order to try to stem the flight of hard currency. During the next six years inflation reached a high of 150 percent, and the economy averaged an annual growth rate of real GDP of minus 4 percent (Pool and Stamos 1989:101).

Mexico's "crisis" of the 1980s was greatly aggravated by the increasing debts accrued in the 1970s. By the 1980s, loan repayments were taking up a major part of the country's foreign currency reserve, a situation found elsewhere in Latin America. In the mid-1980s, mandatory debt restructuring and accompanying structural adjustments of Mexico's economy were demanded by the International Monetary Fund. In most cases, the governments of debt-riddled Latin American countries like Mexico had little choice about implementing structural adjustment. Broadly speaking, structural adjustment was aimed at alleviating the debt crisis and the deteriorating terms of trade as well as limiting soaring inflation. Such policies were supposed to promote economic growth and improve the balance of payments by switching resources to production of tradables through unhindered operation of the market. While such policies did stem inflation by the late 1980s, they never succeeded in stimulating significant improvements in economic growth or in promoting long-term foreign investment in Mexican capital goods.

Important changes in the availability of resources and the conditions of survival for the urban and rural poor were related to other policy aims. As a result of structural adjustment, Mexico was pushed toward shrinking public expenditures and a series of market-oriented policies.[1] An emphasis on cutting government expenditures goes along with the acceptance of higher levels of unemployment, devaluation, and removal of import controls. Drastic cuts in government spending decreased the quantity and quality of government services in basic areas such as health, education, and social security. In 1990, despite the implementation of a major social welfare program targeting Mexico's poorest (PRONASOL, the National Solidarity Program), social expenditures as a percentage of total expenditures amounted to 28.8 percent, contrasted with 38.8 percent in 1980 (Dresser 1991:13n8).

The human costs of a devastated economy were seen in the 60 percent drop in real minimum wages between 1982 and 1988 and a 30 percent drop in the internal consumption of basic grains during the 1980s (Carlsen 1988:36; Stephen 1992). In 1986 it was estimated that 62 percent of the economically active population of Mexico earned subminimum wages (Chant 1991:41). From 1989 to 1993, per capita GDP fell by 13 percent from U.S.$2,633 yearly to U.S.$2,289 (González Amador 1994:10). In 1994 the World Bank estimated that 38 percent of the total population of Mexico lived in absolute poverty. Two out of five households had no water supply, three out of five had no drainage, and one in three had no electricity (Economist Intelligence Unit 1994:13). The 1980s resulted in grim living conditions for many Mexicans.

While these indicators show the concrete effects of structural adjustment at the national level, conventional economic measures seemed to indicate some initial success at the end of the 1980s in stemming economic disaster. By 1993 inflation was down to 8 percent after the government restricted the money supply and controlled wages and prices (de Palma 1994). On the eve of 1994 when the North American Free-Trade Agreement (NAFTA) was to go into operation, many thought the country was economically and politically stable. However, as the next year demonstrated, this was far from true.

In 1994, the increased poverty that had been experienced by a majority of Mexico's population during the 1980s was finally showing up in mainstream economic indicators such as higher unemployment, an unstable stock market, and little economic growth. Such indicators were also responding to a year of exceptional political instability, including the Zapatista rebellion in Chiapas during January and the assassinations of the PRI (Institutional Revolutionary Party) presidential candidate, Luis Donaldo Colosio, and the PRI secretary general, José Francisco Ruiz Massieu. Finally, in December 1994, the peso suffered a 50 percent devaluation and the Mexican stock market nosedived as foreign investors pulled their money out of Mexico. In February 1995 the United States, Canada, and others provided Mexico with an $18 billion credit to shore up the peso. Inflation for 1995 was well over 50 percent, and Mexican wage earners faced a major drop in the value of real wages, which had never recovered from the events of 1982. "La Crisis" had returned.

Government Antipoverty Programs: Concertación Social and PRONASOL   As the Mexican government carried out structural adjustment policies, it simultaneously implemented a series of social welfare programs targeting Mexicans living in poverty. Later it attempted to recuperate a loss of political control by incorporating autonomous organizations into social welfare and other programs and initiating small community organizations responsible for administering and managing resources. As pointed out by the historian Alan Knight, the logic of programs such as PRONASOL fit with policies of privatization not only by emphasizing the ways that selling off state enterprises could provide resources for the poor, but also by emphasizing the notions of "self-help" and "empowering" citizens (1994:31). The distribution of resources, particularly in a climate of scarcity, has always been a way of building political support for the PRI-based government. During the late 1980s, the Mexican government used social welfare programs to develop relationships with grassroots organizations such as the CONAMUP and attempted to incorporate movement leaders into the government. This policy shift was in marked contrast to the rejection, harassment, and even detention of autonomous movement leaders in the past. The following discussion of antipoverty programs of the mid- and late 1980s aims to shed light on how and why the Women's Regional Council of the CONAMUP decided to participate in such programs, but did so while maintaining their autonomy—eating the bait without swallowing the hook, as a popular Mexican saying suggests.

Many analysts have pointed out that the slashing of social welfare resources after 1982 should not be seen as necessarily discontinuous from previous policies (Escobar Latapí and González de la Rocha 1991: 2–3). While there were significant cuts to social welfare programs as a result of the 1982 crisis, Mexico's poor should not be seen as having generous government benefits before the crisis. What is more significant than actual amounts of money pumped into the further-scaled-down social welfare programs of the 1980s are the political practices that characterized their implementation.

The mid-1980s in Mexico were marked by the emergence of a new bargaining relationship between technocrats in the government of President Miguel de la Madrid and semiautonomous social movements. This new relationship, known as the *concertación social* (social agreement), "deliberately favored a mix of official and nonpartisan social movements. This new bargaining style recognized them as legitimate interlocutors as long as they steered clear of overt political opposition" (Fox 1994a:182). This approach was probably a result both of the increasing strength of grassroots movements in the 1980s and the government's conviction that its political control was eroding. A key testing ground for *concertación* negotiations was in the aftermath of the 1985 Mexico City earthquake when the government bargained with urban movements which were focused on procuring housing, land, and basic services. The *concertación social* also resulted in wage and price freezes before the 1988 elections as part of a solidarity pact between government and labor.

While the *concertación social* focused on limited pacts between the government and specific social sectors such as labor, transportation, and government workers, the crowning piece of 1980s social welfare policy was the creation of an umbrella organization called PRONASOL, which was charged with coordinated health, education, infrastructure, and productive projects designed to improve the living conditions of the poor. As pointed out by Nora Lustig (1994:83), most of the projects were designed to "expand, rehabilitate, or improve the infrastructure available for the provision of basic services" (such as hospitals, schools, water supply systems, sewage, electrification, roads, and food distribution stores). A small number of the projects qualified as transfers of income, such as a children's scholarship program, the availability of interest-free loans for productive projects, and food subsidies. Begun in 1988 by President Carlos Salinas de Gortari after a questionable electoral victory, PRONASOL primarily targeted poor peasants, indigenous people, and the urban poor and attempted to directly involve them in the program through local committees that were supposed to design, implement, and oversee local projects (see articles in Cornelius, Craig, and Fox 1994). A majority of the funding came through block grants to state and municipal governments.

PRONASOL programs for the urban poor included such benefits as subsidized tortillas and milk, sold to families earning less than twice the minimum wage (see Cornelius, Craig, and Fox 1994 for more on PRONASOL). The rural poor were targeted through continued funding of CONASUPO (the distribution branch of the National Basic Foods Company) which provided some subsidized food such as beans, corn, and tortillas to rural consumers (see Fox 1992b). PRONASOL also provided funding to the Family Services Agency and to the government's health and nutrition program. In 1990, PRONASOL established three additional programs aimed at the poor: Solidarity Funds for Production, which provided credit to farmers and producer organizations; Solidarity Funds for Indigenous Communities (see Fox 1994a; Hindley 1995b); and Women in Solidarity. A solidarity health program and funds for infrastructural development in poor communities were also set up through Municipal Solidarity Funds. Many evaluations of the program conclude that it did nothing to change the structure of poverty in Mexico and did not reach the poorest communities in the country (Molinar and Weldon 1994; Gershberg 1994). It did, however, have an important sociopolitical role (Knight 1994; Ward 1994; Fox 1994a).

The language used to frame the PRONASOL program and the active recruitment of leaders from autonomous organizations to participate in it can be read in most cases as signals that grassroots movements were being co-opted to maintain ruling-party control. In a few limited instances, calls for coresponsibility between policymakers and low-income communities may demonstrate the presence of genuine reformers (Fox 1994a:179–180). As noted by Moguel (1994:173), the similarities between certain ideas held by those on the social left who are in leadership positions in urban popular organizations and others who are incorporated in the PRONASOL are not coincidental. Key figures in the administration of the PRONASOL program and some movement leaders share common political experience through their participation in the Maoist tendency known as Popular Politics (Política Popular) (see note 6). Moguel notes that "the very structure of Solidarity incorporates fundamental elements of the left's discourse, such as direct or assembly democracy, concertation, noncorporatist organization, horizontal coordinating committees, mass politics, etc." (1994:174).

Living Conditions in Urban Mexico and Women's Individual Struggles for Survival   While an understanding of the dynamics of Mexico's economic crisis and government antipoverty programs is critical for explaining the rise of the CONAMUP, we must also move ourselves closer to the devastating daily-life experience of people living in urban Mexico during the 1980s. We have to look at the special impact the crisis had on women, because their struggles are the motor for many urban social movements.

With roughly a quarter of Mexico's population concentrated in Mexico City, the fiscal crisis of the Mexican government in the 1980s was more manifest there than in other areas. As documented in detail by Diane Davis, when the fall in oil prices brought a debt crisis and forced the government to impose a rigid austerity plan, Mexico City's budget was one of the first to be affected (1994:251). Drastic cuts in public expenditures on transport, potable water, health services, trash collection, and land regularization created an emergency situation for many residents.

Women in Mexico City protesting government economic policies and
demanding the right to a decent living, 1987. The newspaper banners read,
"Everyone against the Pact." The government was asking workers to sign a
solidarity pact in which they would "share the burden" of economic crisis.
Women at the rally objected to the pact.

Making matters worse, at the same time that expenditures on urban services fell, employment dropped, poverty increased exponentially, and the
costs of housing and other much-needed urban goods rose at an unprece-
dented rate as the debt crisis intensified. In the three-year period starting
in 1984, prices of dietary staples in Mexico City rose at a phenomenal
rate—757 percent for beans, 480 percent for eggs, 454 percent for fish,
340 percent for milk, and 276 for cornmeal (Davis 1994:277).

Besides these devastating economic factors, simply living in Mexico
City during the 1980s was a guarantee of continuous health problems.
Because of the extreme centralization of population, industry, manufacture, and government functions, Mexico City had become pollution central, with a wide range of polluters spewing "approximately 6,000 tons
of contaminants into the atmosphere daily" (Nuccio and Ornelas 1990:
40). Thermal inversions and record air-pollution levels in the winters left
many Mexico City inhabitants with permanent respiratory problems,
particularly the elderly and children. One of the worst effects of pollution
is linked to leaded gasoline. A 1988 study of 102 newborns found that

50 percent of those studied had dangerously high levels of lead in their blood; indeed, similar levels found in children in other countries had resulted in slower rates of mental development (Brannigan 1988).

As the material resources, social services, and the real income for maintaining their families dwindled, women in Mexico City developed survival strategies which placed them under increasing stress. Studies conducted on marginalized urban women during the 1980s indicate several major trends which are discussed in detail below (Arizpe 1977; Arizpe et al. 1989; Benería and Roldán 1987; Benería 1992; del Castillo 1993; González de la Rocha 1989, 1991; Gutmann 1994a, 1994b; Sánchez Gómez 1989). These trends include an increase in the number of women and children (especially teenagers) entering the informal and formal wage-labor force, the self-provisioning of goods and services formerly purchased, coerced family cooperation, and continued heavy domestic workloads for women. Women received some help from husbands and children with domestic chores, but the amount of that help varied and did not include the most time-consuming domestic duties such as cooking. Conditions of economic and ecological impoverishment create a harsh living and working environment. Deteriorating health conditions put an increasing physical strain on women as they care for themselves and their often chronically ill children. And lack of access to drinking water, transportation, and food markets in peripheral city areas often further increases the total time women spend trying to finish their unpaid domestic chores.

In urban areas, the unemployed, underemployed, and the poorly paid engage in petty trade and service industries which are labeled "the informal economy." In 1985 it was estimated that the informal sector generated over 38 percent of Mexico's GDP (Vera 1987:81). Mexico had an 80 percent increase in informal employment from 1980 to 1987 with a stagnation in formal employment (Escobar Latapí and González de la Rocha 1991:9). Analysts have found that women's informal-sector participation in Latin America has grown steadily during the 1980s, rising by 24 percent from 1983 to 1987 (Inter-American Development Bank 1990:232). Mexico is no exception to this pattern.

Women in Mexico participate in two major types of informal-sector work. The first is in the area of subcontracting to produce intermediate or finished goods, as documented by Benería and Roldán (1987). The second type includes such self-generated activities as the sale of services (as domestic workers), food, or other petty commodities. In the 1980s, if remunerated household services are included in the definition of "informal" economic activities, women constituted between 52 percent and 62 percent of all informal-sector workers (Berger and Buvinic 1988). Between 1985 and 1988, women's contribution to household income increased from 20 percent to 32.4 percent among lower-income informal-sector families included in a study of low-income families in Mexico City (Jusidman 1988, cited in Inter-American Development Bank 1990:235).

In Mexico overall in 1990, 19.58 percent of women were part of the "economically active population" as reported by the Mexican census (INEGI 1990:316). As pointed out by Gutmann (1994a:23–24) in his reading of the 1990 census material, "statistics by age groups reveal an even starker contrast between Mexico City and the country as a whole: over 40 percent of women between the ages of 40 and 44 in the Federal District were still 'economically active.' In the rest of the country 22 percent of women were registered as 'economically active.'"[2]

And how are urban women coping with an increasingly difficult situation beyond entering the wage-labor force in greater numbers? The working-class women who were subjects of a Guadalajara study carried out from 1982 to 1987 coupled their increased wage-labor participation with a strategy of producing items such as clothing, vegetables, and cooked lunches which they had previously purchased in the market (González de la Rocha 1989). This strategy is reminiscent of women in the rural subsistence sector who subsidize insufficient male wages by remaining at home to farm, care for animals, and produce clothing while their husbands engage in migrant wage labor. In the Guadalajara study, however, women appear to be subsidizing their own as well as their husbands' wages. González de la Rocha also found that women and children ate lower-quality foods than men, concentrating on beans, tortillas, vegetables, and fruits while men ate more meat, eggs, and industrialized food products (1991:119).

Benería and Roldán's study (1987), carried out in Mexico City in 1981–1982, indicates that in spite of their employment in home assembly work, most women workers are constantly thinking of ways to reduce their household budgets. Their pay is extremely low. Workers were not given fringe benefits and in fact were subsidizing the nonlabor costs of production, including use of electricity, tools, and services normally provided at the site of production.

In a follow-up study ten years later, involving some of the same households included in the 1981–1982 study, Benería found that 69.4 percent of the fifty-five households included regularly "bought less food, clothing, [and] shoes, and spent less on other daily expenses such as transportation, drinks, and snacks than during the pre-1982 period" (1992:94).

She also found that households living under extreme poverty or at subsistence levels were not able to keep up with basic house repair and often had to spend their money on food instead of repairing their homes. A majority of households in her sample (which cut across impoverished, working-class, and middle-class households) were cutting back their food purchases. Women's domestic work had increased significantly, and older daughters were also working harder. Benería found, too, that more than half of the households in her sample had "decreased or eliminated trips to visit relatives and friends and attendance at family parties and religious holidays" (1992:96).

A key factor associated with women's individual responses to the economic crisis is a major drop in fertility rates. In her restudy, Benería found that 45.7 percent of the households in her sample of fifty-five had "decided to either stop or postpone having children during the 1982–1988 period" (1992:94). In 1981 the overall average number of children for women twelve years or older was 3.4; in 1988, it was 2.5 (Zavala de Cosío 1992:26, cited in Gutmann 1994a:29). In 1990, in Mexico City, the average was even lower—2 (Gutmann 1994a:29). While birthrates are also related to factors such as education, women both with and without higher levels of education were having fewer children in the 1980s than ever before. Nevertheless, most still have children to care for.

One of the reasons women start doing poorly paid industrial work in their homes is so that they can continue their traditional duties as wives and mothers. Other studies (Sánchez Gómez 1989; Sánchez Gómez and Martini Escolar 1987; Arizpe 1977; Arizpe, Salinas, and Velásquez 1989) demonstrate that women tend to engage in paid activities which facilitate their domestic work. While many women are conscious of their exploitation in the underpaid, informal wage-labor force, they still feel a strong commitment to carrying out their socialized roles as wives and mothers.

When urban marginal women enter the paid labor force they receive some domestic help from their husbands and children, but they still end up working long hours. Just how much help they receive and what "help" means is not entirely clear in the literature. Benería and Roldán found that while a high proportion of husbands help out their working wives, usually this help is concentrated almost exclusively in "activities outside of the home. . . . There was no instance of collaboration in housecleaning or food preparation" (1987:130). Despite their status as "wage earners," women continue to be responsible for procuring and preparing food, obtaining water, providing clothing, taking care of household needs and often covering at least part of their children's educational and medical costs.

Recent ethnographic work done by Gutmann (1996) in the Mexico City working-class *colonia* of Santo Domingo suggests that men are more helpful than Benería and Roldán imply. He documents ample evidence of men assisting in parenting (particularly of boys), laundry, cleaning, and shopping—even buying their daughters sanitary napkins (Gutmann 1994a:25; Gutmann 1996). Gutmann found that men's assistance with household chores was closely correlated with women entering into the wage-labor force. Those men who spent the greatest amount of time doing domestic chores had wives who worked full-time outside the home. Younger unmarried men indicated that if they married someone who worked, they would not have a problem with sharing domestic chores such as laundry and cleaning (Gutmann 1994b, 1996). The more labor-intensive activity of cooking remains a woman's activity except for cooking on festive occasions when men pitch in. Gutmann also suggests that we begin to question our assumptions of what "housework" means. Does unpaid work that men do such as laying bricks, pouring cement, hanging doors, building closets and patios to maintain and improve their homes count as domestic work? (Gutmann 1994b: chap. 5, pp. 3–4).

The unrecognized domestic work that men do, however, does not undercut how hard women are working. Benería and Roldán (1987:124–130), for example, found that women who contribute more than 40 percent of their weekly household income pool spend an average of between 49 and 56 hours per week doing domestic work. When this is added to their paid workload, they work an average of between 105 and 111 hours per week. The issue, Gutmann suggests, is not to deny the long hours that women do work at home, often in addition to wage work, but to also document subtle changes in the division of labor and ways in which men are also carrying out unpaid labor which contributes to family survival.

While Gutmann found strong evidence that men's domestic participation, particularly in parenting, has been underestimated, he remains only cautiously optimistic about what this means for women.[3]

Thus, in large part, the increased domestic workload that women (and, to a limited extent, perhaps men and children) have taken on can be read as an individualization of the economic crisis and as increased individual exploitation. While individualization is one coping strategy used by many, there is another. For some women, the very dynamics of privatization and structural adjustment that resulted in increasing their workloads, decreasing the quality of their diets, and making it even harder for them to take care of their families led them eventually to organize around the struggles of daily urban life. We now move on to the conditions that fostered grassroots organizing in Mexico City.

Collective Responses to the Crisis   Analysts trace the rise of grass-roots urban movements in Mexico City and other major metropolitan areas to a number of factors. The material conditions of the 1980s economic crisis are one set of factors, unresolved problems of land tenure and housing for the poor are another, and a third has to do with the presence of a large cadre of ex-student activists who, after the massacre in Tlatelolco, shifted their focus from confronting the state to working directly with "the masses" (Díaz Barriga 1996; Bennett 1992a; Moguel 1994; Ramírez Saiz 1990). A fourth factor is a decline in government control reflected in the widespread belief that the government was unresponsive to demands from below and that direct action was the only way to achieve change.

The growth of cities through migration in relation to macroeconomic policies favoring urban over rural development is an important factor for understanding the development of political movements around land and housing in Mexico City. In 1970, it was estimated that over 50 percent of those living in Mexico City who were older than twenty had not been born in the city (Muñoz, Oliveira, and Stern 1971). The constant flow of migrants to Mexico City beginning in the 1960s had reached an average of 270,000 people per year in the 1980s (Nuccio and Ornelas 1990:39). This migration flow has contributed to the industrial labor force and to a transfer of surplus labor from the countryside to the city, forming a reserve labor force that is the rank and file of the informal sector (Benería and Roldán 1987:19). In 1990 Mexico City had approximately 20 million inhabitants, making it the largest city in the world at the time. The rapid growth of Mexico City has been repeated in other major urban areas including Monterrey, Tijuana, Ciudad Juárez, and Guadalajara. In fact, by 1990 Mexico's population was 71.3 percent urban (INEGI 1990:10).

Many of those who arrived in Mexico City during the 1960s and 1970s were without housing or basic services. Eugenia Flores Hernández, a founder of the women's movement within the CONAMUP, recalls how the earliest successes they had in the CONAMUP were focused on procuring basic services by negotiating with officials in the appointed (i.e., nonelected) Mexico City government and others. Eugenia is a working-class woman who was active in the student movement before she began organizing in urban neighborhoods. She was unusual in her neighborhood because she finished high school and went to the university:

First, we would fight for a piece of land to build housing on, then fight for the introduction of public services with city officials. And if we got those services, we had to provide labor to install them — like digging the ditches to put in water pipes or drainage pipes. We also had to fight just to get primary schools built in our neighborhoods. The Education Ministry wouldn't listen.

Another organizer of the Women's Regional Council, Carmen Martínez Flores, related a similar story, adding the importance of local activists who got her involved in organizing:

I am a seamstress. I lived in Colonia Ermita Zaragosa. That's where I met several local activists who got me involved. We had to begin working somewhere. I started out working in my colonia *because we didn't have any basic services like water, electricity, sewage, or streets. It's work that doesn't just benefit me, but also other people.*[4]

The presence of male and female organizers in the CONAMUP who had been part of the student movement in Mexico City was also reported as an important moment in history by Eugenia Flores:

In Mexico, as in many countries around the world, there was a large student movement. The repression of the government against this movement was at its worst on the 2nd of October 1968 [Tlatelolco massacre] when four hundred students were killed. This caused some students to leave the movement and they decided to go and support popular organizations.

While activists in the CONAMUP describe the presence of organizers as important, their self-histories do not focus exclusively on links to political organizations. Political analysts of the left have carefully documented the relationship between various strands of the Mexican left and the rise of urban popular movements. Student organizers who worked from a Maoist philosophy called "la linea de masas" (the mass line), emphasizing the building of a mass movement from the bottom up, were particularly successful in areas on the urban periphery. Leaders were somewhat surprised at their success in urban areas because the logic of the Maoist approach was to create revolutionary nuclei in the country-side and use them to encircle the city.[5]

Bennett (1992a) argues that a shared starting point in the Maoist left of post-1968 Mexico City continued to link the leaders of movements in Monterrey, Durango, and Mexico City after their individual destinies became wrapped up with movements in different regions. This shared experience also allowed movements from Mexico City, Monterrey, and Durango to come together for the first national congress of urban popular movements in 1980. The presence of well-trained, dedicated activists who communicated frequently, organized national marches and meetings, and formed long- and short-term coalitions was a critical factor in the formation of the CONAMUP. As discussed below, several different political tendencies came together to form the organization, but they would vie for control throughout the organization's life.[6]

In a useful analysis, Bennett (1992b) divides Mexico's urban social movements into three periods. She places the first wave of urban popular movements in the early 1970s and notes that most of them arose in the northern states of Chihuahua, Nuevo León, and Durango and in the southern state of Oaxaca. What characterizes each of these movements is that they constructed "new channels to express the needs of the urban poor," bypassing government offices and government-controlled organizations that were seen as incapable of delivering urban services. Since many people perceived the state as unresponsive to their needs and as dedicated to maintaining a corrupt maze of bureaucratic black holes, these new movements were initially seen as more responsive to the needs of people, and they created a new relationship between activist leaders and popular bases. All were formed during a post-1972 "democratic" political opening under the administration of President Luis Echeverría Alvarez (Bennett 1992b:244–246).

Bennett's second wave of urban popular movements was formed between 1979 and 1983 after a wave of repression. This period is characterized by the formation of independent popular urban neighborhoods (created through land invasions and self-development projects), the birth of neighborhood-based organizations, and the structuring of regional and national coalitions of urban popular movements (Bennett 1992b: 248). While land invasions and squatter movements were established in Mexico City in the 1970s, they did not develop into stable grassroots movements which acted in coordination.

Nineteen eighty stands out in the history of Mexico's urban movements because it is the year when approximately twenty-one organizations and seven hundred delegates attended the first national congress of urban popular movements in Monterrey (Moctezuma 1983:7). The congress allowed activists and participants in movements from different parts of the country to debate and compare strategies, ideologies, and specific programs. The first congress concluded with a pact of solidarity and a promise to hold a second congress in 1981 (Moctezuma 1983:7; Bennett 1992b). It was at that congress, held in Durango, that the CONAMUP was formally created, by two thousand participants from sixty organizations representing fourteen states. The constituency at the founding congress covered a range of class factions including the urban poor, renters, working-class and some middle-class homeowners, people looking for housing, workers from the informal sector, small-scale vendors and merchants, and more (Ramírez Saiz 1986:175).

The demands of the CONAMUP focused on improving the living conditions of its constituent members, but also on democratizing Mexican society and easing repression against those who organized for change. The CONAMUP had annual congresses to coordinate the exchange of information and strategies. While it was supposed to have many regional assemblies, the one that was most effective was that operating in the valley of Mexico which coordinated sixty organizations that previously had been working separately (Ramírez Saiz 1986:178–179).

During the 1980s, the work of the CONAMUP was wide-ranging. The council focused on procuring land, housing, running water, drainage, schools, clinics, and public transport for the residents of urban marginal zones as well as on rent freezes, sustaining price subsidies, eliminating the value-added tax (IVA), and defending the human rights of those involved in the struggle. A major point of their political program was the fight to allow each neighborhood and community the right to self-government. Mexico City was and is ruled by an appointed mayor. By the early 1980s the CONAMUP claimed to have a hundred thousand participating families (Ramírez Saiz 1986:175).

Groups within the CONAMUP remained divided over whether or not to become involved in electoral campaigns. Some organizations within the CONAMUP continued to view elections as tools of the ruling class; others felt that it was strategically desirable to enter electoral campaigns for particular ends (Ramírez Saiz 1986: 184–185). At the end of the 1980s, some organizations of the CONAMUP, and the Women's Regional Council within it, began to participate in government solidarity programs, taking resources and redistributing them to their constituencies. CONAMUP organizers negotiated regularly with officials from the

Mexican Social Security Institute (IMSS) about medical and health concerns, as well as with the Family Services Agency, the National Solidarity Program, and others.

At the time of its formation, the CONAMUP did not embrace all of the independent urban popular movements in Mexico, but certainly it included a good part of them (see Ramírez Saiz 1986:174 for those not included). The core of the CONAMUP was made up by the Union of Popular Neighborhoods (UCP), formed in 1979 in the valley of Mexico; the Popular Front for Land and Liberty (FPT y L), formed in 1976 in Monterrey; the Committee for Popular Defense, Durango (CDP), formed in 1979; and the Popular Front of Zacatecas (FPZ).

The third wave of popular movements identified by Bennett (1992b) took place between 1985 and 1988, with a majority of the new movements being formed in Mexico City following the 1985 earthquake in which more than ten thousand lives were lost and hundreds of thousands were homeless or had their homes damaged. Within thirty days of the earthquake, the Sole Coordinating Council of Earthquake Victims (CUD) was formed to pressure the de la Madrid government to respond to the housing crisis. Another group, the Neighborhood Assembly (Asamblea de Barrios), was formed in 1987, likewise organizing around housing issues. During this period the CONAMUP also remained active.

The Emergence of Women's Organizing within the CONAMUP   During the 1980s, the CONAMUP emerged as one of Mexico's most powerful "urban social movement" organizations. A majority of the participants in the CONAMUP, however, were seemingly invisible—the women. While a majority of the participants in marches, meetings, sit-ins, and other activities carried out by the CONAMUP were women, they were not represented in the leadership, barely spoke at public meetings, and had few opportunities to give voice to their particular struggles. Some women who came to CONAMUP meetings and activities faced domestic violence simply for leaving their homes. Their husbands accused them of having affairs when they left their neighborhoods to attend regional meetings in the center of Mexico City. Most had to plan for days in advance, preparing food and making sure that their cleaning and washing was done in order to spend a day at a march or a meeting.

These women found urban living a struggle, and spent long hours carrying out domestic work in addition to working in the informal sector, doing home assembly work, or (if they were really lucky) going to a factory job. They were women of different ages, marital status, and ethnic backgrounds (self-labeled *mestizas* and/or, in some cases, identified with specific indigenous groups), but they shared a common experience of trying to manage in an urban environment with a minimum of resources. A few had political experiences with labor unions or the church, but most were simply trying to survive "la Crisis." Similarly, a few had contact with women from feminist organizations, but most did not. Many CONAMUP women members joined the organization in the 1980s. Others joined as a result of women's neighborhood committees that were formed after the Women's Regional Council emerged. What women in the Regional Council came to share was a set of strategies forged with others for ways to improve their daily living conditions. The varied women within the CONAMUP continued to have distinct visions of what their organization was doing and what it meant in terms of each of their lives, but they were agreed on the range of issues their struggle incorporated and on the continued need for a separate organizational space for women within the CONAMUP. The autonomy of the Women's Regional Council allowed women not only to participate more effectively in the particular struggles they identified as their own—improved urban living conditions, domestic violence, and women's health and reproduction—but also to democratize the larger CONAMUP in terms of gender equity by developing a stronger presence in the leadership as well as at the base. The present section describes the development of the Women's Regional Council during the 1980s, focusing on organizational issues in its formation and maintenance. This is followed by a discussion of the key issues around which women have organized. Then we address the role of feminism within the CONAMUP and the different ways that women engaged with feminism and adapted it to their own particular identities.

Initially, the impetus for forming a women's organization within the CONAMUP came out of discussions focused on the theme of democracy. How could an organization claim to be democratic if a majority of its members were not fully participating? According to Eugenia Flores, one of the founders of the Valley of Mexico Women's Council of the CONAMUP, the idea for a national meeting of women first surfaced in 1983.

Lynn: How was the Women's Regional Council formed?

Eugenia: Within the CONAMUP the discussion for having a national meeting of women came out of a discourse on democracy. This has always been a big concern within the CONAMUP. Men and women both realized it was a problem that even though most of the members were women, they were the ones who participated least in decisionmaking.

Lynn: Was it men or women who came up with the idea for the women's group?

Eugenia: It was formed by the women who were there. But there were only a few of them who could speak up and propose anything at a national CONAMUP meeting. That's when it was first recognized that women are the backbone of the urban popular movement.

Lynn: You hear that phrase a lot, women are the backbone of the movement.

Eugenia: Yes, but it means that people accept that women are the backbone, not the head of the movement. We said that it was important for the people who formed the majority of the movement to participate more. Furthermore, there were a lot of problems created for women when they left their houses and began participating in local organizations. . . . (W)omen were beaten just for going to meetings. There was a real need to deal with these types of issues. That's why we decided to have that first national meeting for women.

The First National Women's Meeting of the CONAMUP was held in November 1983 at the headquarters of the Committee for Popular Defense in the city of Durango.[7] The CDP was one of the core groups in the CONAMUP. Several hundred women came together in the first national meeting and made a commitment to keep on sharing their experiences and to organize future events. One of the results of the meeting was to reinvigorate already existing women's groups which had fallen by the wayside. An effort was made to reactivate such organizations as the feminine leagues, formed in Monterrey within various urban popular movements, as well as specific women's organizations in Guanajuato and Zacatecas (Bennett 1992b).

Women at the first national meeting also coordinated regional celebrations of International Women's Day on March 8 and Mother's Day on May 10. After the first national meeting, the Women's Regional Council of the CONAMUP was formed from women who participated in thirty urban organizations in the valley of Mexico. This regional group has remained the most successful instance of women's organizing within the CONAMUP and has had an important presence in Mexico City.

The most striking aspect of the organizing project of the Women's Regional Council of the CONAMUP is the combination of issues activists have focused on since its inception. Workshops and campaigns bring together domestic violence, women's sexuality, and women's political participation together with poverty and urban survival. This range of issues more than anything is responsible for the successful integration of women from a variety of backgrounds into one organization. The issues also reflect the different dimensions of women's lives relating to gender, class, age, and ethnicity. While the larger CONAMUP remained focused on the material conditions of living, often filtered through rhetoric about class and class position, the Women's Regional Council developed a more wide-ranging discourse that incorporated different aspects of women's identities (Stephen 1996b:171).

Following the second national women's meeting of the CONAMUP in 1985, the Women's Regional Council organized several campaigns. From August 1985 until February 1986 they organized their first campaign against violence against women. The activities focused on consciousness-raising about domestic violence and on education through films, flyers, and discussions in and around Mexico City (Brugada and Ortega 1987:101). In 1987, after the Fourth Latin American and Caribbean Feminist Encuentro in Taxco, Mexico, the Women's Regional Council joined women across Latin America in observing an International Day against Violence against Women. It was resolved at the fourth *encuentro* that the day would be observed on November 25, in commemoration of six Dominican peasant women who were killed after resisting sexual violation by military troops (Miller 1991:245).

In 1986 the Women's Regional Council organized a second campaign against inflation. A major focus of this struggle was to persuade the Ministry of Trade and Industrial Promotion (SECOFI) to let them control the distribution and sale of gas used for cooking in thirty neighborhoods. Through such direct actions as occupying the office and picketing, they got SECOFI to donate gas tanks and to give them a distribution contract. This program continued into the 1990s. Also in 1986, the Women's Regional Council began to organize to keep the price of subsidized corn and tortillas down as well as to control distribution of subsidized milk from the government-run LICONSA (CONASUPO, Industrialized Milk Inc.). They achieved these goals by pressuring CONASUPO officials with nonstop visits, sit-ins, and banners.[8]

By the end of the 1980s, the economic situation of Mexico's urban poor and working classes had worsened significantly. The creation of the National Solidarity Program by the government was a turning point for organizations like the Women's Regional Council. While many grassroots organizations were ultimately squeezed out of existence for economic reasons, many women in CONAMUP believe that their participation in PRONASOL was key not only to their own continued

hunger strikes, and other actions to pressure government officials. By the 1990s, when they showed up at the offices of PRONASOL officials, it was well known that these women would not back down and would be willing to stay until their demands had been met.

In 1988 the Women's Regional Council moved into a building occupied by a feminist organization called "New Moon" (Cuarto Creciente). New Moon solicited the support of the CONAMUP in order to avoid being evicted from the house they had taken over in the center of Mexico City. They donated all their materials to members of the Women's Council who valiantly tried to defend the space. Carmen Martínez Flores, age fifty-eight, describes the struggle for the house.

We received notice that we were being evicted. We lost a bitter court battle with the owner, and we were thrown out in the street. We occupied the atrium of the cathedral for fifteen days and got a lot of publicity. That was the beginning of a long fight.

Once they were evicted from their original location, the women decided to petition the mayor, Manuel Camacho Solis, for a space. They maintained a constant presence in and outside of the mayor's office and kept pressure on the mayor to give in to their demands. Their occupation of his office was the first one faced by Mayor Camacho Solis, who capitulated to the pressure and gave them a credit from the city to be used toward a twelve-year mortgage in order to acquire a permanent space. The women used the credit to purchase a large house in the center of Mexico City, and that house is now a women's center housing a wide range of activities (Mogrovejo Aquise 1990:42–43).

The experience of winning the struggle for their space as well as prior confrontations over access to the control of gas distribution, tortilla programs, and milk supply emboldened the women in their efforts. Once they moved into their new center, the Women's Regional Council organized a school for women, a collective kitchen that serves breakfast to schoolchildren and lunch to the elderly, a health clinic, and a wide range of workshops focusing on women's health and sexuality, domestic violence, and strategies for generating household income. Workshops on economic production emphasize clothing manufacture, small crafts, food processing, and tarot card reading. The Women's Regional Council distributes over sixteen thousand government-subsidized breakfasts to children each day and uses the center for weekly meetings with representatives from the neighborhood committees that make up the Regional Women's Council. In 1994 the Women's Council also began organizing cultural outings once a month. They took a trip to the ruins at Teotihua-cán, visited several museums, and went to the state of Morelos to mark the assassination of Emiliano Zapata. The government provided them with transportation for these outings.

The Women's Center of the Regional Council is located in a bustling working-class neighborhood in downtown Mexico City close to the historic Zócalo. One half of the building is dedicated to a collective kitchen that the women organized with the help of the government's Family Services Agency. The DIF's logo is prominently displayed on the building. While the DIF donated stoves, tables, chairs, and tiles, the Women's Regional Council provides labor and pays for, cooks, and distributes the food. Aside from the free meals provided to neighborhood children and to the elderly, the kitchen also sells food which generates enough cash to pay for the phone, light, and water bills of the Women's Center. The kitchen also serves as a local gathering place for political meetings and trading gossip and is a comfortable spot for people in the neighborhood to hang out. It integrates the Women's Center into the daily life of the neighborhood. The Women's Center also has a medical area, a large meeting hall, a library, and smaller rooms for meetings as well as offices.

In 1989, the Women's Center received a $10,000 grant from a religious foundation in Boston. They put this money in the bank and have been using it as well as the interest generated to meet their monthly mortgage payments on the house. Beyond this large donation, they have not received major foundation funding.[9]

The economic crisis of the 1980s affected the Women's Regional Council as well as many other organizations, and they have survived primarily by gaining control of resources offered by the government through various social welfare programs. Even so, programs such as subsidized tortillas and milk were cut in the early 1990s. Subsidized breakfasts from the DIF and resources from the Women's Solidarity Program (a subset of the National Solidarity Program) were the primary government assistance received by women in the CONAMUP during 1994. While activists in the Regional Council complain about not wanting to work with the government, they also acknowledge that they had little choice. Says one neighborhood activist who prefers to remain anonymous:

It's not as if we actively decided to work with the government. We don't really have many other possibilities. We have to take what the government offers and make it work for us. If not, we might not survive. A lot of women's organizations have gone under in the past ten years.

In 1994, several women on the staff of the Women's Center as well as representatives from the neighborhood committees finished negotiating with the government's Women's Solidarity Program to provide funds for repairing the center. They spent a year and a half writing letters, going to meetings, and occasionally occupying government offices to get the agency to pay attention to them and acknowledge their work. One staff member, Carmen Martínez Flores, describes the work:

At first they [Mujeres en Solidaridad] didn't want to support us because they said they wouldn't support a women's center. They investigated us and saw what we were doing. They saw that we really were working with women in the colonias populares. *Now they are finally going to give us some support. We just kept bothering them until they gave in to us. It took one and a half years.*

In late 1994, when I carried out my last visit with women in the Regional Council, their struggle with the government bureaucracy to win recognition of their work had absorbed considerable energy. Nevertheless, they continued to maintain the strong local women's committees they have established in twenty-four neighborhoods. The work of these local committees and their coordination remains the core of the organization. While local committees are independent and are often involved in diverse activities, they also participate in unified campaigns coordinated through the regional office in Mexico City. Interviews with several neighborhood-level activists in 1994 revealed that their struggles were focused on "lo de siempre" (the same old issues) of housing, basic services, health, and domestic battery. Neighborhood committees continue to organize around local campaigns, to hold workshops, and to participate in the regional organization.

Every Tuesday evening, sixty or seventy women from local committees come to the Women's Center to meet, share information, discuss the breakfast-distribution program, and develop proposals for the regional organization. Local committees have an average of thirty to forty members. Some elect representatives to the Regional Council, and others rotate their representatives on a more informal basis. The committees are so well established that some women are even accompanied by their husbands. In some instances, men who started out following their wives downtown to make sure they were really going to meetings (instead of meeting secret lovers or engaging in unladylike behavior as their husbands suspected) now come with their wives to the meetings. As reported by an animated local committee member from Colonia Aragón:

*What happens is the husbands come here with them. They say, "How
can you spend three hours in the Regional Council's office?" Then they
realize that nothing [improper] is going on. . . . There was one man
who started out coming to spy on his wife to make sure she was really
here. Then they came together and now he likes to come here maybe
even more than she does. He says, "I like to come here. I like to be
here." Now his wife doesn't even come any more. . . . And now
sometimes he talks in the meetings. He says things like, "Yes, there
are men who beat their wives." And the women turn to him and say,
"And you don't?" "Well," he answers, "I did before, but now it's a
good thing that I came here because I learned that I shouldn't be
doing that."*

Mixing Class and Gender Issues   The longevity of the Women's Regional Council seems specifically related to the way in which gender and
class issues are both integrated into the organization's activities. While
many women initially join local women's committees in search of economic assistance and ways of improving their marginal existence, they
come in as individuals participating in a wide range of social relations.
They are mothers, wives, workers, daughters, part of an ethnic and
neighborhood community, and may also be politically active in a church
or some other organization. Their participation in the Women's Regional
Council affects their other social relationships. The relationships that
seem to be immediately affected are those growing out of gender in the
home, family, and neighborhood. The very act of leaving their homes,
breaking daily routines, and coming to a meeting can result in difficult
consequences for women. As they increase the amount of time they are
involved in organizing and begin to ask for help with their domestic responsibilities, they often encounter conflict at home and within their organizations. Indeed, many women in the CONAMUP report physical
intimidation by their husbands. Thus, domestic violence and disrupted
household gender relations quickly become a part of women's experience
when they participate in the Regional Council. The organizer Eugenia
Flores reports:

*To leave the house and go to a demonstration causes husbands to get
angry. Women being active causes problems which can even result in
beatings. . . . For example, if there was a woman who took on a leadership position and could speak very clearly, she often had problems later
with her husband. That would be it. She would have to leave the organization, and nothing could be done. It still happens, but today there*

are places where we can discuss these problems — places just for women.

Participation in a political organization brings to light a series of social relations that may have become invisible to women as they went about their daily routines. Getting the cold shoulder or being physically evicted by government officials who do not appreciate their visits to demand basic urban services makes women realize that, because they are poor, they are despised and viewed as unimportant by many in the city. Standing and repeatedly attempting to enter a discussion in a larger CONAMUP meeting and being consistently ignored by the man chairing the meeting pushes women to question just how welcome their participation really is in their own organization. Having a husband or son stand in the doorway and refuse to let a woman leave who has promised to take a turn cooking in a collective kitchen down the block reinforces her knowledge of unequal power relations at home.

When women come to local committee meetings every week, they bring all of these experiences with them and want to talk about them. The space itself is crucial for allowing women to begin thinking about their experiences, sharing them with others, and figuring out if and how they can confront some of the conflicts they endure. While single, childless women and older women with no children to care for may have more mobility than others, for some poor, urban women political participation may bring a price—domestic violence. While the threat of domestic violence is something that many women have felt at one time or another, this does not by any means imply that it is an easy issue to confront. For many, it is simply easier to stop their political participation than to face possible beatings and intimidation if they continue.

The Women's Regional Council of the CONAMUP was one of the first grassroots women's organizations in Mexico which began to systematically take on this issue. In cooperation with a few neighborhood organizations, the council now carries out workshops on women's health, sexuality, and judicial rights. One neighborhood CONAMUP activist, married with two small children, describes the problem. It took Angela, age twenty-four, a long time to convince her husband to let her leave their two-room house to attend meetings:

Women are considered inferior and because of this we are denied rights — the right to walk freely on the street without being attacked, the right to leave our homes without our husband's permission. . . . A lot of times we are treated like humans without any rights of our own.

In some neighborhoods, women carry whistles and when a woman is beaten, the whistles are blown and women go en masse to confront the batterer. In one rare instance, women punished a grandfather who raped his granddaughter by stripping him naked and locking him up overnight in their meeting headquarters (Stephen 1989). But this sort of response is unusual.

Organizing around domestic violence seems to work best where people in the neighborhood have a long history together. Those who engaged in a long struggle for a piece of land, who built their homes together, who were harassed by police and went to jail to obtain basic services have shared a great deal. Women who have participated alongside men have a greater chance of being valued for their individual contributions to a community struggle, rather than being seen simply as anonymous wives, mothers, and daughters. The common thread of shared struggle can provide more optimal circumstances for beginning to organize neighborhoods around issues of violence and women's domestic labor. Eugenia Flores explains:

There are some neighborhoods where it is easier to organize women around violence — where the neighborhood organization was founded with a basic struggle for land, where people worked together for housing, and where they had a vision together. In this type of situation there is a great deal of solidarity and many possibilities. But in other organizations, like where I am currently, people are more physically separated. Where women are separated it is more difficult.

Cohesive neighborhoods with a history of shared struggle may also provide more fertile ground for collectivizing some of the increasingly heavy domestic workloads women have taken on in the face of economic crisis. Throughout Latin America, collective kitchens have been a popular strategy for trying to share the domestic burden of women and to move their labor from the so-called private realm to a more public arena. Promoted in a limited way in China and Cuba after their revolutions—in an attempt to aid women's integration into the formal labor force— collective kitchens have been organized in Peru, Chile, and elsewhere for different reasons (see Fisher 1993; Jelin 1990; Jaquette 1989). Urban survival movements such as the CONAMUP have used collective kitchens to help families pool their economic resources and to get more from economies of scale. They have also been used by some organizers to make visible the reproductive work of women.

The Women's Regional Council seems to have implemented collective kitchens and taken on a government breakfast-distribution program as a strategy for raising class- and gender-based issues. Not being able to afford breakfasts, sending children off to school with half-empty stomachs—these are constant reminders of just how marginally women and their families are living. Time spent shopping and scavenging for food, not to mention fuel and water, can take up many hours in a woman's day. Then there is the cooking itself and the fact that for those consuming the food, the labor behind it is taken for granted, even when it becomes more intensive. Organizers believe that collective kitchens and breakfast programs should both help to provide more resources and help to make women's labor more appreciated and visible. Sometimes they do as the organizer María Váldez reports.[10] María completed junior high and some high school and is a single mother. Her own mother's struggle to make ends meet while engaged in multiple forms of so-called informal employment and while also completing a heavy load of domestic chores has influenced her own perspective:

When women go out into their neighborhoods to feed their own children and other women's children, they begin to recognize and value cooking and domestic chores as work. When they do it in their own houses, they see it only as a natural obligation.

It is not always so simple, however, as women themselves (like their family members) also discredit the long hours spent in the daily struggle for food. They do not see what they do in their own homes as "work." When they have to give up time to work for others somewhere outside their home, as in the breakfast-distribution program, they may object. Collectivizing does not come easily, and even though women may complain about the time they spend providing for their own family, to give up a morning for someone else can seem like a bigger sacrifice even though it may mean time saved in their own homes later. The act of working five hours in someone else's neighborhood or walking door to door distributing breakfast boxes does not translate into an instant consciousness about the hours spent every day at home preparing food. María Váldez reports:

In the breakfast program we have, the women go and distribute the breakfasts in their neighborhoods. This takes time, sometimes all morning. Later, in the meetings, the women get angry about this. They say, "We spend all day doing this; by the time we get back, it's really late." They begin to see it as work because they are all doing it.

The first women to participate in collective kitchens are single mothers. They find it a convenient way to feed their children, and they can bring them along instead of having them wait to eat until mother returns from work. Nor do single mothers have to contend with the problem of providing an explanation to a suspicious husband about why they are participating in the kitchens. Differences in marital status as well as age and political orientation have concrete effects on whether or not women are able to participate in programs of the Women's Council.

The gap between organizers' ideas about what women will see as they engage in such programs as breakfast distribution and how the women actually experience and interpret those programs brings us to a central point of tension in the Women's Regional Council: namely, the ways in which women perceive, experience, and attempt to change gender relations that may be viewed as exploitative and/or unequal. In the world of Mexican leftist politics and social movements, while some might identify improvement of the position of women in unequal gender relationships as the central thrust of feminism, others more intent on recasting the world by eliminating class differences are apt to call feminism an imported, bourgeois strategy which divides women from men and moves away from the central point of the struggle for change. Still, others, as seen in many countries, have attempted to combine class- and gender-based struggles. Most members of the Women's Regional Council did not come into the organization with previous experience in gender-based struggles. And most had no exposure to anyone who labeled herself "feminist." Once in the organization, though, all the women were exposed to ongoing dialogues and relationships with self-proclaimed feminists.

Mexican Feminisms and the CONAMUP The Women's Regional Council of the CONAMUP has interacted with self-proclaimed feminist organizations since its inception. Working sometimes closely and at other times more distantly with several feminist NGOs and political groups in Mexico City, the CONAMUP has engaged in a complex and varied discourse around the topic of feminism. These interactions with feminists (as well as the very existence of the Women's Regional Council) have also been subject to continual tension as male CONAMUP leaders from various political tendencies struggled for control of the organization.

From its inception in 1984, The Women's Regional Council of the CONAMUP has had ties with one of Latin America's best-known feminist NGOs: the Human Development Collective of Latin America

(CIDHAL), founded in 1969 in Cuernavaca. In 1979, CIDHAL opened an office in Mexico City, and its organizational growth there paralleled the growth of the Urban Popular Movement, with which CIDHAL made a decision to establish specific ties in 1982 and to organize activities related to the needs articulated by women within the MUP and also reflecting what CIDHAL called "feminist objectives." These included ending women's oppression in a wide range of areas, transforming women's lives, and supporting women's capacity to organize change. CIDHAL planned to achieve change through "the creation of women's organizations that are plural and autonomous" (Mogrovejo Aquise 1990:49). Thus, its vision of feminism concluded that women live in a world of unequal gender relations, women are clearly exploited and oppressed by those relations, and change can only be brought about through the establishment of spaces exclusively for women that would form a basis for concrete organizing projects.

One of CIDHAL's principal methods of operation is popular education built on the model of the Brazilian Paulo Freire. Its work also exhibits a critical concern with participatory democracy, widespread participation in organizational decisionmaking, and accountability between leadership and base. In the 1980s, CIDHAL's work focused on four main themes: (1) gender relations in domestic work and in the wage-labor force; (2) women's identity and sexuality; (3) family life and forms of reproduction; and (4) women's political participation (Mogrovejo Aquise 1990:50).

CIDHAL began working with women within the CONAMUP before the formation of the Women's Regional Council and was involved in the latter's formation in 1984. In 1985, after the earthquake in Mexico City which strengthened the Urban Popular Movement and spawned new organizations, CIDHAL joined forces with several other feminist groups to support the work of women in a range of organizations dealing with the issues of housing, service procurement, and political participation. Other groups such as the Women's Team for Action in Solidarity (EMAS) focused specifically on the health arena and began working with some of the local committees that participated in the Women's Regional Council of the CONAMUP, such as the one in San Miguel Teotongo.

The profile of feminism within the CONAMUP and the Women's Regional Council has always been varied and somewhat conflictive. A few women within the CONAMUP leadership began and continued with a vision of feminism, while others never thought in those terms. The few women who did identify as feminists were interested in combining class and gender struggles into a "popular feminism." As described below, this brand of feminism takes the concrete daily struggles of poor urban women as its starting point. Different strands of Mexico City feminism had proven extremely divisive in international meetings, such as at the Fourth Latin American and Caribbean Feminist Encuentro held in Taxco in 1987 (Mogrovejo Aquise 1990:118–120), and in other organizations such as the all-women "19th of September" Garment Workers' Union (Carrillo 1990:193). Most CONAMUP women who called themselves feminists were clearly aligned with other feminist organizations that had emerged from a working-class identity and focused on labor issues. Among these was the Integral Revolutionary Project (CRI, Colectivo Revolucionario Integral), which was one of two feminist organizations competing for control of the garment workers' union. Feminist organizations such as CIDHAL which worked with the Women's Regional Council were interested in having the council take on a more explicitly feminist identity. The politics of what this identity would mean, how it was framed, who would embrace it, when, and for what purpose were difficult.

As analyzed in rich detail by Mogrovejo Aquise (1990), the Women's Regional Council was caught between a number of exterior political forces. Women within the CONAMUP were a target group for organizations like CIDHAL, of course, but were also subject to the politics of competing interests that raged within the CONAMUP itself. The ability of some women within the Women's Regional Council to embrace feminism came in part from support offered by the Emiliano Zapata Popular Revolutionary Union (UPREZ), aligned with OIR–LM (see note 4). Male leaders from UPREZ not only supported the existence of the CONAMUP Women's Regional Council (which had its legitimacy continually questioned by other male leaders), but also supported to a limited degree some of the alliances the Women's Regional Council had with feminist organizations. One male leader of UPREZ and the CONAMUP, interviewed by Mogrovejo Aquise (1990:78), stated:

People's conceptions within the CONAMUP have changed with time. In some cases, in some places within the organization we have declared ourself to be a feminist organization. . . . We talk about popular feminism because that is what is happening. . . . We came to a point where we asked the organization to call itself feminist.

Mogrovejo Aquise cites numerous instances in which men from UPREZ supported the Women's Regional Council. Their motivation was perhaps genuine, but their support also meant that they could claim partial credit for the significant gains of the Women's Regional Council. This in turn helped them reinforce their own hegemonic position within the competing political currents of the CONAMUP. In many instances, feminism became the political football that was used as a pretext for discussions calling for the dismantling of the women's organization within the CONAMUP. The long-time activist Clara Brugada stated that

people within the CONAMUP who were opposed to UPREZ had this image of women taking over. This kind of conflict was evident during the Tenth National Meeting of the CONAMUP at Monterrey in October 1989. There, some political groups — such as the "11th of November" Union of Colonos, Renters, and Solicitors of Housing [UCISV "11 de Noviembre"], the Socialist Organization Block [BOS], the Democratic Forces Block [BFD], and other groups — questioned the legitimacy of the Women's Regional Organization, even calling for its dismantlement. (Mogrovejo Aquise 1990:79–80)

Within the ongoing contest for power between male leaders in the CONAMUP, women in the Women's Regional Council also had to struggle among themselves to figure out what the word "feminism" meant to them and whether or not they could agree on some kind of feminist label. The notion of "feminismo popular," or grassroots feminism, was born from internal discussions women from the CONAMUP had with each other. Clara Brugada recalls the process and how women came from many different positions to begin with:

Although some of us who were leaders within the Women's Regional Organization had a feminist vision since the inception of our work in the CONAMUP, not everybody shared this vision, not even all the activists. There were even activists who were clearly antifeminist. They had strong prejudices against feminism. . . . Of course we were influenced by the different political currents within the CONAMUP, particularly by those who said that we shouldn't even exist. They told us that we were dividing the organization, that the work we were doing was petit bourgeois, and that we didn't need to exist. We thought about this and about the work we were trying to do. We had internal workshops to develop our own line of thinking about the work we were doing with women. . . . We talked about how women were specifically exploited within the urban movement because of the domestic work they did and how they were responsible for reproducing the labor force. . . . We talked about this and about different explanations for the

exploited position of women. We analyzed different currents of femi-
nism. Then we started to talk about feminismo popular *as an important*
part of feminism. We were talking about a feminism that comes from
the concrete life conditions women live under. We wanted to concretize
women's problems and redefine what gender struggle means. We were
looking for a different point of departure for our struggle as women.
(Mogrovejo Aquise 1990:117–118)

While some leaders in 1989 declared the organization to be feminist and talked about "popular feminism" as an appropriate label for
the work of the organization, other women were more reluctant to
claim that label. The word remained problematic not only within the
CONAMUP, but in other women's organizations and coalitions as well.
In 1988, the Women's Regional Organization had been one of the pivotal
founders of a wider coalition of women's organizations on the left that
were working to forge a broader movement of grassroots feminism.
Called the Benita Galeana Women's Council (Coordinadora de Mujeres
"Benita Galeana") after a woman who has been active in women's and
popular struggles since the 1930s in Mexico, the group decided not to
use the word "feminist" publicly owing to a lack of consensus about
what the word meant. While some in the coalition openly embraced the
label of "feminismo popular," and while it was used publicly within the
CONAMUP, its content was never agreed upon within the Benita Galeana Women's Council. The program of the Benita Galeana Women's
Council focused on democracy, preventing violence against women,
and the right to a full life (not to be confused with an antiabortion
stance). The central thread of their organizing was devoted to what they
called the "gender/class" struggle (Stephen 1989:106). Extremely active
during the first few years of the Benita Galeana Women's Council, the
Women's Regional Council of the CONAMUP gradually withdrew its
participation. There were disagreements within the council about how
important the work of the coalition was, and the simultaneous struggle
of keeping their own regional organization going led to the council's
withdrawal. In 1993 the Benita Galeana Women's Council shut down.

The legacy of the work of the Benita Galeana Women's Council and
of "feminismo popular" within the CONAMUP and the Women's Regional Council has been mixed. While some key activists who worked
for over a decade with the Women's Regional Council continue to embrace the term "feminismo popular" and integrate the concept into their
work, others are more skeptical and indicate that they never really understood the term.

The following partial transcript of an interview with Carmen Martínez Flores, an administrator and long-time CONAMUP activist, illustrates the position of women who never quite embraced the feminist label and who perhaps continued to believe it was related to lesbianism.
Carmen comes from a poor, working-class background. She is a seamstress in one of Mexico City's marginal *colonias*. She did not complete
elementary school and is married with grown children at age fifty-eight.

Lynn: How did you feel about the term "feminismo popular" that
was being used within the Women's Regional Organization and the Benita Galeana Women's Council?

Carmen: We were one of the initiators of the Coordinadora Benita
Galeana.

Lynn: Yes, I know about your important work there. I understand
that some explicitly feminist groups worked with you but that there
were always differences in perspective.

Carmen: Yes. They always said that we were grassroots feminists
(*feministas populares*). . . . They wanted to interpret us that way, but
that wasn't the way that we thought about it.

Lynn: So for you, the idea of popular feminism doesn't make much
sense.

Carmen: Well, the situation we are in might cause us to be called
feminist, but we never wanted men to be separated from women. They
might have this idea to live as single women, separately. But we didn't
think this. We believe that men and women should be in couples.
Maybe that is why they called us "popular" feminists. . . . We don't limit
our relationship with men. We believe in working with men, but our primary goal is to improve the lives of women, to help them get the basic
things they need in life and prevent them from suffering from violence.

In this exchange, Carmen clearly outlines her own ideas about the
meaning of the work she does. She also signals what she thinks feminism
means for some of the organizers who worked with the Women's Regional Council. A major theme in her characterization of "their" feminism is that activists who worked with the Women's Council believe that
men and women should be separated—"we never wanted men to be
separated from women." Carmen's characterization of the separatism of
feminist activists seems to have two strands. On the one hand, it means
that women should be open to working with men and should not carry
out their political work entirely separately from men—"we believe in
working with men." It is also a positive statement about heterosexuality

and questioning the notion of single women—"we believe that men and women should be in couples."

Using as a point of departure what she perceives to be the separatist position of feminist activists who worked with the Women's Regional Council, she goes on to positively define what her work means to her—"our primary goal is to improve the lives of women, to help them get the basic things they need in life and prevent them from suffering from violence." While Carmen does not accept the term "feminist" in any sense as representative of her work, she uses a negative portrayal of other women's feminism to positively define her own work. What is most interesting is the way in which the boundaries of her discourse are defined by the presence of what came to be known as "popular feminism" within the CONAMUP. Even if most women in the Women's Regional Council did not actively identify as "popular feminists," the concept clearly influenced their thinking. This questioning dialogue with popular feminism is a key element in what unifies the women within the CONAMUP beyond their shared material experience of poverty and struggle.

Another critical element shared by all the women who have participated in the Regional Council for a number of years is their common experience in an autonomous women's organization. The presence of autonomous women's groups within larger organizations allows women of varying ages and with different political skills to discuss their ideas and problems in a manner which lets their existing political style and experience emerge. While such women's groups will clearly also reflect power differences between women, based on age and class and ethnic experience, they nonetheless provide a more open space for political participation than larger mixed organizations which have only allowed women to act as supporters and informal participants. If and when the positions of such autonomous women's groups solidify, then women will be more prepared to participate as a group in mixed-gender organizations. Autonomous women's groups within regional organizations can provide opportunities for women to learn how to do national-level organizing if they participate in regional and national meetings with women from other popular organizations. Links between women's groups are important: they prepare women to take up leadership at higher levels in their own organizations, and they give women training and strategies so that they can work inside their own organizations for changes that will facilitate the full incorporation of women.

Conclusions   Social scientists engaged in studies of gender-based responses to economic crisis in Mexico offer convincing evidence that the most common response is individualization of the crisis (Benería 1992; González de la Rocha 1991). If women can find ways to cut costs (by consuming less) and to increase their incomes (by producing more or by working more hours to increase their cash flow), then they may be able to lessen the impact of falling real wages and rising prices. The decade of the 1980s was marked by a severe decline in the standard of living for most Mexicans, borne most heavily by women, children, the indigenous, and the poor. Increased social and economic inequality in the 1980s was also accompanied by the emergence of regional social movements dedicated to improving urban living conditions. Indigenous and peasant movements also consolidated in some areas of the country. In a few rare instances, women were able to form regional movements—such as the Women's Regional Council of the CONAMUP detailed here. The emergence of the Women's Regional Council—with its concrete emphasis on improving the daily living conditions of poor, urban women—provided an alternative model to individualization of the crisis.

The longevity of the Women's Council points out the importance of a theoretical analysis of social movements that looks at economic development not only in terms of its impact on people as individual consumers and political actors, but also in the context of politics and unequal relations of power. In such an analysis, the complexity and heterogeneity of the state must also be recognized. The ever-changing relationship that the Women's Council had with different state agencies, involving both cooperation and conflict, suggests the importance of examining the flexibility with which different state agencies can deal with collective mobilizations through time. The fact that a particular movement is tolerated by one part of the state is not necessarily an indication of democratization, but may merely reflect an attempt to legitimize otherwise contradictory policies (see Hindley 1995a). Such a moment can also simultaneously present an organization like the Women's Regional Council with an opportunity for obtaining increased resources.

The experiences of the Women's Council suggest that women's involvement in struggles against increased economic hardship, physical violence, and political marginalization does not necessarily bring changes in traditional gender roles or an increase in women's power in the household or in popular organizations. But it can. When women are granted political recognition (i.e., semiautonomous organizing structures within popular organizations) and when conflict between women's traditional domestic responsibilities and their roles as public activists is openly recognized, gender roles may begin to change. What is critical to the success of an organization, however, is that the meaning of these changes not be mandated as identical for all women. Flexibility in the style and interpretation of political and social experience can allow women with very different backgrounds and ideologies to organize together around a common set of daily living experiences. The internal and external politics of the Women's Council were continually rooted in conflict and disagreement, even between women. Conflict, difference, and disagreement, however, do not eliminate the possibility of cooperation. Women like Clara Brugada, who *does* label herself a popular feminist, and Carmen Martínez Flores, who emphatically *does not*, can work together in the same organization because they share a common set of questions focused primarily on women's class and gender relations in urban Mexico.

The practical outcome of programs carried out by the Women's Regional Council has resulted in many shared experiences for women who are active in the organization. These include

1 *leaving their homes several times each week to participate in local and regional meetings, marches, health and nutrition programs;*
2 *participating in workshops and events where domestic violence, women's health, and reproduction are discussed;*
3 *having to renegotiate, at least minimally, the household division of labor with respect to childcare, cooking, and cleaning when they are absent because of organizational activities;*
4 *participating in wider political meetings and events in mixed organizations (male and female) where they are often marginalized; and*
5 *participating in all-female meetings and organizational spaces.*
(Stephen 1996: 173–174)

These shared experiences have provided women with a common set of questions regarding the various dimensions of inequality found within the class, gender, racial, ethnic, and generational social relationships they participate in. These questions—rather than shared answers—provide some common outlines for their varied experiences within the Women's Regional Council. Whether or not all women agree that such questions are "feminist" seems irrelevant. What matters most is their shared commitment to help one another improve their lives.

INTERVIEW

Irene Soto
Women's Regional Council
of the CONAMUP

Irene Soto is a thirty-year-old woman who became politically active as a teenager in high school. She came from a working-class family in Mexico City, surviving but not upwardly mobile. She is a single mother with one child. I first became aware of her work in and around Mexico City in 1987. Later, in 1989, I helped to organize a tour for Irene and another CONAMUP organizer in Boston. I translated for Irene at Northeastern University, where I worked, and at other events in Boston that she attended. We had several conversations in the course of her visit to Boston. This interview took place in my kitchen on a warm fall afternoon. Irene and I were both wearing jeans and sipping coffee. We started out talking about different neighborhoods in Mexico City, and Irene told me how she began to work with the CONAMUP.

Irene: I began working in the Women's Regional Council in 1983. That was when I started working in some of the poorer neighborhoods. I actually started doing political work in high school when I joined a student group. But I began working specifically with women in 1983, when the Regional Council was formed.

Lynn: How did the Women's Regional Council come into existence?

Irene: In our fourth large national meeting we stated that it was important that women begin to take a more active part in decision-making. The CONAMUP has always been very concerned with the question of democracy. So at that meeting it was actually some of the men who said that it didn't make sense that even though women were the majority of the participants that they had the least amount of decision-making power.

Lynn: So was it the men who . . .

Recorded October 10,
1989, in Boston,
Massachusetts.

Irene: No, it wasn't just the men who made the decision to open things up to women. The idea was pushed by some of the women who were there as well. But there were very few women who were prepared to propose that women do their own organizing.

Lynn: But the men realized that there was a problem?

Irene: Yes. They did. That was when they came up with that famous phrase that "women are the support system, the backbone of the urban popular movement."[1] Well, we said that we didn't want to be the backbone, but the head, the ones in charge of the movement. So people agreed that it was important, not only for the collective decisionmaking process in the organization but also for the way that people were socialized in the organization, for women to participate in decisionmaking. We thought it might also be helpful to women who had trouble even coming to and participating in the meetings. Some women would get

Irene Soto, an activist from the Women's Regional Council of the CONAMUP.

beaten just for coming to meetings. After this discussion, we decided
to organize the first meeting of the CONAMUP specifically for women.

Lynn: Could you describe how women began to discuss these issues
in meetings?

Irene: A lot of women begin participating in the organization by
engaging in the simplest activity. They just go to meetings. For them,
just leaving the four walls of their home is a big deal. A lot of the women
who come to meetings for the first time tell us, "I can't come any more
because my husband won't let me." Others say, "Well, I come to these
meetings because I need to figure out how to solve my economic problems, even though my husband doesn't approve of me being here."
When women say they are going to come despite what their husbands
do, it makes some of the other women question their own situation.
They begin to ask, "Why can't I decide to leave my house and come to a
meeting in my neighborhood?" They start to question things at home.

It gets worse for the women when they want to go outside their neighborhood and go to meetings in downtown Mexico City, where the
regional women's meetings are. For a lot of them, it may take two hours
of traveling by different buses and collective taxis to get to the meeting.
But if women participate in the regional meetings, then their world
really begins to open up. They start to hear about national politics. They
really begin to understand the world outside their neighborhood.

Lynn: So there are different ways for women to participate?

Irene: Yes. When a woman begins to be an activist then she has to
give up a lot of her time. She doesn't just go to her neighborhood meeting, but she also has to go to the regional meeting in Mexico City. She
has to negotiate with government officials like those from CONASUPO
(National Basic Foods Company, run by the government) to bargain over
subsidized tortillas. And she has to attend marches and sit-ins.

Right now there are quite a few women who are seasoned negotia-
tors. They have negotiated with officials to get control over the distribution of subsidized milk and tortillas in their neighborhoods. They make
sure that all the women who are eligible have access. So that it doesn't
go to those who shouldn't have it. Often they have to go meet with their
local mayor or congressional representative and discuss issues of food
distribution or other problems with them.

Lynn: Do you ever have to negotiate with people from the PRI
(Institutional Revolutionary Party)?

Irene: Well, we try to treat people in the government as separate
from the PRI—even though they may not be. Usually women who are
activists have to demand that politicians do their jobs as public ser-

vants. I don't think the Constitution specifies that you have to belong to the PRI to have basic civil rights. For us, some of the hardest people to deal with are those corrupt people from the PRI who are not in positions of public service but only belong to the party. They are the most confrontational with us. Sometimes they physically attack people. For example, last year one of our workers was beaten and had her nose broken by a man who was active in the PRI. People who do things like this don't have any rational sense. It's like they are *caciques*[2] or something. Not everyone is like that.

Lynn: I would like to return to the theme of women and what happens to women as they begin to participate in the Women's Regional Council?

Irene: It usually begins when a woman has to deal with trying to leave her home. Her husband always pressures her and says, "Why did you leave the house? Where are you going?" She says, "I went to a meeting in order to find out about getting cheaper tortillas." He says, "Well, why don't you stay here and just cope with the situation?" Then she says, "No. I can't. Why don't you give me more money?" She is fighting for power with her husband, and when he accepts the fact that he can't provide for the family, then she has made an important gain.

A lot of the women say they feel relieved when they reach this point. They don't have to hide their political participation from their husbands, and sometimes their husbands recognize that what they are doing is important—that they are making a concrete contribution to the family.

Other types of recognition come through the work women do. I can give you an example having to do with the collective kitchens we started in a few places. It starts with a group of women who decide they want to run the kitchen. They come to their weekly neighborhood meeting and discuss with the other women what each will have to contribute to the daily meal. They work out daily menus, and have to talk about the specific ingredients of each meal and what they will cost. How much will the chilis cost? The tomatoes? Everything. They have to come up with a budget. Each week they pull the money together and go to the central market, which is the cheapest place to buy the ingredients. Then each one of them cooks one day a week. In return, they get to eat there with their children on the other days and bring food home to their husbands. This experience breaks down a lot of barriers.

By participating in the collective kitchens they save money. For example, a woman who used to spend 45 pesos a week on food has to spend only 27 pesos. Now she can use the difference to buy new notebooks for her children's education. They have more money, and now they only have to cook one day a week.

It actually takes a lot of guts and stamina to participate in the collective kitchens. Because you have to be willing to bring home a meal to your husband that you didn't cook. Most of the women who participate in the kitchens are those who are more conscious of their situation or who are in dire economic straits. It looks like a good idea, but it's hard for some to participate. It's important for other women to see that the kitchens can work, and it helps women to break down barriers at home. A lot of men say things like, "Why aren't you cooking for me, *huevona* (lazy woman)? That is what you are supposed to do."

Single mothers are usually the first ones to participate in the collective kitchens. It's better for a child to have a balanced, collectively prepared meal than to eat just anything or to be waiting around until his mother can come home from work.

There is one other thing I want to say about the collective kitchens. About a year ago, we began to pressure the Ministry of Social Development so that they would create these types of programs. Now the DIF (Family Services Agency) has received money to set up about eight hundred kitchens. This year they were supposed to open forty-five, but only five have opened so far. This is because the PRI doesn't care about the kitchens. It's not a priority. What we have to do is keep pressuring them. If there are no women organized who want to collectivize domestic work, then (the kitchens) won't be opened. We not only want to pressure the DIF, but also to move forward with the idea that domestic work has to be socialized.

Lynn: What are the critical ingredients to building a local neighborhood committee?

Irene: Right now we've been doing a workshop on how to create permanent women's committees in neighborhoods where none exist. The groups that haven't really worked are those where there isn't a basic demand to organize around. The best thing for us to do is to keep focusing on very concrete demands, like getting bus service or drainage. When you call a group of women together just to talk, the group doesn't function for long. . . .

Right now one of our major projects is to give activists who have become local leaders some insights from the women's perspective. We don't mean just being women, but being aware of all of the power relations women are involved in. . . .

Overall, I am really happy with what the Women's Regional Council has been able to accomplish. We have more and more women who are getting involved in local committees and more and more women who are becoming leaders of local women's committees. This is really important and difficult because often women aren't recognized as leaders if they focus only on women's demands. We also have to put in time working on other areas and demands of the organization.

Lynn: What do you mean by "women's demands"?

Irene: That is a key point of discussion within the urban popular movement. I think that women's work has to do with housing, with public services, with health and nutrition. It also has to do with making public officials respond to us. We believe that we have specific needs that are based on class and gender. We need to change our way of thinking. . . . It is still difficult to discuss a lot of our issues within the CONAMUP. What we really need to do is change the structure of the organization, of CONAMUP overall, but we don't have the necessary set of circumstances for doing that right now.

Lynn: How about the theme of democracy we mentioned earlier? How about organizing around the demand of democracy at home between men and women, of women having the right not to be beaten, to control their own sexuality?

Irene: It's very difficult to make concrete gains in the areas of domestic violence and sexual relations.

Lynn: Why?

Irene: Because as women we are taught to believe that we don't have the right to our own existence, to control our bodies. This is one of the problems with just focusing on economic demands that everyone considers basic necessities. But we have begun to have discussions and workshops on women's health, sexuality, women dying in childbirth.

Lynn: Are there any concrete experiences you can point to in those areas?

Irene: There are some experiences, but it's important to point out that our ability to organize in these areas is limited. . . . One thing we do each year is to organize on the International Day against Violence against Women. On this day we organize local discussions in neighborhoods as well as in our regional office. It's a difficult topic to get women to talk about, but now that women in the regional office have started to share their experiences with respect to battering, it may be easier to organize at the neighborhood level. One of the critical things that must happen is that we will have to create more local spaces for women to discuss this topic. . . .

Consolidating existing women's groups and organizing new ones is one of our most important pieces of work. In some of the neighborhoods where the CONAMUP is active, there are men who object to the formation of women's groups. Fortunately, this is the case only in a minority of neighborhoods. We have to get women to protest and form their own groups. We have to take power through action, not just in words.

Lynn: How do you see the relationship between the Women's Regional Council and feminism? What does feminism mean and is it possible to integrate some feminist ideas, maybe from what has been called "popular feminism," into the work you do?

Irene: From my point of view and for more or less most of the women in the Women's Regional Council, what feminism means to us is changing the situation of women, fighting for women's liberation. And this change has to be for all women. I can't say that I am free, even though I have individual liberty. I am not free until the situation of all women has changed. It might be that because I am from a different class or because I have access to something like a washing machine that I can say I am liberated. But the minute I step out into the street it becomes clear that I am not liberated. I can be raped. I have to deal with institutions that are run by men, that are not democratic. Only when we have changed the life conditions of all women can we say we are liberated. And I'm not just talking about ideas, but about a concrete economic condition. It's like what they say about workers. Workers aren't fighting for higher wages so that they can keep on maintaining the boss. We aren't fighting for better nutrition for women and children because we think women should be in charge of nutrition and food. We are fighting for more and better food because we are living without it. And we need to get better nutrition and food so we can transform the other things that need to be changed.

So, what is the most common condition that united us as women? Domestic work. We all have to do domestic work. We all have economic problems, so one of the places we begin organizing is to collectivize some of the domestic work we have to do. We don't want women to work permanently in collective kitchens. No. They are a tool for beginning to organize.

Right now, our domestic work in the collective kitchens isn't being remunerated. We are working for free. We believe that in the future this has to change and that all of this work should be recognized and paid-for. But the first thing we have to do is to collectivize some of this work so that we will be socialized in a different way.

I think that women in the communities we work in, in the popular movement, see feminism as a way to transform the conditions women live under. I'm sure that there are *compañeras* (sisters) who can provide more theoretical elements and who can define feminism more broadly, but for us (feminism) is about concrete, daily-life conditions. That's what we are working for. We can learn a lot from other feminist groups, from feminists who are more theoretical. I hope that they will be interested in using some of their resources to help women in our communities, to help more directly so that we can change the difficult conditions women live under.

Lynn: What kinds of links are being made within the CONAMUP between women in urban areas and in rural areas throughout Mexico? Have any rural women been to the national women's meetings held by the Women's Regional Council?

Irene: There are some urban-neighborhood movements which have relationships with *ejidos* in organizations like the CNPA (National Coordinator of the Ayala Plan, a national independent peasant organization formed in 1979). But there are very few women, maybe two or three, who are active in both movements. There is one person who works in Zacatecas (and) another person who works in Torreón (and they are) active in both the CNPA and the CONAMUP. In Monterrey, there are men who are from the CONAMUP who also have connections with *ejidos*. But very few women. It's very difficult because usually it is men who make the connections and operate at the higher levels of the organization and who therefore have more opportunities to connect with other people. We have to work very hard to get the men in the organization to respect the work that we do. They don't respect our work with the women throughout the organization. This causes many women to stop working with women, because they see that the men don't respect their work. Besides, doing this on a permanent basis is very hard. If one of the *compañeros* sees that you only work with women and not on other things, then they begin to criticize you.

Lynn: Has this happened to you?

Irene: No, it hasn't happened to me because I have always been involved in a lot of different places in the organization. But I have seen it happen to many other women. They constantly have to defend the work they do. They end up doing a lot of different jobs. They have to do their domestic work at home, often they have a paid job, they work with women in the organization, and then they also do general organizational work.

Lynn: So they are working triple or quadruple time.

Irene: Yes, that is true for a lot of women. I do very little in my own house. When I have the time I do, but it's hard.

Lynn: Do you have any children?

Irene: I have one daughter.

Lynn: So you have to do some work at home.

Irene: I do the least possible. At least once a week I clean up, and I have to take her to and from school every day. There are a lot of women who do all this and more and who also participate politically. We are going to keep on doing what we have to do. We have to consolidate our organization and really begin challenging violence against women. Oppression against women never stops, so we can never stop our work.

CHAPTER 5

The Unintended Consequences of "Traditional" Women's Organizing
The Women's Council of the Lázaro Cárdenas Ejido Union, Nayarit

The proclamation of the United Nations International Decade for Women in 1975 and the Percy Amendment to the U.S. Foreign Assistance Act in 1973 made women a specific category for receiving aid (Alvarez 1990:79). During the 1980s, the Ford Foundation, the World Bank, and the Agency for International Development all had programs that targeted the area of women and development as did many nation-states, including Mexico. The objective of many "women's projects" was to increase household subsistence production through animal, vegetable, and fruit production and/or to involve women in small income-producing projects, often called "microenterprises," that would give them small amounts of disposable income to be used for food, clothing, and other fixed costs. The goals of most projects were focused on very limited economic benefits and operated on the assumption that if women were contributing to the household income then they might have greater leverage in household decisionmaking and, hence, indirectly gain more control over other areas of their lives.

In 1995 at the Fourth United Nations World Conference on Women, held in Beijing, the theme was "Women's Rights Are Human Rights." Thus, in the twenty years since the major push for "women and development" began, while economic rights for women and efforts to provide them with income-generating employment have continued, what some have called the "unintended consequences" of such economic projects—viz., women's double and triple workloads, their lack of control over reproductive decisionmaking, domestic violence, and political marginalization—have come to the fore. These issues have often emerged in the process of efforts to organize small-scale economic projects. The present chapter documents how women's attempts to improve household income and nutrition through participation in collective bakeries, poultry projects, and sewing cooperatives—organized through the Women's Council of the Unión de Ejidos "Lázaro Cárdenas" (UELC) in the state of Nayarit, Mexico—resulted in challenges to the household division of labor, to women's marginal roles in local-community and regional-coalition meetings, and to women's scant participation in formal political campaigns.

The Women's Council of the UELC provides an interesting contrast to the case of the Women's Regional Council of the CONAMUP, discussed in Chapter 4 above. Like the Women's Regional Council of the CONAMUP, the Women's Council of the UELC was created out of a larger regional organization that included men as well as women. Both cases involved the creation of local committees that were articulated into larger regional units. Both involved a struggle for identity, agendas, and decisionmaking power for women that distinguished their local committees and regional organization from the larger mixed groups they were part of. The political, cultural, and historical contexts they emerged from, however, are the source of important differences which have significantly influenced the trajectory of women's organizing in each case and the language that is used to discuss it.

While the CONAMUP and UELC both were created with the significant involvement of people active in the student movement of 1968, those who worked with the UELC were integrated with official state organizations, while for the most part those who helped found the CONAMUP maintained organizational autonomy in the 1970s and early 1980s. The UELC was incorporated into state rural-development programs since its inception, whereas the CONAMUP became integrated into government programs at a later stage of development.

Part of the political milieu surrounding the emergence of the Women's Regional Council of the CONAMUP were several overtly feminist organizations which explicitly decided to target women in the CONAMUP. In the Nayarit countryside of Ahuacatlán, no feminist organizations operated or had ongoing contact with the rural women who came to form the Women's Council of the UELC. The most gender-conscious ideological source was state programs that targeted women (e.g., the "Women in Solidarity" program, briefly discussed in Chapter 4 above).

What is most interesting in the comparison is that the issues which emerged in the work of the Women's Council of the UELC resembled those of the CONAMUP. While women's discussions of their experiences in rural Nayarit focused initially on economic issues in relation to their productive projects, with time and experience their concerns also encompassed political marginalization, domestic conflict, and control over household decisionmaking. They were not using what others might call "feminist" or even "grassroots feminist" rhetoric to describe their problems and experiences, but how they talk about their participation in the UELC Women's Council is reminiscent of some women's descriptions of their struggles in the Women's Regional Council of the CONAMUP.

The political factionalism which characterizes the region through divisions in the ruling party (PRI), as manifested by splits in the official peasant organization (CNC, Coordinadora Nacional Campesina) and the National Educational Workers' Union (SNTE), has also affected women's experiences in their projects and in their attempts to build and maintain a regional organization. In addition, varying levels of education (and thus power) between women in the same local committee have also been important in defining diverse positions and tendencies toward fracture rather than greater unity.

More than anything, the present chapter highlights the difficulty of creating and maintaining a regional women's organization built primarily within state and local structures that have systematically excluded women from participating and from holding positions of power. A summary of rural economic and political history is offered before going into the specifics of how the UELC was formed. After explaining the origins of the Women's Council within the UELC, the types of economic projects the council has undertaken, and women's struggle to maintain the council, I discuss the varied experiences of women within the council. The chapter concludes with a discussion of the unintended consequences for women from their participation in the council and with a suggestion of what the future may hold for them.

Mexico's Rural Economy   Without a doubt, the most enduring legacy of the Mexican Revolution was the agrarian reform constituted under Article 27 of the Constitution (and formally in a 1920 law) that allowed for the formation of *ejidos* as collective entities with a legal stature, specific territorial limits, and representative bodies of governance (Baitenmann 1995). *Ejidos* were created to satisfy the demands of landless peasants who had seen their communal village lands eaten up by large agricultural estates and/or who served as laborers on those estates. An *ejido* is a communal form of land tenure to which members have use rights, usually in the form of an individual plot of land. The formation of *ejidos* since the Mexican Revolution has involved the transference of over 70 million hectares from large estates to slightly more than 3 million peasant beneficiaries (Stavenhagen 1986:262). In addition to *ejido* lands, another important part of the rural sector is made up of agrarian communities that hold indigenous common lands based on historical claims usually dating back to pre-Columbian and colonial times (see Barry 1995:5).

Ejido land is held corporately by the group of people constituting the *ejido*. Such land can be worked collectively or parceled individually (see De Walt et al. 1994). Heads of household are awarded use rights to land and are known as *ejidatarios*. Their rights can be inherited by their offspring, and many families have consistently worked the same parcels of land through several generations. Until the change in Article 27 in 1992, *ejido* land could not be legally sold or rented to outsiders. A majority of *ejidatarios* in Mexico are men, although increasingly women are becoming *ejidatarias* as their husbands die and leave use rights to them. Nationally it is estimated that 15–30 percent of *ejidatarios* are female (Stephen 1994b, 1996a; Botey Estapé 1993).

Today, Mexico's agrarian structure is characterized by both proletarianization and the continuation of a subsistence-oriented agricultural sector. After 1940 the state's rhetoric made continued references to the legacy of Emiliano Zapata, but policy shifted to accommodate dependent capitalism (Barry 1995:25). Many have labeled the structure of Mexican agriculture as "bimodal," with a huge gap existing between the large-scale commercial producers and the majority of farmers, who depend on family labor. As Barry points out, the term "trimodal" suggests a better categorization of farmers: "1) capitalist producers, 2) medium- and small-scale farmers who are surplus producing but rely primarily on family labor and 3) infrasubsistence or subsistence farmers together with the landless, many of whom work regularly as *jornaleros*, or wage farmworkers" (1995:28). Most *ejidatarios* who participate in the Unión de Ejidos "Lázaro Cárdenas" fall primarily into the third category, what Fox has called "nonirrigated smallholders with less land than needed to provide the equivalent of a full year's employment even at minimum wage" (1994b:286). A smaller number fit into Barry's second category and none are in the first.

For those holding land in agrarian reform or *ejido* communities, access to land has not been a guarantee of survival. While in 1950 about 85 percent of those working on *ejidos* earned more than half of their income from farming, in 1985, less than 40 percent did. By the early 1980s, the continued expansion of capitalist agriculture in Mexico begun in the 1930s and 1940s and subsidized by the state, along with a lack of feasible economic possibilities in the countryside, resulted in the marginalization of a vast portion of the rural smallholder sector. Cockcroft (1983:191) estimated that in 1983 nearly 80 percent of Mexico's *ejidos* and indigenous communities could no longer support themselves on farming alone.

Most who remained in the countryside made their living from a combination of local and regional wage labor, migration, and subsistence and small agriculture (Grindle 1988). Cash income was particularly critical for those farmers who produced slightly more than half of the total national corn output on rain-fed plots using traditional farming methods. Even subsistence corn production came to depend increasingly on the ability of rural households to generate off-farm income to finance such inputs as fertilizer and machinery rental (Hewitt de Alcántara 1991:19). As pointed out by Fox (1994b:244), "For landholders, government production support programs were uneven in coverage, unreliable in quality and often conditioned on political subordination." Thus, the little assistance that the government did offer provided no long-term security and left even those lucky enough to hold land scrambling for other sources of income.

In 1992, the government issued reforms to Article 27 of the Constitution that would permit but not require the privatization of previously inalienable, community-held *ejido* land. The law also allows foreign firms to buy, rent, or lease land for agriculture and forest use and ends the government's constitutional obligation to redistribute land. Most significant, for individual *ejidatarios* who have had use rights to land, it allows the possibility of holding an individual title to land once they receive a certificate.

To facilitate the proposed changes in landholdings among Mexico's 28,058 *ejidos* and indigenous communities, a new government office was created, the Procuraduría Agraria, or Agrarian Attorney's Office. The certification program of the Procuraduría is built around protecting the rights of *ejidatarios* by providing them with certificates specifying that particular plots of land belong to them as individuals. The possibility of holding individual title to a piece of land, however small, has motivated some *ejidatarios* to formally enter the government's certification program. Upon signing up, they are deluged with information, official visits from lawyers and agronomists, advice, teams to measure their community boundaries and individual plots, invitations to participate in programs to "help" peasants, and a pile of paper to document the entire process.

Agrarian restructuring comes together with free-trade policies when subsistence and small-scale commercial farmers have to compete with highly subsidized U.S. agricultural products on the Mexican market. Owing to protests generated by producer organizations during the process of negotiating NAFTA (North American Free-Trade Agreement), the Mexican government initiated a program for peasants in 1993 called PROCAMPO (Support Program for the Mexican Farm Sector). This program promised Mexican farmers of corn, beans, wheat, rice, soybeans, sorghum, and cotton a subsidy (about $65 per hectare) for the period from 1993 to 2008. Guaranteed price supports for these crops, however, were phased out by autumn and winter seasons of 1994–1995, thus pitting Mexican producers against cheaper U.S. imports and aligning Mexican crop prices with international prices. Corn production has stagnated owing to a lack of commercial viability and the large debt loads carried by producers (Legler 1995:4; Ovalle Vaquera and López Gámez 1994).

In the state of Nayarit, the total cultivated area dedicated to corn production has fallen from 48.8 percent in 1975 to 21.4 percent in 1990. The amount of land dedicated to the cultivation of vegetables, fruit, and such export commodities as sugar, sorghum, and tobacco has increased in proportion to the reduction of corn production—from 28.6 percent in 1975 to above 50 percent in 1990 (Sifuentes Ocegueda 1995:42). The small farmers who joined the UELC live in the corn belt of Nayarit and although they have continued corn production at levels higher than those seen in other areas of the state, they have been handicapped by a lack of irrigation and by relatively low-tech cultivation techniques. During 1990 in the *municipio* of Ahuacatlán, where the UELC is centered, farmers devoted 39.29 percent of their land to cultivating corn (Sifuentes Ocegueda 1995:50). The concentration of land under corn cultivation in Nayarit is also related to out-migration from the area, both to other areas of the state (for work in more intensive agriculture such as sugarcane and melons) and to the United States. This is discussed below in greater detail.

In 1995, Mexico had to import a record 10 million tons of grain, more than 25 percent of its total annual grain consumption (Reuters 1995). Since price supports have been phased out, the small subsidy offered by PROCAMPO clearly does not offset the loss of higher crop prices for small farmers. In 1995, Longino Olivera, a corn farmer in Ahuacatlán who is a member of the UELC, estimated that after farmers paid all of their expenses to cultivate one hectare, if they got a yield of 3 tons of corn per hectare and included the subsidy from PROCAMPO, they would still have a net loss of 320 pesos (approximately $52 per hectare). Some farmers reported that they would simply plant enough for their own consumption. This provides some insight into Mexico's need to import record amounts of corn during that year.

By the end of the Salinas de Gortari government in 1994, the future was looking bleak for many of Mexico's farmers and rural workers. As stated succinctly by Tom Barry (1995:145), Mexican farmers faced six major changes: "1) the withdrawal of government-subsidized inputs, 2) high interest rates and lack of access to credit, 3) the end of land distribution and the new status of ejidal land, 4) an increased flow of cheaper food imports, 5) inadequate government measures to upgrade productivity and competitiveness, and 6) a widely criticized new subsidy program called Procampo." A clear signal had been sent that future policies would weed out the weak from the strong in the countryside.

The Formation of the Lázaro Cárdenas Ejido Union in Nayarit   The UELC emerged historically from three waves of peasant and indigenous organizing focused on recuperating land lost by indigenous communities to large haciendas and mines (Hernández 1988). From 1857 to 1881 an unsuccessful indigenous insurrection raged in the Nayarit area, initially stimulated by the reform laws of 1856 which called for abolishment of the property rights of all corporate organizations. The primary targets of the legislation were properties controlled by the church and administered by town councils and indigenous communities. John Tutino suggests that the economic liberals who promoted the reform laws had a well-known goal of ending community landholding and were clear about their objectives (1986:259).

From 1933 to 1939, there was a significant land reform movement under the presidency of Lázaro Cárdenas that resulted in the creation of many *ejidos*. In 1933 the state of Nayarit had 78 *ejidos*, and by 1939 some four thousand campesinos were organized in 233 *ejidos* covering an area of 730,000 hectares (Hernández 1988:12). The power of the hacendados was broken, and Nayarit became known as the "state of the *ejido*."

The 1960s were marked by a successful movement for the restitution of communal lands that had been taken over by private farmers and ranchers (Fox and Hernández 1989:11). In the late 1950s, a charismatic leader from Nayarit known as "El Cora"—characterized as a mixture of social bandit and honest peasant leader who led a band dedicated to stealing cattle and supporting agrarianists in their struggles against the *caciques* and large landowners—began organizing a campaign to regain land by petitioning for communal land (Hernández 1988:16–18). At first dedicated to forming new *ejidos*, when El Cora discovered the colonial maps and titles of indigenous communities from Nayarit in the archives of Guadalajara and Chapultepec, the struggle shifted to restitution of communal lands. He renamed an earlier organization of indigenous and *ejido* communities the Adolfo López Mateos League, after the president at the time (Hernández 1988:18–19). In 1962, thirty-five communities from Nayarit participated in the League, including that of Jomulco, which has been a prime mover in the UELC.[1] Several women from Jomulco who participated in the League were later active in the UELC and in the formation of the Women's Council. Most of those petitioning for land were peasants without land, agricultural workers, people taking care of cattle for large landholders, children of *ejidatarios* who were tired of waiting for land, and those who had small amounts of land without legal title (Hernández 1988:19). The League was part of the CNC until 1965. Little by little, land solicitations were resolved and indigenous communities moved ahead faster than those of *mestizos*, particularly after 1966. In 1970 the politics of El Cora changed and he encouraged, for example, the *comuneros* of San Jerónimo Jomulco to invade the lands of smallholders with parcels of one or two acres, leaving large holdings intact (Hernández 1988:21). This action and his increased tendency to support large landholders are known as the "Betrayal of El Cora."

The 1970s were marked by the creation of several important regional peasant organizations which built on prior agrarian struggles. Though aided by organizers with government ties, some of the regional groups came to adopt a semiautonomous stance in relation to state agencies and agricultural policies. The Unión de Ejidos "Lázaro Cárdenas" was created in 1975 with the assistance of a dynamic team of community organizers working under PIDER (Rural Development Investment Program), an antipoverty program of the Luis Echeverría Alvarez administration. *Ejido* unions like the UELC brought two or more *ejidos* into regional organizations. The *ejido* communities that joined in these unions had received the right to their land under Article 27 of the Mexican Constitution. But most actually received their land during the 1930s under the presidency of Lázaro Cárdenas.

Ejido unions like the UELC were always in an odd position. While the government did not intend for regional organizations such as the UELC to become autonomous, some degree of independence could clearly arise, depending on the politics of those who worked in the organization. Many of the young PIDER organizers who worked in the UELC and elsewhere had emerged from the radical student movement of the 1960s and were committed to organizing, consciousness-raising, and helping to transform the country from below (Hernández 1990:13–14). PIDER's projects were also structured to encourage the participation of rural communities in decisionmaking and in a coordinated set of activities and services that included the development of organizational skills, credit, training in small-scale industry, and marketing rural products (Hernández 1990:15). The PIDER organizers encouraged the UELC to take on an independent identity, and they tried to foment autonomous regional organizations under the cover of a government agency. But because the *ejido* union had been tied to state programs and resources since its inception, it was also consistently influenced by state policy and political pressures. Moreover, its leaders were continually tempted to accept favors in exchange for political loyalty to PRI officials sitting in the governor's mansion.

Older members of the UELC, like Doña Kata Moreno of Jomulco, recall the work they did with PIDER organizers to pull the *ejidos* into a regional organization:

We were going around day and night talking to ejido *assemblies. We had to convince them of how important this was. In Marquesado when they didn't want to participate, I told them, "We are going to show the government that we can work hard and with honor. We will fight for our rights as peasants."*

After months of organizing, in September of 1975 ten *ejidos* and one indigenous community came together to form the Lázaro Cárdenas Ejido Union. *Ejidos* from the *municipio* of Ahuacatlán included Ahuacatlán, Uzeta, Tetitlán, Heriberto Jara, La Ciénaga, and Marquesado. From the *municipio* of Santa María del Oro the *ejidos* of Chapalilla and Tequepexpan joined. From the *municipio* of Ixtlán del Río came the *ejido* of San José de Gracia. And from the *municipio* of Jala, the *ejido* of Jomulco and the indigenous community of San Jerónimo Jomulco came on board. The *ejido* of Zoatlán, from the *municipio* of Ahuacatlán, joined after 1977. By 1988 the UELC had a total of 4,752 members from the eleven *ejidos* and one indigenous community that participated. More than half of these members (2,891) were from San Jerónimo Jomulco. (See table.)

At the time the UELC was formed, the official peasant organization (the CNC) was splintered and ineffective in the state of Nayarit. In 1976, the involvement of some community leaders and PIDER promoters in that year's gubernatorial opposition movement in Nayarit led the UELC to be identified with an unsuccessful electoral challenge. After the loss of the popular opposition, the governor expelled the PIDER organizers from the state (Fox and Hernández 1989:12). From this point onward,

Number of members of UELC and hectares held in each *ejido*, 1985

Municipio	Ejido or Indigenous Community	Members	Moist Hectares	Irrigated Hectares	Rainfed Hectares	Pasture/ Woods Hectares
Ahuacatlán	Ahuacatlán	148	146	150	1,506	1,993
Ahuacatlán	La Ciénaga	31	381	—	572	—
Ahuacatlán	Heriberto Jara	123	112	—	1,114	3,627
Ahuacatlán	Marquesado	158	305	—	1,117	1,892
Ahuacatlán	Tetitlán	254	288	391	2,657	1,749
Ahuacatlán	Uzeta	191	—	140	1,250	1,390
Ahuacatlán	Zoatlán	24	—	34	223	334
Jala	Jomulco	111	—	—	1,013	8,912
Jala	Indigenous Community of San Jerónimo Jomulco	2,891	—	—	3,000	77,374
Santa María del Oro	Chapalilla	161	—	80	495	1,370
Santa María del Oro	Tequepexpan	573	682	—	1,408	4,836
Ixtlán del Río	San José de Gracia	87	—	—	1,069	2,930
TOTAL		4,752	1,914	795	15,424	106,773

Source: Hernández 1990:38.

the *ejido* union was more vulnerable to intervention by the state government of Nayarit.

During its initial years, the UELC repeatedly confronted the government by winning rights to a major government fertilizer distributorship, challenging corn prices with regional road blocks, and creating autonomous community-development projects (see Fox 1992a; Fox and Hernández 1989; Hernández 1990). The early political leadership of the UELC consistently chose autonomy over incorporation and appeared to be achieving concessions with this strategy. After weathering a difficult period in the late 1970s, when authorities cracked down on two of the most active communities in the *ejido* union and temporarily took over the UELC's fertilizer outlet, a new federal food-distribution program brought fresh external allies to the region in 1980 (Fox and Hernández

1989:12). Organizers who came in to form community food councils worked with the leadership of the UELC (in one case taking them to visit one of the most successful coalitions of *ejidos* in the country) and redoubled efforts to regain the leadership from state-installed authorities. A democratically oriented leader from Jomulco won elections for the presidency of the *ejido* union and ushered in "an extended period of broadened participation in decision-making" (Fox and Hernández 1989:13). During this period the UELC launched a community housing project with government loans and pushed for higher corn prices; the Women's Council was also organized, as is detailed below.

In the late 1980s, a newly elected president of the union began using the organization as a launching pad for his political career. He formed links with a faction of the National Peasant Confederation (CNC) that was aligned with the state governor, personally met with President Salinas de Gotari in 1989, and negotiated several projects for the UELC, including funds for women's development projects. When he declared his candidacy for the municipal presidency of Ahuacatlán in 1990, the reasons for his strategy of negotiation with the state were clear—he was preparing to take municipal office while he was president of the *ejido* union. The context of his election was a larger effort on the part of the state government to eliminate a political faction of organized teachers from key political posts. Factionalism within the PRI in relation to the teachers' group permeated the UELC as well as the women's groups within it.

From the mid-1980s until 1995, the UELC went from being a semi-independent organization to one that deliberately traded its autonomy for access to state agricultural resources (Fox 1992a). By 1995 the UELC was looking to sell one of its large fertilizer warehouses in an attempt to raise capital. Continued direct links with the state and to the CNC and PRI have also affected the trajectory of women's organizing within the UELC.

Social and Economic Composition of the UELC   The UELC is a regional peasant organization that represents about half of the peasants in its area of influence (Fox 1992a:9). Other strata such as a small commercial elite, teachers and bureaucrats, and landless farm workers are not represented and do not participate in the UELC. The majority of members in the organization are dryland corn farmers who sell small and medium amounts on the market and who produce for their own subsistence as well. The area produced about 38 percent of the state's total corn yield in the 1980s (Hernández 1988:5). Some also grow other cash crops such as garbanzos, soybeans, sugarcane, peanuts, and small quantities of vegetables to sell in local markets. The average household allotment is about 4 to 4.8 hectares of unirregated land, with a range of 1–10 hectares (Fox 1992a:9; Hernández 1988:6). Average irrigated holdings are .35 hectare per household (Hernández 1988:6). There is some variance in the type of farming households represented, but most are small to medium holders.

Both those with and without land migrate seasonally to work in Mexican agribusiness and in the United States. During the dry season, significant numbers of people will migrate to the coastal region to work in bean and tobacco harvests (Hernández 1988:7). There are also internal flows of migrants within the four *municipios* that participate in the *ejido* union. Interviews in December 1990 with forty households revealed that an average of one person per household was actively migrating to other parts of Mexico or to the United States. In December, many migrants return home for the holidays. Several holiday events such as *posadas* and fairs saw major contingents of young people, both men and women, who had returned from the United States and were sporting U.S. fashions.[2] Local dances looked like an encounter between the L.A. club scene and the more traditional Mexican fiesta.

Some women in the area work in coastal harvests, but many are also employed in harvesting dried corn husks which, after being processed, are shipped to the United States to be used for tamales. Others travel to the state capital of Tepic or to Mexico City to labor as domestic workers.

In the mid-1980s, squeezed between inflation and falling government subsidies, corn production became less profitable for farmers in Nayarit (Fox 1992a:18). Initially encouraged through government credit programs that were then scaled back, families decreased the variety of what they produced, focusing primarily on corn production both for the market and for their own consumption. As a result, they had to buy other household food products such as milk, cheese, eggs, bread, fruit, vegetables, beans, and meat that they had previously produced. They lost some of their self-sufficiency. In the late 1980s, the government began to cut subsidies from all but the most basic food products. Migration remained the primary cash-earning strategy and generated income to pay for ever more expensive food products, agricultural inputs, and other goods such as clothing and machinery.

The Gendered Division of Labor and Differences between Women

In southern Nayarit, peasant women engage in a wide range of productive and reproductive tasks. Women participate in agricultural labor, frequently working in the fields planting, weeding, and harvesting. The amount of time that women spend working in the fields varies according to household composition by gender and age and in relation to migration. High levels of migration by men and women mean that household labor forces are reduced. When men migrate, women may take their place in the fields, particularly if they cannot afford to hire laborers.

Women in Nayarit raise vegetables and care for animals including chickens, ducks, pigs, goats, and sheep. They also engage in a host of tasks related to reproduction, including

preserving, processing, and preparing food; washing, repairing and often producing clothing; socializing and providing for children's school needs; participating in kin networks on ceremonial occasions; cleaning houses and courtyards; hauling water and firewood; transporting food to market to be sold; maintaining household ties with the church; providing medical and psychological care; and negotiating family conflicts. (Stephen 1992)

These reproductive tasks are not separate from production in the minds of peasant women, yet they are seldom the focus of organizing efforts.

Household decisionmaking may follow a variety of patterns dependent on economic status, ethnicity, and individual household dynamics (Stephen 1991). While men tend to dominate decisionmaking about production, in some cases women also have considerable say. Inheritance patterns tend to favor men who receive rights to land, houses, agricultural machinery, and animals. Most women take up residence in the house of their husband or their husband's family in cases of common-law marriage. The marriage may or may not be officially formalized through a church wedding or civil ceremony. A couple which begins to cohabitate is considered married.

Varied landholding patterns within the *ejidos* that make up the UELC as well as income from migration and wage labor have produced some economic stratification between households. Increasingly those who have been able to generate small amounts of capital are sending their children to the state capital or to Mexico City for high school and college education. Different levels of education as well as differences in family economic resources can thus be found among those who are potential leaders in the Women's Council and in the UELC.

Many (but not all) women who have taken on leadership roles within the Women's Council are educated. In two of the *ejidos* active in the Women's Council, the leaders are teachers; the woman who was elected to the presidency of the Women's Council in the early 1990s and who also served as its technical advisor for six years, is a veterinarian. In the arena of productive projects for women, those who have some technical experience with animal and plant production and/or experience in marketing, finance, math, and institutional relationships have a clear set of skills which makes them stand out. Thus, within one *ejido*, important differences between women in skills, experience, and resources may affect their individual experiences within the projects they participate in.

UAIMs: The Mexican State's Development Plan for Rural Women
The historical gendered dynamics of *ejido* law and organization in Mexico are consistent with a cultural ideology that subordinates women's decisionmaking to men and sees women as having their interests represented by male family members (Baitenmann forthcoming). While the original Article 27 of the Constitution does not specify beyond "nucleos de población" (population sites) just who is to receive rights to *ejido* and communal land, the Ejido Law of 1920 establishes for the first time that land should be divided equally between "jefes de familia," or household heads. While some analysts such as Carlota Botey point out that the introduction of "jefes de familia" suggests that the original intent of the *ejido* law was to grant land as the right of families and not of individuals (Botey Estapé 1991), in many rural areas of Mexico the term "jefe de familia" culturally implies a *male* household head. As pointed out by Helga Baitenmann (1995:22), the cry to return to the original Zapatista spirit of the 1917 law does nothing to help women: it merely reproduces previous agrarian constructs which stripped women of their rights. The notion of a household head representing his or her family as a democratic entity has been soundly criticized by anthropologists who have pointed out repeatedly that hierarchies of gender and age which characterize social relations outside the household also permeate relations within the household (Stephen 1993b).

While the term "jefe de familia" does not linguistically signify the gender of the "head," culturally in Nayarit and elsewhere it is assumed to be male. If it is a "jefa de familia" (female head of household), that is a special case which has to be explained. Article 97 of the Ley de Dotaciones y Restituciones de Tierras, a law written in 1927 interpreting the implementation of Article 27, specified that those eligible to be members of an *ejido* had to "be Mexican, males over eighteen years of age or single women or widows who are supporting a family" (Botey Estapé 1991). The 1927 law spells out specifically the assumption that heads of household are male and that all males can function as symbolic heads of families, whether or not they in fact have a family. Women qualify to become members of *ejidos* not on the basis of age or gender alone, as is the case for males, but because of their reproductive status as mothers or widows supporting a family. In this capacity they become substitute males because they are supporting the remaining human capital and property of a male (see Baitenmann forthcoming; Stephen 1996a; Vásquez García 1995).

It is not until 1971 under the Federal Law of Agrarian Reform, Article 200, that men and women become equal under the law with regard to their ability to qualify for ejidal rights. The law was changed to state that in order to receive land rights one must be "Mexican by birth, male or female, older than sixteen or of any age if they are supporting a family" (Botey Estapé 1991). Under the 1971 law, women are no longer required to be mothers or widows maintaining a family in order to qualify for land rights.

The law also allowed women to hold any position of authority (*cargo*) within *ejidos*, and called for the creation of Agro-Industrial Units for Women (UAIMs). These units provided special agricultural and small industrial projects for those women (the majority) who did not have access to *ejido* land as *ejidatarias*. The language of the law suggested that "the organization of women would be stimulated because they would be incorporated into the 'productive process.' In some cases, government rhetoric went on to suggest that this would eventually lead to reducing gender inequalities" (Villarreal 1994a:6). As pointed out by Villarreal (1994a: 5–7), the number of UAIMs that have been established in Mexico is difficult to ascertain. One study found that 8,000 UAIMs had been legalized, but only 1,224 were officially registered and 1,112 had received credit (Arizpe and Aranda 1986, cited in Villarreal 1994a:6–7). In 1988 there were 64 UAIMs officially registered in the state of Nayarit according to the Ministry of Agrarian Reform (Aranda Bezaury 1993: 206–207). In 1993 only 15 percent of Mexico's *ejidos* had any registered UAIMs. And an even smaller number are actually functioning (Robles, Aranda, and Botey 1993:32).

The logic behind the fomentation of UAIMs appears vaguely to reflect the assumptions of economic development programs such as those in Cuba, where pushing women into agricultural production was supposed to reduce inequality between men and women. In Mexico little was done, outside of changing the law, to make UAIMs a reality. No effort was made to organize women, to defend their rights within *ejidos*, or to provide them with credit, technical training, or access to markets for their products. In addition, the law did nothing to address continued inequities in local political cultures where community assemblies and decisionmaking was the province of men.

In her discussion of the formation of UAIMs, Magdalena Villarreal points out how the creation of UAIMs helped to legitimate the Mexican state at a particular point in time. She writes: "The UAIMs allowed the state access to a sector of the population that was previously inaccessible in many ways. It created women's organizations in state terms, and through state support" (Villarreal 1994a: 170). The creation of UAIMs as well as other government programs that involved women through their role in the family created a new constituency that could receive resources and be cultivated to support the PRI politically. This happened quite clearly in Nayarit. While the UAIMs languished in the mid to late 1980s, in the 1990s they were reclaimed by the official peasant organization (CNC) and, in some states, by the "Women in Solidarity" program.

UAIMs allow women as a group to receive communal land from agrarian communities and plots from *ejidos*. The amount of land they receive as a group, however, is equivalent to the amount given to one *ejidatario*. It matters not whether the UAIM has four members or forty members: the women still receive the amount of land allocated for one *ejidatario*. The existence of a UAIM also allows the group of women who formed the UAIM to have one vote in the *ejido* organization—equivalent to the vote of one *ejidatario*. If women are not official *ejidatarias* (having use rights to *ejido* land), they have no representation in the public assemblies of *ejidos*, despite the fact that they may have worked on *ejido* land all their lives as daughters and wives. Women's very presence in the UAIM is dependent on their relationship to an *ejidatario*—usually male. On the official enrollment document for legally forming a UAIM, each woman's name, age, marital status, occupation, and relationship to an *ejidatario* has to be specified. In the case of women in the UAIMs of the Women's Council of the UELC, the relationship was always "daughter" or "wife."

The 1971 law also allowed women in UAIMs to receive credit and government resources for small development projects, but these funds were usually funneled through the *ejidos*, often resulting in problems for women who did not have direct access to the funds but had to depend on male leadership. In some cases, UAIMs were created by a group of male *ejidatarios* who saw it as a way of obtaining additional resources. In other cases, *ejido* presidents or other local government officials established UAIMs as "proof of their success in carrying out government policies" (Villarreal 1994a: 178).

In 1991, UAIMs were given independent judicial and financial status that allowed them to directly receive funds from the government and other sources such as international development agencies. While this decreased their dependence on local *ejidos* and other peasant organizations with respect to procuring funding, it also resulted in the increased reliance of UAIMs on government bureaucrats from such places as the Ministry of Agriculture and Water Resources or the Ministry of Agrarian Reform. Rather than increase their autonomy, this change often strengthened their direct clientalist relations with the state and made them more directly accessible to be mobilized for political purposes.

During the 1990s, under the Salinas de Gortari government, many UAIMs became dependent on social welfare for their funding. Women's participation in the "Women in Solidarity" program and in community solidarity committees had mixed results in Nayarit. While it made them politically dependent on the state governor and his supporters, the fact that women participated in local committees oriented toward public works and providing credit gave them a set of skills that they are now transferring to their own projects.

Under the 1992 changes in the Agrarian Reform Law, Article 27 of the Mexican Constitution, UAIMs could decide to privatize their plots of land and/or negotiate joint-capital ventures with outside parties using UAIM property and resources. However, women continue to be denied access to land as individuals unless they become *ejidatarias* by taking over someone else's land-use rights. Their only access to land besides inheriting *ejido* use rights continues to be through the limited form of the UAIMs. As pointed out by Carlota Botey (1991:3), allowing male *ejido* members to make decisions about land that is regarded as family property continues to marginalize women from agrarian decisionmaking and results in outsiders having easier access to *ejido* land than the very women who often worked to make it produce. In sum, although the creation of UAIMs allowed women a new channel for limited participation in local agrarian politics, the constraints on UAIMs and now the marginalization of a majority of women from decisions about privatizing *ejido* land have set up consistent roadblocks in the way of rural women's organizing efforts.

Building the Women's Council of the UELC   The formation of a women's council of UAIMs within the organizational structure of a union of *ejidos* is unusual. Few UAIMs in Mexico are organized into regional councils. The Women's Council of the UELC began by building on the existence of state-sponsored Agro-Industrial Units for Women. In the *municipio* of Ahuacatlán, Nayarit, three UAIMs emerged among communities affiliated with the UELC in the early 1980s. In 1985, at the urging of male leaders of the UELC, two female organizers originally affiliated with DICONSA (Distributor for the National Food Program) began to discuss organizational options with women in these three UAIMs. Their initial organizing strategy was to mobilize women through a series of small economic projects designed to increase household and community production of basic food goods in order to help combat the impact of the Mexican economic crisis of the 1980s. These included vegetable gardens, chicken raising, small orchards, and bakeries. Promotion of these projects was accomplished by training a local group of organizers who then tried to establish UAIMs in their own communities. That same year, the UAIM in the indigenous community of San Jerónimo Jomulco began its turkey-raising project. With funds from the Inter-American Foundation, they obtained 1,150 small turkeys to raise and market. The project functioned well at first—the turkeys were raised and consumed locally (Hernández 1990:107). Other projects were to follow.

In 1987, a large regional meeting of women was held that was critical in helping different UAIMs to define themselves and their interests. This meeting was the culmination of an organizing effort in which one female promoter from each community was chosen to support the formation of a UAIM that would operate within each *ejido* in the UELC. By that time, the *ejido* union had grown from the original ten *ejidos* and one indigenous community to incorporate eleven *ejidos* and the indigenous community. At the meeting, UAIMs from four *ejidos* formally created the Women's Council, pulling women from diverse *ejidos* into one organization. This was the first instance of any kind of organized women's presence in the UELC (Stephen 1991:236–240).

In 1988, a total of twelve UAIMs joined together.[3] The legalization of local women's groups as UAIMs made it possible for them to receive resources from the Ministry of Agrarian Reform (SRA) to be used in productive projects. One of the DICONSA organizers spoke with a subsecretary of the SRA about the formation of the UAIMs, and he facilitated their formation within the space of six months. However, as soon as the women began to receive SRA resources, funneled through the *ejido* union, they began to have problems with the UELC leadership. Some members of the all-male directorate were only providing selective information and resources to some of the UAIMs. This was an effective way for the *ejido* union to maintain control over the Women's Council, and it caused considerable dissatisfaction among the women who participated in the council. In June of 1988, women from five of the UIAMs met and resolved to do the following:

- *Solicit documents from the Ministry of Agrarian Reform that would provide them with information about the particular project each group was to undertake.*
- *Investigate why the resources they were supposed to receive had not arrived.*
- *Request that their resources be turned over to them immediately and that each group receive the money they needed directly, without having it funneled through their* ejidos *or through the UELC.*
- *Attend the next assembly of the* ejido *union to state their dissatisfaction with the lack of information and to declare their disagreements with the leadership of the* ejido *union.*

Representatives from the five UAIMs met with officials from the Ministry of Agrarian Reform and found that resources for their projects were already available but that information had not been passed along to them. They invoked the superior authority of the SRA to back their position as they complained to the male leadership of the UELC.

Part of the male leadership of the *ejido* union was not pleased with the independent politicking of the women. These men told the women that the leadership could have intervened on their behalf and that they should not be carrying out actions without consulting them. The treasurer of the UELC told the women at the UELC assembly that they did not even have the right to complain there because they were not elected delegates (Hernández 1990:111). The president of the *ejido* union intervened, however, and after a heated meeting stated that women ought to have a space in the assembly and that the statutes of the organization should be changed to give them a voice.

After this meeting, women from the UAIMs met again with representatives from a wide range of official entities including the Ministry of Agrarian Reform, the Ministry of Agriculture and Water Resources (SARH), and the League of Agrarian Communities, representing the CNC. The women decided to divide the resources equally among themselves and to form a regional council including the original twelve UAIMs plus two more and the two women who served as their technical advisors. Thus the Women's Council included fourteen UAIMs in total.

After the summer of 1988, representatives from each of the fourteen women's UAIMs would meet together as the Women's Council once a month to compare notes on their respective projects, plan future projects, and discuss organizing strategies. At the height of their unity, from 1988 to 1989, the Women's Council included 401 official members, with the following numbers in each community:

Ahuacatlán	45
Chapalilla	67
La Ciénaga	24
Ejido Jomulco	26
Heriberto Jara	30
Marquesado	31
San Jerónimo Jomulco	43
San José de Gracia	12
Santa María del Oro	31
Santa Isabel	19
Tequepexpan	21
Tetitlán	20
Uzeta	13
Zoatlán	19
(UELC 1990)	

Women's Council meetings drew an average of fifty people, with representatives coming from each UAIM. Training workshops on topics such as family health and nutrition drew more people. Local meetings

Panel from a UELC comic book showing the turkey-raising project of the San Jerónimo Jomulco UAIM.

were usually attended by ten to thirty women, depending on the size of the local UAIM. On paper, the numbers of women in some *ejidos* (esp. San Jerónimo Jomulco, Chapalilla, and Ahuacatlán) were impressive, but the active cores of these UAIMs were much smaller and continue to be. Most have an active membership of ten to twenty women.

The political project of the Women's Council involved integrating women into the political assemblies of individual *ejidos* and having a voice and a vote in the larger assemblies of the UELC. The UELC president who eventually left to become municipal president of Ahuacatlán finally agreed to let the women have one representative in the assemblies of the *ejido* union, but only after a considerable amount of pressure was applied by women within the UAIM as well as by outsiders who were funding some of the UAIM projects. And this concession still only gave women from the council one delegate for all their members, despite the fact that they represented fourteen *ejidos*.

Political factionalism within the UELC and within individual *ejido* communities also influenced the UAIMs. In the mid-1970s, the rise of an opposition gubernatorial candidate caused the governor to shut off electricity and water in communities supporting the opposition. Discontent spread to the PRI itself, and PRI groups in Ahuacatlán and Jala protested the imposition of PRI candidates for municipal president, declaring their intentions to vote for the opposition both at the local level and for governor (Hernández 1990). Despite a promise from President López Portillo, fraud was widespread and the opposition candidate was declared the loser even though many voters believed he had won. The PRI candidate took office and ushered in a period marked by strong efforts to repress independent organizations and movements.

Within the *ejido* union, those who had declared their independence from the PRI continued to coexist with those from other *ejidos* who had their own particular interests. Some *ejidatarios* from one of the most important *ejidos*, Uzeta, were aligned with a very powerful group from the National Educational Workers' Union (SNTE) who were attempting to further their control in the state by winning municipal presidential seats and by controlling the League of Agrarian Communities, the organization run by the CNC. This powerful group of teachers had close ties to a succession of governors who had attempted to shut down opposition politics and autonomous organizations. Several of the UAIMs, including that of Uzeta and Heriberto Jara, remained seriously divided by the presence of the teachers and their female CNC allies and leaders.

At two different times in the life of the UELC, political divisions between different PRI factions—those for and against the teachers and, therefore, for and against the CNC—were used to divide the *ejido* union and impose leadership. This tactic was used in 1976 when, in exchange for the release of several UELC leaders who had been jailed on false charges of fraud, the government used elections to impose its CNC-aligned candidates for leadership of the union. Because half of the delegates within the UELC already supported the CNC, the government's imposition was made that much easier.

In 1989, after a period of unity in which individual projects began to move forward and women gained a small political space in the UELC, an intense political battle resumed within the UELC as well as within the Women's Council. The outcome of all this turmoil was the expulsion of the two outside advisors, leadership of the Women's Council being turned over temporarily to a female representative of the CNC. Eventually a permanent split occurred in the Women's Council between those UAIMs that remained loyal to one of the outside advisors, and thus distanced themselves from the *ejido* union, and those UAIMs that continued to relate to the *ejido* union. The latter group worked closely with a local woman, a veterinarian, who began as a technical advisor to the turkey-raising project in San Jerónimo Jomulco and was later elected president of the Women's Council.

In 1989 when the *ejido* union president was preparing to launch his campaign for the municipal presidency of Ahuacatlán, he used a local female CNC leader to eliminate the two outside organizers who had been critical in consolidating the Women's Council. The process confirmed the continued ability of the CNC to influence the internal workings of the UELC and of the Women's Council. In some measure, the basis for the expulsion seems to have been a dislike on the part of the then-president of the UELC, for the advisors' efforts to establish the Women's Council as an autonomous entity. If the Women's Council became independent of the *ejido* union, then the women in the UAIMs could no longer be counted on as campaign workers and supporters in his forthcoming quest to become municipal president. The president of the UELC sought to consolidate his political power and to create a solid political base for his campaign. The small economic projects of the Women's Council were important political capital that he did not want to lose. If he could not take credit for helping to secure their resources, he could not ask for their political loyalty and labor.

After the problems women had experienced in 1988 with respect to gaining control of the funds destined for their projects, the advisors wanted to find a way for the Women's Council to receive financial resources directly. One of the advisors stated in an interview in 1990:

At the time, the women didn't have any legal status. We wanted to have some autonomy, and that collided with the agenda of the UELC president.

At the time the advisors suggested that the Women's Council become independent, women from many of the UAIMs in the Women's Council felt that they should remain formally part of the UELC. They felt political loyalty for the *ejido* union and for its president. Some, such as a few women from San Jerónimo Jomulco, had worked intensely in the 1970s to help organize the UELC. They opposed the idea of autonomy in the Women's Council. Said one UAIM member in the community of Jomulco:

We have to stay with the union. We owe our loyalty there because the union was the first organization that helped us improve our communities. We have to stand by it. They [the advisors] wanted us to sign a document so that we would be independent, but we couldn't do it.

In some cases, women who felt loyal to the UELC were also supportive of the CNC. The strategy of the UELC president for getting rid of the advisors relied on the women's loyalty to both the UELC and the CNC. He invited the district women's representative of the CNC to a meeting and used her to expel the advisors. Ironically, in that meeting she told the Women's Council that they and the UELC should be free from outside interference. Some women in the council felt extreme loyalty to the CNC, so they listened to her and temporarily rallied behind her. The two women technical advisors as well as two men were expelled in that meeting. Shortly thereafter, however, when the CNC representative no longer served his purposes, the UELC president got rid of her.

Throughout this process, it was clear that the political culture in which the UELC and the Women's Council evolved militated against an autonomous identity for the women's organization and reinforced gendered power relations in which women were subordinate at best and invisible at worst. Although women did important organizing work during the creation of the UELC, they never had representation on a par with men because of the historical structure and decisionmaking processes within the *ejidos*. Yet their sense of emotional loyalty was one of the primary ways in which they experienced their relationship with the UELC, despite their marginalization within it. Only later, when the UELC president actually became municipal president (in part owing to the loyalty and labor of women in the Women's Council) and abandoned them completely, did they rethink their position. For he did not hold up his end of the bargain. They provided him with political support, but he did not secure ongoing resources for them. This was in part because of his lack of interest in their projects, but also because of a rapidly diminishing pot of federal funds.

In the 1990s, when the CNC could not count on automatic loyalty because there were fewer and fewer resources to hand out, the leadership reinvigorated its programs to incorporate organized rural women into CNC ranks. Successful UAIMs as well as local committees that received money from the "Women in Solidarity" program initiated by Salinas de Gortari were among the CNC's prime targets. In the mid-1990s, a Nayarit state leader of the women's section of the CNC supported the UAIMs in the Women's Council, but also tried to interfere in the council's political process by imposing her preferred leaders. This time around, however, women in the council were not responsive. They became suspicious when the CNC leader claimed the UAIMs were "hers" and called on them to attend mobilizations of the CNC because of the "support" the organization had offered them.

The interest of the CNC in the Women's Council also may have intensified after several leaders attended activities sponsored by the Union of Regional Autonomous Peasant Organizations (UNORCA, Unión Nacional de Organizaciones Regionales Campesinas Autónomas), a national independent peasant organization of small and medium-size producers battling for control of the production process. After being used by both the UELC president and the CNC for political purposes, more women in the council became open to working with a range of peasant organizations. For those whose projects had gotten under way somewhat successfully, their primary concern in the mid-1990s was to work with people and organizations that could move them forward.

Since the 1989 expulsion, the Women's Council has existed as one block of five UAIMs that works occasionally with one of the expelled advisors and another block of nine that has worked with the technical assistance and leadership of Esmeralda Avalos, a local woman who is a veterinarian. Esmeralda has worked with the Ministry of Agriculture and other government agencies on women's development projects. In 1990 she was elected president of the Women's Council and was the disputed coordinator of the UAIMs in 1995. She retained close ties to the CNC and to PRI in the early 1990s but, like other women in the council, grew tired of being used politically with no reciprocation.

By 1995, Esmeralda was openly critical of the CNC for its repeated intervention in the Women's Council. She stated: "Outside people like those from the CNC create divisions and problems. They come and promise the sun, the moon, and the stars. . . . It's difficult and tiring to deal with." Esmeralda also noted in 1995 that the government's "Women in Solidarity" program did nothing for the UAIMs, and "we didn't want to put on their T-shirts and wear them around or go to CNC rallies." She observed that because the UAIMs now have their own judicial and financial status, they do not need such programs: now they can get credit on their own. After years of struggle to control their own resources, this was a major step for women in the council. Once they established their ability to directly obtain resources, they no longer needed to focus on the *ejido* union.

By 1995, most women's interest in the UELC had waned and few women wanted to attend the meetings. Many felt that the *ejido* union had offered them little support in recent years and was too eager to take credit for their successes. Since the UAIMs no longer needed to go through the *ejido* union in order to gain access to state officials, it was unclear just what the purpose of their relationship with the union would be. The nine that are aligned with Esmeralda have continued to work together in some fashion, continuing to meet occasionally as the council. Some of the UAIMs have evolved into strong, locally based projects of ten to twenty women who participate in the political life of their own *ejidos* but have little interest in or motivation for belonging to a regional peasant organization. Their most important business is now conducted directly with agents of the state.

The end result of the council's trajectory has been to foster some strong, locally based economic projects where women have control. In the process, women have developed skill in working within their *ejido* assemblies but have weakened as a regional organization. The *ejido* union is in a significant decline, and women feel most focused within their communities and only secondarily as part of the Women's Council. What is most interesting is the types of changes they have experienced indirectly at home and in their local political participation as they have struggled to create and maintain small economic projects.

Development Projects Focused on "Family"   Both state policy on rural women as well as the attitudes of bureaucratic officials and many men in the *ejidos* encouraged women to undertake projects that reinforced their roles as wives and mothers. While focusing on what might be viewed as very traditional projects, women in the Women's Council nevertheless found that simply carrying out their projects resulted in a challenge to household gender roles and to their marginal political status. They did not create a new ideology that prioritized gender, but used the roles outlined for them within small economic projects as a way of gaining more political space and authority.

As discussed above, the creation of UAIMs was a state-sponsored program in Mexico designed to give women access to some of the land and resources from which they were excluded by the Agrarian Reform Law. As noted by Villarreal and others, the creation of UAIMs also allowed the state direct access to a sector of the rural population with which it had no formal links: "Using procedures similar to those found in the construction of ejidos, UAIMs were created as institutions linked to state legislation and subject to government authorities to gain access to resources, to resolve conflicts, and to establish their internal forms of organization" (Villarreal 1994b:2). While the particular union of *ejidos* which the Women's Council was a part of had been semiautonomous for a portion of its existence until the late 1980s, by the time the UAIMs received sufficient funding to begin working on their own projects and functioning in a strong way, they were directly linked with and obligated to the state for the funds they were receiving. Beyond this, the ideology surrounding the projects of the UAIMs was geared toward improving the position of peasant families, not aimed specifically at improving the lot of Mexican rural women as individuals. Government development programs funded through PRONASOL as well as the Women's Council's own agenda assumed that women's specific problems could be successfully addressed within the context of the rural family. Women were assumed to be unpaid domestic producers who would best be served by small economic projects.

A 1989 document outlining the goals of the UAIMs that are part of the UELC included the following objectives:

- *To raise the nutritional levels of families in the region.*
- *To increase the economic and social development of families.*
- *To improve the production of nutritious food and make sure that it is available for consumption throughout the year.*
- *To generate employment for families in their communities.*
(UELC 1989)

The emphasis on small economic projects to increase household nutrition and provide employment was promoted not only by the two original organizers who set up the UAIMs, but also by the Inter-American Foundation (which subsidized several women's projects), the National Solidarity Program, and the Ministry of Agriculture and Water Resources (which paid for the development of most of the projects functioning under the aegis of the Women's Council during the 1980s and 1990s).

Esmeralda, long-time Women's Council president, trainer, and advisor, worked with the former president of the UELC to obtain a grant of over $119,000 from several government agencies (primarily the Ministry of Agriculture and the National Solidarity Program) for a wide range of projects including corn mills, vegetable plots, orchards, chicken and turkey hatcheries, and sewing workshops. Most, but not all, of the projects are in the block of nine UAIMs she works with. Most of the projects were operating by late 1991, and by 1995 several of them (including two bakeries and a poultry project) had successfully borrowed and paid back the money that was used for operating expenses. Two of the projects took out second loans from the National Solidarity Program. By the early 1990s, women in a number of UAIMs had proven themselves capable of maintaining small-scale projects and repaying credit. In most cases, though, this was a long and difficult process, with failures preceding successes.

The progression of one UAIM's project in the community of Heriberto Jara provides a useful example of the ups and downs of women's small-scale enterprises. Formed in 1988, the UAIM began with a sheep-raising project. Antonia, a fifty-year-old woman who used to be president of this UAIM, tells of the difficulties of their first project and its relationship to a functioning beekeeping project:

We started out with about thirty women who received different kinds of training. By the time we had a concrete idea for a small-scale economic project there were only twelve of us left. Then two more young women left after they got married and their husbands wouldn't let them attend. . . . We started working with the sheep, but everything was very poorly planned. They [government officials] promised us training and materials to build a corral for them, but neither of these things ever materialized. One of the group members loaned us a corral, but then there were problems with taking care of the animals. She had to take on more responsibility because the sheep were at her house. And because we had no training in how to take care of them, some of the sheep died. . . . Finally, we divided up the animals and each [one of us] took some home. Only two people were able to successfully breed the sheep. . . . Then we had a lot of problems in the group when we had to pay back the loan. Those who had animals that died didn't think we should pay back the cost of the animals because we never received the training and materials we were promised. Those two women who were able to successfully breed the sheep didn't see why they should pay for the rest of us. . . .

Later we started up a beekeeping project. We used our savings to buy three hives and then three more. After working in the project for five years, we earned enough money to purchase another fifty hives. Last year, in 1994, we received a credit from the [National] Solidarity Program which we used to maintain our hives and to buy a honey extractor and an electric knife for cutting into the hives. . . .

The work we have to do now to maintain the hives isn't too bad. We only have to work a few hours per week, except when we have to move the hives. That is very intensive work and our husbands have to help us. Not all of them do, but we do have help. We don't divide up the work of maintaining the hives. We all do it together.

Thus, after the ups and downs of the sheep-raising project, some women in the Heriberto Jara UAIM settled on a product and a technology that they felt comfortable with. They began with their own capital and only later took on a PRONASOL loan. While the economic benefits of the project were hard to deduce from interviews in 1991 and in 1995, the beekeeping project has endured and grown over a five-year period and women are receiving some income.

A second group of women in the same UAIM have run what is apparently an even more successful project—a bakery that sells locally in several communities. Begun in 1990, the bakery came about because of a local political split in the *ejido* of Heriberto Jara which permeated the UAIM. Women in the bakery project backed the UELC president's political campaign and were opposed to the entrenched teachers' faction which occupied statewide political posts—"los maestros." Thus, political factionalism within the *ejido* split the projects of the UAIM. By 1995, the bakery project had successfully paid back 100 percent of their government loan. Teresa, a young woman who served as coordinator of the bakery while she studied nursing, spoke of their success:

When we started, we slowly lost women from the group. We had to work very hard, and they left because they couldn't find the time to participate and their husbands wouldn't let them. Right now we have nine members. . . . Because we paid back 100 percent of our loan on time, we got a visit from the governor of Nayarit and his wife. . . . This also allowed us to cosign for the credit that was given to the other group of women [i.e., those doing beekeeping].

Later in the conversation, however, it became evident that the success of paying back the loan had not necessarily translated into long-term economic stability. The woman cited above was accused of theft, and the bakery began to produce less frequently. Women in the bakery project have a contract once a week with a local secondary school, and during Holy Week their sales rise; yet they have had problems building a steady market. Local stores do not have confidence in the group's stability and will not make long-term commitments to them. The women have to sell the bread as they make it, going out into local communities in teams of two.

Marketing their products has remained a consistent problem for women in the UAIMs, as seen above. Having finally worked their way through their marginal status in the individual *ejidos*, in the *ejido* union, and often in government agencies, women have run into further obstacles—a combination of larger cultural prejudices against women in the business world and the fact that their projects have been small in scale, vulnerable, and dependent on government support.

In another example, sewing cooperatives from UAIMs in several communities received a six-month contract in 1994 from the Mexican Social Security Institute (IMSS) to produce surgical clothing. The contract was extended to a full year and a new contract was being negotiated in 1995, but was uncertain of approval. Such contracts are negotiated through personal connections; as political personnel change, so do the possibilities for marketing.

In addition to confronting the uncertainties of local markets, women in the UAIMs have also been subject to significant resistance and ridicule from the very state officials who are supposed to be assisting them. Esmeralda and the local leaders of the UAIMs developed their projects and political strategies surrounded primarily by male engineers and bureaucrats from state offices such as the Ministry of Agriculture and Water Resources. They also worked closely with male leaders of the UELC, some of whom consistently opposed their existence. After the 1989 expulsion of the two female technical advisors from the UELC, the Women's Council had no women advisors. Understanding the difficult daily context in which Esmeralda and others worked to carry out their economic projects makes their work all the more admirable.

While conducting fieldwork in December 1990, I went with a Mexican field assistant to interview the head of the local SARH office who was supposedly supervising the projects that the UAIMs were carrying out. He had daily contact with Esmeralda. During the discussion, he pulled out a picture display showing the progress of all the projects and described how wonderfully the women's groups were doing. We ended up talking about the big difference that having a corn mill can make for rural women all over Mexico. Then he turned to us and said:

Speaking of corn mills, I am going to tell you a joke. There was a Mixe woman in Oaxaca who didn't wear a bra. You know how they don't wear anything. Well, she and her friend were grinding corn together on a metate. *She says to her friend, "You know, grinding corn on a* metate *is really hard. It makes my arms hurt a lot. But what hurts the most is when my breast gets caught on the grindstone and pulled way out to the end."*

He laughed heartily and told us that he would be happy to offer any support he could in the research because he was very enthusiastic about the women's projects. He assumed that his racist and sexist remarks regarding indigenous women from southern Mexico would not offend us since we were clearly from another class and race. What they did was to clue us into the kind of daily environment people like Esmeralda had to work in.

Later that day, Esmeralda complained repeatedly about this official, saying that she had to beg for everything she got and ask repeatedly for payment for the projects. She remarked that he often made fun of the women's projects, and she was convinced that he didn't really care if they succeeded or not. She pointed out that his attitude was typical of government officials with whom she had to work.

Studies and development projects carried out in the 1980s revealed that the poor—particularly poor women—were avid savers and participated in a wide variety of informal credit institutions. Projects like the popular Gremin Bank in India have proved that women can and do participate in small-scale finance. Yet while loans such as those granted to the UAIMs in Nayarit do provide small amounts of capital for women, they continue to be structured with the idea that the economic activity of women is exclusively small-scale, supplementary, and tied to domestic needs. And they do nothing to affect larger neoliberal economic structures which continue to reproduce gross inequities in income (see Cosgrove 1995). As a result, even the "successful" projects of the UAIMs that received second loans do not appear to be economically empowering women in any significant way. Women who participate in the projects receive very little pay for the two or three hours of daily labor they put in—sometimes as little as ten or fifteen dollars a month. Free bread or discounted chickens may be the most tangible benefits. The pressure

to repay the loans quickly and to save money for other improvements—
say, a truck to increase bread distribution—have limited financial returns for project members. Perhaps the most important "returns" have
been the small advances women have made in the ways they have subtly
challenged gender inequalities in the relations of power at home and in
their *ejidos*.

Domestic Conflict and Participation in the Larger World   Women I
interviewed and observed often spoke about the difficulties of participating in political organizing and development projects because of their responsibilities as wives and mothers. Domestic relations and the heavy
burdens they shouldered at home were pressing concerns for women in
their individual lives. Most of the productive projects of the UAIMs required women to put in volunteer labor of at least eight hours per week
as well as to attend meetings of their local UAIMs. Representatives
from the UAIMs in the Women's Council had to leave town to go to
the *ejido* union building in Ahuacatlán for monthly meetings. Women
who were serving as part of construction committees or marketing
committees for their projects would also have to leave town to purchase materials or negotiate with bureaucrats in the state capital for
resources. The political difficulties women faced in getting their projects
off the ground and maintaining them also required them to leave their
homes. This was not looked upon favorably by many men, although if
the time away from home resulted in some form of income, it could be
tolerated. In 1995, the president of the *ejido* union said of the women's
projects: "We men don't want the women to leave and work. We let them
participate in the projects because it was just for a little while and it
brought in some income. The advisors told us we should let them do it,
so it's fine."

For many women, participating in the projects is their first experience outside their homes and gives them a sense of accomplishment and
a reason to break their domestic routine. A discussion I had with a
woman in the community of Marquesado illustrates the importance of
this process.

At the time of our discussion, Ana María Rodríguez was thirty-nine
years old and lived with her husband, one daughter, and father-in-law.
Her husband worked as a bracero in the United States. The UAIM in the
community of Marquesado began a tortilla factory with funds from the
"Women in Solidarity" program, channeled through female leaders of
the CNC. The tortilla factory had been up and running for about a year
when we talked.

Woman from the Marquesado UAIM weighing tortillas to be sold to a young customer. The tortilla factory supplies women in the local community.

The eleven women who run the factory work from two to six hours per day, depending on the season. During the corn harvest season they sell fewer tortillas because women are making more of their own. They work in teams of two people per week, so they have to work about one week per month. They earned the equivalent of about thirty dollars a week, for the weeks they worked, plus getting free tortillas. For Ana María, who barely finished elementary school, the project has been quite significant.

Lynn: What did you learn in the project, if anything?

Ana María: I didn't know how to run anything before the project. I never left the house. I learned how to work the machines and everything. The main reason I participated was to earn some money for our family and now I am earning some.

Lynn: Has your family been supportive of your working here?

Ana María: My husband supports my participation, but others do not. They complain that their wives aren't around to do their work at home and they scold them or even hit them. This even happens now to the current president of our UAIM. Her husband constantly scolds her for participating.

Domestic conflict can result in physical confrontations between men and women as men threaten or actually beat women for their participation in organizing efforts. This was reported by women from several communities in the Women's Union in Nayarit. Other women reported going to the offending man's house and confronting him as a group, convincing him of the utility of the woman's participation in productive projects.

A few women stated that they came to an understanding with their husbands. Eulalia, forty-eight years old and a UAIM president in the community of Jomulco stated:

I got married in 1969 and endured ten years of subjugation. I had to do whatever my husband wanted. When I couldn't take it anymore, after we got more active in the ejido *union, I talked to him. I told him, "You do one kind of work and I do another. Let me be." Now we are getting along.*

Women's participation in productive economic projects and in the politics of the UAIMs and the *ejido* union increased their workload. This is ironic since the idea of grassroots development projects for women is that they will somehow make women's lives easier. In some cases, women are performing triple labor as activists, agricultural wage laborers, and unpaid domestic laborers—a phenomenon which has been noted elsewhere in studies of women who are activists in popular movements (see Stephen 1992). A majority of the forty-three women I interviewed in the Women's Union in Nayarit reported that they coped with conflicts between domestic chores and political work by simply getting up earlier and preparing food in advance. Thirty-seven-year-old Natividad, from Chapalilla, said:

Finally our husbands let us go, but they didn't lift a hand to help us at home. It meant we had to pay a personal price. We have to get up really early in the morning to cook everything that is needed during the day so that all of their needs are met.

A few women reported that their husbands split the cooking with them, and one man reported that he had learned how to cook and that his marriage had improved in the process. While such renegotiations of the domestic division of labor appear to be happening in some households, the topic has not reached the organizing agenda of the Women's Council.

Political Marginality   The reception that women from the council got within their own *ejidos* and by the *ejido* union was sometimes very hostile. All had to struggle for a voice and a vote within their individual *ejidos* and within the larger UELC. Women interviewed in twelve of the fourteen UAIMs that make up the Women's Council all had stories of how they had been challenged by male *ejidatarios* within their *ejidos* as they tried to carry out their projects. In some cases they were denied access to *ejido* land, in other cases they had equipment such as sewing machines taken away from them after the projects were started, and in one extreme case they were even locked out of the *ejido*-owned room they met in and had to coerce someone into letting them in every time they wanted to meet.

In almost all the fourteen communities in the Women's Council, support for the women's group was dependent on men who were in leadership positions. They were usually the husbands of women active in the local UAIM. When these supportive men were rotated out of their positions of influence, such as commissioner of communal land, women often had to reclaim their land. In one community, a regional politician struck back at *ejido* members who did not support his political campaign, sending in his allies to squat on a piece of land which was designated for a women's tortilla factory. Women in the UAIM spent almost a year petitioning to retrieve their land. They gained significant political experience in the process. One of the women involved related the story:

We had meetings with the governor, a lot of meetings. Sometimes we would go with ten or twenty or thirty women. We would fill up two big trucks just with women. We had some savings we had earned from selling tamales, having fairs, and selling our vegetables. We have spent all our resources and lot of time going to the capital trying to work this out.

Many of the UAIMs were also used as political footballs in local political struggles. In the community of Chapalilla, women in the UAIM got caught in a political quarrel between the PRI and the Partido Auténtico de la Revolución Mexicana (PARM), a semiofficial party that provides an outlet for local disagreements with the PRI.

Four women in the Chapalilla UAIM who were involved with establishing an agricultural plot were assaulted by members of the PARM political opposition. One of the women was pregnant. In the *ejido* of Uzeta, *ejidatarios* voted to turn over a local building to women in the UAIM to use as a tortilla factory. According to a local leader of the UAIM, when it became clear that the credit made available would go directly to the UAIM and not to the *ejido*, male *ejidatarios* became angry and forbade their wives to participate. *Ejidatarios* had thought the women in the tortilla factory would be working for them. When they discovered this was not the case, they withdrew their support and actively resisted the project. In short, women's dependent status both within their *ejidos* and within the larger *ejido* union put severe constraints on their organizing projects, but it also made them determined to secure the rights of representation and access to land they were supposed to have.

Reproducing Male Political Culture   The fact that the Women's Council of the UELC is partially dependent on and integrated with the largely male organizational structure of the *ejido* union is also reflected in the style or political culture of the UAIM meetings and of the meetings of the Women's Council. Observation of several local UAIM meetings as well as of a larger meeting of the Women's Council revealed a meeting style dominated by one leader who narrated past accomplishments, and future aims, and encouraged little discussion. Exchanges that involved questions were flavored with an attitude of friendly authority by the person chairing the meeting and, in many cases, humble ignorance by the questioner. In interviews, some women elected as leaders in UAIMs also expressed notions of superiority and distance from the women they worked with. In part this was because of educational and skill differences. Women elected to leadership positions generally had more education, often having finished at least the equivalent of middle school or high school. Several local leaders were observed constantly telling other women, "Fijense bien niñas" (pay attention girls); these leaders had taken on the role of an authoritative teacher who expected obedience. Workshops and hands-on types of activities, however, seemed to generate more spontaneous and participatory discussion.

In the case of the larger Women's Council, while there were often two or three representatives from each community, one woman from each community was clearly the acknowledged leader and her opinion was consistently followed. Few new proposals or debates came from the wider group of women, the majority of whom did not speak. Two male representatives from the UELC were also present, the secretary and the treasurer, and their opinions were often solicited.

The wider meetings of the Women's Council as well as the smaller formal meetings of individual UAIMs observed in 1991 tended to reproduce the style of the mostly male *ejido* meetings and *ejido* union meetings in which an authority, usually the president of the group, dominated discussion while the others usually agreed with him.

Conclusions   Women of the UELC entered an organizing process where there was little overt challenge to a dominant gender ideology that defined them as wives and mothers dedicated to improving the material and social conditions of their families. Although as an organization they did not generate a gender-based ideology, they did broaden their political roles and increase their participation in local *ejidos*, in the *ejido* union, and in political campaigns. In the process, they spent long periods of time discussing the gendered relations of power—at home, in the *ejidos*, and in the larger world. Although their questions about gender were not always clearly formulated, their ongoing experience incorporated a questioning and renegotiation of gender roles along with the day-to-day reality of running their projects and struggling to find a political voice.

The various identities of individual women in the Women's Council with respect to party affiliation, economic position, education, and family interests were evident in the variety of ways in which they attempted to accomplish their goals and in which they described one another. At times women within one UAIM would be in conflict or the UAIMs that made up the council would disagree—as, for example, in the debate about whether or not the Women's Council should be autonomous from the *ejido* union. Different UAIMs within the council also had varying levels of experience. In the indigenous community of San Jerónimo Jomulco, where women had a longer tradition of agrarian struggle, the UAIM is rooted in the previous experience of a core of activist women. They are important in maintaining the UAIM and its chicken-raising project through the ups and downs of economic and political crisis.

Women in the UELC never participated in opposition organizations or parties and had little contact with Mexican women's movements. For the most part the participants in the Women's Council belonged to the PRI and to various factions of the CNC, although in 1995 that relationship began to sour. None of these factions seriously challenged the government or made any effort to organize women on a grassroots level until the 1990s, when the CNC reinvigorated its women's programs in some states in an apparent effort to bolster its own position vis-à-vis independent organizations and to mobilize women's support for government programs. The organization of women in the UAIMs and in the Women's Council did not result in a focused challenge to gender subordination, but it certainly did have an impact on gender relations as women struggled for simple representation and for permission to leave home and carry out their economic projects.

One of the greatest obstacles to women's continued personal and political development was the continued structural dependence of their projects on government agencies and personnel. The Women's Council, its constituent UAIMs, and their projects have counted on various state officials as their allies since the very beginning. While officials from the Ministry of Agrarian Reform, the Ministry of Agriculture and Water Resources, the CNC and, later, the National Solidarity Program could serve as counterweights to entrenched male resistance in local *ejidos* and in the UELC, their involvement clearly had costs. The women in the UAIMs were constantly claimed as political capital and constituents by various state actors, and over time they saw that their own long-term interests did not often coincide with those of the officials they worked with. Nevertheless, as with CONAMUP, their ability to continue to extract resources from state programs, particularly in the 1990s when resources became scarce, allowed their projects to continue to function. This is an accomplishment in and of itself. And it is within their daily experience with the small economic projects—the daily breadbaking, beekeeping and harvesting, tortilla making, the sale of their products and the improvement of their small enterprises—that women continue to question a wide range of inequities in their lives.

By participating in a project as simple as a small turkey farm, women increased their workload and added to their reproductive responsibilities. This put a strain on their domestic relations and at some level resulted in attempts to renegotiate the domestic division of labor. They also questioned political structures that left them marginalized in *ejido* and *ejido* union meetings within their communities. The women who participated in the Women's Council have been in process. They are not the same now as when they began to participate. The process of participating has in part transformed who they are. The case of the women of Ahuacatlán, Nayarit, suggests that the path to grassroots change may not always be direct, but that the potential for transformation can be found in even the most conventional places. If the women of Nayarit are able to sustain their projects, they will have a continued space for the exploration of alternatives. This may bear even more radical results in the future.

Doña Kata Moreno and Aurora Cruz
Lázaro Cárdenas Ejido Union

Doña Kata is a chipper seventy-year-old woman.[1] She has been very active in the Unión de Ejidos "Lázaro Cárdenas" since its formation in the 1970s. In 1967, after working as a domestic servant in several large cities, she returned to her hometown of Jomulco to claim her grandparents' land and become a *comunera*. The community was then engaged in a struggle for the restoration of communal lands. In 1965 Jomulco had been declared a "comunidad indígena" and anyone who could demonstrate that he or she was a descendant was eligible to receive title to communal land. This struggle is briefly described in Chapter 5 above. Kata had returned to claim land which her grandparents had purchased but which was to be converted to communal property under its new legal definition as part of an "indigenous community." Unfortunately, the struggle for communal land in San Jerónimo Jomulco pitted small property holders against those filing communal land claims, but left large landholdings intact.

Before the formation of the Women's Council of the Lázaro Cárdenas Ejido Union, Doña Kata was a pivotal member of a local women's organization that worked within the community of Jomulco for fifteen years, later becoming a UAIM. While she cannot officially belong to a UAIM, since she is a *comunera*, Kata has been a leader and advisor to women in the community of Jomulco, where there is a long tradition of women working together. Doña Kata served as an advisor to and supporter of the Women's Council highlighted in Chapter 5.

On the day of our conversation she wears her white hair in a long braid that trails below her waist. She is wearing a cotton dress, a smock apron and, loosely draped around her shoulders, a black shawl. It is late afternoon. As the sun fades, the air inside her adobe house grows cool. I pull a cotton shawl up over my shoulders to cover the sleeveless cotton

Recorded December 12, 1990, in Comunidad Indígena Jomulco, Jala, Nayarit, Mexico.

Doña Kata Moreno (second from left) relaxes with friends from the San Jerónimo Jomulco UAIM.

blouse I have on with a skirt. Pilar López, a Mexico City–based researcher who is working with me in Ahuacatlán, sits on a low stool in jeans and a T-shirt. We are sitting near the front door to Doña Kata's house, facing the street. Kata does not want to miss any of the action going by. She likes to keep track of who is coming and going near the center of town where she lives.

The second part of our conversation takes place at the home of Aurora Cruz. Aurora is about forty-eight years old. She is a charismatic woman with a powerful voice and presence. People listen to her when she speaks. Her black hair is worn in a single braid. Like Kata, she is dressed in a cotton dress with an apron over it. Aurora participated in the formation of the *ejido* union and was an important figure in the Jomulco women's group, which went from being a women's auxiliary within a CNC-based regional peasant organization to a UAIM. She spent years trying with other women to get a turkey farm constructed and functioning.

As we begin, Kata talks about her land and the history of the two-room adobe house we are sitting in.

Lynn: Do you own the land we are sitting on here?

Kata: This was my grandparents' land and home.

Lynn: So you inherited this house and land from your grandparents?

Kata: Yes.

Lynn: Is it the custom here to give inheritance equally to sons and daughters?

Kata: That depends on whether or not there are sons. When there are sons, they inherit the house and the land. For example, my father was from a family with three sons, and they got the land.

Lynn: So did you inherit the house when your parents died?

Kata: My parents died while my grandparents were still alive. We were the only grandchildren my father's parents had. There were eleven of us, but only eight of us lived. Some of us lived with my grandparents. I lived with my grandparents and so did two of my brothers who now live in the other part of this house, here in front.

Lynn: So your grandparents divided up the house between you?

Kata: Yes. I got this part and a brother of mine got the other part. He died, but his family still lives here. Other siblings inherited other land and houses nearby on this block.

Lynn: Did you inherit any land to plant on as well?

Kata: My grandparents didn't leave the land directly to me. The land was supposed to be inherited by my uncle, who was a priest, by my father and by his sister, but she died. Since a priest doesn't work land and the sister died, this left all the land for my father. When he died, the land was left to my brothers; but one of them couldn't work in the countryside because he was handicapped, and the others stayed on the coast and didn't return. I came back here with the idea of defending my grandparents' land when they converted the town to an indigenous community. We didn't have titles for the property my grandparents owned, but everyone knew where their land was. . . .

Lynn: How old were you when you came back to claim your grandparents' land?

Kata: Maybe thirty, or more than thirty, because I was born in 1920. I came back here in 1965.

Lynn: I think you were forty-five when you came back. You returned and joined the newly formed indigenous community in order to hold onto your grandparents' land.

Kata: That's right.

Lynn: Were there any other women who did the same thing?

Kata: Three of the women are still alive.

Lynn: How many women were claiming communal land when you first returned?

Kata: There were about six.

Lynn: Were they all unmarried?

Kata: Four were *solteras* (unmarried), and two were widows. They were all there to claim their land rights and the land they owned. . . .

Lynn: Why did you feel it was important to defend your grandparents' land rights?

Kata: My grandparents were very poor, hardworking people who bought this land with the sweat of their brows. I remember my grandmother saying to me, "Listen, my granddaughter, we got all of our land, our house, and our animals through a great deal of personal sacrifice. So please take care of it." I always hear her words in my head.

Lynn: When you returned, they were going to turn over the land your grandparents had planted to other people?

Kata: If I hadn't returned here, they would have given the lands my grandparents planted to other *comuneros,* people who claimed membership in the indigenous community. Now their land is written down in my name in the book which documents how the land was divided up when they created the indigenous community here in 1967.

Lynn: I want to change the subject a little bit here. I imagine that many of the women here are married. You told me that you never married? Was that something you chose? Did you prefer it that way?

Kata: No. It wasn't really something I chose. It came about because of the obligations I felt toward my parents. My mother died when I was still young enough to be unmarried. My brother was an invalid. He couldn't walk. He was only six years old when my mother died. I thought my father would remarry and take his children with him and that if I found the right person to marry, I would get married. Unfortunately, it didn't turn out that way. Two years after my mother died, my father got sick. He died four years later.

Lynn: So you took care of him?

Kata: I took care of him, but I was also working in a store to make money. My sister took care of him too. My sister and I were in charge of him and my brother at a very young age. That's how we spent our youth, taking care of my father and brother and working. After you get older and you look back, you can see how difficult situations like this are. My time to get married just passed me by. . . . Apart from this situation, I remember some advice my grandmother gave to me while my parents were still alive. She said to me, "If you don't get married, don't ever leave this house." She said that because the house was mine. She said,

"Don't go to live with your brother or your sister-in-law. Stay here in your own house because it is yours."

Lynn: You really admired this grandmother, didn't you?

Kata: Yes. And now I can see that she was right. All the advice she gave me was magnificent.

Lynn: How old were you when your grandmother died?

Kata: She died in 1944. My mother died right after my grandmother, and then my father got sick and died. My oldest brothers were already dead by this time. So during this period I was taking care of everyone. I was in my twenties.

Lynn: So did there ever come a moment when you accepted the fact that you probably would not get married?

Kata: Yes, absolutely. There came a moment when I didn't think about marriage anymore. I dedicated myself to domestic work, to working where I could, to cooking for people or selling things to eat—like here on the corner next to the theater, (where) I sold little snacks. Sometimes my nieces who live in Villa Hidalgo would come here and help me out before they were married. Now that they are married they can't come, because they have their own families to take care of.

Lynn: Was it easier to be involved as a *comunera* since you weren't married?

Kata: Yes, it was. . . .

Lynn: Can you tell us a little bit about the formation of the union of *ejidos* and your participation?

Kata: I first participated as a delegate to the union. There were five delegates in the beginning. I was one of the first delegates and I participated openly in organizing the union of *ejidos*. That is when those young organizers were here from PIDER. They came here from Mexico City and the governor kicked them out. After they left, we founded the Lázaro Cárdenas Ejido Union. It was a beautiful process that we went through in each *ejido*. Each day, some of us would go to a community. Many people participated in community visits to talk about joining the union. Even women went. I visited with three different *ejidos*.

Pilar: What did you tell people when you visited?

Kata: We told them that the *ejidatarios* were living in a very depressing situation and that we needed to organize ourselves and fight together to improve our lives. We told people about the government resources we were supposed to have access to. At that time, the only people whose lives seemed to be improving were the state governors and their senators. They were living high on the hog. When we started telling people about all the things that they had a right to and weren't receiving—like credit, loans, and fertilizer—they began to get angry and discontented. Then we had the period where the government bank didn't pay us for our harvests or for planting and there was a shortage of fertilizer. Only the rich could get fertilizer. The fertilizer shortage really helped to unify us so that, one by one, the *ejidos* joined and we went to protest in front of the Governor's Palace and at the government fertilizer offices.

Lynn: What concrete actions did you engage in?

Kata: One of the things we decided was to take over the fertilizer-distribution offices in the state capital of Tepic.

Lynn: How many people went there?

Kata: All kinds of people went. Men, women, children. We went in buses. There were about twenty people from our community, and fifteen, ten, twelve, and so on from each *ejido*.

Lynn: So there were at least a hundred forty to a hundred fifty?

Kata: Yes, at least. We divided ourselves up between occupying the Governor's Palace and the fertilizer offices and we were successful. We won the rights to distribute the fertilizer, and so more people wanted to join. Even though the original PIDER advisors left, we still got visits from other organizers who came to see us from Sonora and Sinaloa. They came to help us get unified.

Lynn: And through this process were you the only woman who was a delegate in the union?

Kata: Yes.

Lynn: And did the men take you seriously?

Kata: Yes, they always did.

Lynn: Why do you think that they treated you well, but when the women's group from your community went to the union for help in continuing their turkey-raising project, the union treated them poorly?

Kata: The way I see it is that they don't want to see women making any progress or thinking for themselves. They always kept us quiet. But there comes a moment when you say, "Why should we always be subject to their opinions?" Some of us took on the responsibility of telling them that they don't have any reason to oppose the decisions that we make just because they are "muy machitos" (just to show off their manhood). We have to keep moving ahead with our work.

Lynn: Let's return to your previous experience as a delegate representing men in the union. Do you think that if you had been representing women instead of men that you would have been treated differently?

Kata: As you know, when the women from my community asked the union for help in moving forward with their turkey-raising project, they suddenly turned deaf. So we said to them, "Don't be so extreme. Your children and your families will benefit from our project. . . . Stop being so stubborn and help us out." So finally we convinced them, and some of them started to say "Yes, let's help out the women. They are going to help us too." That is when we could start working on the project again. . . .

The second part of our conversation takes place in Aurora Cruz' house. Aurora is present along with another woman named Mercedes, who is about forty-five years old. They both have their black shawls wrapped around their heads to guard against the rain coming down outside. For the most part they listen, deferring to Kata. Aurora occasionally joins in.

Lynn: You began telling me before about how women in the indigenous community of San Jerónimo Jomulco were organized well before the formation of the UAIM.

Kata: The community was legally constituted in 1965, and the women began to work together in 1967. We formed a peasant organization in 1967 that included all of the *comuneros* (those with access to communal land) and their wives. It was a statewide organization called the Brigada Aldolfo López Mateos.

Lynn: And how did women participate in this?

Kata: We formed a directorate that included a president, a general secretary, and yours truly as the treasurer. We started to work together.

Lynn: Was there anyone in particular who came and promoted the organization?

Women in unison: The CNC.

Kata: It was the CNC (National Peasant Confederation). They encouraged us. In 1967 we began to work together. We got together every Friday. Each woman who participated paid dues of twenty-five centavos, and this money was given to the leaders to carry out their work. To help them pay for their expenses, travel, or whatever. Look, I still have the books. Here's a page from a meeting from April 12, 1967. I was the treasurer and I wrote everything down. So we organized ourselves. For, as Señor Arvizo from the CNC told us, "Organize yourselves so that you lose your shame and fear. Organize yourselves so that in the not so distant future you yourselves can do something for your community."

Lynn: What kinds of work did you do in the organization?

Kata: We would get all of the women together every week and discuss what was going on in the community.

Lynn: So you didn't just focus on things particular to women, but talked about community politics as well?

Kata: Yes. We talked about all kinds of politics. And we made our opinions known.

Aurora and Mercedes: Yes, we did.

Lynn: Did women go to community meetings?

Kata: Well, the women participated with the women, and the men with the men, because that is how they set up the meetings. Each was separate. We formed a committee, and the women who participated said to the men, "We are very glad to participate, but we want you to tell us in a general meeting with all of the men the reasons why we are going to organize as women." The women said this because our husbands still had a lot of machismo and they didn't let us leave the house.

Lynn: Was it difficult to get women to participate in the beginning because they weren't used to going out?

Kata: No. It wasn't. Most of the husbands let their wives come to the meetings.

Lynn: What did you do to convince the men?

Kata: We put together a plan to convince them that women's participation was important. They started to see that women's participation in politics and social events was urgent and necessary. No one here was accustomed to participating in politics or in social groups. The initiator of the group, Concepción Aguilar, who is still alive, came and told the men to shed their machismo. She told them to allow their wives to participate in the women's group so that the community would be stronger. After that, little by little the men began to give permission to their wives to participate. That's how we came to participate in social events, in political events, and we were able to initiate the turkey-raising project. There were twenty-five women or more who came to the meetings. Here are the lists of those who attended the meetings.

Lynn: What kinds of social activities did you undertake?

Kata: The first activity was to sell supper in the local plaza. Then we also organized raffles. When the *compañeros* had to go to Mexico City, we would each donate five pesos, which was a lot of money. Everyone would give what they could. Some people would give two pesos, some three, some five. That is how we helped to finance the work of the men as well.

Lynn: What kinds of political activities did women participate in?

Kata: Well, we participated in the elections and campaigns for mayors of the municipality. It was hard for married women. Since I am not married, I can just say, "Well, I'm going," and I walk out the door. Married women have to get their husband's permission to leave. The men finally came to trust the women who were leaders and would let their wives go with them.

Lynn: Did women have a hard time leaving their houses to participate?

Kata: When we started participating in political campaigns and our other activities, some of the husbands began to see that there was nothing wrong with women participating in the community and doing more than just staying at home.

Lynn: When women were leaving to participate in political campaigns, did their husbands help them out by cooking?

Three women in unison: No. They didn't then and they don't now. They don't like to help us out.

Kata: No. The women would tell their husbands ahead of time that they were leaving and would leave everything ready.

Aurora: We still do that. When we are going somewhere, we get up really early in the morning, maybe at four o'clock, and we make the food and leave it. If we have older daughters, then they help us out, grinding corn into tortilla dough, making the tortillas, and heating them up for everyone.

Lynn: What kind of political support did you get from the candidates you worked with?

Kata: Well, some of the candidates we supported didn't win. So we didn't ask them for anything. When a candidate we supported did win, we asked him to help us with our turkey farm. And one of the municipal presidents did support us. . . .

Lynn: When did the women here in Jomulco get a piece of land they could work on together?

For the next five minutes, the three women argue about who was municipal president of Jomulco when they went to request a piece of land. Finally someone breaks in.

Kata: Well, the truth is that the idea of getting a piece of land for the women came from a group of ten organizers who were here from Mexico City. They went around to all of the *ejidos* and gave people ideas about what to ask for.

Lynn: So you hadn't asked for a piece of land yourselves before they arrived?

Aurora: No. They came here and, just like you, they were going from *ejido* to *ejido* and community to community to see what kinds of projects could be successfully carried out. After they were here, they gave the women the idea that they should have a piece of land too. . . .

Lynn: And there weren't any problems when you asked for the land?

Kata: Right. There wasn't any problem because the plot of land was one where I had the rights. When I realized that they had given the land to the women, I didn't contest it at all because I realized that the land was going to benefit the community. . . . I wasn't here when they made the transfer. It was communal land. I was in Villa Hidalgo. . . .

Lynn: How did the women organize around the land?

Kata: It started when the organizers were here. We began work on the turkey farm. All of the women got together and we worked clearing the ground and dug out a hole for the foundation. Some women worked carrying sand, others hauled water to the site. We constructed a foundation one meter deep. This was in the early 1970s; but then we stopped working. The project stopped because the governor kicked out the organizers. They were doing good work.

Aurora: That governor never helped us. He wouldn't listen to anyone from this community.

Kata: These were the same organizers who helped us start the *ejido* union. They made us realize what we had to fight for as peasants. They helped us to understand our rights. It was around the same time that we had a mass meeting and action in the offices of FERTIMEX.

Aurora: Then, when they kicked out the organizers, the project stopped. We were just sort of stunned and saddened.

Kata: The women kept on meeting, but we didn't have the same kind of enthusiasm as before.

Aurora: Then later in 1982, I was named as president of the Women's League (Liga Feminina) of the Adolfo López Mateos League. . . . At the time, we were trying to get our turkey farm started again. The governor gave us some materials and the mayor of Jomulco did also, but we couldn't get much help in terms of labor. We had a lot of internal problems in our organization, because there was a lot of machismo. The commissioner of communal lands (*comisariado de bienes comunales*) didn't help us out. It was his responsibility because it was a project on communal lands. When they assigned men to come and work on the turkey farm as part of their *cargo* responsibilities,[2] they wouldn't come. . . . They didn't think what we were doing was important because we are women. . . .

Lynn: How did you come to be organized in a UAIM?

Kata: Well, it was because of the efforts of an organizer who came to visit, a woman.

Aurora: And the other organizers as well. When these people were here from Mexico City helping us to organize the *ejido* union, it began. Before, it used to be that the man was the *ejidatario* and the women were only recognized as wives of *ejidatarios*. But when these organizers were here and they went from house to house, they held meetings where they offered ideas to the women about what they could do. After this, the women were better organized than before.

Kata: And then later, there was a woman from Sonora who came to visit the union. . . . We invited her to come and she realized that there were a lot of women getting organized here. She told us, "I like your organization." She came here once in a while, I don't know why, and she pushed us to organize ourselves and present ourselves as an organization to the union of *ejidos*. I think this was in 1983. . . .

Aurora: Then in 1984 or 1985 this woman and her husband helped us create a document that made us into a UAIM. They took care of it in Mexico City. . . . We finally finished our project in 1986. We got our first bunch of little turkeys. . . .

Lynn: Can you tell me how and why the Women's Council of the Lázaro Cárdenas Ejido Union was organized?

Kata: The Women's Council was organized with the help of the *ejido* union. It was when the women organizers were here, (with) their husbands and several other people. They helped to formalize the UAIMs and then the Women's Council. The council was formed in 1988 with fourteen UAIMs. The men who were leaders in the *ejido* union really started the Women's Council.

Lynn: How were the meetings? Did you participate in them?

Kata: They were great meetings, and we were working together really well. I thought our projects were excellent, but then we began to have problems. Things seemed to go well for about two years, but then the problems began.

Lynn: How did the problems begin?

Kata: I think it started when the women who helped us to organize began suggesting that the Women's Council should become independent of the *ejido* union. Some women agreed with this idea, but others said no. They said, "If the *ejido* union supported us and helped us to get started, how can we turn our backs on it? . . .

Aurora: The real problem came when these organizers told us that we should become independent. Some of us just didn't want that.

Lynn: How did participating in the council and all the women's groups feel to you personally? What was your experience?

Kata: Well, I think working with the women's organizations and working in the community have changed me. I started doing things in the community when I was in my forties and now I am seventy. I used to be very timid. When I was elected treasurer of the first women's group and had to go to Mexico City on business for the group, I was really afraid and embarrassed. People here in Jomulco didn't approve of women being active in politics and going to Mexico City. But I have learned a lot. I know that it is important to decide to do things, to make changes. I know what the problems in my community are and what needs to be done to fix them. I am not silent anymore.

PART III BRAZIL

CHAPTER 6

Class, Gender, and Autonomy
The Rural Women Workers' Movement of Southern Brazil

Political and cultural context can be extremely important in shaping the content of women's movements and ultimately encouraging their autonomy. One of the most impressive regional movements of rural women is found in southern Brazil in the state of Rio Grande do Sul. The Movimento de Mulheres Trabalhadoras Rurais (MMTR, Rural Women Workers' Movement), begun in 1989, grew out of women's activism in land-recovery movements, antidam movements, labor unions, and church-based organizations. By 1992 the movement had over thirty thousand members and was functioning in more than 110 counties. It has an active local leadership of about five hundred, making it one of the strongest regional women's movements in Brazil, and outstanding in the Americas. The movement's agenda has moved from procuring equal working conditions and benefits for rural women to reproductive health rights, domestic violence, representation of women in the political system, and general women's rights. Here we will try to understand the important factors that resulted in the MMTR having an agenda that ultimately challenged gender hierarchy and allowed issues such as abortion and women's sexuality to be taken up in a movement that was initially nourished by the Catholic church.

Four key points will be explored to clarify the evolution of this organization and its varied meanings to its base members and leadership:

1. *The MMTR of southern Brazil has its roots in a strong opposition organized in rural labor unions and in the landless movement with ties to the Partido dos Trabalhadores (PT, Workers' Party). These movements share a strong ideology that emphasizes confronting the state and organizing the rural working class.*

2. *Leaders of the MMTR had significant and consistent contact with activists from similar movements throughout Brazil. They also worked consistently with staff from NGOs who were familiar with feminism and who encouraged them to broaden their organizational agenda to change oppressive gender roles.*

3. *During their involvement in other movements, leaders of the MMTR were marginalized. Having analyzed their experience, they have deliberately built an organizational model and structure that will not leave out the women they are trying to organize.*

4. *The MMTR emerged as an autonomous women's movement that related to but was no longer dictated to by other regional movements, including those of the landless, the rural labor unions, and the church.*

Before we discuss the specific history of the MMTR, its emergence will be related to the gendered political economy of southern Brazil.

Economic Development and the Gendered Division of Labor in Southern Brazil   After the 1964 military coup in Brazil, the agricultural sector was reoriented to serve as a market for agrochemicals and machinery produced in the prioritized industrial sector. It was also supposed to produce export crops that would help reduce Brazil's foreign debt (Spindel 1987: 52–53). A large-scale credit program provided subsidized credits and fiscal incentives to landed power holders while the military's national security program managed agrarian conflicts (Grzybowski 1990: 20–21). Most assessments of Brazil's agricultural modernization program find that it has exacerbated socioeconomic inequalities. The subsidized credit was unequal and was used primarily by those who already had land to acquire still more land. Land prices rose 2,000 percent between 1971 and 1977 (Martine 1983, cited in Spindel 1987: 53). By 1985, the .09 percent of the agricultural enterprises in Brazil that had 1,000 hectares or more controlled 44 percent of the land. The 53 percent of the agricultural enterprises that had less than 10 hectares accounted for 2.7 percent of the total land (Grzybowski 1990: 21).

In the southern part of Brazil, the economy followed these same general trends, with the notable exception of the preservation of a small but significant group of peasant households which have been able to become part of the capitalized smallholder sector. The remainder have become landless and/or migrated elsewhere, primarily to the Amazonian region. Beginning in the late 1950s, the agricultural economy of the state of Rio Grande do Sul changed significantly. As in much of the south, the rich, fertile landscape of the southern part of Rio Grande do Sul was gradually consolidated into larger farms; mechanized production of soybeans and wheat pushed out small-scale subsistence agriculture.

In Rio Grande do Sul, land fragmentation brought about by inheritance, continued colonization, and population growth has resulted in a significant landless population. It is estimated that in all of Brazil there are over 10 million landless or nearly landless people (Grzybowski 1990: 21). Other estimates place this figure as high as 24 million (McManus and Schlabach 1991:174). By 1989, 26,466 peasants in Rio Grande do Sul were reported to be involved in land conflicts, more than in any of Brazil's other states (*Quinzena* 1990:8; Brooke 1990). The state is home to one of the largest landless movements in the country, the Movimento dos Trabalhadores Rurais sem Terra (MST, Landless Rural Workers' Movement).

In those parts of Rio Grande do Sul that were not suitable for large-scale, mechanized agriculture, smallholders were able to hang onto their land and some were even able to mechanize, purchasing small tractors and other machinery that allowed them to make the transition to capitalized agriculture. It was not in capital's interest to completely destroy the smallholder sector, which still provides 70 percent of basic foodstuff production in addition to raw materials for agro-industry. Smallholders have been integrated into the process of agro-industry, and although this allows smallholders to survive, it is highly exploitative of family labor and makes small producers dependent on agro-industry (Spindel 1987: 54). The hilly, northern part of the state has retained a significant population of smallholders. It also contains a young generation of landless people, some of whom have joined the MST in occupying former ranches and creating new communities in such locations as Anonni, Nova Ronda Alta, and Cruz Alta. These different landholding patterns and levels of political activism are associated with varying patterns of gender relations at home.

While little has been written on household decisionmaking among smallholders in rural Brazil, activists and feminists have a different assessment than that of some rural sociologists. In a discussion of family decisionmaking, the sociologist Mauro William Barbosa de Almeida states that the Brazilian peasant family is relatively democratic (1986: 71, 77) and that his findings support Santos' suggestion (1978:32) that "'the fact that the peasant family is a collective enterprise implies many times that decisions about labor allocation are communal,' indicating that peasant women also participate in work decisions." Almeida states that it is illusory to look for social inequality within the peasant household; in his own experience, he says, the authoritarian declarations of male heads of household do not correspond to the practical reality (1986:71). My research and the experience of MMTR activists suggests otherwise. Household decisionmaking is not necessarily democratic, and as women become politicized domestic conflict increases between men and women.

Smallholder women at various levels of the MMTR stated that household decisionmaking is generally dominated by men. Men usually hold the title to land as well. Literature from the MMTR as well as that from other rural women's unions in Brazil demand equal decisionmaking power in the household and the right to hold land titles. Discussions and role-playing skits I observed in local meetings of the MMTR, however, revealed that gender roles in household decisionmaking and the titling of land, machinery, and houses to women varied by ethnic group. Women of Italian, Polish, and German descent stated that men dominated household decisionmaking and that only sons inherited land and agricultural machinery. Women of Portuguese-Brazilian descent stated that they had received land from their parents and felt they had a more equal say in household decisionmaking.

The gendered division of labor within land occupations and settlements is different from that of smallholder households. In the case of land occupations which have turned into new settlements, the prolonged process of political struggle, the active physical presence of women in land occupations and confrontations with the police and army, and an emphasis on collective production have changed some aspects of the gendered division of labor. In many settlements, there is an emphasis on collective production, reciprocal work relations, and property sharing. Women work directly in agricultural production, and specific economic projects (e.g., milking co-ops, craft production, vegetable farming) have been created for women. Decisionmaking with respect to production is done by consensus among those who work together in the group. Production groups often include men and women. In some MST settlements, entire families (including children) attend community meetings where productive activities are discussed. In general, male-directed households no longer appear to be the norm. In some settlements, though, women are still struggling to be named with men as having use rights in collective land and to be included in community meetings.

The Gendered Politics of Grassroots Movements in Southern Brazil
The decade of the 1980s was an important one in the political history of Brazil. A resurgence of grassroots social movements resulted in significant challenges to the status quo of government. The depth and breadth

of the change in Brazil via the creation of a network of social movement organizations, many aligned with the opposition Workers' Party, provided a base for the fomentation of new rural women's organizations.

In the state of Rio Grande do Sul, the late 1970s and 1980s saw the rise of a variety of grassroots social movements that openly confronted the state with demands for land, resources, and political recognition. The MST, founded in the early 1980s, occupied abandoned ranches and then pressured the government to legalize their claim to the land and legitimize their resettled communities. Rural workers who had belonged to official state unions began to join the rural branch of the CUT labor federation (Central Unica dos Trabalhadores), formed in the mid-1980s as part of Brazil's new unionism. An antidam movement mobilized those who were displaced by large-scale flooding to lobby the government electricity commission (ELETROSUL), take over their buildings, and demand the right to participate in future regional planning (see Marcondes de Moraes 1994; Z. Navarro 1994). Finally, the liberation theology branch of the Catholic church continued the work begun in the 1960s and 1970s, organizing people in rural communities into neighborhood committees that demanded economic justice and engaged in self-help projects. The previous work of the church had provided foundations and support for many of the movements that took off in the 1980s. The emergence of these movements coincided with the rise of the Workers' Party in 1979, and the broadening discourse of that party appealed "to workers not only on the basis of their workplace and union experience, but also on the basis of their involvement in a broad spectrum of social organizations in poor neighborhoods" (Keck 1992:25).

"New unionism" gained strength and unions such as the Central Workers' Organization (CUT) began recruiting programs to challenge state-controlled labor unions. In Rio Grande do Sul, CUT was rather successful in broadening its membership in the agrarian sector during the mid-1980s. Traditionally, in state-controlled and opposition unions, women were not included as members on the principle that they were dependents of male heads of household. Because female agricultural wage workers are uncommon among the smallholder and landless sectors organized by unions (both state-controlled and opposition), women were simply not viewed as workers. This was reinforced by existing social welfare policy as well.

Wage workers officially registered with FUN-RURAL (Brazilian Rural Social Welfare System) receive a pension equal to 75 percent of the prevailing wage upon retirement for reasons of age or disability. Because only one household member is entitled to retire for old age, the only way that rural women can benefit from this provision is if they are official heads of household or registered as wage workers (Spindel 1987:57). Because female wage laborers are rare in the smallholder and landless sectors, women are effectively denied the right to a pension. Maternity leave is extended only to those who are registered as wage workers, as are maternity benefits. National laws that were supposed to help rural female wage workers who were active in the commercialized sector ended up discriminating against smallholder and landless women. Their productive work, critical to household income, was not counted as work. Changing these discriminatory laws was the basis for beginning to incorporate women into opposition rural unions. It also required making women's productive work visible.

At the base of these social movements in Rio Grande do Sul was an identification of the struggles for land, economic justice, and political recognition as working-class struggles. These movements also presented themselves as clearly opposing the state and as forming part of a new political process that would open up the political system to the disenfranchised (see Z. Navarro 1992).

Political theorists have often noted the complexity of social movements with respect to how they may be differently perceived by movement leaders and the base membership (Fox and Hernández 1989). For example, as Zander Navarro (1992:21) notes, differences in production in rural areas of Rio Grande do Sul created a wide array of interests and demands that opposition rural unions were not prepared for. There is no homogeneous class identity among the group of individuals that both the CUT and the MMTR call "rural workers." The membership of the MMTR includes smallholders, landless women, and a few women from households with larger holdings. Leaders of the MMTR include women from smallholder as well as landless families. This complexity supports the notion that global capitalism creates a broad spectrum of possible social identities (Hall 1995).

As part of their organizing strategies, movements such as the MST and the rural CUT deliberately recruited women and set up special committees and organizational structures for them within each movement. The rural department of CUT followed the example of FETAG (Federation of Agricultural Workers), a state branch of the official CONTAG (Confederation of Agricultural Workers). FETAG was the first group to mobilize women around a recognition of the economic contributions of rural women, procuring rights and services already available to urban women workers and demanding access to healthcare.

*A family outside their temporary home in a land-reclamation settlement of
the Landless Rural Workers' Movement in Cruz Alta, Rio Grande do Sul.*

Women were also critical in the land occupations and organization of
new settlements by the MST during the 1980s and in the antidam movement. Activists who recall early occupations such as at Encruzilhada
Natalino in 1981 and 1982 constantly reiterate the important role of
women. MST literature of the mid-1980s also emphasized the role of
women in the struggle for land. An MST document from 1986 reads:
"We will fight for a just and equal society . . . reinforcing the fight for
land, including the participation of all rural workers, and stimulating the
participation of women at all levels" (cited and trans. in Z. Navarro
1992:29).

This is not unlike the strategy of creating women's organizations
within revolutionary parties, as in Cuba, Nicaragua, El Salvador, and
elsewhere. Some of the political leaders of the MST worked in Cuba and
received a political education that clearly emphasized including women
in the political process. This is no guarantee, however, that women's demands will be taken seriously. The reason why formal attention to wom-
en's rights in Brazil resulted in some concrete changes is clearly linked to
the presence of a strong women's movement. In Brazil, a wide variety of
grassroots women's organizations emerged in the 1970s and 1980s as
part of the largest, most diverse, and perhaps most successful women's

movement in Latin America (see Alvarez 1990). The creation of many state entities devoted to women's issues (e.g., State Councils on the Status of Women) as well as a National Council on Women's Rights also raised the profile of women's oppression in Brazil, at least in the 1980s. Some of the state-organized initiatives to address women's issues later stagnated and became lower priorities for subsequent governments. The existence of a strong and diverse women's movement and of state entities devoted to women's rights provided an important legitimating context for the MMTR and other rural women's organizations that sought to specifically address women's concerns in the late 1980s.

Perhaps the most important legacy of the women's movements of Brazil in the 1970s and 1980s was the creation of a national array of such nongovernmental organizations as Rede Mulher (Women's Network), which persisted through time and provided ongoing support and training to women in a variety of organizations and movements. Sonia Alvarez, Evelina Dagnino, and Arturo Escobar discuss the importance of networks and webs as a means of conveying the intricacy of the manifold connections "established among movement organizations, individual participants and other actors in civil and political society and the State" (1996:25). In Brazil, women's movements as well as other movements are clearly linked through steadily growing networks which may not be visible to conventional students of social movements who rely on a large public presence to document the ongoing existence of movements and organizations.

The liberation theology branch of the Brazilian Catholic church has emphasized some women's issues as well. The Pastoral Land Commission (CPT) of the Catholic church, closely linked to the MST, organized women and young people into groups and encouraged their participation in resolving issues of landlessness, production, and family. While the church's discourse on the participation of women in political and community activities was quite strong, it emphasized traditional roles for women. The following passage is from a book by the Pastoral Commission of Poor Women which was used in mothers' clubs in several communities of Rio Grande do Sul:

The pages of this book offer a small example of what poor women can do when they are united and organized in their communities. . . .
Women who fight for land for crops and for housing. Women who build community ovens to guarantee bread for the unemployed.
Women who build nurseries to confront the problem of abandoned

children. Women who organize teams to sew quilts to keep the sick
warm. These activities and others are coming from communities and
are signs of the reign of god in action. A new woman is being born. . . .
She is a community woman. (Pastoral da Mulher Pobre 1988:8)

Although the book also provides instructions for how to confront the
police and set free those who have been jailed for illegal land occupations, a majority of the proposed activities for women work well within
prescribed gender roles and do not question traditional family structures
in which males are the primary decisionmakers. This ideology, coupled
with the reluctance of the church to deal with women's health (specifically, family planning and abortion), ultimately resulted in a major distancing of women activists from the church.

The Rise of the MMTR   Rural women in Rio Grande do Sul were organized in a variety of movements during the mid-1980s but continued to
lack their own leadership within these movements. Many had participated in large mobilizations within their specific organizations, such as
the large-scale land occupations of the MST or the short-term mobilizations of women coordinated by temporary coalitions. In 1985, ten thousand women gathered in Porto Alegre for the First State Meeting of Rural Women Workers, organized by FETAG and the CPT. In 1987, rural
women from Rio Grande do Sul participated in a caravan to Brasília of
twelve thousand strong in order to secure the constitutional rights of
rural women workers. They joined a large number of grassroots organizations which were determined to have a say in revising the Constitution
after the movement to hold direct presidential elections was defeated.
Participating in the rewriting of the Constitution was seen as critical to
the effort to democratize Brazil. The caravan was preceded by many local and regional preparatory meetings that drew as many as a thousand
women, as did the preparatory meeting in Ronda Alta. It was thus evident that rural women could be mobilized by rural unions and the
church, but these mobilizations did not result in locally based organizing
projects that specifically addressed the needs of rural women.

Some women who rose to leadership positions within the MST, the
antidam movement, and the rural unions felt frustrated by their inability
to have their gender-specific demands considered important. In interviews, they recalled being told that if they joined in the struggle for rural
workers, then the problems of women would be solved as well. Some
remembered realizing in the mid-1980s that they were developing a dif-

ferent set of concerns from those within CUT, the church, the MST, and the antidam movement. The MMTR leader Gessi Bonês (highlighted in the extensive interview following this chapter) reflects on this issue:

We started to talk about other issues like women's health, sexuality, and our bodies that were not taken up by these movements. There wasn't any room to discuss these issues. . . . [T]hey were always considered secondary: the price of agricultural products, occupying land, [and] the dams were more concrete things. They were economic demands that got people involved. These were seen as the important issues.[1]

Others simply recalled feeling that it was hard to participate in meetings of any kind because of the limitations at home. Isabel, a thirty-five-year-old smallholder member of a local MMTR committee, remembers:

It was hard to go to meetings because I didn't have anyone to take care of my children. If my husband went to a meeting and I wanted to go too, then there was no one to be at home with the children.

In order to move forward with issues that were gender-specific, a group of women from a largely CPT-based organization called the Organização das Mulheres da Roça (Organization of Country Women) began a discussion with other women about the possibility of forming an autonomous movement for rural women workers. In 1988 a temporary council was formed by CPT women and others who had been active in the MST and CUT. They then engaged in a series of discussions and meetings with people from all the regional social movements of Rio Grande do Sul. There was significant resistance to the formation of an autonomous women's movement, including resistance from some of the regional leaders. Many people, men and women alike, felt that women should be organized as part of existing movements that were focused around labor and class issues. The faction that was arguing for an autonomous movement finally convinced the others, and in August 1989 the MMTR was created in a statewide meeting. The understanding of many men who agreed to the creation of the movement was that it was to be a training ground for preparing women to participate better in other movements.

Part of the initial organizing of the MMTR involved a distancing from the church. Before 1989 they had been receiving technical assistance and advice from the church, particularly in some regions. The MMTR leadership was also significantly influenced by training and support they received from two women activists from CAMP (Centro de Assessoria Multiprofissional, Center for Multiprofessional Advising), an NGO that supports regional social movements. It is based in the city of Porto Alegre. CAMP organizers urged the young leadership of the MMTR to deal openly with issues of women's health, sexuality, unequal work roles at home, and general discrimination. Fabiana, a twenty-eight-year-old CAMP organizer who has worked with the MMTR for several years, commented on the change in emphasis by the MMTR:

I remember when I first got the document that was the basis for their formation as an autonomous movement. . . . I felt that this document had a much bigger emphasis on questions of production, work, or economy than it did on discrimination against women. This was when the movement was really deciding if it was part of the labor movement, part of the church, or a women's movement. . . . A lot of women in the leadership were listening to a critique of just focusing on production and felt that the movement should begin to pay attention to questions that no other movement looked at, such as questions of sexuality, women's bodies, and discrimination. . . . We distinctly felt that the movement should be autonomous and treat questions that were specific to women.

Ultimately, the leadership of the MMTR chose CAMP and their organizers to be their primary advisors and trainers. This move immediately put them into contact with other rural women's movements such as the five-state coalition they belong to. Through their association with NGOs like CAMP and the five-state coalition, the MMTR leadership quickly became linked to the wider Brazilian women's movement and readily exposed to the ideas of popular feminism associated with such organizations as Rede Mulher in São Paulo.

When it began in 1989, the MMTR was active in eighty counties; it had about fifteen thousand women participating in its activities and a leadership of about five hundred. Many of the local leaders had been active in their communities through the Catholic church, CUT, the anti-dam movement, or the landless movement. About 80 percent of the participants were from smallholder households, and 19 percent were landless; a small minority of 1 percent were landless salaried workers in small businesses. The elected leadership represents about the same class proportions. The original focus of the movement was on women's health, paid maternity and retirement benefits equal to those of urban workers,

1.º ENCONTRO DO MOVIMENTO DE MULHERES TRABALHADORAS RURAIS DO RS

DATA: 10 a 12 de agosto de 1989

LOCAL: Seminário Na. Sra. Aparecida
km 3 - RS 153 - Passo Fundo - RS

Poster advertising the first statewide meeting of the Rural Women Workers' Movement in Rio Grande do Sul, August 1989. The poster says, "Women who struggle collectively will give birth to a new society."

recognition of rural women's labor as work, and the integration of women into unions and cooperatives (MMTR 1992:5).

Since its inception, the MMTR has undergone a major transformation in terms of its agenda and political perspective. While still firmly rooted in an analysis that stresses the place of the working class (even though it has a clear multiclass base) in global capitalism, the movement has come to work more specifically with the social and cultural aspects of gender inequality in Brazil. By 1992, MMTR literature envisioned:

> *an autonomous movement where women themselves propose, discuss, and decide their own course of action. This autonomy allows women to make the transformation of women's position a priority in their work and practical decisionmaking. We see ourselves as having a complementary relationship to other movements. . . . The advances we have made (since 1989) have resulted in . . . the examination of new questions such as the functioning of our bodies, sexuality, production and reproduction. . . . These themes led us to . . . a new ideology, equal socialization for men and women: enfin, new relationships between men and women. (MMTR 1992:5)*

The 1992 platform discussed by the MMTR at their second statewide assembly directly questions gender inequality and calls for fundamental changes in gendered culture and social life. These more abstract themes were important, but difficult to operationalize. They also caused tension with male leaders in other movements who criticized the MMTR for not contributing to the economic struggles they were engaged in. At the same time, the MMTR became increasingly active in a five-state coalition of rural women's movements, including movements from the states of Paraná, São Paulo, Santa Catarina, and Mato Grosso do Sul.

During 1993 and 1994, the MMTR concentrated heavily on women's health benefits, in part to have a concrete campaign to mobilize their base and in part because obtaining paid maternity leave for rural women (it already existed for urban women workers) had become the major project of the five-state coalition they participated in. In August and September of 1993, 120 women from the MMTR went to Brasília and participated in a lobbying campaign to pressure federal representatives and senators to approve paid maternity leave (MMTR 1994a:3). The campaign also included an effort to establish the Single Health System (SUS, Sistema Unico de Saúde) which would provide general healthcare for rural women and make family-planning methods available at the local level. In addition to occupying the Senate balconies as it debated the is-

Drawing from MMTR educational material showing what a more equal domestic division of labor might look like. A man washing dishes and boys and girls playing with the same toys are seen as positive changes.

sue, women sent hundreds of telegrams and letters supporting paid maternity leave and urging that it be available to rural women workers (AIMTR–Sul 1994:16). Legislation for implementing four months of paid maternity leave through the National Social Security Institute (INSS) was finally approved by the president in July 1994.

During 1994 the MMTR continued its broad program of obtaining further rights for rural women workers in the area of health and childcare, and held workshops on nonsexist education, abortion, sterilization, and violence against women. They also worked on issues of internal democratization and tried to strengthen their links with other rural movements such as the MST, CUT, and other women's movements. Finally, they identified the relationship between gender and class as an ongoing practical and theoretical puzzle that needed more work, specifically raising the question, "When does gender supersede class?" (MMTR 1994b).

In October 1995, the MMTR and the five-state coalition took part in a national meeting that included rural women workers from seventeen states in Brazil. At the meeting, they formed a national coalition of rural women workers' movements to coordinate their work. They declared "the urgency of being conscious of the fundamental intersections of class and gender not only in relation to the construction of new gender relations, but also for the creation of a democratic society." Furthermore, they stated, an integrated gender and class consciousness can provide a countermodel to "the current authoritarian and macho practices of many working-class organizations" (*Carta as trabalhadoras rurais do Brasil* 1995). They vowed to continue their struggle to recognize the full range of rights for rural working women and to intensify their action at all levels of society. On March 8, 1996, International Women's Day, they led a coordinated set of debates, presentations, protests, and public rallies throughout Brazil.

At the end of six years of organizing in 1995, the MMTR could point to several concrete victories they had helped win for rural women: guaranteed rights to retirement benefits, to disability leave and pay, and to paid maternity leave. They also connected their statewide movement to a national coalition and helped make the labor of rural women workers visible to the state. Making that labor visible to women themselves and to members of other rural social movements is the ongoing work of the MMTR.

In 1995, the movement could point to activities in over 110 counties in the state of Rio Grande do Sul and to a base membership of from thirty thousand to thirty-five thousand women. They established a statewide leadership structure with ten regional councils—in Sananduva, Erechim, Tres Passos, Cruz Alta, Dr. Maurício Cardoso, Roque Gonzalez, Sarandi, Cachoeira do Sul, Julio de Castilhos, and Torres. They have a statewide office in Passo Fundo. Each regional council is in turn made up of local councils with ten to seventy women in each. Local councils elect leaders who then come together at the regional level to elect two or three regional leaders who represent their region in the statewide directorate. In 1995 twenty-three regional leaders made up the statewide directorate. Thus, all leaders at local, regional, and state level are elected.

The statewide directorate is made up of women from a variety of class, ethnic, and educational backgrounds. Some are long-time activists, and others are women who first became active in their local councils. In relation to other social movements in the region, the MMTR is the only one that has continued to grow and strengthen into the 1990s (see Z. Navarro 1994).

Dueling Discourses: Christ, Class, and Gender   As seen in the political history of the MMTR, women's organizing is tied to a specific set of political discourses and ideologies surrounding its inception and growth. These discourses have provided both constraints and resources for women as they fashioned their struggles at home and within their respective organizations. The competing discourses on class and feminism that the leadership of the MMTR were exposed to (as well as their own experience of marginalization within the leftist movements they were part of) resulted in overt ideological contradictions. The leaders of the MMTR confronted these contradictions and, in the process of organizing, created a new ideology that prioritized gender concerns as they related to a multiclass female population. This new ideology was also informed by the daily-life experiences of women in local communities.

An interview with MMTR participants about the document they created as the basis for organizing an autonomous women's movement reveals the source of their original ideological framework. Twenty-five-year-old Gessi Bonês states:

In the beginning, our companheiros *imagined that the movement would depend on the unions and other existing organizations for its structure and that it would remain subordinate to these organizations. We didn't have any resources at the beginning and no new ideas to work with. As a matter of fact, the first document we created was simply copied from CUT documents. . . . This also helped to reassure the men that we were not going to break from existing movements.*[2]

Thus, the founding document of the MMTR was in fact just a reformulation of CUT documents that focused on how to organize women of the rural working class. Indeed, the importance of class as a category was built right into the name of the organization as a movement of *trabalhadoras rurais*, or rural workers. This was a deliberate and marked difference from one of the MMTR's predecessor groups, a group that designated *mulheres da roça*, or country women.

An examination of MMTR documents from 1989 through the present reveals a consistent concern with class as a category, but also a reworking of class to include gendered concerns and women's issues. The evolution of the organization reveals a consistent effort to look at the interconnections between class, gender, and culture. The 1989 document that formed the basis for the formal incorporation of the MMTR as a movement was loaded with references to the working class. Discussion questions included the following:

> *How should we be participating in the workers' struggle? How do we guarantee women's participation in other movements? (MMTR 1989:8)*
>
> *How do we organize our women's movement so that we won't be controlled by the bourgeoisie? (MMTR 1989:12)*

A working document one year later continues to identify women as part of the working-class struggle, but focuses more specifically on questioning the power relations within some of the institutions women work in. Discussion questions include these:

> *What kinds of discrimination against women do we find in the family, in unions, and in political parties?*
>
> *How do we overcome different kinds of discrimination? (MMTR 1990a:11)*

Discrimination against women in the left, in the church, and at home was also the subject of a 1990 bulletin published by the movement. Says Mariza Scariot, a participant in a local council who is interviewed in the bulletin:

> *I think that a majority of women suffer from discrimination. One of the most concrete forms of discrimination can be seen in the different kinds of education found in the family, where women are taught only to cook and to take care of children. This kind of work doesn't earn money, so it isn't valued. (MMTR 1990b:6)*

Interviews with movement participants in local councils revealed a similar perspective when women reflected on the socialization of many of the smallholder and landless women who make up the base of the movement. Elenice, a twenty-seven-year-old smallholder states:

Women were socialized from the beginning with the idea that they are in charge of the children and the man has no responsibility. . . . It's a cultural question. It's hard for women to realize that we are discriminated against. . . . I know women who have had fifteen children and never knew what it meant to have a sexual relationship or to feel pleasure in a relationship. They get married with the idea that it is their duty to reproduce people . . . have children. The church reinforces this idea, even today.

Domestic violence and issues of female sexuality have also become part of the MMTR's organizing agenda, categorized as issues of reproduction. According to the elected statewide leadership of the MMTR, a focus on issues of sexuality, domestic violence, and women's health was a three-part process.

First of all, through contact with sociologists, psychologists, and other instructor-facilitators in national meetings and local workshops, elected regional leaders of the MMTR began to consider the gendered relationships that men and women have both at home and in their organizations. Thus, in 1989, the MMTR joined a five-state coalition that included rural women's movements from the states of Rio Grande do Sul, Mato Grosso, Paraná, São Paulo, and Santa Catarina. This coalition had annual workshops and meetings that included representatives of NGOs and women's organizations from other parts of Brazil. Activities of the coalition were the first training ground for the MMTR regional leaders.

Second, these regional leaders would educate local leaders, using videotapes, role playing, and discussion. The local leaders would in turn disseminate information and training through local councils. One particularly popular video, a tool for examining gender relations in the home, was titled *Acorda Raimundo* [Wake Up, Raimundo]. In it, a working-class couple wakes up one morning to find that they have switched roles. The wife goes off to work in a factory, stays out drinking, demands dinner, and ignores the husband. He stays at home all day with the children, washing, cooking, and waiting for the wife to return. In the end, the whole scenario turns out to be a dream, and life goes on as usual with husband and wife playing their traditional roles. The video was quite successful in generating discussion among women in a humorous manner.

Finally, local leaders would organize activities with women in their communities in order to discuss topics that women had expressed interest in, sometimes using tools like the *Acorda Raimundo* video. Popular topics among local discussion groups were childbirth and pregnancy, problems between husbands and wives, and women's health.

Beginning in the 1990s, sexuality and reproductive and maternal health gained prominence in the movement's literature. The training manual from one workshop, done by a sexologist from Rio de Janeiro, included the following questions:

When are women unable to fulfill themselves sexually?
When is there sexual violence in a relationship?
Why do women have to stay home while their husbands leave to
participate in political struggles? *(AAMTRES 1990:11)*

At the same time, the training manual talked about sexuality in relation to four classes of women—dominant class (*mulheres dos patrões*), peasant women and rural workers (*camponêsas e trabalhadoras rurais*), working class (*operários*), and modern middle class (*classe média moderna*)—thus continuing to link gender issues with class (AAMTRES 1990).

These workshops and later meetings also included discussions of sterilization, birth control, and abortion. While Mulheres da Roça, one of the MMTR's parent groups associated with the Catholic church's CPT, had an explicit stance against abortion and divorce, beginning in 1990 and 1991 the MMTR began to deal more openly with these issues under the guise of maternal health. Abortion had been discussed openly, in relation to women's health, by the National Commission on the Question of Women Workers of CUT in 1988. Some women from the MMTR were present at that discussion. The 1992 working document for the second statewide meeting of the MMTR follows the CUT initiative, stating:

Within the question of women's health, we also see thousands of
women searching for any form of contraception who are subjected to
sterilization. . . . Today nationally, 27 percent of women of fertile age
are sterilized. . . . Another issue of relevance to a lack of healthcare for
women is the fact that Brazil has the seventh-highest level of deaths
from clandestine abortions in the world. (MMTR 1992:3)

A 1994 document from the five-state coalition dodges the issue of abortion in a lengthy discussion of maternal health, focusing instead on the more flexible notion of "family planning." Specific recommendations about family planning are made cautiously, signaling the continued difficulties and divisions among women as to just what "reproductive control" means:

> We understand that it is important, beginning now, to fight for the introduction of family planning that respects the cultural and economic differences of each region, always defending the preservation of life. Public authorities are responsible for creating conditions so that men and women have access to contraceptive methods and information. (AIMTR–Sul 1994:14)

Introducing "family planning" while "preserving life" leaves it ambiguous whose life is being preserved—that of the mother, the fetus, or both. The ambiguous language no doubt allows those with different positions on abortion to work together in a broader effort to support women's health.

While the MMTR's elected leaders are clear that they are not endorsing abortion, they see it as an important issue to discuss. Says Gessi Bonês:

> Our discussion is just that. It's not a question of the movement saying that we are in favor of abortion. In our understanding, abortion is a question that should be discussed today as part of women's health. People should know the consequences and causes of abortion.

Activists such as Gessi take this position publicly while privately indicating that they do support a woman's right to abortion. Some other women within the MMTR, however, are strongly opposed to abortion. They are willing to talk about abortion because of their opposition to it, but they realize this is a point of disagreement among women within the movement.

Discussion and consideration of the abortion issue by the MMTR obviously reflects a major distancing from the Catholic church by the movement's leadership and some members. It also reveals the continued influence of the Catholic church's proscription of abortion in that it is such a divisive issue. While MMTR members acknowledge some of the positive results of working with the church—such as a strong commitment to the participation of all base members of the organization in decisionmaking and discussion—they also blame the church for some of the most difficult problems women face. Marlene, an elected regional representative from Erechim in 1990, reflects on this:

I can say openly that the church has a great deal of responsibility for those years in which women were dominated. . . . Today we work in the area of family planning which is a question the church also dealt with. . . . The church had a big effect on people that you can see when you work with women on religious questions, and there are people who grew up believing that you never question anything a priest or nun tells you. . . . [B]ut today, even at the base level, people are questioning what the church taught.

Marlene and others acknowledge that their current organizing strategy is bound to result in conflict not only with the church but also with political parties, unions, families, and society at large as they begin to seriously question inequalities in gender roles. A key ingredient in this questioning has been their ongoing contact with the ideas of "popular feminism" disseminated through NGOs.

The reception of popular feminism by MMTR participants varies significantly. Some women from local committees I interviewed were uncomfortable calling themselves feminists. A typical response to the question "What do you think of popular feminism?" was the following, from twenty-five-year-old Lucinha, a landless married mother of two who has participated in a local MMTR committee for two years:

I don't really know what that means. We are all working with men. In my community we are working to make women's lives better. Getting our husbands and children to help us more, learning about our bodies, this is what we are working on.

Many MMTR leaders are also reluctant to call themselves feminists, yet because of their exposure to the language of feminism their speech is peppered with such terms as "gender," "production and reproduction," and "women's oppression." A 1994 document outlining the future work plans of the MMTR identified the interconnected relationships between "gender," "production," and "reproduction" as key. In the document there is a diagram with arrows connecting the three terms in a circular fashion. At the local level, such issues are discussed in terms of "how I get treated by my husband and children," "how I have more work responsibilities than my husband at home," and "feeling like things aren't fair for women." What seems to be working is that the issues the organization has focused on are very real in the lives of women in the communities. They are eager to talk about them and to make some changes in their daily lives.

Political Marginality and Its Influence on MMTR Political Culture

Significant numbers of women in the MMTR had experience within a variety of organizations before forming an autonomous women's movement. Part of their frustration with opposition unions, the church, the antidam movement, and the landless movement was because they were being left out of discussions and major political decisionmaking. This was because of exclusionary structures and methods of selecting representatives, but also because of their own socialization. Many were not prepared to speak in public and challenge authoritarian leaders. This experience was influential in how they structured their own organization. Women as well as men have to be taught how to participate in meetings and to create democratic political cultures. These two themes are reflected in the following conversation with Gessi and another MMTR activist, Marlene.

Lynn: Do you think men and women have different concepts of democracy?

Gessi: I'm not sure they do because there is no democracy. For example, let's say that there is a labor union with fifteen hundred members. Of all those people, only four or five will be able to develop proposals, raise points of debate and speak in a meeting. Small farmers have this political culture where you have to wait for the authorities to tell you what to do. Women are also brought up to believe that they should wait for someone to tell them what to do. They are taught that they should wait for men to tell them what to do. As rural farmers or workers, we are always waiting for someone to tell us what to do: someone from the cooperative, the priest, the police, or whatever. I think that the issue of democracy is a challenge for the women's movement as well as for the union movement.

Lynn: Do you think that the women's movement can set an example for other movements about how to operate democratically?

Marlene: I'm not sure how much our experience can serve as an example for other movements. I think we are showing through our interactions with other movements that, in practice, the exercise of democracy in the women's movement is different. . . . People seem to think that in some of the other movements the leadership decides everything alone and just goes ahead and does whatever it wants. They don't consult with people at the grassroots level. We worry about connecting with people at the base of our organization. A lot of times, people at the grassroots don't even understand the process of democracy. . . . We don't have any illusions about having an ultimate democratic system for everyone to copy, but we are trying to create a different kind of democratic process within the women's movement. . . .

Lynn: How do you establish a democratic culture for women? Don't you need to have a political space to do that?

Gessi: I think it is easier to do with a smaller number of people. Many of the women who are working in the women's movement today used to work in other movements. They tried to raise issues of democracy and gender in these other movements. Usually their discussion of these issues remained at a very personal level. It was never elevated to the level of an internal political discussion that everyone participated in. That's how women felt working inside the other movements. That's not to say that you can't experience democracy outside the women's movement, it's possible. Ultimately, if we can get women into positions of power in the landless movement, in the labor movement, and elsewhere then the need for the women's movement ends. Our purpose really is to change the ideology and social relations within these other movements.

MMTR leaders such as Gessi and Marlene state that they have a major commitment to making sure that women in communities participate in the organization. Local community meetings take the form of consciousness-raising sessions where individuals share experiences and stories around a particular topic such as health or childbirth. Much of their initial organizing is done through workshops and sharing sessions. Personal experience is the basis for organizing.

In the official structure of the organization, issues that are identified as the primary focus of the group are also discussed at the local level, the regional level, and then at state-wide meetings. Issues are thus discussed at all levels of the organization, and state leadership is composed of representatives from local and regional groups. From what I observed in 1990 and 1991, this tended to work. The primary problem for the MMTR seemed to be twofold: (1) the extreme autonomy of some local groups, which did not always hook up consistently with the regional organizational structure, and (2) differences of opinion among women from the same community on issues like abortion. Local groups seemed free to disagree with regional program priorities and free to develop their own projects.

The unusual organization of the MMTR highlights the difference between mobilization and participation and the importance of viewing social movements as networks or webs. While capable of mobilizing thousands of women for rallies (indeed, they mobilized thirty thousand women statewide for International Women's Day on March 8, 1994), the MMTR devotes a major portion of its organizing effort to continued grassroots discussion, workshops, and community-based campaigns. Such tactics do not result in a highly visible movement like the MST (which has an international profile because of leadership emphasis on public image), but in a less visible, solidly supported movement whose membership seems to feel informed and included in the decisionmaking.

The MMTR does not have permanent paid staff who act as statewide leaders. The leadership of the movement simultaneously participated in local and regional groups as well. As a result of this structure and process, the political culture of the MMTR has been distinctly more democratic in nature than the more vertical organization of other regional movements.

Conclusions   The particular set of ideologies that women in the MMTR were exposed to (feminism, class demands of the left, the Catholic church in both the traditional and the liberation theology form, traditional-rural gender ideology) in part shaped the outcome of the political process they were involved in as well as their individual senses of identity. The particular "multiple selves" of these women in turn modified these ideologies as they were reinterpreted in accordance with local and individual reality. The contradictions inherent in the competing ideologies and discourses that women experienced, however, did not operate in isolation.

Those contradictory ideologies and conflicting discourses were strongly connected to the larger political, economic, and cultural power relations of the region and the nation. The original entrance of MMTR women into politics was largely prompted by the presence of a leftist political opposition represented in a variety of regional movements and by the organizing efforts of the church. These efforts by the left and the church were responses to a long period of military dictatorship and to widespread socioeconomic inequality linked with Brazil's agricultural modernization plan in the region. The presence of an organized left-wing opposition in Brazil, plus the existence of a strong feminist movement with far-reaching networks as well as NGOs linked to social movements, provided a significant part of the context necessary for the emergence of an autonomous MMTR.[3] While this opposition did not organize women as a conscious challenge to gender subordination, the politicization of women in union, landless, and church-based movements resulted in one of the strongest and most viable regional women's movements in Brazil.

In Rio Grande do Sul, as landless and smallholder women entered political activity because of their roles as rural "working-class women" and were encouraged as equals by organizers who spoke a discourse of gender equality, they were awakened to a new kind of political action— one that questioned their subordinate gender status within the church and within the leftist unions and social movements they participated in. Different class sectors of the MMTR also resulted in varying formulations of the gender-based ideology of the MMTR and colored how women experienced the class-based analysis of other social movements. Differences were also found in how individual women interpreted the MMTR's discussion of abortion, tied in part to their views of the Catholic church.

The contradictions experienced by MMTR women in other movements had two important outcomes with respect to how they built their own movement. First, they decided to create an autonomous women's movement rather than continue to organize as women within the mixed organizations they were a part of. Autonomy allowed them more space for the transformation from a class-based political ideology to one based on gender. Second, their experience as participants within the left—recruited but then marginalized—led them to consciously create a different kind of political structure and culture.

By 1995, through their coalition work with similar organizations from seventeen states in Brazil, women in the MMTR were not only redefining their own internal political culture but were actively working to change the hegemonic political culture within the Brazilian left. Arguing for the need to systematically analyze and create strategies based on the intersections of class, gender, and culture, they are seeking to redefine political culture—"the particular social construction in every society of what counts as political; . . . the domain of practices and institutions, carved out of the totality of social reality, that historically comes to be considered as properly political" (Alvarez, Dagnino, and Escobar 1996:10).

Gessi Bonês and Marlene Pasquali
Rural Women Workers' Movement

Gessi Bonês has just stepped down from the speaker's platform at a large rally held at an encampment sponsored by the Landless Rural Workers' Movement (Movimento dos Trabalhadores Rurais sem Terra). She is wearing a T-shirt, and sweat is dripping from her brow as we walk toward the shade. It is a hot day.

Gessi began political organizing as a teenager in a Catholic youth organization and then moved on, at age twenty-one, to work in rural unions and become a founder of one of the largest grassroots organizations for rural Brazilian women. While at first she comes off as everyone's kid sister, she quickly establishes herself as a seasoned organizer who can work with a wide cross-section of social movements; she is slowly convincing them to integrate the concerns of women into their agendas. The interview begins after the rally and continues during a discussion that includes Marlene Pasquali, another pivotal member of the MMTR.

Gessi: My name is Gessi Terezinha Bonês. I am from Sanandi, which is in the Alto da Serra region of the state of Rio Grande do Sul. I was born in 1968. I am going to be twenty-three years old.

Lynn: How were you brought up? Could you tell me about your family?

Gessi: My family is Italian on both my mother's and my father's side. There are nine children in my family, seven women and two men. I am the youngest. My family still works on a farm. We produce small amounts of food for our own consumption and to sell on the market. One thing I remember, even from when I was still in a crib, is that the boys and girls in my family had very different socializations. It was always clear to me that we had very different roles. There were certain

Recorded March 13 and 18, 1991,
in various locations
of the state of
Rio Grande do Sul, Brazil.

things that my brothers could do that we girls couldn't. Maybe this rigid socialization is why I began to fight for changes for women when I became older and started to understand how the world is put together.

Lynn: When did you start organizing?

Gessi: I started participating when I was about sixteen, in 1984. There was a lot of talk about how young people should participate in politics. Later, in 1986, there were going to be elections for state and federal representatives and we started talking about the role of young people in the elections, in labor unions, and in city politics.

There was also an important problem in my city which affected my entrance into politics. A lot of people in and around my community were going to have to leave their land because of the flooding they were doing to set up a new dam. As young people we participated in acts of civil diso-

MMTR leaders Gessi Bonês (right) and Marlene Pasquali at an outdoor rally.

bedience to prevent the dam from being built. We tore down markers they put up, took over buildings, and held demonstrations to prevent the government electrical company, ELETROSUL, from coming in.

Lynn: How did these mobilizations against the dams begin? Was there an equal number of women and men in the group?

Gessi: More of us were women. The movement of young people was very active in 1985 because that was the International Year of Youth promoted by the Brazilian Bishops' Council. The Bishops' Council didn't just promote local youth groups, it coordinated them. There were 655 groups of young people who came together in a statewide meeting of youth at Passo Fundo in 1985. At that meeting, we decided that all of the youth organizations should support one candidate for federal representative from our state. In 1985 there were also a lot of debates going on about whether or not sixteen-year-olds should get the vote. At that time, people who were sixteen couldn't vote. In 1988 the Constitution was changed to give sixteen-year-olds the vote in Brazil.

In 1986 the youth groups also decided to support an opposition candidate for a rural union. We participated in the union election and lost. But in the process we also started to meet as women. In 1986 we started to really organize women. Our big objective was to validate women's work and make sure that they had a space for political participation. We also began to discuss how to unionize women and how to get women into leadership positions in labor unions.

Lynn: Was this process of organizing women initiated by men or by women?

Gessi: The idea came out of a discussion we had in the youth group. Three women who participated in the Pastoral Youth decided that they wanted to make the organization of women their priority. I was one of these three women. After this meeting, we formed a commission and began visiting communities. There we held meetings to discuss the specific problems faced by women as rural workers and how to resolve these problems.

Lynn: Who supported you in this work?

Gessi: The Pastoral Youth and the antidam movement. And we also got support from the rural union people who lost the election. All the work we did was very local. Then we pulled together several counties. In 1987 we created a regional organization and we also began to hook up with other women's groups in the north.

Lynn: What was the movement called at this time?

Gessi: It was called the Organization of Country Women (Mulheres da Roça). We got support from the church and from the antidam movement, but we were already discussing the possibility of an autonomous women's movement. We thought that women knew the most about their own problems. After all, it was women who experienced these problems on an everyday basis. They should be the ones pushing for their own organization.

Lynn: How did this process work? Was it hard to hook up with other women's groups from other states? How did other movements feel about the idea of an autonomous women's movement?

Gessi: I think a critical time for our consolidation was in 1987. That year, rural people went in a caravan to the national capital of Brasília in order to guarantee the rights of all workers in the Constitution. Ten thousand rural men and women participated in the caravan. All of the movements from here went, including the landless movement, the rural unions, the antidam movement, the Pastoral Land Commission, (Pastoral) Youth, and our women's movement.

When we returned from Brasília, we had a meeting with a group of women's organizations from the north. We felt that we didn't want our movement to be dependent on other organizations. Our movement needed to have its own legs, so to speak—to be able to walk alone. In May of 1988, we called a meeting with all of the other movements. Everyone wanted to direct the work of women, but there was no agreement on what women should be organizing around. At that meeting, each movement had its own agenda for women.

Lynn: So each movement was competing to see who would be in charge of women's work?

Gessi: Each one of them wanted to set the agenda for women's organizing. We analyzed all of this information and got all the movements to agree to support the initiation of a women's movement. It was a long process. We had a whole series of local and regional meetings and two statewide meetings, in 1988 and 1989. In 1989 we approved the final proposal for an independent movement.

Lynn: What was this process like? What were some of the doubts about building a women's movement?

Gessi: People argued about whether or not women should be organized inside or outside the other movements. Whether or not we should be autonomous was a big point of contention. . . . There was a big argument about whether or not a women's movement would be dividing the working class. People said that if women had a specific movement just for themselves, then they would divide the working class and that was just what the bourgeoisie wanted. When we started telling people that we didn't want these kinds of divisions, just our own organization that would focus on women's specific problems, then they started to understand what we were proposing. . . .

Lynn: And how were they convinced?

Gessi: That happened when we began to show clear examples of how the majority of women who were part of the women's movement were also participating in other struggles. They were part of the union movement, the landless movement, the youth movement, the Pastoral Land Commission, and the antidam movement. We explained that these movements didn't have a political space that allowed for the discussion of issues which are particular to women. And women in these movements didn't have the experience to bring their issues forward. Then people started citing specific instances, and they began to see that the issues we were bringing up were very real on a day-to-day basis.

Lynn: And how long have you been working in the women's movement?

Gessi: I started doing this work in 1987. In 1988 I worked on local meetings and on the statewide conferences to form the women's movement in 1988 and 1989. I think that if I hadn't become involved with the women's movement, then I couldn't have tolerated the union movement anymore. When I was working in the union movement, there were fourteen of us who were regional leaders. Only two of us were women. The good part of my experience with the labor movement was that I learned a lot about the economy.

Lynn: So why did you leave the labor movement?

Gessi: I stopped working with the labor movement in 1989 because the opposition I was working with won and became the leadership. . . . Then, that same year, I saw that the women's movement really needed someone to work with it. I felt like I was needed in the women's movement. . . . At one level, I had to choose between the two movements. I chose to prioritize the women's movement. . . .

Lynn: Can we talk for a moment about the economic and social composition of the women's movement?

Gessi: According to a survey that we just carried out, about 70 to 80 percent of the women in the movement are small-scale producers. The movement also includes some landless women and some who are salaried workers.

Lynn: How is it different for small-producer women than for landless women in the movement?

Gessi: It is more difficult for women who are small-scale producers to leave their homes. They are responsible for daily maintenance of the house and of the crops. In addition to carrying out housework and childcare, they are also responsible for working in the fields.

Lynn: Don't landless women have some of these problems as well?

Gessi: Women who have participated in the land occupations of the landless movement have the benefit of some of the discussions that have occurred there about the importance of women's roles in the movement. Women who are small producers are usually isolated and are seldom hooked into a political organization. For both groups, there are issues of culture and religion as well. . . . Now we are working to bring together women from different sectors. There are important differences, but there are also ways that we suffer in common from discrimination as women, no matter what sector we are from. . . .

During this part of our conversation, we are joined by Marlene Pasquali, a founding member of the MMTR who is also of Italian ancestry. She comes from a family of small producers. Like Gessi, Marlene was also active in the labor movement before becoming involved with the women's movement. She was a regional leader in the CUT labor federation (Central Unica dos Trabalhadores). She has long dark wavy hair tied back in a pony tail, and she sits with her legs crossed. Marlene was twenty-eight years old and single at the time of this discussion.

Gessi: Sometimes women themselves participate in creating stereotypes about the life of women leaders. When a woman becomes a leader and begins to travel a lot, then other women may not see her as a small producer any more. And the fact that she travels around alone without being accompanied by a man can make people, even other women, talk about her.

Marlene: This still happens. . . . For example, Gessi is single and she goes to a lot of meetings with married men. Sometimes people talk about this. Or it might be even worse if Gessi were a married woman. What would it mean if she was going out at night alone, traveling a lot, and being absent from home and not taking care of her domestic responsibilities? She ends up looking like a tramp, like a woman who will go with anyone she meets. When women first become regional leaders, they run the risk of being seen as loose women. There was a woman who lived by my mother who always talked about women going out just to have a good time. Married women get labeled as whores if they don't come home and do what they are supposed to. Just because they didn't come home, people say they are out on the streets looking for men and cheating on their husbands. This kind of name-calling still goes on a lot.

Lynn: Are there cases where women are physically threatened for their political participation, by their husbands or others?

Gessi: Physical violence? I think this still exists in the countryside. Women at the grassroots level still suffer from this. There are women who say quite clearly that they are coming to meetings against the wishes of their husband. In a lot of communities they can suffer violence. And it can happen to women who are leaders. If a woman who is a leader has gone to a meeting and her husband has been out drinking all night, he will come home and beat her and throw her out.

Marlene: Sometimes men use violence against women without being drunk. They just don't like the fact that women go to meetings. They don't like what they are doing. There are women who tell us that when they leave the house, they don't tell their husbands where they are going. They don't say where they are going so there won't be a big ugly fight when they get home.

Gessi: At the beginning of the women's movement we had women who would tell us, "I came to this one meeting, but I'm not coming back." "Why don't you come back?" we asked. "Because at home things are getting out of hand. If I have to separate from my husband, will the women's movement take care of me?"

Some people have been able to participate in the movement and have gone through a process with their daughters, husbands, and other family members and got them to accept their participation. But sometimes this takes two or three years, and every now and then there is a backlash.

But there are some men who are changing, especially young men. I was in one community recently where four years ago they were saying that the women's movement had to end. This time when I visited the community, the same men were defending women's rights in a public meeting. . . . Today women in that community are demanding more and participating in community politics. They say, "I don't accept the story that I will marry and become the property of my husband." Even my own mother tells my father, "I will not just do as you say. Forget it." Twenty-five years ago she would never refuse my father's wishes. Things are changing.

PART IV   CHILE

CHAPTER 7

Sweet and Sour Grapes
The Struggles of Seasonal
Women Workers in Chile

The impact of commercialized agriculture on women in Latin America is consistent with two primary trends found elsewhere in the world. When subsistence agriculture is subordinated to cash crop production for export, women's labor either becomes invisible as part of the subsistence labor force (Deere 1979; Evers, Clauss, and Wong 1984; Mies 1988; Stephen 1991) or is channeled into such appropriate "feminine" tasks as fruit or vegetable picking and packing, as in the case of female seasonal workers in Chile (Arizpe and Aranda 1986; Nash 1989). Workers in "natural" feminine jobs are usually remunerated less than their male counterparts because they are classified as unskilled (Nash and Fernández Kelly 1983; Ong 1987).

Contrary to common ideas, women have not been marginalized in the agricultural wage-labor force with the development of global capitalism, but are being increasingly employed "as seasonal workers in the most labor-intensive tasks of export agriculture" (Deere 1987:5). One study suggests that almost half of all seasonal commercial agricultural workers in Mexico during the late 1980s were female (Arizpe, Salinas, and Velásquez 1989:237). Until the 1980s, commercial agricultural firms seemed to prefer young and childless women for seasonal work (Arizpe and Aranda 1986). Recent research in Chile suggests this is no longer the case. One study found that among seasonal fruit workers in Chile, 66 percent of female workers are or have been married and nearly 20 percent are heads of household (Venegas and Sepúlveda 1991:11, cited in Collins 1994:27). Whatever their marital status, however, when women do enter the paid labor force their work is defined in terms of their domestic responsibilities. Women are seen as appropriate seasonal workers who do not need a full-time income. As pointed out by Nash (1989:32), "Even in those societies where women's productive activities are complementary to those of men and highly valued in noncapitalist institutions, their role in wage-paying work in capitalist enterprises is prejudiced by assumptions regarding the priority of their domestic responsibilities and the devaluation of their labor at home."

Even when they are major income earners, women are still seen as bringing in secondary income, if they are married, or "lipstick money" if they are young and unmarried. Employers tend to see women as "special workers" who have infinite flexibility in their schedules. As pointed out by Collins (1994:3), transnational firms involved in commercial agriculture have their own gendered propositions about women and their labor: "that women are special (usually by virtue of their relation to home and family), and that labor practices should be shaped—not by prevailing labor legislation and market forces—but by that special status. What special means can then be redefined as necessary to assess women's skills levels, set their wages, and arrange their work hours and working conditions."

While many studies have explored the ways in which transnational firms reproduce myths about women's nature and labor flexibility (Fernández Kelly 1982; Barrón 1991; Arizpe and Aranda 1986; Rodríguez and Venegas 1989; Venegas 1992), few have focused on "what women are saying back to capital" and to others who occupy positions of power (Collins 1994:5; Collins 1995). For women in the Santa María Seasonal and Permanent Workers' Union explored here, the subordinate female gender roles found in international, national, and local cultures are being challenged by the more egalitarian discourse on gender roles promoted by the movements and organizations these women participate in. The rural seasonal workers who labor in export fruit production in Santa María are participating in the first-ever union of seasonal workers in Chile. The Seasonal and Permanent Workers' Union emerged in response to the conditions of capitalist agricultural development in Chile during the 1970s and 1980s.

This case study suggests that women's participation in grassroots organizations that offer a more egalitarian gender ideology can, over time, transform women's vision of themselves as political actors at home, at work, and in the organizations they participate in. Some women in the Seasonal and Permanent Workers' Union of Santa María have challenged notions about the "natural" character of their own gender roles. In addition, their political activism has (1) led them to challenge the traditional gendered division of labor, (2) caused them to question their relative power and authority in the family, in local firms, and in formal organizations, and (3) raised issues of reproductive control and sexuality within their homes and organizations.

To set the context for the emergence of the Seasonal Workers' Union, we open with a discussion of the feminization of commercial agriculture and its impact on gender roles in Chile. The union organization is then looked at in detail and the last section is devoted to a discussion of how women's experience in their union is challenging subordinate gender roles in production, reproduction, sexuality, and local politics.

Commercial Fruit Production and Traditional Gender Roles in Chile   The swearing in of Patricio Alywin as president of Chile in March 1990 widened the democratic opening which began with the vote to oust Augusto Pinochet from presidential power after sixteen years of brutal dictatorship. From 1964 to 1973 Chile carried out an extensive land reform that in large part broke down the traditional agrarian social order. This was made possible through the weakening of right-wing parties in the 1960s, the elimination of the latifundio system, the unionization of peasants, and the promotion of laws guaranteeing the rights of rural workers—first under the Christian Democratic government of Eduardo Frei and then accelerated under the Popular Unity government of Salvador Allende. Rural development policy under Frei and Allende favored a permanent peasantry living on appropriated estates, run collectively and known as *asentamientos* (agrarian reform communities). Smallholders outside the *asentamientos* were paid little attention to during the agrarian reform period (Silva 1990b: 197). During the 1970s, Pinochet dismantled agrarian reform communities, leaving many peasants without land. In some areas of Chile, more than 50 percent of those who had benefited from agrarian reform under Salvador Allende lost land under Pinochet's allotment scheme. Many of them were rejected for political reasons. By 1978, only about 22.4 percent of those marginalized in the Pinochet allotment program were able to find permanent employment (Silva 1990a: 27).

Many of these former peasants, men and women, became the labor pool for vegetable and fruit export production, one of the leading sources of foreign exchange for Chile. Smallholders, or *minifundistas*, who were never beneficiaries under Allende's agrarian reform or that of his predecessor had a deteriorating standard of living beginning in 1973. Many of them have also been forced to earn income by selling their labor to augment subsistence production, often working in large fruit-growing operations (Gómez 1982).

During the 1980s, fresh fruit export was one of the most dynamic sectors of the Chilean economy, ranking third in exports behind copper and fish (Gómez and Echenique 1988:152). Chile is now the premier fruit exporter of South America, competing with South Africa, Australia, and New Zealand. The United States is the largest market for Chilean fruit. Along with plums, peaches, nectarines, apples, grapes, and pears, Chile is even exporting kiwifruit. Fruit exports grew from $198 million in 1981 to $477 million in 1986 (Gómez and Echenique 1988:299) to over $900 million in 1992 (Falabella 1992:2).

The dramatic increase in fruit production for export during the late 1970s and 1980s was accompanied by a rise in the number of temporarily employed workers. In 1965, 65 percent of rural Chilean workers had full-time work and 37 percent had seasonal work. By 1976, only 44 percent had full-time work; 56 percent had seasonal work (CEM 1987: 88). And by the late 1980s, over two-thirds of Chile's rural workforce was made up of seasonal workers (Gómez and Echenique 1988). In 1992, 12 percent of the total Chilean labor force worked producing fruit for export, most of them as seasonal workers (Falabella 1992:2).

This increase in the number of seasonal workers involves a large-scale entry of women into the labor market beginning in the 1970s. By 1987 there were from seventy thousand to a hundred thousand women employed in the fruit business according to some estimates (Valdés 1988: 390). Employment statistics from 1982 show that a majority of female rural workers lived in those areas with the greatest concentration of fruit plantations—i.e., in the central and north-central parts of Chile. Most women employed as seasonal workers in capitalist enterprises are from households that have either lost their land or never owned any (Lago 1987:28).

Why did large numbers of women enter the seasonal wage-labor force to work in fruit production for export? As explained by Valdés (1987a: 46–47), the labor force of the fruit-production export sector was segmented by gender to make it competitive with those of other fruit-exporting countries. The competitive edge lies in a lower wage rate. This lower rate can be accomplished by exploiting female laborers who are viewed as mere housewives working to help support their families (Valdés 1987b:28). Employing the same logic as electronics manufacturers in Latin America and Southeast Asia who cite women's biological propensity for delicate tasks requiring patience, orderliness, and responsibility, the Chilean fruit growers cite women's domestic talents as housewives and mothers in order to justify the work they do clipping trees, picking fruit, and carefully packing it in crates. Ximena Valdés (1992, cited in Collins 1995:187–188) describes how a technical division of labor becomes gendered by imbuing certain tasks with innate male and female abilities. Women's monitoring of the quality of fruit in the packinghouses, for example, is seen by employers as akin to the kind of selection that women shoppers do in the market. Valdés also discusses how the tasks men and women do entail different levels of prestige, salary, forms of payment, and working conditions. Men's jobs involve great spacial mobility, greater use of tools of all sorts, and their positions are more likely to offer opportunities for advancement (Valdés 1992:109–110).

Men, as Valdés notes, are concentrated in mechanized jobs and in jobs that are permanent and better-paying. Overall, however, women have better employment possibilities than men, and in general their work in the packing plants pays better than much of the work available to the male labor force. As a result, women are often the major contributors to household income.

Seasonal workers are employed from three to eight months per year. Many are paid at piece rates and usually do not receive benefits. While seasonal workers in theory have the same rights as permanent workers, those rights are guaranteed only when a contract is signed. Few employers sign contracts, however, and most contracts, if they are signed, last only a few weeks and are confined to one kind of fruit. When the fruit is picked, the contract ends. Despite extremely long days, moreover, no overtime is paid (Falabella 1992:2). And many women are not aware of the benefits they are entitled to, such as paid maternity leave, health protection, nursing rooms on the job, and so on (CEM 1987:93–94).

While Chilean women were slowly being moved into commercial-export agriculture in the 1960s, the state disseminated its ideals of traditional gender roles by creating thousands of Mothers' Centers. These centers did nothing to promote more equal treatment of women workers. Instead, they were meant to anchor women in the home as service providers. The Mothers' Centers espoused an ideology that rural women were the link between the family and the market. Women were granted credit so that they could manage family consumption, buying sewing machines, gas cookers, and other domestic appliances (Valdés 1987b: 33). Courses offered by the Mothers' Centers focused on domestic arts and activities that women could do at home to increase household income—painting, embroidery, sewing, hair care, nutrition, and health. Women over forty who remember the Mothers' Centers promoted under Frei and Allende state that they were "helpful in terms of services in that they made it possible for women to leave their houses, but useless in helping them develop as women or in establishing their own specific demands. Women state that the Mothers' Centers didn't help them understand their own condition or the enormous changes taking place in the countryside during those years" (Valdés 1987b: 35).

Under Allende, women were organized into Social Welfare Committees as well as in Mothers' Centers. The Popular Unity government reorganized the agrarian reform communities (*asentamientos*) as Centers of Agrarian Reform (CERAs). One of the committees of the CERAs was for social welfare, conceptualized as the most important strategy for organizing women (Garret 1982:283). Women's participation in these committees, however, was not without problems:

Most male agriculturalists showed hostility toward the participation of women in any official capacity or leadership position in the agrarian reform communities. One of the most frequent criticisms of the CERAs was precisely the fact that they let women participate. While the government tried to combat these types of criticisms, popular opinion, particularly of men, went against government policy. (Garret 1982:283)

As a result, Social Welfare Committees were often marginalized and not given sufficient funds to operate with (Garret 1982:283). The proper place for rural women was seen to be within Mothers' Centers, where traditional gender stereotypes were not challenged.

After 1973, the Mothers' Centers abandoned any pretext of providing women with training for the commercialization and distribution of their products (a focus of some prior programs) and moved wholeheartedly into the ideological, social, and economic control of women and their products. The state turned the Mothers' Centers into more exclusive institutions, where women had to pay for courses, and the centers began to control women's artisanal production, putting their profits as intermediaries into state coffers (Valdés 1987b: 35).

Focusing on the role of women as the reproducers of future soldiers and as housewives, the Mothers' Centers became mouthpieces for the military to promote women's duty as mothers to defend the integrity of the Chilean family and to save the fatherland. Levy and Lechner (1986: 86) state that the government considered women to be "a natural category (sex), whose permanent and unchanging essence is determined (by biology). Women are not subjects, but objects of history." Women are defined exclusively in reproductive terms, thus reducing them to mothers, caretakers, and sexual beings in the service of husbands for the primary purpose of procreation.

In 1973, Pinochet reorganized the Mothers' Centers, which had been

community-based and grassroots organizations, into a national structure. He also created the National Secretariat of Women, an organization
directed at middle- and upper-class women who (as volunteers) disseminated patriotic and family values to working-class and peasant women.
Pinochet's wife became the director of both organizations. By 1983 it
was estimated that there were ten thousand Mothers' Centers throughout Chile with two hundred thirty thousand members and six thousand
volunteers. The members were primarily urban-working-class and peasant women while the 6,000 volunteers who directed the programs were
middle- and upper-class women, many of whom were military wives
(Chuchryk 1989:160). The social influence of the Mothers' Centers and
the sustained images they promoted for more than twenty years should
not be underestimated in trying to understand the behavior of rural
women.

The Seasonal and Permanent Workers' Union of Santa María   In
central Chile, a push toward commercial fruit production for export
promoted under the dictatorship of Augusto Pinochet has resulted in
large rural enterprises run primarily with part-time female labor. The
community of Santa María began to show patterns of urbanization, proletarianization, and the establishment of capitalist relations of production long before the rest of Chile, as early as the 1960s (Lago and Olavaría 1982:185). Located in the fertile valley of the Aconcagua river and
close to Valparaíso, the principal port of Chile, Santa María was an ideal
location for commercialized agriculture. The use of part-time female
wage laborers is also not new to the area. One researcher documented
the presence of seasonal female laborers up to sixty years ago (Lago and
Olavaría 1982:183).

In 1991, Santa María had a population of 9,700 inhabitants and the
greatest concentration of fruit trees per hectare in all of Chile (Falabella
1991:1). Most people in the community work in fruit production. A
majority of women's work is in the packing plants, though some work in
the fields when the trees require thinning. Women work twelve to fourteen hours a day in the packing plants and, in 1991, earned an average
of four dollars per day. Women seasonal workers often work until two
or three in the morning or even until dawn, depending on how much
fruit they are required to pack. They are often exposed to pesticides that
result in severe headaches and eye pain. Outside of the few months when
seasonal work is available, there are few employment opportunities for
women.

Studies conducted of grape firms in the Aconcagua Valley found that a majority of female seasonal workers are married and 30 percent are heads of household (Venegas 1992:102, cited in Collins 1995:187). A majority of others, classified as "multi-occupational" women who combine fruit packing during the harvest with other seasonal work, are heads of household or from families where men are unemployed or underemployed (Collins 1995:187).

Although many women in Santa María and other communities in central Chile work as wage laborers, their domestic workloads have not adjusted accordingly. Women who work in the packing plants may begin their wage work at two o'clock in the afternoon after having worked eight hours in their homes preparing food, cleaning, doing laundry, and working in gardens. They often return home at midnight. Ximena Aranda Baeza says of the semiproletarian women in Putaendo, many of whom labored in fruit-packing plants: "Women who are wives and mothers have other obligations that exist outside of those derived from selling their labor. . . . Sixty percent of women workers had to make meals for their families, clean their houses, and take care of the clothing. On Sundays they wash. The other tasks are done by the eldest daughters. Children are taken care of by daughters and neighbors" (1982:173). Aranda Baeza (1982:175) found also that the average number of hours worked daily by female seasonal workers from semiproletarian houses was 17.5. This includes wage work and domestic chores. Childcare which was compatible with women's work in family plots is not compatible with work in the fruit orchards because of the dangers of damaging the fruit (Lago and Olavaría 1982:189).

While women's wage work and income have caused some changes in terms of household interactions, the norm remains that men will have the leading role in household decisionmaking. In smallholder households where women also work as seasonal wage laborers, land is titled to and inherited by men. In a 1986 meeting of rural women called by the National Peasant Commission (CNC), one of the primary demands of young women was that inheritance laws be changed so that women could inherit land (Valdés 1987a:48).

In fruit-growing enterprises, management is almost exclusively male. Many women workers complain of sexual harassment on the part of owners, supervisors, and foremen (Acuña and Riquelme 1986). Thus, in spite of their new status as wage laborers in large numbers, women in Santa María and other communities have virtually no control over their working conditions and treatment.

In 1989, the first-ever union of seasonal workers in Chile was formed in Santa María. By 1992, the union had approximately nine hundred

*The author sitting with her co-researcher Jonathan Fox (*third and second from right*), two women leaders of the Seasonal and Permanent Workers' Union, and two staff members from the Casa del Temporero in Santa María.*

members, representing about 36 percent of the seasonal workers in the community. A majority of the union members are women and, to date, almost half its leaders have been women. Born with the help of a non-governmental organization, the House of the Seasonal Worker (Casa del Temporero), the union is working to carve out its own identity.

Because the union grew out of a community-based NGO, its structure and program are unusual for the labor-union sector. It functions not only as a labor union but as a community organization offering a wide range of services to its members, both during the off-season months and when they are working. The model of a nongovernmental organization supporting local union affiliates has been reproduced outside of Santa María. During 1992, financing was received from a U.S. foundation, the government of Norway, and the Chilean government to build thirteen more such "houses," modeled on the House of the Seasonal Worker, "La Casa." The idea is to support the type of organizing carried out by the Santa María Seasonal and Permanent Workers' Union and to set up affiliate unions in other communities.

In Santa María there has been an ongoing tension between La Casa and the union, particularly regarding the demands of women workers.

Some of the union leaders, particularly women, felt that the staff of La Casa was overly paternalistic and did not listen to the gender-specific needs of women workers. Some of these tensions are detailed below in relation to the place of women in the culture and politics of the union.

In 1990 when the new government of *concertación* (harmony) organized a trilateral agreement between government, business, and labor, the resulting new labor law denied the right of collective bargaining to seasonal workers. This has placed the union in a difficult position, but has not prevented it from acting on workers' behalf. The union negotiates on behalf of individual workers in local packing plants and has been quite successful in hitting management with "lightning strikes" of from three minutes to several hours in which people suddenly stop work as a way of pressuring for higher salaries and improved working conditions. These work stoppages are usually realized during the peak of the picking season and at the hottest part of the day, when many trucks are waiting to take the fruit to port (Falabella 1992:6). During the high season and with the heat, time is of the essence in getting the fruit off the trees, packed, into refrigerated transport, and on its way before it begins to spoil. A hundred women sitting down for an hour while fruit rots in the sun has proven quite effective in gaining salary increases at local plants. These actions are usually spontaneous, however, and are not coordinated with large campaigns. During the off-season, the union has solicited the collaboration of employers in communal kitchens, asking for assistance in procuring food and firewood.

Participation in the union has not been without costs for some members, particularly those who are leaders. Many who took on leadership positions in the union were blacklisted by employers and unable to obtain employment. In some cases, leaders were able to work—but only in the lowest-paying jobs. For the majority of women who are leaders in the union, particularly those who are single heads of household, blacklisting had severe consequences and influenced their search for alternative sources of employment (Valdés 1991).

In 1990, the union affiliated with the Confederation of Peasant Workers' Unity (UOC, Confederación Unidad Obrera Campesina), an independent union confederation. The union has not affiliated with the large United Workers' Center of Chile (CUT, Central Unitaria de Trabajadores de Chile), which represented 12.6 percent of the Chilean labor force in 1992 (Falabella 1992:10). Large federations such as CUT do not have organizational structures which facilitate participation from the base. As discussed by Falabella (1992:10), only the representatives of national federations have any say in the politics of CUT and, unlike the union in Santa María, CUT separates salary issues from the rest of the workers' needs. This has important implications for women workers, as seen below.

Union-sponsored activities that take place outside the packing plants include workshops on labor law and workers' rights (held once a week, with childcare provided), workshops on health, and help with transportation, food, and daycare during the high point of the harvest season. During the off-season, programs include collective kitchens, theater, housing construction, and organic gardens. The union has a women's group that meets once a week, offering workshops on health, reproductive, and legal issues and a crocheting and knitting project.

Challenging Subordinate Gender Roles In Chile, the expansion of fruit production for export created a predominantly female labor force that is beginning to be wooed by independent rural unions. These unions have only been able to operate without repression since 1989. In Chile this "new unionism" under a seemingly democratic regime can be distinguished by its inclusion of women. This inclusion is not directed toward helping women workers with specifically female issues of production and reproduction, but toward broadening union membership. An unintended consequence of such organizing, however, in conjunction with the presence of instructors and facilitators versed in some of the principles of feminism, has been the emergence of women's groups within unions.

Such groups can result in a challenge to subordinate female gender roles by women who, through the political process or organizing with other women, come to have more egalitarian visions of what women's lives can be like. For women participating in the Seasonal Workers' Union of Santa María, challenging traditional gender roles promoted by state policies and local rural cultures has become an important organizing focus.

PRODUCTION AND REPRODUCTION Perhaps the biggest struggle for women who participate in the Seasonal Workers' Union is to have their responsibilities as workers *and* mothers recognized and valorized. The deepest part of the struggle has to do with getting women themselves to recognize their heavy burden. The socialization of rural women through the Mothers' Centers in the 1970s and 1980s reiterated the ideal that women's natural and primary responsibilities were in the

A local union member (far right) with her daughter and husband outside their home in Santa María. The two women participated actively in the collective kitchens run by the Casa del Temporero.

domestic sphere and focused on domestic arts. Many felt that they should be able to handle the double workload of twelve to fourteen hours a day in the packing plants plus four to eight hours of housework.

Initial efforts to organize collective kitchens within the Seasonal and Permanent Workers' Union illustrate the difficulties some women have in overcoming their acceptance of the double workload as a natural responsibility. In 1990, several collective kitchens were organized in different parts of the town of Santa María, providing hot meals for union members. The kitchens functioned successfully for a few months, but required the hard work of several women who essentially became full-time cooks. Other women used them reluctantly. One fifty-year-old union member explained:

It made me feel ashamed to walk past everyone with food from the kitchen. I was sure they thought I was so poor that I couldn't even feed my children. It was like admitting that I couldn't provide for them as a mother should.

When the kitchens began to fall into disuse, many women admitted that they didn't like to use the kitchens in the first place, because it hurt their pride to be seen carrying pots of food across town. The kitchens were later reorganized and had higher levels of participation. One source of tension between La Casa and women in the union was over whether or not to permit contributions to the kitchen in the names of individuals. La Casa argued against this, while the women maintained that it was important to know who was and who was not contributing. Attaching people's names to their contribution made it public knowledge who had contributed. If such information was public, then it was clear that women who participated and provided contributions were not freeloading and could provide for their families.

While La Casa has proven supportive of some of the women workers' needs, such as daycare and kitchens, it has not provided other types of support women need—in the areas of health and reproduction. In 1991, when a "popular education" professional contracted by La Casa went to begin a course on women and work, union leaders and other women requested a special meeting with her, specifically requesting that the meeting be held in the union building, not at La Casa. There, not only did participants ask for information about how to commercialize the products from their weekly knitting and sewing workshop, but several also asked for contacts with respect to getting an abortion as well as sources of financial support for the abortion (Valdés 1991:18). Much of the meeting was also spent criticizing La Casa and the union for not supporting women's needs.

At a later point during the course on women and work, two women who are leaders in the union spoke to the women in the class about the difficulties they had in making men from the union federation to which the Seasonal Workers belonged (the UOC) understand how they were workers, leaders, and mothers all in one. The two women had been attending a day-long workshop which was predominantly male. One of them reported to the women in the class:

The men started to share their opinions and we were just quiet. Then during the coffee break we started to talk with the other union leaders. . . . A president of one union told me, "As president, I am very opposed to the idea that women participate in unions because it just causes problems. Besides that, you are mothers." "Yes," we answered. "We are mothers, but we are also union leaders." "No," he said. "When a woman goes out, she has to define herself as either a mother or a union leader." (Valdés 1991:12)

The other woman who had gone with her to the workshop chimed in:

That's not true. When a woman leaves her house, she is an owner of the house, a mother, and a union leader. When she is in the house, she is a union leader, a mother, and an owner of the house. The men who were in the workshop just didn't understand that. (Valdés 1991:12)

SEXUALITY   Within the union, some women have begun to question their traditional submissive roles in relation to sexuality and reproduction, as indicated by the request for information on abortion noted above. In rural Chile, an ideological emphasis on women's roles in reproducing future soldiers, laborers, and sons for the fatherland placed them under the strict control of their husbands. Female sexuality was to be directed toward reproduction only. An interesting contradiction between this ideology, promoted in the Mothers' Centers, and the reality of the nightlife of women working in the packing plants began to emerge in Santa María during the 1970s and 1980s.[1]

Because of their schedules, many women emerge from the packing plants at two or three in the morning, sometimes returning home as late as five o'clock. Traditionally, any women seen out on the streets at night were assumed to be prostitutes and up to no good. The current reality is that a majority of the people out on the streets at night during picking and packing season are women, both married and unmarried. While some go home, others go out to eat, drink, and socialize. Women have reclaimed the streets at night and broken the pattern of being confined to their homes. Some have also begun to have relationships outside of marriage. Walking around with a group of women at midnight in the town, one very much has the feeling that the streets are theirs. They talk to and flirt with men they encounter, treating them as they themselves might have been treated earlier.

Within the Seasonal Workers' Union, women use their sexuality to assert their right to participate in the union and be absent from their homes. When men questioned their right to remain absent from their homes and neglect their household duties, union women would belittle them publicly, even commenting on the size of their sexual organs. I repeatedly heard women refer to men as unprincipled weaklings, and threaten that they would take other lovers if the men did not cooperate with their demands. The female culture that has evolved among women who work in the packing plants is reinforced by their predominant position in the union. Sometimes the talk at union meetings I observed seemed to dissolve into pure sexual banter.

Because of high levels of repression against trade unionists, some men remain cautious in their political activity and remain silent when told by women that they are cowards.[2] In addition, because men are more likely than women to have permanent jobs (if they have jobs), they have more to lose by joining unions, a material basis for fear. These circumstances have perhaps reinforced a change in the gendered culture of women's sexuality that was already under way.

POLITICAL CULTURE   A final arena where women in the Seasonal Workers' Union have challenged local gender hierarchy, trying to redefine the nature of political culture, is in the organizational forms and processes of the union. Even in this predominantly female organization, the presence of an autonomous space for women has been critical in the integration of some women into the larger union. In Santa María, a women's knitting-and-crocheting workshop was started as a space to give women a chance to speak and to learn political skills. A former president of the union related how, in her experience, if there were a meeting of forty people that included twenty-five women and fifteen men, only three or four of the women would speak. She stated, "It is important to create small spaces just for women as well as spaces for men and women together. Women talk more in small groups."

The knitting-and-crocheting workshop was also begun by the women in an effort to find ways of generating income during the off-season. Although they had complained to staff of La Casa about the need for developing productive projects for women, little had been done to address that need (Valdés 1991). Incorporating the handicraft skills they had learned by participating in the Mothers' Centers, women from Santa María were attempting to develop some source of self-sufficiency for the winter months. Having no materials, little guidance, and no marketing outlet they were not successful. The weekly meetings served other important purposes, however.

The knitting-and-crocheting workshop functions primarily as a non-threatening space for inexperienced women to speak in public for the first time and express their confusion and frustration about the slow process of organizing in Chile—feelings that are less permissible in the larger union culture. Such feelings which may be stereotyped as "female" have to be expressed in an intimate, more comfortable setting before they can be safely expressed in larger meeting spaces where the political culture may be more "male," a likely outcome of women's exclusion from rural unions until recently.

Several women related how they cried with fear and joy after having spoken in public for the first time in their lives in the women's group. Through the group, women are trained to feel stronger and more legitimate when expressing their feelings in general union meetings. This example suggests that integrating women into rural worker organizations is related not only to the physical presence of a group of women, but also to the nature of the organizational political culture (something similar happened in the case of the MMTR in Brazil). The political training and affirmation women get for their own forms of expression in the women's group can be infused into the larger Seasonal Workers' Union as they become more active in assemblies and committees. Like women in the MMTR, though in a more limited sense, women in the Santa María Seasonal and Permanent Workers' Union are redesigning the political culture they became active in. Just what is deemed a political issue, the style that concerns are expressed in, accountability to those who bring forth new and different ideas—there are the sort of cultural changes women are introducing into the political culture of the union.

What has proven to be an ongoing challenge for women leaders, however, is how to bring the concerns of women from the weekly workshop into the union meetings and to consistently integrate the multiple mother-worker-leader aspects of their identities into a strategy for participating and guiding the larger union. As pointed out by Valdés (1991:

18), because female leaders must continually challenge the dichotomy between mother-wife and worker–union leader, women's demands sometimes get left behind or weakened.

Conclusions   The experiences of the women in the Seasonal and Permanent Workers' Union of Santa María, Chile, provide examples of how women can begin to challenge traditional gender roles through grassroots organizing. The conditions of commercial agriculture include gendered roles for rural women that leave much of their work unrecognized and that often render them second-class citizens in their own homes, communities, and organizations. The degree to which this is true can vary locally in relation to landholding patterns and levels of political activism. At the same time, though, the conditions of commercial capitalism in conjunction with other factors such as democratizing processes have also encouraged grassroots opposition movements. In a few cases, these movements and organizations have focused specifically on the plight of rural women workers. Through the process of organizing, some women have come to see new possibilities for themselves as workers, as family and community members, and as political actors who should be on a more equal footing with men.

When rural women have their own political spaces—either as women's groups within mixed organizations or as autonomous movements—they often begin to experience their gendered identity in a different light as they collectively confront discrepancies between the more egalitarian gender roles promoted in their organizations and those they experience at home, at work, and even in mixed organizations. While the conditions of commercial agriculture have clearly placed political, legal, economic, and cultural constraints on women's social roles, through their involvement in grassroots organizations women have come to see their work, household responsibilities, and family and community relations as "political," and they have pushed this integrated vision into the political culture of their own union.

Capitalist agriculture can create conditions whereby women simultaneously occupy their homes, the packing plants, and the so-called public space of the street. In Santa María, where commercial fruit production has been going on for more than fifty years, analyzing women as part of "the domestic sphere" makes little sense. The integration of women's identities as both mothers and workers, stated so clearly to male union leaders, demonstrates the synthetic nature of women's social, political, and economic world. Their political concerns also demonstrate this integration as they combine an interest in income-generating projects with reproductive health. Finally, their continued concern with the material conditions of their work as well as with their health and sexuality suggests the importance of an analytical perspective on social movements that puts political mobilization in an economic and political context while simultaneously validating the importance of political culture and identity formation as an ongoing process.

Antonia Gómez
Interindustry Union of Seasonal and Permanent Workers of Santa María

Antonia Gómez[1] is a self-described Mapuche Indian who moved to Santa María in the 1970s after she and her husband fled the south, where they had both participated in labor struggles within the fishing industry. Antonia is about fifty years old. She lives with several daughters, one of whom also works in the packing plants. At the time of the interview, she was the president of the Santa María Seasonal and Permanent Workers' Union. We are sitting around her kitchen table at nine in the evening after a union meeting which I observed. It is cold outside. I have on a pair of blue jeans, a turtleneck sweater, and a jacket. Antonia has on a sweater and a shawl. Another worker, Cecilia, has come by for a visit and walks in and out of the room during our conversation, sometimes joining in.

Antonia's house is a simple wooden structure with three rooms. There is a living room with a low stuffed couch and a wooden chair, a bedroom with two double beds, boxes, and a bureau, as well as a kitchen with a small square table and four chairs. We sit for quite some time without the tape recorder turned on, sipping tea and talking about the meeting. When we begin discussing conditions inside the *parrones* (special structures built to house grapevines), Antonia indicates to me with her hand that I can turn on the tape recorder. I do so.

Lynn: What does it feel like to work among the grapevines and in the packing plants?

Antonia: Well, they say that working in the *parrones* where the grapes are housed involves eight-hour shifts. But that isn't always so. We go in at eight o'clock in the morning and come out at noon for two hours. Then we go back to work at two o'clock in the afternoon and are supposed to leave at six. In the morning it is really cold. There is a lot of

Recorded October 1,
1990, in Santa María, Chile.

fog and humidity and the grapes are watered at night. So you spend the whole morning walking around in cold, wet mud carrying around heavy wooden crates to put the grapes in. By the time the afternoon rolls around, the sun comes out. It's not good for your body to move from cold to hot so quickly. Once the sun comes out, it gets hot and often the food we have with us gets spoiled because of the heat. By that time, the water we have with us to drink is quite warm as well and not very refreshing. So sometimes we decide to drink out of the irrigation ditches because the water is nice and cool. We wet ourselves with the irrigation water when it is hot, and we drink it even though we know it is dirty. It must be contaminated because they are constantly using insecticides on the grapes.

Working inside the packing plants is also difficult. When you work there, you usually are running out the door at midday and you have to take your meals with you.

Lynn: What time do you finish working at night in the packing plants?

Antonia: Sometimes we finish at one or two in the morning.

Cecilia: Not always. One time I went to work at 1:30 in the afternoon and I didn't leave until five o'clock in the morning. I spent the whole night working. Other times I leave at two or three in the morning. We always finish really late. It takes a lot out of you to work in the packing plant.

Antonia: You really kill yourself to earn a few *pesitos*.

Lynn: What is it like inside the packing plant?

Antonia: When you are inside you are thinking about what is going on at home. How are my children? What are they doing? Is everything okay? Sometimes when you are there working, a big load of grapes arrives and they have to be cleaned for packing. Then, later, no grapes come in and you don't have anything to do for two hours. If you don't work, you don't get paid even though you are hanging around inside the packing plant. We are just waiting there for the grapes. They run our lives.

In general you only get work when you sign a contract, and this contract doesn't give you any benefits. As Cecilia said, sometimes you don't finish until five or six in the morning. You never know. When the grapes are picked, they have to be packed and sent off immediately.

There is something else that can happen as well. Sometimes the quality control people arrive out of the blue. They look at all of the grapes and if they find one bad grape then they take everything out of the box and you have to repack it all. Or they may empty a lot of boxes looking for bad grapes. Then the woman packing loses all the time it takes to repack everything. And this time isn't paid for. It's her problem. We don't get paid while we eat either. Sometimes the owners get really pissed off when we have to repack the grapes, and they forget that we have to eat. They don't give us breaks and we are really hungry. Inside the packing plant, they give you a cup of tea or some water. Sometimes they have sandwiches as well.

Lynn: Do they give you the sandwiches?

Antonia: No, they take it out of your paycheck. Sometimes they don't give you anything and the hours are very long. When I was working at Agrovalle (company name) we used to go to work at 1:30 in the afternoon and leave at three in the morning. They didn't give us anything. Nothing at all.

Lynn: So you worked fourteen hours straight?

Antonia: Yes. They didn't give us anything to eat or drink and just wanted us to keep on working. So we protested. Imagine how we felt. It was really cold, and we had nothing to eat or drink.

Lynn: Who is in charge of the packing plants?

Antonia: Usually they are men. The grapes are almost always examined by men for quality. Generally, inside the plant, there are women who are in charge of each line of women workers, who are cleaning and packing in teams. The owners don't really get involved with the workers. They leave that up to the bosses. And these bosses are much more annoying than the owners. They walk around doing their "quality control," exhorting us to hurry up and to work harder. These men have a lot of power inside the packing plants and they use it. They treat the people working there badly. . . . The other people inside the plant who are watching us are the people in charge of each line.

Lynn: These people are the same as you, aren't they? Aren't they hired from among the workers in the packing plant?

Antonia: Yes. But they are paid a lot more than people who clean and pack the fruit. All they do is watch us to make sure that we are always working. They check to see that we aren't talking too much and that our hands are moving quickly. They tell us to hurry up. That's what they get paid for, just to tell us this.

Lynn: How long have you been working in agriculture?

Antonia: For ten years. I have worked thinning and pruning plants, taking leaves off, and cleaning fruit and packing. I have done all of these things. . . . I have also worked in asparagus. My job there was to pull weeds. I did the work on my hands and knees in the cold and the fog.

You know, a lot of women went out to work during the dictatorship because our husbands were afraid to go out, especially if they had been in any kind of union. So a lot of women began working in agriculture, and we didn't know much about labor laws and our rights. Most people were not unionized, and a lot of people were afraid of unionizing because of the consequences. So a lot of people didn't speak up at all for their rights as workers.

I originally came here from another region way to the south. Before I came here to work, I thought the people in the south were completely forgotten and abandoned in terms of knowing about their rights. But once I got here and started working in the packing plants, I saw that the workers here didn't have very much consciousness and that there was a real need to organize people.

Of course, I also think specifically about the women workers here. They earn very little, while the owners are accustomed to earning a lot of money. The working conditions are quite dismal. When I first came here, I thought that there would be a separate place for us to eat. On the first day I worked, I said to my *compañeras*, "Where is the lunchroom? Where should I go to eat?" They looked at me as if I were nuts and said, "We eat right here in the *parron* with the grapes." I started to complain about a lot of things—the water, the lack of bathrooms, no place to eat, everything. They were all accustomed to the conditions and didn't know that they could ask for anything else. It was all normal for the women working in the packing plants.

Lynn: Can you tell me about the Mothers' Centers?

Antonia: The central activity of the Mothers' Center here is knitting. I belonged to the Mothers' Center here in Santa María called "La Amistad" (Friendship). I went for a year, but I had to stop going after I became more active in the Seasonal Workers' Union. We used to come together to knit, to talk, to sew things.

Lynn: Were the Mothers' Centers helpful to women?

Antonia: Yes, in a sense. You would go all afternoon from two until six, and you could forget about all of your problems at home. I guess that is good for women.

Lynn: How is the women's knitting-and-crocheting workshop that the union has organized different from the Mothers' Centers?

Antonia: It's different from a Mothers' Center because we aren't just going there as individuals. We are all members of the Seasonal Workers' Union and we talk about the organization there. We also talk about women's rights as workers while we are knitting and weaving. It has also been a space where we have had special classes on women's rights within labor law and on women's health. We also encourage women to go to the women's school, even though their husbands don't want them to. There are some husbands who don't like it when their wives come to the knitting workshop. They are suspicious. There are even some men who refuse to give their wives permission to go. Some of these women come anyways, but they are very quiet. It's very hard for them to say what they think, even in our meetings.

Lynn: What happens when men and women both participate in the broader meetings of the union? Do women speak up?

Antonia: There are some women who have been participating ever since the union began. But most women do not speak up. Most of the women who are really quiet in the general meetings of the union don't come to the knitting workshop. The knitting workshop has a different feel to it than the union meetings. Because only women come to the workshop, usually all the women present eventually let loose and participate.

I remember one woman who was completely silent. Her name is Carmen. When she first started coming to the knitting workshop, she never said anything. Then one of the other women, Josefa, invited us all to sit around a table so that we could get to know one another. This woman was so shy that when her turn came to introduce herself around the table, she cried. She had never spoken in a group before. But now she is changed. Now she speaks with everyone in the women's knitting workshop and isn't afraid to say what she thinks. There are a lot of women like her who are afraid to go to the union meetings. And they are also afraid to participate in a union.

Lynn: What do you think needs to be done to give more women a chance to participate in general union meetings?

Antonia: Well, that entails a lot of work. Because it is always the same women who are actively participating. In a general meeting, about forty or fifty of the five hundred members show up. . . . (W)e meet about once a month.

Lynn: When you have a meeting, how many women and how many men come?

Antonia: About twenty-five women and about fifteen men.

Lynn: How many women speak?

Antonia: Only about four of them will participate. The other twenty-one will be quiet.

Lynn: How many of the fifteen men speak?

Antonia: About eight or ten of the men will speak. . . .

Cecilia walks back into the room after we have discussed different men and their styles of leadership.

Cecilia: Well, you know that a man came to one of our meetings. He went to our workshop, picked up some knitting needles, and began to knit. He is the only man who has come and listened to us.

Lynn: So men don't come into women's spaces very often, but women go into the union space. How can you create more spaces for women to be active?

Antonia: To get women to participate, we have to create more small groups and spaces like the knitting workshop. We also have to create places for men and women to participate together. They can't just be isolated. But we have to have other kinds of experiences for men and women together besides meetings. For example, when you have a theater group, people like to come. They have a good time together. That's important. . . . Men and women have to learn to get along before they can feel comfortable together in meetings. Now, they just don't know what to say to one another.

CHAPTER 8

Conclusions
Women in Action

Feminist social scientists have been engaged in a conversation about the nature of gender relations, economic development, political mobilization, and women's identity and experience for quite some time. This conversation includes not only an evaluation of what is observed by women researchers in what is conventionally termed the "field situation," but also an exploration of power relations between women in the process of conducting research. The experience of Latin American women and grassroots organizations represented in the present book offers six thematic contributions to this ongoing conversation:

1. *The social, cultural, and political worlds of individual women are characterized by a unity of experience. It does not make sense to divide women's experience into a public sphere associated with maleness and a private sphere associated with femaleness.*

2. *Women's economic participation includes a wide range of activities that crosscut unpaid domestic labor, work in the so-called informal sector, and in the formal economy. They do not conceptualize or experience their economic participation as segmented. The abstract division of economies into "informal" and "formal" genders the economy by incorporating the dichotomy of female-private and male-public into economic analysis and distorts the context and meaning of women's economic participation.*

3. *Latin American women's activism, like that of many women in other places and times, often combines a commitment to basic material survival for women and their families with direct or indirect challenges to women's subordination to men. The nature of the women's political activism highlighted in this book suggests the futility of trying to project abstract categories onto women's mobilization, particularly those* *categories which characterize mobilizations as either a strategic-feminist activity that challenges women's subordination or a practical-feminine activity that reinforces women's traditional gender roles associated with the domestic sphere. It is often both simultaneously.*

4. *Women's ability to carry out collective action is based on forging a common argument in a particular time and place, often by agreeing to disagree. Unity is not necessarily achieved by the formation of an organic identity which automatically emerges out of the process of collective action. Rather than assume the formation of collective identities which take on a life of their own, women's political participation should be examined in context and viewed as a process of constant negotiating and repositioning. The heterogeneity of women within one organization that embraces differences in age, class, ethnicity, sexuality, and political experience are all part of the context within which political action is negotiated.*

5. *Women's political action is also embedded in the larger power relations of community, nation, region, and world.*

6. *The Latin American women's organizing reflected in this book as well as the spirit of the research behind it suggest the possibility of remaining committed to the support of women's struggle yet also projecting a political analysis that works across cultural divides and acknowledges the differences of women's experience in contemporary global relations.*

This chapter will be devoted to a discussion of each one of these themes, drawing on the lessons to be learned from a comparative discussion of the movements included in this book and using those lessons to contribute to the feminist conversation on women in grassroots movements.

The Unification of Public and Private   The ethnographic record of social life in many rural and working-class urban communities in Latin America defies the division of the social world into public and private. Anthropologists who have worked with marginalized and disenfranchised societies or social groups have documented these trends for quite some time.[1] In Latin America, the vast literature on civil-religious *cargo* systems which describes the merging of civil-government hierarchies with cult religious ceremonies sponsored by male/female pairs of household heads has documented the changing history of merging household religion with civil government—a prime example of politics blurring the boundaries between public and private. The institution of *compadrazgo,* or ritual kinship, has served as a basis for extending family ties and influence within and between communities, for political and other ends.

To understand how the merging of public and private works for women, let us look at some specific examples from the case studies. Is a heated discussion on how to occupy a public building in Mexico City, by ten CONAMUP women on one of their front stoops, taking place in the public sphere or the private sphere? When women in Chile are chopping vegetables to serve to a group of thirty people who will come to eat at a communal kitchen, are they engaged in a private-domestic activity? Is the entry of military police into a woman's home to drag her son out of bed in the middle of the night and take him to a clandestine prison in El Salvador a private act? The daily-life routines as well as the planned political actions of the women in the organizations represented in this book often defy a neat division of social space or behavior into public or private. The same is true of the economic activities of women.

Defying Women's Development as Part of the "Informal" Sector   Women in all of the organizations represented here have rotated in and out of the formal economy, and many have worked simultaneously in what are often billed as three different sectors of the economy: the waged formal sector, the waged informal sector, and the unpaid domestic sector. Women from the CONAMUP may work in collective kitchens, may sell processed food in the evenings, and may have spent time before they were married working as cashiers in local stores. Women from the MMTR in Brazil have worked in subsistence farming, in production for the market, and in unpaid housework; they may also hold part-time positions (e.g., as beauticians) in small towns. Almost all the women in this book have worked as wage laborers.

Yet despite this fact, they were often not viewed as important economic actors or producers by those who designed development projects for them, whether those project designers worked within international agencies such as AID (Agency for International Development), national governments, or progressive nongovernmental organizations and labor organizations. As summarized by Carmen Diana Deere and Magdalena León in their discussion of development projects for rural women in Latin America:

Rural women were perceived only as housewives who were responsible for the domestic realm. The state resources directed toward them focused solely on their roles of wife and mother. Thus home economists were trained throughout Latin American to teach rural women health and nutrition and sewing and handicrafts and at best to introduce home gardens. Programs for agricultural technical assistance and access to credit were directed overwhelmingly toward rural men. Thus, rural extension services reproduced the socially constructed — and idealized — gendered division of labor in which men were the agriculturalists and women were the housewives. (1987:7)

In Mexico, the creation of Agro-Industrial Units for Women (UAIMs), which gave a group of women access to a small piece of land either for planting vegetables and fruit (occasionally corn and beans) or for developing a small industry such as a bakery or tortilla factory, often reinforced traditional notions of women's proper domestic roles. The National Solidarity Program created in the 1990s also confined its women's projects largely to the areas of health, nutrition, and domestic productive activities. The culture of women and development begun at the level of international monetary and development agencies and filtered down to states also permeated many independent peasant, labor, and urban survival organizations, not to mention the revolutionary left.

In El Salvador, the women's projects of the FMLN focused on providing women with health and nutrition training and promoting income-generating projects. Later projects included communal banks (Cosgrove 1995). In Mexico, women in the CONAMUP began to organize around obtaining access to government-subsidized food and other services. Under Salvador Allende in Chile, Mothers' Centers encouraged women's craft production. Strategies that were often repeated by official as well as by independent peasant organizations for women reproduced the notion that the domestic or private sphere belonged to women while the public world of markets, credit, and finance belonged to men.

Nevertheless, the dual reality of (1) women's own work lives, which crosscut different economic sectors, and (2) the daily-life obstacles, both within families and within larger organizations, to actually implementing even the most conservative women's development projects can result in a sustained challenge to the relegation of women's work and economic-political activity to some sort of "informal-domestic" sphere. In Brazil and Chile, women workers' rights are part of an explicit organizing agenda that includes pressuring for old-age pensions, maternity leave, and health benefits. Making women's labor visible and formalizing it is part of a strategy for gaining official recognition as workers and for having the rights of those employed in the "formal" sector extended to them. Since these women have always viewed their labor as public and formal, why should they not receive the benefits other workers receive?

A second way in which the association of women with a private economic sphere continues is through analyses of "women and economic crisis" which confine their focus to the household. In addition to the well-documented fact that the household is an undemocratic institution riddled by the age and gender hierarchies of the world outside it, any exclusive focus on women's changing roles in the household as a response to economic crisis eclipses women's efforts to organize collectively in other social constellations (e.g., communal kitchens in Mexico City and in Santa María, Chile, notwithstanding their initial problems). While many women are certainly increasing their self-exploitation by assuming greater domestic workloads and increasing the amount of time they spend in paid employment, some are also simultaneously organizing to reallocate resources and hold Latin American states accountable for the minimal social welfare obligations they still owe to the poor. When neighborhoods or communities have a history of common struggle, as in some areas of Mexico City, economic crisis may trigger a shared effort at confronting the sources of the crisis. Women's tactics for participating in these struggles crosscut the household as a unit and result in neighborhood webs of action which can form a counterbalance to the individualization of economic crisis.

Women in Social Movements   The problems inherent in characterizing women's economic activities as belonging primarily to one sector (formal, informal, domestic) are repeated when abstract categories are applied to their grassroots mobilizations—as with the feminine-practical versus feminist-strategic distinction often made to categorize women's collective action (see Chapter 1 for a discussion of these terms). The actual process of any type of women's organizing, whatever the content, is likely to challenge conventional gender roles at some level.[2] As suggested by the prevalence of threats against and actual domestic violence encountered by many of the women from the organizations discussed here, the simplest act of organizing, regardless of its content or intent, often has the result of disrupting domestic routines and divisions of labor. Such disruptions bring to the surface domestic divisions of labor and gender roles which have often been invisible to women and men alike. If family members are able to work out an accommodation for women who need to leave the home and go to meetings, demonstrations, government offices, hospitals, prisons, and elsewhere, then women will be able to continue their organizational participation. If there is no familial accommodation (as is often the case), domestic conflict is the result. When domestic conflict occurs, if there is support within a woman's organization to discuss it, or if there are connections to other groups such as feminist NGOs which carry out education about domestic violence, women's physical subordination to their husbands usually becomes a source of future group activity. Thus, women in the CONAMUP who set out to organize communal kitchens and breakfast programs for their children also ended up holding workshops on domestic violence and participating in the International Day against Violence against Women. Because many kinds of organizing activity inevitably contain public aspects and disrupt normal routines, they also disrupt the apparent cultural logic of women's confinement to the private sphere. The totality of women's experience as political organizers will very likely include "strategic" as well as "practical" interests, for the fact of their organizing is inevitably tied to challenging gender subordination at some level.

The suggestion that we reconsider the strategic-versus-practical dichotomy and, by implication, the categorization of social, economic, and political relations as either public or private fits well with recent writing on women's mobilizations. In an article on popular women's organizations in Ecuador, Amy Conger Lind suggests that although women's organizing projects may focus on procuring basic needs, those "basic needs are not tied solely to survival, but rather to constructions of identity and relations of power." She criticizes Maxine Molyneux's paradigm based on its assumption that a "practical or survival strategy cannot simultaneously be a political strategy that challenges the social order" (Lind 1992:137).

In an edited collection on women and popular protest in Latin America, Sallie Westwood and Sarah Radcliffe (1993) reject the strategic/practical dichotomy for two reasons. First, they suggest that such a dichotomy is founded on a linear view of progress rooted in a post-Enlightenment evolutionary perspective that posits a hierarchical relationship between feminine and feminist movements: progress is made when a women's organization moves from practical to strategic interests. This view, moreover, "tends to maintain the distinction between public and private, and between the personal and the political, the deconstruction of which has always been so central to feminist politics" (Westwood and Radcliffe 1993:20). Instead of dichotomies between public and private, practical and strategic interests, they propose understanding women as political subjects and actors in relation to "the multiplicity of sites wherein women are engaged in power struggles" (1993:20). In the same volume, analyzing the CO-MADRES and the CONAVIGUA Widows of Guatemala, Jennifer Schirmer also raises the question of how we understand women who have multiple "strategic" and "pragmatic" interests which change over time and which "they themselves do not deem as separate" (1993b:61).

In all of the cases analyzed in this book, women's continual occupation of what are seen as public spaces—squares, political forums, state capitals, government offices, etc.—disrupts cultural readings of what the proper gendering of public space should be. Many people such as Jean Franco have read the so-called motherist movements (often, movements of mothers and relatives of the disappeared) as "transforming mothering and transferring it from the private to the public sphere" (n.d., cited in Miller 1991:8). In the 1980s, the general interpretation of the "motherist" movements was to see them as using "traditional" expectations about mothers to get away with conducting political protest in times and places where no one else could. Capitalizing on *marianismo*, or the cult of the Virgin Mary, women such as the Mothers of the Plaza de Mayo were portrayed as making an appeal based on "the most conservative aspects of feminine identity" (Feijoo 1989:88).

The response of mothers to the kidnapping of their children was described as being based on the simple fact of their motherhood:

They were compelled to act not on moral or political grounds or out of a concern for gross human rights violations, as in the case of other groups, but because they were mothers. Their refusal to acquiesce in the loss of their children was not an act out of character, but a coherent expression of their socialization, of their acceptance of the dominant sexual division of labor and of their own subordination within it. True to themselves, they had no other choice but to act, even if it meant confronting the junta. (M. Navarro 1989:256–257)

While many mothers were no doubt strongly affected by the loss of their children and extremely militant in their efforts to find them, we cannot conclude that their motherhood somehow imbued them with a uniform identity or interpretation of what they were doing. Hegemonic gender constructions in Argentina and elsewhere no doubt did facilitate women's ability to tread on political terrain where others dared not go during such repressive times as "el Proceso." But such hegemonic constructions of motherhood also have internal contradictions, and motherhood has always varied by age, class, ethnic affiliation, and race.

Women's presence within a political movement or confrontation in what is culturally labeled a public space makes visible the fact that mothering has always been both public and private. While hegemonic interpretations of women's proper behavior may confine "mothering" to the domestic realm, that is no guarantee that women themselves see mothering as a solely private activity. Motherhood has always had a public identity in Latin America, at least for many women engaged in it.

As seen among the women of the CO-MADRES, for example, mothering can mean bringing four children with you to a stall in a public marketplace, staying there all day, walking home with them after dark, and stopping to visit relatives on the way. Among the upper classes in El Salvador, mothering can mean having a live-in domestic serve your children lunch while you supervise a gardener's arrangement of flowers in the patio. Hegemonic constructions of gender do reinforce virginity and biological motherhood, do connect them to the Catholic church and various virgin cults, and do encourage the idea that women should be protected, at home, and serving their families. There are, however, alternative cultural discourses of motherhood continually spun out of the different daily lives of women in Latin America.

Should we thus label women's political participation on the basis of being mothers as being limited to "practical ends"? If women such as the CO-MADRES repeatedly question male military authority and in the process lead other sectors of society in protest marches against repressive regimes, are they still merely shifting their "mothering" from the private to the public realm? Is their agenda simply aimed at recovering their children? In reality, their very authority in the public realm comes from the fact that mothering is a public activity and their loss is generalizable to people who are not mothers. The ability of groups like the CO-MADRES to vigilantly maintain public opposition to the military regime in El Salvador was also a result of their influence in a wide range of movements and of their ongoing understanding and readjustment of a coherent political project: to be simultaneously a human rights and a women's rights movement.

The use of gendered ideology by those in power to justify the repression of women (e.g., by using rape as a method of torture because the women involved are no longer seen as proper mothers) can, of course, reinforce in terrible ways larger cultural messages about women's lack of rights and can severely limit their ability to organize. This is well documented in the systematic rape of the CO-MADRES under detention and the continued and escalating domestic violence many women experience when they become politically active. It is also seen in the resistance of the Catholic church, even in its progressive mode, to women's work concerning reproductive health and rights.

At the same time, though, the use of gendered ideology by those in power to justify the repression of women can trigger a questioning not only of the military culture of terrorism, but of the legal codes that prevent women from prosecuting for rape or domestic violence. The CO-MADRES are a case in point. There, some women slowly came to terms with the contradiction between denouncing the military for various forms of torture, but not confronting their own family members for rejecting them as damaged goods after their rape under detention. In a very different example, the presence of women on the street at night in Santa María, Chile, some of whom have become sexually active outside of their marriages, also provides an avenue to challenge the ideology that would label them as "whores" for being on the street at night. In both cases, the actions of women are working against the biologizing of gender and rejecting the notion that women's proper place is at home.

Another way in which the case studies demonstrate the *unity* of women's organizing experience, rather than its dichotomization between practical and strategic interests, is the combination of daily-life survival issues specific to women's experience with a questioning of various forms of gender subordination including rape, domestic violence, and a lack of reproductive knowledge and control. This convergence of issues found in many of the organizations studied here is perhaps the best evidence of how women can incorporate a wide range of issues and experiences into one struggle that might not appear logically compatible to outsiders. The integration of seemingly contradictory gender interests—in that they simultaneously reinforce and challenge traditional roles—is a hallmark of the movements analyzed here.

As Hall (1989, 1995), Roseberry (1994), and others working from a Gramscian perspective have reminded us, power and hegemony are not absolute. The presence of ideological contradictions within any system of unequal power relations both validates the power of forms of domination and provides the potential for challenging them. The possibility for the emergence of new political and social subjects is dependent upon the contradictory and uneven ways in which structures of domination function. Because power can come from below, because it comes into play through a wide range of institutions and throughout the social body (Foucault 1990:94), challenges to unequal relations of power come logically in contradictory packages. Such is the case of the women's movements analyzed in this book.

Forging Temporary Unity out of Heterogeneity   Recent work which attempts to get at the integrated nature of individual women's experience in political activism by eliminating the application of abstract categories to collective action also suggests that we avoid re-essentializing women by declaring them unified within a shared collective identity. The variety of individual experiences and interpretations of political activity and ideology (including feminism) expressed by the women in the case studies also points to the need for moving beyond the notion of assumed collective identities as an explanation for how women can act together.

In many of the organizations studied here, important differences can be found among women participating in the same organization with respect to age, class, sexuality, political experience, ideology and, in some cases, ethnicity and location (urban/rural). These differences result in varying senses of identity (each woman having several) when women enter the organization as well as varied interpretations of events and strategy. They also suggest that the process of mobilization involves internal power negotiations, shifting alliances, and processes of accountability between leaders and base. Here, two common themes found running through the organizations will be used to illustrate the importance of both respecting and negotiating difference in order for collective action to take place. The first theme has to do with the range of opinions often found within one organization in relation to varying definitions of feminism. The second is a focus on internal democratization and the creation of new forms of political culture in many of the organizations.

With the exception of the Women's Council of the UELC in Nayarit, Mexico, all of the organizations studied have had contact with varying types of self-identified feminists, either through workshops and training they received with NGOs or through their participation in wider political coalitions that included self-described feminist organizations. In many instances, the reactions of women to the feminists and their ideas have been quite diverse. If they had forged a completely unitary collective identity, their reactions would perhaps have been more uniform. Such differences of opinion, however, did not prevent them from engaging in discussions, arguments, and actions around many issues which others have labeled "feminist."[3]

Within the MMTR, even women who privately would say they were feminists would not do so in public, fearful of public surmises about their stance on controversial issues such as abortion. Women within the MMTR remain divided on abortion, and they have advanced the debate on abortion by including it in discussions of women's reproductive health. They agree that it is an important topic of continued discussion and do not feel it is necessary to have a unified position.

Women within the CONAMUP have quite contradictory visions of what feminism means. While some have embraced "feminismo popular" (popular feminism) as a way of integrating class- and gender-based concerns, others associate feminism with separatism and feel it threatens their heterosexual marriages and distinctiveness as women. Nevertheless, they are all capable of working within the same organization and have agreed to disagree. Women in the CO-MADRES manifest a similar division concerning whether or not to embrace feminism, and they have expressed important differences in their ability to assimilate discourses on women's sexuality and pleasure.

Ironically, while it is clear both to the women in grassroots movements and to their observers that participation in organizing is a continued process of negotiating difference, the need to create unitary names, symbols, and goals can result in the essentialization of women—as "mothers" in the case of the CO-MADRES or as "female rural workers" in the case of the MMTR of Brazil. The political necessity of "sameness," such as that projected to people outside the movement, however, does not offer an explanation of how a movement operates, what it means to those involved, or what it is able to accomplish. We cannot explain how women in self-labeled "motherist" movements act simply on the basis of the shared label of "mother." We have to explore the internal negotiation of difference between women to understand the process of their publicly constructed unity.

In most of the organizations studied here, there is a preoccupation with the internal process of democracy, and this highlights the importance of negotiating differences among women. The issue of democratization was a major political concern in each of the countries represented here, and it is quite logical to think that national political concerns have a significant influence on the internal processes of social movements. They certainly have had such an influence over the past decade in Latin America (Escobar and Alvarez 1992; Jaquette 1994). At the same time, however, a significant preoccupation with processes of internal democratization also indicates the necessity of mediating, not erasing, difference.

The term "participatory democracy" is used in this book to denote widespread citizen participation. It is not confined to electoral democracies in which the primary exercise of citizenship is voting. Politics as participatory and citizenship as the active engagement of peers in the public realm assume a notion of democracy that is neither the negative liberty of noninterference nor the legitimization of every individual interest (see Dietz 1992). Democracy "takes politics to be the collective and participatory engagement of citizens in the determination of the affairs of their community" (Dietz 1992:75).

For the women represented here, the issue of internal democracy has arisen through various avenues. First, it has arrived via the brutal treatment of many opposition organizations by governments. Second, it has arisen through the exclusion and marginalization of women within opposition organizations, primarily those of the left in the cases studied here. In many cases, a fairly obvious contradiction emerged as independent labor, peasant, and revolutionary organizations called for the democratization of *national* politics, but reproduced vertical structures of decisionmaking *within* the organization. In two of the cases explored here—the DIGNAS in El Salvador and the Women's Regional Council of the CONAMUP—women's organizations grew either directly or indirectly because of women's exclusion from structures of power within mixed organizations.

In order to understand the importance of internal democratization in the women's grassroots organizations explored here, it is useful to continue the previous discussion of the term "political culture." As described by Alvarez, Dagnino, and Escobar, political culture is the "domain of practices and institutions carved out of the totality of social reality that historically comes to be considered properly political" (1996:10). Internal democratization efforts by women in the Regional Council of the CONAMUP, the DIGNAS, and the MMTR consist of creating alternative forms of political culture and process that do not reproduce the marginalization they experienced in mixed organizations. Alvarez, Dagnino, and Escobar write that

the cultural politics of social movements unsettle the dominant political culture. To the extent that the objectives of contemporary social movements go beyond perceived material and institutional gains; to the extent that social movements shake the boundaries of cultural and political representation and social practice, calling into question even what may or may not be seen as political; to the extent, finally, that the very cultural politics of social movements enact cultural contestations or presuppose cultural difference—then we must accept that what is at stake for social movements, in a profound way, is a transformation of the dominant political culture in which they have to move and constitute themselves as social actors with political pretensions. (1966:10)

Described as such, social movements have truly radical potential. While they can and do unsettle dominant political culture, they can also reproduce (albeit often unintentionally) exclusionary dominant political practices.

While in some cases women may believe that they have the potential to be less hierarchical and more inclusive, they often have few resources to work with. If they were socialized with little participatory experience as women and came into political organizations where it was the norm for women to remain silent, then developing an alternative political culture had to take place in gender-separate spaces where new rules could be enacted. Even with the best of intentions, however, activists in groups such as the DIGNAS found themselves speaking for other women and initially unable to incorporate the differing visions of rural women into their political culture. Efforts at creating "new" political cultures can themselves turn out to be exclusionary. Only a more open conceptualization of who "we" are allowed urban, working-class DIGNAS activists who came from authority positions within the FMLN to rethink their relationship with their rural *compañeras* who formed the core constituency of their organization. In fact, it was only after they rejected the "feminist" versus "feminine" analysis of their own organizing projects that they were able to reevaluate and appreciate the contributions of the rural women they worked with, acknowledging their differences but not forcing a unified vision on them.

While grassroots women activists have raised important questions about how to generate a democratic political culture, it should not be assumed that just because they are women and have a common experience of exclusion from political structures of power, that they will automatically be able to democratize their own organizations easily or come up with ideas that all find acceptable. As women in the MMTR indicated, they must cast aside their own socialization and begin with very different forms of political culture, such as small group discussions and new definitions of leadership that focus not on charisma and public-speaking ability, but on patience, listening ability, and a capacity for unifying diverse factions (see Sacks 1988).

These examples further suggest that it makes little sense to assign women within the same organization an automatic collective identity. Organizational unity at specific conjunctures does not necessarily correspond with homogeneity in experience, interpretation, or personal-identity building. The sharing of a common set of questions directed at unequal relations of power which frame the broader experience of each woman within an organization may be a more accurate formulation of what allows women to engage in collective action. They agree to construct a common argument at a specific point in time. As pointed out by Alvarez and Escobar (1992:319), "the production of oppositional and alternative meanings as a political fact is a realization that has to be brought to bear on social movement theory and methodology."

Linking Women's Political Action to Larger Social Forces   Theorizing about social movements purely on the basis of identity formation leaves politics without roots in social forces and transforms social movements into unitary actors devoid of internal contradictions: identity becomes a mobilizing force on its own (see Hindley 1995b). Larger social, political, and economic forces significantly influenced but did not determine the formation, strategy, content, and outcomes of the women's movements highlighted in this book. Such movements in turn have sometimes also affected agencies of the state, other political organizations or movements, and the formation of policy.

The case studies from Mexico, for example, highlight the complexity of the state and the necessity of seeing how contradictory tendencies within the state can provide a complex terrain for negotiation by movements. Laws aimed at providing access to land and credit for women, through the creation of UAIMs, coexisted with the historical political structure of the *ejido*, which marginalized women in decisionmaking. The UAIMs were also created as a political strategy on the part of the state to widen its web of clientist relations to incorporate women. These and other contradictory factors linked to the state, as well as the varying positions of different state agencies and individuals, all affected the trajectory of women's organizing projects in the Women's Council of the UELC. Complaints from women that they had no control over their own resources, as well as further legal reforms, also led to a change in Mexican law in 1991 that allowed UAIMs to directly receive resources, rather than having them funneled through *ejidos*.

In El Salvador, the CO-MADRES resisted the torture and disappearance of relatives and children, and brought public attention to the brutal human rights abuses carried out by government troops and police. Their success in the global arena at times helped to force an easing in government repression and helped to keep the Salvadoran civil war alive as an issue in the international news media and in diplomatic circles. After the civil war had been declared "over" with the signing of peace accords between the FMLN and the Alfredo Cristiani government, and after civilian elections took place, the DIGNAS used the elections as a tool for raising national consciousness about legal discrimination against women in the Constitution and as a way to train women for positions in future municipal elections.

In Mexico, women from the CONAMUP sought collective alternatives for dealing with increased individual economic hardship brought on by structural adjustment policies. They were also courted by a state agency to participate in a national antipoverty program known as

PRONASOL, or the National Solidarity Program. They were no doubt targeted for inclusion in the program because of their organizational effectiveness. Through their participation in the National Solidarity Program, they tried to hold state agencies such as the Family Services Agency (DIF) and the distribution branch of the National Basic Foods Company (CONASUPO) accountable for the services and goods they were supposed to deliver.

In Brazil, women in the MMTR took notice of how the state had responded to urban workers by extending them benefits; they pressured the state to grant rural women workers the same rights. In Chile, the end of the Augusto Pinochet dictatorship signaled an opening for labor organizing, and so women seasonal workers in Santa María demanded the same rights as permanent workers. In each of these cases, women's organizations responded specifically to larger political, economic, and cultural circumstances.

In an attempt to explain the "constructedness" of identity, some new social movement theorists seem to go overboard in their rejection of structure in order to move human agency to center stage. Laclau and Mouffe (1985), for example, suggest that collective action can only come about contingently through the chance and temporary articulation of competing discourses which actors with multiple subjectivities encounter.[4] Because each actor has a plurality of positions or orientations (identities are never given) and because the articulation of this plurality of positions is contingent (not to be taken for granted or read off of structural conditions), the main political problem becomes "exploring the kinds of articulations that may result in the formation of identities and collective mobilization" (Escobar 1992:79).

Contesting the idea that structure determines experience and identity is one thing. But rejecting any link between materially based relations of power and collective action is another. As stated by John Gledhill in his evaluation of Laclau and Mouffe, "this brand of deconstructionist theorizing, if taken at face value, leaves politics without roots in social forces" (Gledhill 1994:186). If everyone has radically different subject positions and is open to a wide range of antagonisms that never line up in similar experiences, how likely are people to unify around a common objective, even for an afternoon?

A different piece of writing by Chantal Mouffe (1988), however, suggests that she by no means sees social movements as completely disconnected from economic, political, and cultural process and, perhaps somewhere underneath, even from structures. The strong influence of Antonio Gramsci in her work comes through here and provides a way to link the process of identity creation to the larger political economy and to competing ideologies.

In her discussion of hegemony and its relation to new social movements, Mouffe outlines antagonisms reflected in the relations of subordination people experience. These antagonisms are central sources of conflict and struggle in new social movements and can result in a higher level of awareness on the part of political actors of their situation. Collective struggles against inequality occur when "subjects constructed in subordination by a set of discourses are, at the same time, interpellated as equal by other discourses. . . . [I]t is the subjectivity-in-subordination that is negated, which opens up the possibility for its deconstruction and challenging" (Mouffe 1988:95). The awareness generated through conflicting discourses can in turn generate new ideologies and forms of struggle that often fall outside traditional categories of political analysis.

"Subjects constructed in subordination . . . at the same time interpellated as equal" presumably have a relationship to the contradictory structural and ideological contexts in which they exist. New forms of struggle come out of transactions, experiences, events, and discussions posed in structural contexts, but the process of engaging in them also involves the attachment of meaning and interpretation as mediated by the multiple selves of each person involved. Here, the integrative types of actions, strategies, and ideals generated through women's political mobilization are a result of contradictory structural processes of political economy as well as multiple and often contradictory cultural ideologies concerning appropriate gendered behavior. In Brazil, women in the MMTR became politicized in organizations such as labor unions and the antidam movement, fighting the process of unequal economic development. While these organizations often espoused the general notion of gender equality, they did not target women's gender subordination. As subjects constructed in inequality who came to hear discourses about gender equality while not being granted equal participation as members and leaders, and who later were exposed to discourses challenging women's political, economic, and domestic subordination to men, the women in the MMTR faced major contradictions. These contradictions helped bring about an autonomous women's movement that self-consciously tried to create alternative forms of political culture. The actions, reactions, and creation of new political forms and culture by the women of the MMTR cannot be divorced from the material and cultural conditions out of which their initial and continued politicization emerged.

The women from the organizations presented here came to their collective mobilizations from different positions, with varied understandings and interpretations, but the commonalities of some of the themes they are organizing around suggest that gendered relations of power are operating with some similarity in different parts of Latin America and are linked to larger social, cultural, and political relations which can limit women's political activities. One common area of gendered relations of power, for example, is the traditional Catholic church.

For women in many Latin American countries, notions of proper female behavior, particularly with respect to motherhood, are tied to the Catholic church. With the exception of some parts of the church of liberation theology, the Roman Catholic hierarchy has reinforced public perceptions about the appropriateness of a male-directed society in which women remain confined to the home. In El Salvador, Argentina, Chile, and other Latin American countries where women organized as mothers confronting military regimes in search of the disappeared, women were uniformly raped in the process of their torture and detention (see Schirmer 1993b; Agosín 1993; Bunster-Burotto 1986). If women were not living up to the traditional Catholic image of the Virgin Mary as an obedient, pure, and self-sacrificing mother, then they could be interpreted as the opposite—as a whore, an aggressive, impure, sexual object. Rape becomes a justified treatment of women who are behaving incorrectly.

Other examples of how political, economic, and cultural relations influenced the movements explored here include economic development programs for women which were focused on small-scale productive activities tied to the home, women's consistent marginalization within organizations of the left, and the domestic violence which often accompanied women's increased political activism. The limits and resistance to women's political participation—faced by women in all the case studies—suggest some shared cultural resources on the part of men and in the gendered behavior of men and women which can be formidable obstacles to women attempting to change their lives for the better.

We should not throw the baby out with the bathwater and "disappear" all forms of inequality by deconstructing hierarchies of power to the point of nonexistence and delinking them from collective action.[5] It is possible to refrain from projecting identities and experience onto women while simultaneously acknowledging structures of power. In the end, "disappearing" the structures of repression which are experienced as the interlocking forces of racism, sexism, classism, and heterosexism may be more of a disservice to women than reproducing gender as biologically constituted. The concept of collective identity does little to explain the "how" of social movements if it is removed from the larger context within which such movements operate.

Acknowledging Difference in Research and Politics   Just as the Latin American women discussed here have worked to bridge differences without declaring uniform identities between themselves, feminist researchers have sought to find ways to remain committed to feminism yet acknowledge the differences of experience they and the women they work with have. Grappling with the meaning of power differentials between women in the process of research is a topic which has sometimes provoked honest and pessimistic appraisals from ethnographers, whether working close to their own "location" or abroad where the relations of research are supersaturated with economic, racial, and political differences. Evaluating whether or not her work collecting oral histories from sixty poor, Brazilian women of color could result in ethical research, Daphne Patai (1991) begins and ends her essay with an emphatic "No!" Patai rejects the notion that researchers can partially empathize with their subjects, as proposed by Maria Mies (1983), and she forewarns those tempted to "situate" themselves in the text with a summary of their identity (e.g., white, working-class mother and academic; middle-class Chicana researcher) that rhetorical maneuvers do not erase difference.

Judith Stacey, who carried out fieldwork on gender and family relationships in California's Silicon Valley, believed at first that this situation might present her with fewer problems and allow her to work closer to her feminist principles than following up her doctoral dissertation on patriarchy and revolution in China. Her intensive ethnographic experience led her to conclude, however, that "the ethnographic method exposes subjects to far greater danger and exploitation than do most positivist, abstract and 'masculinist' research methods" (1991:114).[6] A pessimistic reading of Patai's and Stacey's work might lead one to conclude that feminists should simply give up doing research—something that neither author proposes. Instead, they maintain the importance of being able to do research, but they abandon the project of trying to develop "*the* feminist methodology" with which to accomplish the job.

In their volume titled *Scattered Hegemonies: Postmodernity and Transnational Feminist Practices*, Interpal Grewal and Caren Kaplan (1994) provide plenty of provisos about the dangers of glossing difference with feminist universals. At the same time, they propose that women take responsibility for differences between the researchers and those researched, situate what they are doing in the transnational economy of texts and theories, and get on with doing work that clarifies the different ways in which gender is encoded in transnational structures of capital, power, and culture.[7] Their underlying call for responsibility rather than guilt or a simple rhetoric of "location" is important to consider, and was something pointed out to me on many occasions by the Latin American activists I worked with.

One of the dangers in pursuing a radical politics of identity is the re-creation of essentialist categories. If the only people who ever have the right to speak are those who have direct experience in all aspects of whatever it is they are addressing, then we will find ourselves participating in smaller and smaller conversations. And we will be in the position of believing that we can read people's political perspectives off of some visible aspect of their identity which lines up with our notions of gender, race, class, ethnicity, and sexuality. Put another way, if we can only represent ourselves, then we end up re-essentializing categories we maintain are socially constructed because we will "know" how someone thinks and acts by "who" we perceive them to be. Rather than reject the possibility of people exploring each other's lives and sharing their mutual insights, feminist research must have as its goal methods of inquiry and knowledge production that are able to illuminate difference without falling into extreme relativism.[8]

Just as universal theories and typologies are of little use for understanding the lives of women, it makes no sense to project a set of universal feminist guidelines for how all research with women should be conducted. The rule of thumb is that one must recognize differentials of power and the varying access that researcher and researched have to the larger world; one must think about how to take some responsibility for this realization in accordance with the specific situation each person is working within. Instead of viewing research as offering an opportunity for equal exchange, researchers can think carefully about the kinds of resources and skills they have which may be useful to people and about the political implications of sharing their resources and access.

The experience of the women highlighted between the covers of this book suggests that we bring together the worlds of experience and structure. Our theorizing about women's collective action has to flow from the particulars of specific cases, not from abstract categories that attempt to impose a universal order and interpretation on different women's political projects. While it is important both to consider how and why women come into social movements and to seek an understanding of how their perceptions of themselves and those around them are changed in the process of organizing, we cannot leave the initiation, process, and consequences of women's grassroots organizing disconnected from the larger context of power relations within which it occurs. Gendered relations of power built out of other, overlapping relations of class, ethnicity, race, age, and sexuality are part and parcel of the life of women's organizing—as are the range of institutions through which these relations are mediated, including the church and the state. If we are to do justice to the complexity of women's grassroots organizing, we have to take on these larger structures of power as well as the topics of group process and identity building.

The critical issue of difference—not only among women within one organization and across countries and regions, but between women who are researchers and those who are researched—pushes us to find creative means for constructing connected political projects devoted to improving the lives of women, but not to demand uniformity in goals and interpretation. We can compare "multiple, overlapping and discrete oppressions" rather than come to a common understanding of our hegemonic oppression as women (Grewal and Kaplan 1994:17). That has been the spirit of this book and of the work behind it, and it offers hope that women can indeed communicate and shape future possibilities for global feminist practices.

NOTES

1. Introduction

1. Temma Kaplan brought home the importance of placing the demands and strategies of the women's movements I study within the historical context of Latin American feminism in the 1980s and 1990s. The notion of a "feminine consciousness" resonated more with the content and emphasis of women's movements formed in the 1970s, before the strong emergence of Latin American feminism in the 1980s. Her comments came in response to a paper I delivered at the 1995 annual meeting of the New England Conference on Latin America, held at Dartmouth College in October 1995.

2. In her book *Translated Woman: Crossing the Border with Esperanza's Story*, Ruth Behar offers a creative and insightful discussion about whether or not feminism translates across borders. While some readers have criticized Behar for including a section which discusses her life and experience as a tenured professor within the academy in a book focused on Esperanza (a charismatic rural Mexican woman whose story Behar publishes), Behar's honest and sensitive treatment of the dialectic of the relationship offers much to the field of feminist ethnography. I was inspired by her to publish conversations with activists rather than the seamless prose of an edited testimonial in the style of an earlier book, *Hear My Testimony: María Teresa Tula, Human Rights Activist of El Salvador*. The notion of a dialectic is woven throughout Behar's book.

3. "If feminism is to be different, it must acknowledge the ideological and problematic significance of its own past. Instead of creating yet another grand tradition or a cumulative history of emancipation . . . we need to be attentive to how the past enters differently into the consciousness of other historical periods" (Samgari and Vaid 1990:33, cited in Grewal and Kaplan 1994:18).

4. As noted by Di Leonardo (1991:7), Rayna Rapp Reiter's *Towards an Anthropology of Women* (1975) was the other bible of second-wave feminist anthropology in the 1970s along with the Rosaldo and Lamphere book. Di Leonardo (1991) provides a useful overview of feminist anthropology.

5. Rosaldo (1974:22) specifically asked, "Why is sexual asymmetry a universal fact of human societies? What is its importance and how is it related to other aspects of men's and women's lives?"

Her response: "In what follows, it will be seen that an opposition between 'domestic' and 'public' provides the basis of a structural framework necessary to identify and explore the place of male and female in psychological, cultural, social, and economic aspects of life. 'Domestic,' as used here, refers to those minimal institutions and modes of activity that are organized immediately around one or more mothers and their children; 'public' refers to activities, institutions, and forms of association that link, rank, organize, or subsume particular mother-child groups. Though this opposition will be more or less salient in different social and ideological systems, it does provide a universal framework for conceptualizing the activities of the sexes. The opposition does not *determine* cultural stereotypes or asymmetries in the evaluations of the sexes, but rather underlies them, to support a very general (and, for women, often demeaning) identification of women with domestic life and of men with public life" (Rosaldo 1974:24–25).

6. This definition is the inverse of that given for the informal sector by Portes and Sassen Koob (1987:31).

7. This argument has been used to justify the exploitation of women, children, and others in the segmented labor market, not only in the current era of transnational capitalism but in earlier periods of capitalist development.

8. See the work of Cynthia Enloe (1989, 1993) for a discussion of the symbolic aspects of gendered categories in international politics and economics. Arturo Escobar (1995:171–192) provides an insightful analysis not only of the gendered assumptions of development policy overall, but of the relations between women in different positions of the development discourse.

9. See Jaquette 1989; Jelin 1990; Logan 1990.

10. Researchers such as Francesca Miller date the first wave of Latin American feminism from 1890 to 1938. Miller states of the period: "[W]hat is evident is that, from the first feminist congresses in Mérida in 1873, in Buenos Aires in 1910, in Lima and Havana and Mexico City in the 1920s to the passage of the resolution affirming the right of women to equal civil status with men in Lima in 1938, Latin American women were deeply involved in trying to achieve broad-based political reform within their nations and no nation was completely untouched by their work. A history of activism existed, an activism that bore the special stamp of feminism as it developed in Latin America, with insistence on issues of social justice and the preservation of the feminine" (1991:108–109).

11. The word *encuentro* is difficult to translate. It means more than simply a "meeting," implying a sense of encounter and shared participation as well.

12. Melida Anaya Montes was a guerrilla commander for the FPL who was brutally murdered while exiled in Nicaragua in 1983, presumably on orders from the head of the FPL (New Americas Press 1989:130–131).

13. By 1990, the year of the fifth *encuentro*, feminism had a presence in almost every Latin American and Caribbean nation. The continued growth of the *encuentros* along with the earlier promotion of women's concerns through the United Nations International Decade for Women (1976–1985) affected not only grassroots organizations but governments and First World foundations that funded organizing projects in Latin America. In the 1980s, organizations such as the Ford Foundation had begun to specifically target women. As foundation support for women's organizing grew, nongovernmental organizations (NGOs) began to form in order to support women's organizing projects. Some of these NGOs worked from an explicitly feminist perspective. Many were quite active in the Latin American and Caribbean feminist *encuentros* and made contact with a wide range of grassroots women's organizations.

14. Christina Gilmartin, who was in Beijing just before the United Nations Conference on Women and Human Rights in September 1995, reported that newspapers in Beijing followed a similar strategy to discredit women arriving for the conference. In China, women attending the conference were described as prostitutes, lesbians, and AIDS carriers; special police were even trained to cover women with blankets who might take off their clothing and parade naked in the streets (Christina Gilmartin, oral report on U.N. World Conference on Women at Beijing, Northeastern University, Boston, October 1995).

15. I thank Helga Baitenmann for drawing my attention to this reference.

16. She also warns us, however, that "the demand that the Other expose itself (vulnerability) and the desire to know (power/knowledge) that guides the ethnographic project inevitably create a hierarchical field of forces" (Salazar 1991: 100), a topic taken up by many feminist ethnographers and proponents of a new ethnography.

17. At her request, Doña Kata's actual name has been altered in the text.

2. Women's Rights Are Human Rights

1. I have found the work of Jennifer Schirmer (1993a, 1993b) to be extremely helpful and rich.

2. All data in the preceding two paragraphs are taken from Barry 1990: 177–178.

3. The Chicana writers Gloria Anzaldúa and Cherríe Moraga have commented at length about the power of this dual-gender image not only in Mexico but also among Chicanos/as (see Anzaldúa 1987, 1990; Moraga 1983, 1993; Anzaldúa and Moraga 1983). In popular Mexican historical accounts the figure of Malinche, a Maya noblewoman given to Cortés as a slave, is regarded as a whore and a traitor for consorting with Cortés. She is also held responsible for the creation of the "mestizo" race. Her counterpart is the Virgin of Guadalupe, who is emblematic of all that is desirable in a woman—obedience, devotion, passivity, and motherhood. Anzaldúa, Moraga, and others have offered feminist reinterpretations of Malinche and the Virgin of Guadalupe.

4. "Christian base community" refers to a neighborhood or community organized around the self-help, participatory model of liberation theology. As described by Jenny Pierce, "one of the key elements of the grassroots communities was the way they sought to involve lay people in church functions previously closed to them. . . . Delegates of the Word—men or women—were lay preachers who could do most of the tasks of a priest . . . although not the sacramental functions" (1986:113). The base communities provided a structural organization for the poor, facilitated the organization of collective production and consumption projects (e.g., agricultural cooperatives), and helped forge links between communities. Many of the lay church workers began to connect religious work with political work and became critical players in the organizing of peasants and labor.

3. Women for Dignity and Life

1. Later documents of AMPRONAC cited specific demands including equal pay for equal work, an end to using women as sex symbols and commercializing their bodies, elimination of all forms of prostitution, and eradication of the sources of women's economic misery (AMPRONAC 1979 program, cited in Maier 1985:72–73).

2. AMNLAE participated along with seventy-seven other Nicaraguan women's groups in a national coordinating body (Coordinadora "Voces de Mujeres" sobre Población y Desarrollo, or Women's Voices Coordinating Committee on Population and Development) which held a national meeting in 1993, met throughout 1994, and attended two preparatory meetings for the meeting in Cairo. The coordinating body sent seven delegates to Cairo (Coordinadora "Voces de Mujeres" sobre Población y Desarrollo et al. 1995).

3. See Arnson 1982, Booth and Walker 1989, Montgomery 1994, North 1985, Pearce 1986, and Armstrong and Shenk 1982 for descriptions of popular mobilization, government repression, and the formation of armed guerrilla organizations in the 1970s.

4. For a summary on how economic conditions were affecting Salvadoran women, see Ready 1994.

5. The following discussion of popular organizations, left-wing coalitions, and their links to guerrilla organizations draws from Arnson 1982 and North 1985. See also Montgomery 1994 for further detail.

6. This estimate comes from Van Gosse, a political scientist who has studied the U.S. movement for solidarity with El Salvador. His estimate was checked against the records of CISPES (Committee in Solidarity with the People of El Salvador), the Center for Global Education, Witness for Peace, and CRISPES (Christians in Solidarity with the People of El Salvador). The CISPES delegations include those associated with the Sister Cities and Sister Parishes projects as well as those put together by Share and Nest, two foundations which helped direct delegations and aid to FPL-linked organizations and communities. The Center for Global Education and CRISPES were not aligned with any particular parts of the FMLN. See Gosse 1994 for a detailed analysis of U.S. solidarity movements.

7. The ERP has a U.S. organization called Voices on the Border.

8. In the United States, the RN has a foundation called Fundación Flor de Isote (formerly called El Rescate).

9. This estimate is also provided by Van Gosse (personal communication, February 1995). It was checked against the records of the four largest solidarity fund-raisers.

10. The following discussion draws heavily from Stephen (1994a:206–210) and Mujeres por la Dignidad y la Vida (1993:87–93).

11. Other women's organizations created during this time included the Mélida Anaya Montes Union of Women (1987) which worked in Mexico and elsewhere to foster international solidarity for the FMLN. Over the next two years, other organizations were formed, among them the Association of Marginal Women (AMMA, Asociación de Mujeres Marginales), the Movement of Salvadoran Women (MSM, Movimiento Salvadoreño de Mujeres), the Democratic Association of Women (ADEMUSA, Asociación Democrática de Mujeres Salvadoreñas), and the Salvadoran Women's Association (AMS, Asociación de Mujeres Salvadoreñas).

12. The COM included CONAMUS, AMS, MSM, ADEMUSA and ORMUSA. See note 11 above.

13. In their studies, these activists read the work of Marta Harnecker, a Chilean theorist who in a book titled *Vanguardia y crisis social* [Vanguard and Social Crisis] questions the concept of a vanguard in revolutionary movements. Gloria Castañeda says of Harnecker's work: "By reading Marta's work and that of other people, we came to realize that we couldn't go on considering ourselves to be the only ones that knew what was going on. We weren't the only ones who knew the truth. From there we began to question ourselves about our style of leadership, how our organization was run, how people participated, all kinds of things. . . . We concluded that we couldn't continue using traditional methods of organizing, of using a sectarian type of strategy. We had entered a new political period and we needed some new tools to work with."

In addition to Harnecker's work, some of the DIGNAS also began reading the Chilean feminist Julieta Kirkwood, whose work was introduced to them by Nicaraguan women. They concluded: "Kirkwood tells us that to create politics for women, we have to develop individual and collective practices that are capable of confronting all forms of power that are exerted over us as women in all aspects of our lives" (Mujeres por la Dignidad y la Vida 1993a:81).

Interview with Morena Herrera

1. ANDES refers to the Asociación Nacional de Educadores Salvadoreños (National Association of Salvadoran Educators) which was tied to the FPL (see note 2 below).

2. The FPL–FM (Fuerzas Populares de Liberación "Farabundo Martí") was formed in 1970 and was part of the FMLN.

3. The RN, also known as FARN, refers to the Armed Forces of National Resistance (Fuerzas Armadas de Resistencia Nacional). In discussing her recruitment away from one revolutionary party to another, Morena underlines the intense competition that existed within the left in the 1970s. In 1980, a coalition of four guerrilla groups (including the two discussed here: i.e., the FPL and the RN) and the Salvadoran Communist Party formed the FMLN (Farabundo Martí National Liberation Front). The FMLN carried out coordinated military and political actions during the twelve-year civil war in El Salvador that ended with the signing of peace accords on January 1, 1992. The FMLN became a legal political party as part of the accords and ran presidential, senatorial, and mayoral candidates in the 1994 elections. At the end of 1994 the FMLN broke apart owing to long-standing political differences among several of its constituent parties.

4. Over a hundred people were killed in this demonstration on February 28, 1977, which protested the fraudulent election of General Carlos Humberto Romero to the presidency. Later, a small revolutionary organization, LP-28 (Popular Leagues "28th of February," Ligas Populares "28 de Febrero"), would commemorate the massacre in their name.

5. In response to the Latin American Episcopal Conference in Medellín in 1968, the progressive Salvadoran Catholic church began to define poverty and oppression of the masses as a sin. The organization of hundreds of Christian base communities that discussed and organized around the problems of poverty in relation to biblical teaching politicized both the rural and the urban poor.

6. Families in El Salvador were rarely notified when someone had been killed in a military confrontation, whether real or staged. Many women I have interviewed who reported finding out about a family member's death read about it in the newspaper. The local papers were an indirect means for communicating the latest slaughters, as were routine visits to the local morgue by those whose family members were missing.

7. It is quite possible that Morena used Depo-Provera, or a similar drug, to prevent pregnancy. During the early 1980s Depo-Provera was not long approved for use in the United States, but was being exported for use in Latin America by its manufacturers.

8. CIDHAL and EMAS are two feminist groups which also worked with the Women's Regional Council of the CONAMUP.

9. Morena is referring to the Fifth Latin American and Caribbean Feminist Encuentro, which took place in 1990 in San Bernardo, Argentina. This *encuentro* (loosely translated as "meeting" or "happening") attracted about three thousand women from thirty-eight countries. For a description of this and other *encuentros*, see Saporta Sternbach et al. 1992.

10. Oxfam England is a nongovernmental organization that supports human rights, grassroots development, and social and community organizing work around the world.

11. The Fourth Latin American and Caribbean Feminist Encuentro was held in Taxco, Mexico, in October 1987. It was attended by over fifteen hundred women. It was the first *encuentro* where significant numbers of women attended who were organized within a wide variety of peasant, labor, urban squatter, and other movements.

4. The Politics of Urban Survival

1. For a good overall discussion of the impact of structural adjustment on women worldwide, see Afshar and Dennis 1992. See also Benería and Feldman 1992.

2. A comparative study done in Guadalajara between 1982 and 1987 found a 25 percent increase in the number of women over fifteen years of age who entered the wage-labor market (González de la Rocha 1989:165). In 1985, 47 percent of the households interviewed had female heads who participated in the wage-labor force, almost exclusively in the informal service and industrial sector (1989:166). Their work consisted primarily of extensions of their domestic duties: cooking, cleaning, and washing. This has been corroborated by Oliveira and García (1990), who found that the participation of women between the ages of twenty and forty-nine in the workforce increased nationally from 31 percent in 1981 to 37 percent in 1987 (cited in González de la Rocha 1991:117).

3. "The expression used by nearly all to describe men's activities in the home is *ayudar a la esposa*, helping the wife. Men generally do not equally share in these responsibilities, in word or deed, and the cultural division of labor between women [and men] is still regarded as important and therefore enforced by many. The female *doble jornada*, second shift (literally double day), is an ongoing and significant feature of life in many households in Santo Domingo. In addition, and related to their often privileged position in Mexican society, men in particular sometimes admit to trying to take advantage of the situation, by attributing greater natural energy to women and greater natural *flojera* (laziness) to men" (Gutmann 1994a:25).

4. The local activists Carmen refers to are from the Emiliano Zapata Popular Revolutionary Union (UPREZ). Carmen stated that the Women's Regional Council lets UPREZ use their Women's Center for meetings because "they always supported us through our formation and struggle, and now we have to do the same for them." UPREZ is part of a larger organization called the Revolutionary Organization of the Left–Mass Line (OIR–LM) which grew out of earlier Maoist movements described below (see note 6).

5. Vivienne Bennett, personal communication.

6. Linea de Masas (Mass Line), formed in 1976 out of a split in another Maoist political current known as Política Popular (PP), was of critical importance in the formation of the CONAMUP. As noted by Neil Harvey, Política Popular has its roots in the 1968 student movement. Founded in 1969, PP sought to apply "the Maoist 'mass line' to Mexico in a nonviolent struggle for socialism." Clandestine brigades of students were sent to poor urban neighborhoods and to the countryside to build bases of popular power (Harvey 1994:29).

Efforts to organize a single revolutionary party following Maoist ideology in the 1970s failed and led instead to the formation of a coordinating body to discuss ideology and strategy for the urban popular movements. This body was called COLIMA (Coordinator of the Mass Line). Movement leaders within COLIMA were quite involved in the creation of the CONAMUP (Bennett 1992a).

7. The following description of the first national meeting and early programs of the CONAMUP is taken from Brugada and Ortega 1987:100–102.

8. LICONSA distributed milk to urban families earning less than twice the minimum daily wage. As noted by Fox (1992b:114n68) LICONSA was one of the few government "safety net" programs to grow after the 1982 economic crisis, increasing its coverage from 680,000 families in 1983 to 1.7 million in 1987.

9. In 1994, the Women's Regional Council paid $787 per month toward their mortgage with the city. At that time, the minimum daily wage was about $4 per day (before the peso devaluation at the end of the year). The monthly rent would thus be the full-time wages of about nine people.

10. This woman's name has been changed at her request.

Interview with Irene Soto

1. The term *popular* in Spanish means "of the people" or "popular" in the sense of being populist or of the people.

2. Here the term *cacique* refers to a political boss and is often associated with the use of violence and intimidation in order to maintain political authority.

5. The Unintended Consequences of "Traditional" Women's Organizing

1. The Adolfo López Mateos League is mentioned in the interview with Doña Kata Moreno which follows this chapter. It was in the League that Doña Kata and other women gained their first political experience, and the skills they learned there proved quite important in forming the Women's Council.

2. A *posada* is a religious celebration before Christmas commemorating Mary and Joseph's search for shelter.

3. The following two paragraphs are summarized from Hernández 1990: 100–112.

Interview with Doña Kata Moreno and Aurora Cruz

1. The names of the two women interviewed here have been changed at their request. In their discussions of history, their dates for events may not coincide exactly with those given in Chapter 5. These women are more concerned with temporal relationships between events rather than with the exact date or year in which something happened.

2. *Cargos* are voluntary labor requirements that all members of the community have. Everyone is required to fulfill service on rotating committees and to commit a certain number of days per year to voluntary labor. The men assigned to work on the turkey farm would not carry out the assignment.

6. Class, Gender, and Autonomy

1. This quotation is from an interview conducted by Zander Navarro in March 1992.

2. This quotation is from an interview conducted by Zander Navarro in March 1992

3. See Sarti 1989 for an overview on Brazilian feminism. Sonia Alvarez' (1990) excellent monograph on women's movements in Brazil also provides a good overview of Brazilian feminism and the various movements related to it, both in the realm of popular feminism and that of more liberal feminism.

7. Sweet and Sour Grapes

1. Gonzalo Falabella provided this insight in a conversation.

2. Chuchryk (1989:156) notes that "men were the victims of repression more often than women, in part because women had tended to play what were considered marginal or secondary roles in the targeted organizations, principally political parties and trade unions."

Interview with Antonia Gómez

1. Antonia's name has been changed because I could not reach her to get permission for the publication of this interview.

8. Conclusions

1. See the work of Ann Bookman and Sandra Morgen (1988); Susan Borque and Kay B. Warren (1981); Christine Gailey (1987); Holly Mathews (1985); June Nash and Helen Safa (1986); Karen Brodkin Sacks (1988); and Lynn Stephen (1991).

2. According to most social scientists, gendered behavior also involves the creation of gender roles. A "social role" is any pattern of behavior a specific individual in a specific situation is expected to perform. A "gender role" is any social role linked with being female or male. The socialization of most children into gender roles begins at birth or sometimes before if the gender of the child is known before they are born.

3. I have not attempted to define "feminist" ideas here because they vary tremendously both within and between countries. Miller (1991) and Saporta Sternbach et al. (1992) provide good descriptions of the variety of issues and perspectives included in Latin American feminism.

4. In order to come up with a useful formulation of how collective identity operates, Arturo Escobar (1992) proposes blending Alberto Melucci's (1988) proposal for how collective identities are constructed with Laclau and Mouffe's (1985) conclusion that collective identities can only be built through the articulation of meaning. Melucci states that the construction of collective identities "has two aspects: the internal complexity of the actor (the plurality of orientations that characterizes him), and the actor's relationship with the environment (other actors, opportunities and constraints)" (Melucci 1988:342, cited in Escobar 1992:79). Johnston, Laraña, and Gusfield, interpreting Melucci, state about collective identity: "It is built through shared definitions of the situation by its members, and it is a result of a process of negotiation and 'laborious adjustment' of different elements relating to the ends and means of collective action and its relation to the environment. By this process of interaction, negotiation and conflict over the definition of the situation and the movement's reference frame, members construct the collective 'we'" (1994:15).

5. As stated by John Gledhill, "What we should avoid doing is transforming social movements into unitary actors devoid of internal contradictions and contradictory tendencies, and isolating them from the larger social, cultural, and political fields within which they experience their ebbs and flows" (1994:190).

6. Stacey states that ethnography which builds on participant observation, long-term relationships, and in-depth interviews which require high levels of intimacy is most dangerous because of the greater "apparent mutuality of the researcher/researched relationship" (1991:114). Following the work of critics such as James Clifford, she warns that ethnographic products are not constructed in relations of equality, but aim for only "partial truth—committed and incomplete" (Clifford 1988:7). Stacey points out, however, that poststructural ethnographers and feminists suffer from the delusion of alliance, although she believes feminists are even more liable to succumb to it.

7. See Carr 1994 for an interesting discussion of testimonials, their production and use in the global marketplace of the academy, and First World literary consumption. Also see Stephen 1994a.

8. It should be noted, however, that ethnographers and researchers can be asked by activists to paint a homogeneous picture of them, reproducing an essentialized collective identity. This may be part of the political strategy of movement leaders to further their external image. In one case of collaborative team research that I participated in, leaders of a movement censured a document written by a researcher because it focused on internal disputes over hierarchical leadership practices. Furthermore, the researcher was not permitted any further access to the movement. Engaging in collective, negotiated research essentially incorporates the researcher into the political process and requires him or her to assume some of the risks and frustrations activists have in carrying out their own work.

BIBLIOGRAPHY

AAMTRES (Articulação dos Movimentos de Mulheres Trabalhadoras Rurais dos Cinco Estados do Sul)
1990 Relatorio do Seminário Sobre Afetividade e Sexualidade. Curitiba, Paraná.

ACUÑA, L., and VERÓNICA RIQUELME
1986 *La violencia contra la mujer*. Santiago de Chile: Centro de Estudios de la Mujer.

AFSHAR, HALEH, and CAROLYNE DENNIS
1992 *Women and Adjustment Politics in the Third World*. New York: St. Martin's Press.

AGOSÍN, MARJORIE
1993 *Surviving beyond Fear: Women, Children and Human Rights in Latin America*. Fredonia, Vt.: White Pine Press.

AIMTR – Sul (Articulação de Instâncias de Mulheres Trabalhadoras Rurais dos Cinco Estados do Sul)
1994 Nenhuma trabalhadora rural sem documentos! *Cartilha Formação e Informação*, no. 1 (August). Curitiba: AIMTR–Sul.

ALARCÓN, NORMA
1983 Chicana's Feminist Literature: A Re-Vision through Malintzin; or, Malintzin: Putting Flesh Back on the Object. In *This Bridge Called My Back: Writings by Radical Women of Color*, ed. Cherríe Moraga and Gloria Anzaldúa. San Francisco: Kitchen Table Press.
1989 Traddutora, Traditora: A Paradigmatic Figure of Chicana Feminism. *Cultural Critique* 13:57–97.
1990 The Theoretical Subject(s) of *This Bridge Called My Back* and Anglo-American Feminism. In Anzaldúa 1990.

ALMEIDA, MAURO WILLIAM BARBOSA DE
1986 Redescobrindo a família rural. *Revista Brasileira de Ciências Sociais* 1(1):66–83.

ALVAREZ, SONIA E.
1990 *Engendering Democracy in Brazil: Women's Movements in Transition Politics*. Princeton: Princeton University Press.

ALVAREZ, SONIA, EVELINA DAGNINO, and ARTURO ESCOBAR
1996   Introduction. The Cultural and the Political in Latin American Social Movements. Manuscript.

ALVAREZ, SONIA E., and ARTURO ESCOBAR
1992   Conclusion: Theoretical and Political Horizons of Change in Contemporary Latin American Social Movements. In Escobar and Alvarez 1992.

ANDERSON, THOMAS
1971   *Matanza: El Salvador's First Communist Revolt of 1932.* Lincoln: University of Nebraska Press.

ANZALDÚA, GLORIA
1987   *Borderlands/La Frontera: The New Mestiza.* San Francisco: aunt lute books.
1990   *Making Face, Making Soul/HACIENDO CARAS: Creative and Critical Perspectives by Women of Color.* San Francisco: aunt lute books.

ANZALDÚA, GLORIA, and CHERRÍE MORAGA (eds.)
1981   *This Bridge Called My Back: Writings by Radical Women of Color.* Watertown, Mass.: Persephone Press.

AQUINO, MARÍA PILAR
1993   *Our Cry for Life: Feminist Theology from Latin America.* Maryknoll, N.Y.: Orbis Books.

ARANDA BAEZA, XIMENA
1982   El díptico campesina-asalariada agrícola. In *Las trabajadoras del agro: Debate sobre la mujer en América Latina y el Caribe. Discusión acerca de la unidad producción-reproducción,* ed. Magdalena León. Vol. 2. Bogotá: Asociación Colombiana para el Estudio de la Población.

ARANDA BEZAURY, JOSEFINA
1990   Políticas públicas y mujeres campesinas en México. Manuscript.
1993   Políticas públicas y mujeres campesinas en México. In *Mujeres y relaciones de género en la antropología latinoamericana,* ed. González Montes. Mexico City: PIEM, Colegio de México.

ARIZPE, LOURDES
1977   Women in the Informal Sector: The Case of Mexico City. *Signs* 3(1): 24–37.

ARIZPE, LOURDES, and JOSEFINA ARANDA
1986   Women Workers in the Strawberry Agribusiness in Mexico. In *Women's Work: Development and the Division of Labor by Gender,* ed. Eleanor Leacock and Helen Safa. South Hadley, Mass.: Bergin & Garvey.

ARIZPE, LOURDES, and CARLOTA BOTEY
1986   Las políticas de desarrollo agrario y su impacto sobre la mujer campesina en México. In *La mujer y la política agraria en América Latina,* ed. Magdalena León and Carmen Diana Deere. Bogotá: Siglo XXI–ACEP.

ARIZPE, LOURDES, FANNY SALINAS, and MARGARITA VELÁSQUEZ
1989   Efectos de la crisis económica 1980–1985 sobre la condición de vida

de las mujeres campesinas en México. In *El ajuste invisible: Los efectos de la crisis económica en las mujeres pobres*. Bogotá: UNICEF.

ARMSTRONG, ROBERT, and JANET SHENK

1982   *El Salvador: The Race of Revolution*. Boston: South End Press.

ARNSON, CYNTHIA

1982   *El Salvador: A Revolution Confronts the United States*. Washington, D.C.: Institute for Policy Studies.

BAITENMANN, HELGA

1995   Rural Agency and State Formation in Modern Mexico: The Agrarian Reforms in Central Veracruz (1914–1994). Paper presented at the Center for U.S.-Mexican Studies, La Jolla, Calif., May.

Forthcoming   Rural Agency and State Formation in Modern Mexico: The Agrarian Reforms in Central Veracruz (1914–1994). Ph.D. dissertation, New School for Social Research, New York.

BARRIG, MARUJA

1989   The Difficult Equilibrium between Bread and Roses: Women's Organizations and the Transition from Dictatorship to Democracy in Peru. In Jaquette 1989. Boston: Unwin Hyman.

BARRÓN, MARÍA ANTONIETA

1991   The Impact of Globalization on the Mexican Labor Market for Vegetable Production. Working Paper no. 11. Fresh Fruit and Vegetables Globalization Network, University of California–Santa Cruz.

BARRY, TOM

1987   *Roots of Rebellion: Land and Hunger in Central America*. Boston: South End Press.

1990   *El Salvador: A Country Guide*. Albuquerque: Inter-Hemispheric Education Resource Center.

1995   *Zapata's Revenge: Free Trade and the Farm Crisis in Mexico*. Boston: South End Press.

BEHAR, RUTH

1993   *Translated Woman: Crossing the Border with Esperanza's Story*. Boston: Beacon Press.

BENERÍA, LOURDES

1992   The Mexican Debt Crisis: Restructuring the Economy and the Household. In Benería and Feldman 1992.

BENERÍA, LOURDES, and SHELLEY FELDMAN

1992   *Unequal Burden: Economic Crises, Persistent Poverty, and Women's Work*. Boulder: Westview Press.

BENERÍA, LOURDES, and MARTHA ROLDÁN

1987   *The Crossroads of Class and Gender: Industrial Homework, Subcontracting, and Household Dynamics in Mexico City*. Chicago: University of Chicago Press.

BENNETT, DAVID

1994   Billionaires in Mexico Up, Forbes Reports. *San Antonio Express News*, July 12.

BENNETT, VIVIENNE
1992a   The Origins of Mexican Urban Popular Movements: Political
Thought and Clandestine Political Organizing of the 1960s and
1970s. Paper presented at the 17th International Congress of the Latin
American Studies Association, Los Angeles, September.
1992b   The Evolution of Urban Popular Movements in Mexico between 1968
and 1988. In Escobar and Alvarez 1992.
BERGER, M., and M. BUVINIC (eds.)
1988   *La mujer en el sector informal: Trabajo femenino y microempresa en
América Latina.* Caracas: Nueva Sociedad.
BERRYMAN, PHILLIP
1986   Religion, the Poor and Politics in Latin America Today. In *Religion
and Political Conflict in Latin America*, ed. Daniel Levine. Chapel
Hill: University of North Carolina Press.
BOOKMAN, ANN, and SANDRA MORGEN
1988   *Women and the Politics of Empowerment.* Philadelphia: Temple University Press.
BOOTH, JOHN, and THOMAS W. WALKER
1989   *Understanding Central America.* Boulder: Westview Press.
BORQUE, SUSAN C., and KAY B. WARREN
1981   *Women of the Andes.* Ann Arbor: University of Michigan Press.
BOTEY ESTAPÉ, CARLOTA
1991   La parcela ejidal es un patrimonio familiar. *Uno más uno* supplement:
El ejido a debate. November 18.
1993   La proletarización de la mujer en la última década del siglo XX. Paper
presented at the 13th International Congress of Anthropological and
Ethnological Sciences, Mexico City, August.
BRANNIGAN, WILLIAM
1988   Bracing for Pollution Disaster. *Washington Post*, November 28.
BROOKE, JAMES
1990   Land Program: What's Yours Is Mine. *New York Times* (International
Edition), November 3.
BRUGADA, CLARA, and ZENAIDA ORTEGA
1987   Regional de Mujeres del Valle de México de la Coordinadora
Nacional del Movimiento Urbano Popular (CONAMUP). In *Partici-
pación social, reconstrucción y mujer: El sismo de 1985*, ed. Alejan-
dra Massolo and Martha Schteingart. Mexico City: Reproducción de
Documentos de El Colegio de México.
BUECHLER, HANS C., and JUDITH-MARIA BUECHLER
1992   *Manufacturing against the Odds: Small-Scale Producers in an Andean
City.* Boulder: Westview Press.
BUNSTER-BUROTTO, XIMENA
1986   Surviving beyond Fear: Women and Torture in Latin America. In
Nash and Safa 1986.
CARLSEN, LAURA
1988   Grassroots Social Movements in Mexico. *Radical America* 22:
35–52.

CARR, ROBERT
1994   Crossing the First World/Third World Divides: Testimonial, Transnational Feminisms and the Postmodern Condition. In Grewal and Kaplan 1994.

CARRILLO, TERESA
1990   Women and Independent Unionism in the Garment Industry. In *Popular Movements and Political Change in Mexico*, ed. Joe Foweraker and Ann L. Craig. Boulder: Lynne Rienner.

Carta as trabalhadoras rurais do Brasil
1995   Mimeographed. São Paulo, October.

CASTELLS, MANUEL, and ALEJANDRO PORTES
1989   The World Underneath: The Origins, Dynamics and Effects of the Informal Economy. In *The Informal Economy: Studies in Advanced and Less Developed Countries*, ed. Alejandro Portes, Manuel Castells, and Lauren A. Benton. Baltimore: Johns Hopkins University Press.

CEM (Centro de Estudios de la Mujer)
1987   The Condition of Rural Women in Chile. In *Rural Women in Latin America*. Rome: Isis International.

Central America Information Office
1982   *El Salvador: Background to the Crisis*. Cambridge, Mass.: Central America Information Office.

CHANCE, JOHN
1990   Changes in Twentieth-Century Mesoamerican Cargo Systems. In *Class, Politics, and Popular Religion in Mexico and Central America*, ed. Lynn Stephen and James Dow. Washington, D.C.: American Anthropological Association.

CHANT, SYLVIA
1991   *Women and Survival in Mexican Cities: Perspectives on Gender, Labour Markets and Low-Income Households*. Manchester: Manchester University Press.

CHINCHILLA, NORMA
1990   Revolutionary Popular Feminism in Nicaragua: Articulating Class, Gender, and National Sovereignty. *Gender and Society* 4(3):370–397.
1992   Marxism, Feminism, and the Struggle for Democracy in Latin America. In Escobar and Alvarez 1992.

CHUCHRYK, PATRICIA
1989   Feminist Anti-Authoritarian Politics: The Role of Women's Organizations in the Chilean Transition to Democracy. In Jaquette 1989.

CLIFFORD, JAMES
1988   *The Predicament of Culture: Twentieth-Century Ethnography, Literature, and Art*. Cambridge: Harvard University Press.

COCKCROFT, JAMES
1983   *Mexico: Class Formation, Capital Accumulation, and the State*. New York: Monthly Review Press.

COLLINS, JANE L.
1993   Gender, Contracts, and Wage Work: Agricultural Restructuring in Brazil's São Francisco Valley. *Development and Change* 24:53–82.

1994 Transnational Labor Process and Gender Relations: Women in Fruit and Vegetable Production in Northeastern Brazil. Manuscript.

1995 Transnational Labor Process and Gender Relations: Women in Fruit and Vegetable Production in Chile, Brazil, and Mexico. *Journal of Latin American Anthropology* 1(1):178–199.

COMAROFF, JEAN

1985 *Body of Power, Spirit of Resistance: The Culture and History of a South African People.* Chicago: University of Chicago Press.

Comité Centroamericano Organizador del VI Encuentro Feminista Latinoamericano y del Caribe

1994 *Memorias: VI Encuentro Feminista Latinoamericano y del Caribe, El Salvador 1993.* Managua, Nicaragua.

Comité Nacional Feminista

1994a *Aquelarre del Primer Encuentro Nacional Feminista.* Managua, Nicaragua.

1994b Letter dated November 10. Comité de Disolución.

Coordinadora del IV Encuentro Feminista Latinoamericano y del Caribe

1987 *Memoria del IV Encuentro Feminista Latinoamericano y del Caribe, Taxco, México, Octubre 1987.* Mexico City: Coordinadora del IV Encuentro Feminista Latinoamericano y del Caribe.

Coordinadora "Voces de Mujeres" sobre Población y Desarrollo, Iniciativa de Mujeres Hacia la Cumbre Social, Comité Nacional Hacia Beijing

1995 Las cumbres mundiales y nosotros. Pamphlet. Managua, Nicaragua.

CORNELIUS, WAYNE A., ANN L. CRAIG, and JONATHAN FOX (eds.)

1994 *Transforming State–Society Relations in Mexico: The National Solidarity Strategy* La Jolla, Calif.: Center for U.S.-Mexican Studies.

COSGROVE, SERENA

1995 Women, Credit and the Urban Informal Sector of El Salvador: An Ethnography of Two Communal Banks. Master's thesis, Department of Sociology and Anthropology, Northeastern University.

CRASKE, NIKKI

1993 Women's Participation in *Colonias Populares* in Guadalajara, Mexico. In *"Viva": Women and Popular Protest in Latin America*, ed. Sarah A. Radcliffe and Sallie Westwood. London: Routledge.

DANNER, MARK

1994 *The Massacre at El Mozote.* New York: Vintage Books.

DAVIS, DIANE

1994 *Urban Leviathan: Mexico City in the Twentieth Century.* Philadelphia: Temple University Press.

DEERE, CARMEN

1979 Rural Women's Subsistence Production in the Capitalist Periphery. In *Peasants and Proletarians: The Struggles of Third World Workers*, ed. Robin Cohen, Peter C. W. Gutkind, and Phyllis Brazier. New York: Monthly Review Press.

DEERE, CARMEN DIANA, and MAGDALENA LEÓN

1987 Introduction. In *Rural Women and State Policy: Feminist Perspectives on Latin American Development*, ed. Carmen Diana Deere and Magdalena León. Boulder: Westview Press.

DEL CASTILLO, ADELAIDA R.
1993   Covert Cultural Norms and Sex/Gender Meaning: A Mexico City Case. *Urban Anthropology* 22(3–4):237–258.

DE PALMA, ANTHONY
1994   Mexico Slips Quietly into Recession. *New York Times*, March 15.

DEWALT, BILLIE, and MARTHA W. REES, with ARTHUR D. MURPHY
1994   The End of Agrarian Reform in Mexico: Past Lessons, Future Prospects. Ejido Reform Research Project, Transformation of Rural Mexico no. 3. La Jolla, Calif.: Center for U.S.-Mexican Studies.

DÍAZ BARRIGA, MIGUEL
1996   *Necesidad:* Notes on the Discourses of Urban Politics in the Ajusco Foothills of Mexico City. *American Ethnologist* 23(2):291–310.

DIETZ, MARY
1992   Context Is All: Feminism and Theories of Citizenship. In *Dimensions of Radical Democracy*, ed. Chantal Mouffe. London: Verso.

DI LEONARDO, MICAELA
1991   Introduction. Gender, Culture, and Political Economy: Feminist Anthropology in Historical Perspective. In *Gender at the Crossroads of Knowledge: Feminist Anthropology in a Postmodern Era*, ed. Micaela di Leonardo. Berkeley: University of California Press.

Doble Jornada
1994   La ley revolucionaria de las mujeres. *Doble Jornada*, February 7.

DRESSER, DENISE
1991   Neopopulist Solutions to Neoliberal Problems: Mexico's National Solidarity Program. Current Issue Brief no. 3. La Jolla, Calif.: Center for U.S.-Mexican Studies.

Economist Intelligence Unit
1994   *Mexico. Country Report, 1st Quarter 1994*. New York: The Economist Intelligence Unit.

Edición Mujeres
1994   Suplemento especial. *Edición Mujeres*, March. San Salvador.

ENLOE, CYNTHIA
1989   *Bananas, Beaches, and Bases: Making Feminist Sense of International Politics*. Berkeley: University of California Press.
1993   *The Morning After: Sexual Politics at the End of the Cold War*. Berkeley: University of California Press.

ESCOBAR, ARTURO
1992   Culture, Economics, and Politics in Latin American Social Movements Theory and Research. In Escobar and Alvarez 1992.
1995   *Encountering Development: The Making and Unmaking of the Third World*. Princeton: Princeton University Press.

ESCOBAR, ARTURO, and SONIA ALVAREZ (eds.)
1992   *The Making of Social Movements in Latin America: Identity, Strategy, and Democracy*. Boulder: Westview Press.

ESCOBAR LATAPÍ, AGUSTÍN, and MERCEDES GONZÁLEZ
DE LA ROCHA
1991   Introduction. In *Social Responses to Mexico's Economic Crisis of the
         1980s,* ed. Mercedes González de la Rocha and Agustín Escobar
         Latapí. La Jolla, Calif.: Center for U.S.-Mexican Studies.
EVERS, HANS-DIETER, WOLFGANG CLAUSS, and DIANA WONG
1984   Subsistence Reproduction: A Framework for Analysis. In *Households
         and the World Economy,* ed. Joan Smith, Immanuel Wallerstein, and
         Hans-Dieter Evers. Beverly Hills: Sage Publications.
FALABELLA, GONZALO
1991   Organizarse y sobrevivir en Santa María: Democracia social en
         un sindicato de temporeros y temporeras. Paper presented at the
         47th Congress of Americanists, New Orleans, July.
1992   Reestructuración y respuesta sindical: La experiencia en Santa María,
         madre de la fruta chilena. Paper presented at the 17th International
         Congress of the Latin American Studies Association, Los Angeles,
         September.
FEIJOO, MARÍA DEL CARMEN
1989   The Challenge of Constructing Civilian Peace: Women and Democ-
         racy in Argentina. In Jaquette 1989.
FERGUSEN, KATHY
1990   Women, Feminism and Development. In Staudt 1990.
FERNÁNDEZ KELLY, MARÍA PATRICIA
1982   *For We Are Sold, I and My People: Women and Industry in Mexico's
         Frontier.* Albany: State University of New York Press.
FISHER, JO
1989   *Mothers of the Disappeared.* London: Zed Books.
1993   *Out of the Shadows: Women, Resistance, and Politics in South
         America.* London: Latin American Bureau.
FOUCAULT, MICHEL
1990   *The History of Sexuality.* Vol. 1: *An Introduction.* New York: Vintage
         Books.
FOX, JONATHAN
1992a   Democratic Rural Development: Leadership Accountability in
         Regional Peasant Organizations. *Development and Change* 23(2):
         1–36.
1992b   *The Politics of Food in Mexico: State Power and Social Mobilization.*
         Ithaca: Cornell University Press.
1994a   Targeting the Poorest: The Role of the National Indigenous Institute
         in Mexico's Solidarity Program. In *Transforming State–Society Rela-
         tions in Mexico: The National Solidarity Strategy,* ed. Wayne A. Cor-
         nelius, Ann L. Craig, and Jonathan Fox. La Jolla, Calif.: Center for
         U.S.-Mexican Studies.
1994b   Political Change in Mexico's New Peasant Economy. In *The Political
         Economy of Restructuring: State–Society Relations and Regime
         Change in Mexico,* ed. Maria Lorena Cook, Kevin Middlebrook, and

Juan Molinar Horcasitas. La Jolla, Calif.: Center for U.S.-Mexican Studies.

FOX, JONATHAN, and LUIS HERNÁNDEZ

1989   Offsetting the Iron Law of Oligarchy: The Ebb and Flow of Leadership Accountability in a Regional Peasant Organization. *Grassroots Development* 13(2):8–15.

1992   Mexico's Difficult Democracy: Grassroots Movements, NGOs, and Local Government. *Alternatives* 17(2):165–208.

FRANCO, JEAN

n.d.   Gender, Death, and Resistance. Working paper.

GAILEY, CHRISTINE

1987   *Kinship to Kingship: Gender Hierarchy and State Formation in the Tongan Islands.* Austin: University of Texas Press.

GARCÍA, ANA ISABEL, and ENRIQUE GOMARIZ (eds.)

1989   *Mujeres centroamericanas.* Vol. 1. San José, Costa Rica: FLACSO.

GARRET, P.

1982   La reforma agraria, organización popular y participación de la mujer en Chile 1964–1973. In *Las trabajadoras del agro: Debate sobre la mujer en América Latina y el Caribe,* ed. Magdalena León. Vol. 2. Bogotá: Asociación Colombiana para el Estudio de la Población.

Gente

1993   ¿Vienen las lesbianas? *Gente* 1(21):38–42. San Salvador.

GERSHBERG, ALEC IAN

1994   Distributing Resources in the Education Sector. In *Transforming State–Society Relations in Mexico: The National Solidarity Strategy,* ed. Wayne A. Cornelius, Ann L. Craig, and Jonathan Fox. La Jolla, Calif.: Center for U.S.-Mexican Studies.

GLEDHILL, JOHN

1994   *Power and Its Disguises: Anthropological Perspectives on Politics.* London: Pluto Press.

GÓMEZ, SERGIO

1982   *Instituciones y procesos agrarios en Chile.* Santiago de Chile: Facultad Latinoamericana de Ciencias Sociales.

GÓMEZ, SERGIO, and JORGE ECHENIQUE

1988   *La agricultura chilena: Las dos caras de la modernización.* Santiago de Chile: Facultad Latinoamericana de Ciencias Sociales/Organismo de Desarrollo Campesino y Alimentario.

GONZÁLEZ AMADOR, ROBERTO

1994   Income Inequality in Mexico Grows. *La Jornada,* May 9. Translated in *Mexico Newspak* 2(8):10.

GONZÁLEZ DE LA ROCHA, MERCEDES

1989   Crisis, economía doméstica y trabajo femenino en Guadalajara. In *Trabajo, poder y sexualidad,* ed. Orlandina de Oliveira. Mexico City: Colegio de México.

1991   Family Well-being, Food Consumption, and Survival Strategies during

Mexico's Economic Crisis. In *Social Responses to Mexico's Economic Crisis of the 1980s*, ed. Mercedes González de la Rocha and Agustín Escobar Latapí. La Jolla, Calif.: Center for U.S.-Mexican Studies.

1994   *The Resources of Poverty: Women and Survival in a Mexican City.* Oxford: Blackwell.

GOSSE, VAN

1994   "The North American Front": Central American Solidarity in the Reagan Era. In *Reshaping the US Left: Popular Struggles in the 1980s*, ed. Mike Davis and Michael Sprinker. London: Verso.

GREWAL, INTERPAL, and CAREN KAPLAN

1994   *Scattered Hegemonies: Postmodernity and Transnational Feminist Practices.* Minneapolis: University of Minnesota Press.

GRINDLE, MERILEE

1988   *Searching for Rural Development: Labor Migration and Employment in Mexico.* Ithaca: Cornell University Press.

GRZYBOWSKI, CÂNDIDO

1990   Rural Workers and Democratization in Brazil. *Journal of Development Studies* 26(4):19–43.

GUTMANN, MATTHEW

1994a   The Meanings of Macho: Changing Mexican Male Identities. *Masculinities* 2(1):21–33.

1994b   The Meanings of Macho: Changing Male Identities in Mexico City. Ph.D. dissertation, University of California–Berkeley.

1996   *The Meanings of Macho: Being a Man in Mexico City.* Berkeley: University of California Press.

HALL, STUART

1989   The Meaning of New Times. In *New Times: The Changing Face of Politics in the 1990s*, ed. Stuart Hall and Martin Jacques. London: Lawrence & Wishart.

1995   Cultural Identities in Question: Ethnicity and Difference in Global Times. Paper presented at the Seminar in Ethnic Studies, University of California–San Diego, April.

HARVEY, DAVID

1989   *The Condition of Post-Modernity.* Cambridge: Basil Blackwell.

HARVEY, NEIL

1994   Rebellion in Chiapas: Rural Reforms, Campesino Radicalism, and the Limits to Salinismo. Ejido Reform Research Project, Transformation of Rural Mexico no. 5. La Jolla, Calif.: Center for U.S.-Mexican Studies.

HERNÁNDEZ, LUIS

1988   *La Unión de Ejidos Lázaro Cárdenas: Autonomía y liderazgo en una organización campesina regional.* Report. Mexico City: Inter-American Foundation.

1990   Autonomía y liderazgo en una organización campesino regional. In *La Unión de Ejidos "Lázaro Cárdenas."* Cuadernos de Desarrollo de Base 1, no. 2.

HEWITT DE ALCÁNTARA, CYNTHIA

1991 Introduction: Economic Restructuring and Rural Subsistence in Mexico. In *Economic Restructuring and Rural Subsistence in Mexico*, ed. Cynthia Hewitt de Alcántara. Ejido Reform Research Project, Transformation of Rural Mexico no. 2. La Jolla, Calif.: Center for U.S.-Mexican Studies. Copublished with the United Nations Research Institute for Social Development.

HINDLEY, JANE

1995a Contesting Development: A Political Ethnography of Nahua Mobilization in Contemporary Mexico. Ph.D. thesis, Department of Government, University of Essex, England.

1995b Towards a Pluricultural Nation: The Limits of *Indigenismo* and Article 4. In *Dismantling the Mexican State*, ed. Rob Aiken, Nicki Craske, Gareth A. Jones, and David Stansfield. London: Macmillan.

INEGI (Instituto Nacional de Estadística, Geografía e Informática)

1984 *Agenda estadística 1984*. Mexico City: Instituto Nacional de Estadística, Geografía e Informática.

1990 *Estados Unidos Mexicanos. Resumen general, XI censo general de población y vivienda, 1990*. Mexico City: INEGI.

Inter-American Development Bank

1988 *Economic and Social Progress in Latin America: 1988 Report*. Washington, D.C.: Inter-American Development Bank.

1990 *Economic and Social Progress in Latin America: 1990 Report*. Washington, D.C.: Inter-American Development Bank.

JAQUETTE, JANE

1989 (ed.) *The Women's Movement in Latin America: Feminism and the Transition to Democracy*. Boston: Unwin Hyman.

1994 (ed.) *The Women's Movement in Latin America: Feminism and the Transition to Democracy*. Rev. ed. Boulder: Westview Press.

1995 Rewriting the Scripts: Gender in the Comparative Study of Latin American Politics. In *Politics in Latin America in Comparative Perspective*, ed. Peter Smith. Boulder: Westview Press.

JELIN, ELIZABETH

1990 Citizenship and Identity: Final Reflections. In *Women and Social Change in Latin America*, ed. Elizabeth Jelin. London: Zed Books.

JOHNSTON, HANK, ENRIQUE LARAÑA, and JOSEPH R. GUSFIELD

1994 Identities, Grievances, and New Social Movements. In *New Social Movements: From Ideology to Identity*, ed. Enrique Laraña, Hank Johnston, and Joseph R. Gusfield. Philadelphia: Temple University Press.

JOSEPH, GILBERT, and DANIEL NUGENT (eds.)

1994 *Everyday Forms of State Formation: Revolution and the Negotiation of Rule in Modern Mexico*. Durham: Duke University Press.

JUSIDMAN, C.

1988 Women and Labor in the Mexico City Metropolitan Area: Effects of the Economic Crisis. Paper presented at a conference, "Weathering

Economic Crises: Women's Responses to the Recession in Latin America and the Caribbean," Racine, Wisconsin, June.

KAPLAN, CAREN
1994   The Politics of Location as Transnational Feminist Critical Practice. In Grewal and Kaplan 1994.

KAPLAN, TEMMA
1982   Female Consciousness and Collective Action: The Case of Barcelona, 1910–1918. *Signs* 7(3):545–560.
1990   Community and Resistance in Women's Political Cultures. *Dialectical Anthropology* 15:259–264.

KECK, MARGARET
1992   Brazil's PT: Socialism as Radical Democracy. *NACLA Report on the Americas* 25(5):24–29.

KNIGHT, ALAN
1994   Solidarity: Historical Continuities and Contemporary Implications. In *Transforming State–Society Relations in Mexico: The National Solidarity Strategy*, ed. Wayne A. Cornelius, Ann L. Craig, and Jonathan Fox. La Jolla, Calif.: Center for U.S.-Mexican Studies.

LACLAU, ERNESTO, and CHANTAL MOUFFE
1985   *Hegemony and Socialist Strategy: Towards a Radical Democratic Politics.* London: Verso.

LAGO, MARÍA SOLEDAD
1987   Rural Women and the Neo-Liberal Model in Chile. In *Rural Women and State Policy: Feminist Perspectives on Latin American Agricultural Development*, ed. Carmen Diana Deere and Magdalena León. Boulder: Westview Press.

LAGO, MARÍA SOLEDAD, and CARLOTA OLAVARÍA
1982   La mujer campesina en la expansión fruticultura chilena. In *Las trabajadoras del agro: Debate sobre la mujer en América Latina y el Caribe. Discusión acerca de la unidad producción-reproducción*, ed. Magdalena León. Vol. 2. Bogotá: Asociación Colombiana para el Estudio de la Población.

LEGLER, THOMAS
1995   Contending Approaches to the Politics of Economic Restructuring in Rural Mexico. Paper presented at the 19th International Congress of the Latin American Studies Association. Washington, D.C., September 25–27.

LEVY, SUSANA, and NORBERT LECHNER
1986   CEMA Chile y Secretaría Nacional de la Mujer. In *La otra mitad de Chile*, ed. M. Angelica Meza. Santiago de Chile: CESOC and Instituto para el Nuevo Chile.

LIND, AMY
1992   Power, Gender, and Development: Popular Women's Organizations and the Politics of Needs in Ecuador. In Escobar and Alvarez 1992.

LOGAN, KATHLEEN
1990   Women's Participation in Urban Protest. In *Popular Movements and*

Political Change in Mexico, ed. Joe Foweraker and Ann Craig. Boulder: Lynne Rienner.

LOVERA, SARA
1993   Intentan cancelar en el Salvador el encuentro feminista de AL. *La Jornada*, December 15, p. 15.

LUSTIG, NORA
1994   Solidarity as a Strategy of Poverty Alleviation. In *Transforming State–Society Relations in Mexico: The National Solidarity Strategy*, ed. Wayne A. Cornelius, Ann L. Craig, and Jonathan Fox. La Jolla, Calif.: Center for U.S.-Mexican Studies.

MAIER, ELIZABETH
1980   *Nicaragua: La mujer en la revolución*. Managua: Ediciones de Cultura Popular.
1985   *Las sandinistas*. Mexico City: Ediciones de Cultura Popular.

MARCONDES DE MORAES, MARIA STELA
1994   No rastro das aguas: Pedagogia do movimento dos atingidos pelas barragens da bacia do rio Urugai (Rs/SC) 1978–1990. Ph.D. dissertation, Departamento de Educação, Pontificia Universidade Catolica de Rio de Janeiro.

MARTINE, GEORGE
1983   As transformações na estrutura de produção agrícola paulista: Determinantes, consequencia e perspectivas. Mimeographed. Brasília: ILO/UNDP (International Labour Office/U.N. Development Program).

MARTÍNEZ DEL CASTILLO, JESÚS
1989   La modernización llega al campo. *Pira Política* 39:22–26.

MASSOLO, ALEJANDRA (ed.)
1988   *Memoria del pedregal. Memoria de mujer: Testimonio de una colona.* Mujer, Vida y Movimiento series, no. 1. Mexico City: Mujeres para el Diálogo.
1994   *Los medios y los modos: Participación política y acción colectiva de las mujeres*. Mexico City: Colegio de México.

MATHEWS, HOLLY
1985   "We Are Mayordomo": A Reinterpretation of Women's Roles in the Mexican Cargo System. *American Ethnologist* 17:285–301.

McCLURG MUELLER, CAROL
1992   Building Social Movement Theory. In Morris and McClurg Mueller 1992.

McMANUS, PHILLIP, and GERALD SCHLABACH (eds.)
1991   *Relentless Persistence: Nonviolent Action in Latin America*. Philadelphia: New Society Press.

MELUCCI, ALBERTO
1988   Getting Involved: Identity and Mobilization in Social Movements. In *International Social Movements Research: From Structure to Action — Comparing Social Movements Research across Cultures*, ed. Hansperter Kriesi, Sidney Tarrow, and Bert Klandermans. Vol. 1. London: JAI Press.

1989   *Nomads of the Present.* Philadelphia: Temple University Press.
MEYER, JULIE
1994   Breaking Many Taboos: Women in Solidarity. *Crossroads* 40:11–14.
MIES, MARIA
1983   Towards a Methodology of Feminist Research. In *Theories of Women's Studies*, ed. Gloria Bowles and Renate Duelli Klein. London: Routledge & Kegan Paul.
1988   Capitalist Development and Subsistence Production: Rural Women in India. In *Women: The Last Colony*, ed. Maria Mies. London: Zed Books.
MILLER, FRANCESCA
1991   *Latin American Women and the Search for Social Justice.* Hanover, N.H.: University Press of New England.
MMTR (Movimento de Mulheres Trabalhadoras Rurais–R.S.)
1989   *Cuaderno de formação no. 1.* Rio Grande do Sul.
1990a   *Resoluções e propostas do Movimento de Mulheres Trabalhadoras Rurais do Rio Grande do Sul.* Porto Alegre: MMTR.
1990b   *Despierta Mulher* 3(1). Boletim Informativo do MMTR.
1992   *Pre-tese para a Segunda Assembleia Estadual do MMTR/RS.* Passo Fundo: MMTR.
1994a   Historia do MMTR/RS. Mimeographed.
1994b   Texto sobre o MMTR/RS (Reelaboração a partir da discussão do dia 17/05/94). Mimeographed.
MOCTEZUMA, PEDRO
1983   Breve semblanza del Movimiento Urbano Popular y la CONAMUP. *Testimonios* 1(1):5–17.
MOGROVEJO AQUISE, NORMA
1990   Feminismo popular en México: Análisis del surgimiento, desarrollo y conflictos en la relación entre la tendencia feminista y la Regional de Mujeres de la CONAMUP. Master's thesis, Facultad Latinoamericana de Ciencias Sociales, Seminario Movimientos Sociales Generación 88–90.
MOGUEL, JULIO
1993   Procampo y la vía campesina de desarrollo. *La Jornada del Campo* 2(20):8–9.
1994   The Mexican Left and the Social Program of Salinismo. In *Transforming State–Society Relations in Mexico: The National Solidarity Strategy*, ed. Wayne A. Cornelius, Ann L. Craig, and Jonathan Fox. La Jolla, Calif.: Center for U.S.-Mexican Studies.
MOLINAR HORCASITAS, JUAN, and JEFFREY A. WELDON
1994   Electoral Determinants and Consequences of National Solidarity. In *Transforming State–Society Relations in Mexico: The National Solidarity Strategy*, ed. Wayne A. Cornelius, Ann L. Craig, and Jonathan Fox. La Jolla, Calif.: Center for U.S.-Mexican Studies.
MOLYNEUX, MAXINE
1985   Mobilization without Emancipation? Women's Interests, the State and Revolution in Nicaragua. *Feminist Studies* 11(2):227–254.
1986   Mobilization without Emancipation? Women's Interests, the State,

and Revolution. In *Transition and Development: Problems of Third World Socialism*, ed. Richard Fagen, Carmen Diana Deere, and José Luis Coraggio. New York: Monthly Review Press.

MONTGOMERY, TOMMIE SUE

1994   *Revolution in El Salvador: Origins and Evolution.* 2nd ed. Boulder: Westview Press.

MORAGA, CHERRÍE

1983   *Loving in the War Years.* Boston: South End Press.

1993   *The Last Generation.* Boston: South End Press.

MORRIS, ALDON D., and CAROL McCLURG MUELLER

1992   *Frontiers in Social Movement Theory.* New Haven: Yale University Press.

MOUFFE, CHANTAL

1988   Hegemony and New Political Subjects: Toward a New Concept of Democracy. In *Marxism and the Interpretation of Culture*, ed. Carl Nelson. Urbana: University of Illinois Press.

Mujeres por la Dignidad y la Vida

1993a   *Hacer política desde las mujeres.* San Salvador: Mujeres por la Dignidad y la Vida.

1993b   *Los proyectos productivos y la autonomía económica de las mujeres.* Colleción Debate. San Salvador: Mujeres por la Dignidad y la Vida.

1994   Cambios para todos. Demandas de las mujeres del municipio Víctor. San Salvador: Mujeres por la Dignidad y la Vida.

Las Mujeres Tenemos la Palabra . . .

1988   III Encuentro Nacional de Mujeres de la CONAMUP, 20, 21 y 22 de noviembre de 1987, Zacatecas. Mexico City: Ediciones Pueblo.

MUÑOZ, HUMBERTO, ORLANDINA DE OLIVEIRA, and CLAUDIO STERN

1971   Categorías de emigrantes y nativos y algunas de sus características socioeconómicas: Comparación entre las ciudades de Monterrey y México. In *Migración y desigualdad social en la ciudad de México.* Mexico City: Universidad Nacional Autónoma de México and Colegio de México.

Naciones Unidas

1993   *De la locura a la esperanza: La guerra de 12 años en el Salvador. Informe de la Comisión de la Verdad para el Salvador.* San Salvador and New York: United Nations.

NASH, JUNE

1970   *In the Eyes of the Ancestors: Belief and Behavior in a Maya Community.* New Haven: Yale University Press.

1989   Cultural Parameters of Sexism and Racism in the International Division of Labor. In *Racism, Sexism, and the World System*, ed. Joan Smith, Jane Collins, Terrence K. Hopkins, and Akbar Muhammad. New York: Greenwood Press.

1992   Interpreting Social Movements: Bolivian Resistance to Economic Conditions Imposed by the International Monetary Fund. *American Ethnologist* 19(2):275–293.

NASH, JUNE, and MARÍA PATRICIA FERNÁNDEZ KELLY
1983   *Men, Women, and the International Division of Labor.* Albany: State University of New York Press.
NASH, JUNE, and HELEN SAFA (eds.)
1986   *Women and Change in Latin America.* South Hadley, Mass.: Bergin & Garvey.
NAVARRO, MARYSA
1989   The Personal Is Political: Las Madres de Plaza de Mayo. In *Power and Popular Protest: Latin American Social Movements*, ed. Susan Eckstein. Los Angeles: University of California Press.
NAVARRO, ZANDER
1992   Democracy, Citizenship, and Representation: Rural Social Movements in the State of Rio Grande do Sul, Brazil, 1978–1990. Center for International Studies Working Paper. Cambridge: MIT, Center for International Studies.
1994   Democracy, Citizenship and Representation: Rural Social Movements in Southern Brazil, 1978–1990. *Bulletin of Latin American Research* 13(2):129–154.
New Americas Press
1989   *A Dream Compels Us: Voices of Salvadoran Women.* Boston: South End Press.
NORTH, LIISA
1985   *Bitter Grounds: Roots of Revolt in El Salvador.* 2nd ed. Westport, Conn.: Lawrence Hill.
NUCCIO, RICHARD A., and ANGELINA M. ORNELAS
1990   Mexico's Environment and the United States. In *The U.S. Interest: Resources, Growth, and Security in the Developing World*, ed. Janet Welsh Brown. Boulder: Westview Press.
OLIVEIRA, ORLANDINA DE, and BRÍGIDA GARCÍA
1990   Recesión económica y cambio en los determinantes del trabajo femenino. Mimeographed. Mexico City: Colegio de México.
ONG, AIWA
1987   *Spirits of Resistance and Capitalist Discipline: Factory Women in Malaysia.* Albany: State University of New York Press.
OPPENHEIMER, ANDRÉS
1994   Crisis Battering Economy. *Miami Herald*, April 18.
OVALLE VAQUERA, FEDERICO, and EMILIO LÓPEZ GÁMEZ
1994   La reestructuración de la producción maicera nacional. Paper presented at the Primer Seminario Nacional de Maíz-Tortilla, Centro de Investigaciones Interdisciplinarias en Humanidades, Universidad Nacional Autónoma de México, Mexico City, November.
Pastoral da Mulher Pobre
1988   *Mulher e comunidade: A nova mulher.* Petrópolis: Editora Vozes.
PATAI, DAPHNE
1991   U.S. Academics and Third World Women: Is Ethical Research Possible? In *Women's Words: The Feminist Practice of Oral History*, ed. Sherna Berga Gluck and Daphne Patai. New York: Routledge.

PIERCE, JENNY
1986   *Promised Land: Peasant Rebellion in Chalatenango, El Salvador.*
        London: Latin American Bureau.
POOL, JOHN CHARLES, and STEVE STAMOS
1989   *The ABCs of International Finance: Understanding the Trade and
        Debt Crisis.* Lexington, Mass.: Lexington Books.
PORTES, ALEJANDRO, MANUEL CASTELLS, and LAUREN A.
BENTON
1989   Conclusions: The Policy Implications of Informality. In *The Informal
        Economy: Studies in Advanced and Less Developed Countries,* ed.
        Alejandro Portes, Manuel Castells, and Lauren A. Benton. Baltimore:
        Johns Hopkins University Press.
PORTES, ALEJANDRO, and SASHA SASSEN KOOB
1987   Making It Underground: Comparative Material on the Informal Sec-
        tor in Western Market Economies. *American Journal of Sociology*
        93(1):30–61.
Quinzena
1990   A falsa pacificação no campo. *Quinzena,* July 15:7–8.
RAMÍREZ SAIZ, JUAN MANUEL
1986   *El movimiento urbano popular en México.* Mexico City: Siglo Vein-
        tiuno Editores.
1990   Urban Struggles and Their Political Consequences. In *Popular Move-
        ments and Political Change in Mexico,* ed. Joe Foweraker and Ann L.
        Craig. Boulder: Lynne Rienner.
RANDALL, MARGARET
1981   *Sandino's Daughters: Testimonies of Nicaraguan Women in Struggle.*
        Vancouver, B.C.: New Star Books.
RAPP REITER, RAYNA
1975   *Towards an Anthropology of Women.* New York: Monthly Review
        Press.
READY, KELLEY
1994   It's a Hard Life: Women in El Salvador's Economic History. In *Hear
        My Testimony: María Teresa Tula, Human Rights Activist of El Sal-
        vador,* ed. Lynn Stephen. Boston: South End Press.
REDCLIFT, NANNEKE, and ENZO MINGIONE (eds.)
1985   *Beyond Employment: Household, Gender, and Subsistence.* Oxford:
        Basil Blackwell.
Reuters
1995   Corn. Anenecuilco, Mexico. October 24. From the Internet.
ROBLES, ROSARIO, JOSEFINA ARANDA, and CARLOTA BOTEY
1993   La mujer campesina en la época de la modernidad. *El Cotidiano* 52:
        25–32.
RODRÍGUEZ, DANIEL O., and SILVIA L. VENEGAS
1989   De praderas a parronales: Un estudio sobre estructura agraria y mer-
        cado laboral en el valle de Aconcagua. Santiago de Chile: Grupo de
        Estudios Agro-regionales.

ROSALDO, MICHELLE ZIMBALIST
1974   Woman, Culture, and Society: A Theoretical Overview. In Rosaldo
         and Lamphere 1974.
1980   The Use and Abuse of Anthropology: Reflections on Cross-cultural
         Understanding. *Signs* 5(3):389–417.
ROSALDO, MICHELLE ZIMABALIST, and LOUISE LAMPHERE (eds.)
1974   *Woman, Culture, and Society.* Stanford: Stanford University Press.
ROSEBERRY, WILLIAM
1989   *Anthropologies and Histories: Essays in Culture, History, and Politi-
         cal Economy.* New Brunswick: Rutgers University Press.
1994   Hegemony and the Language of Convention. In Joseph and Nugent
         1994.
SACKS, KAREN BRODKIN
1988   *Caring by the Hour: Women, Work and Organizing at Duke Medical
         Center.* Urbana: University of Illinois Press.
1989   Towards a Unified Theory of Class, Race, and Gender. *American Eth-
         nologist* 16(3):534–550.
SAFA, HELEN
1990   Women's Social Movements in Latin America. *Gender and Society*
         4(3):355–369.
SALAZAR, CLAUDIA
1991   A Third World Woman's Text: Between the Politics of Criticism and
         Cultural Politics. In *Women's Words: The Feminist Practice of Oral
         History*, ed. Sherna Berga Gluck and Daphne Patai. New York:
         Routledge.
SAMGARI, KUMKUM, and SUDESH VAID (eds.)
1990   Recasting Women: An Introduction. In *Recasting Women: Essays in
         Indian Colonial History.* New Brunswick: Rutgers University Press.
SÁNCHEZ GÓMEZ, MARTHA JUDITH
1989   Consideraciones teorético-metodológicas en el estudio del trabajo
         doméstico en México. In *Trabajo, poder y sexualidad*, ed. Orlandina
         de Oliveira. Mexico City: Colegio de México.
SÁNCHEZ GÓMEZ, MARTHA JUDITH, and M. F. MARTINI ESCOLAR
1987   Trabajo doméstico y reproducción social: Un estudio de caso en la
         colonia Santa Ursula Xitla. Master's thesis, Escuela Nacional de
         Antropología e Historia, Mexico City.
SANTOS, JOSE VINCENTE TAVARES
1978   *Colonos do vinho — Estudo sobre a subordinação do trabalho campo-
         nês ao capital.* São Paulo: Editora Hucitec.
SAPORTA STERNBACH, NANCY, MARYSA NAVARRO-ARANGUREN,
PATRICIA CHUCHRYK, and SONIA E. ALVAREZ
1992   Feminisms in Latin America: From Bogotá to San Bernadino. In Esco-
         bar and Alvarez 1992.
SARTI, CYNTHIA
1989   The Panorama of Feminism in Brazil. *New Left Review*, no. 179:
         75–90.

SCHIRMER, JENNIFER

1993a   Those Who Die for Life Cannot Be Called Dead: Women and Human
Rights Protest in Latin America. In Agosín 1993.

1993b   The Seeking of Truth and the Gendering of Consciousness: The
CO-MADRES of El Salvador and the CONAVIGUA Widows of Gua-
temala. In *"Viva": Women and Popular Protest in Latin America*, ed.
Sarah A. Radcliffe and Sallie Westwood. London: Routledge.

SCOTT, JAMES

1985   *Weapons of the Weak: Everyday Forms of Peasant Resistance.* New
Haven: Yale University Press.

1990   *Domination and the Arts of Resistance: Hidden Transcripts.* New
Haven: Yale University Press.

SIFUENTES OCEGUEDA, EMMA LORENA

1995   Mercados de fuerza de trabajo agrícolas en Nayarit (1970–1994).
Condiciones laborales, características socioeconómicas y demográfi-
cas de los jornaleros asalariados. *Revista de Investigación de la Universidad Autónoma de Nayarit* 1(1):37–81.

SILVA, PATRICIO

1990a   The Military Regime and Restructuring of Land Tenure (special issue
on Chile). *Latin American Perspectives* 18(1):15–32.

1990b   Agrarian Change under the Chilean Military Government. *Latin
American Research Review* 25(1):193–205.

SMITH, GAVIN

1991   The Production of Culture in Local Rebellion. In *Golden Ages, Dark
Ages: Imagining the Past in Anthropology and History*, ed. Jay
O'Brien and William Roseberry. Berkeley: University of California
Press.

SPINDEL, CHEYWA

1987   The Social Invisibility of Women's Work in Brazilian Agriculture. In
*Rural Women and State Policy: Feminist Perspectives on Latin Ameri-
can Agricultural Development*, ed. Carmen Diana Deere and Magdalena León. Boulder: Westview Press.

STACEY, JUDITH

1991   Can There Be a Feminist Ethnography? In *Women's Words: The Feminist Practice of Oral History*, ed. Sherna Berga Gluck and Daphne
Patai. New York: Routledge.

STAUDT, KATHLEEN

1990   Gender Politics in Bureaucracy: Theoretical Issues in Comparative
Perspective. In *Women, International Development, and Politics: The
Bureaucratic Mire*, ed. Kathleen Staudt. Philadelphia: Temple Univer-
sity Press.

STAVENHAGEN, RODOLFO

1986   Collective Agriculture and Capitalism in Mexico: A Way Out or a
Dead End? In *Modern Mexico: State, Economy, and Social Conflict*,
ed. Nora Hamilton and Timothy F. Harding. Latin American Perspectives Readers, vol. 1. Beverly Hills: Sage Publications.

STEPHEN, LYNN

1989   Popular Feminism in Mexico. *Z Magazine* 2:102–106.

1991   *Zapotec Women.* Austin: University of Texas Press.

1992   Women in Mexico's Popular Movements: Survival Strategies for Eco-
        logical and Economic Impoverishment. *Latin American Perspectives*
        10(1):73–96.

1993a   Challenging Gender Inequality: Grassroots Organizing among
        Women Rural Workers in Brazil and Chile. *Critique of Anthropology*
        13(1):33–55.

1993b   Gender and Class in Zapotec Households. *Anthropology of Work
        Review* 13(4):5–8

1994a   (ed.) *Hear My Testimony: María Teresa Tula, Human Rights Activist
        of El Salvador.* Boston: South End Press.

1994b   *Viva Zapata: Generation, Gender, and Historical Consciousness in
        the Reception of Ejido Reform in Oaxaca.* Ejido Reform Research
        Project, Transformation of Rural Mexico no. 6. La Jolla, Calif.: Cen-
        ter for U.S.-Mexican Studies.

1996a   Too Little Too Late: The Impact of Article 27 on Women in Oaxaca.
        In *The Reform of the Mexican Agrarian Reform*, ed. Laura Randall.
        New York: M. E. Sharpe.

1996b   Democracy for Whom? Women's Grassroots Political Activism in the
        1990s, Mexico City and Chiapas. In *Neoliberalism Revisited: Eco-
        nomic Restructuring and Mexico's Political Future*, ed. Gerardo
        Otero. Boulder: Westview Press.

1997   Pro-Zapatista and Pro-PRI: Resolving the Contradictions of Zapa-
        tismo in Rural Oaxaca. *Latin American Research Review* 32(2).

STEPHEN, LYNN, and JAMES DOW

1990   Introduction: Popular Religion in Mexico and Central America. In
        Class, Politics, and Popular Religion in Mexico and Central America,
        ed. Lynn Stephen and James Dow. Washington, D.C.: American
        Anthropological Association.

TUTINO, JOHN

1986   *From Insurrection to Revolution in Mexico: Social Bases of Agrarian
        Violence, 1750–1940.* Princeton: Princeton University Press.

UELC (Unión de Ejidos "Lázaro Cárdenas")

1989   Archivo de la Unión. Unidad Agrícola Industrial de la Mujer, de la
        Unión de Ejidos "Gral. Lázaro Cárdenas." Ahuacatlán, Nayarit.

1990   Archivo de la Unión. Coordinadora de UAIMs, Censo Básico de las
        Integrantes de la Unidad Agrícola Industrial para la Mujer del Ejido.
        Documents for San Jerónimo Jomulco, Heriberto Jara, San José de
        Gracia, Ahuacatlán, Tequepexpan, Ahualamo, Santa Isabel, Tetitlán,
        Uzeta, Marquesado, Zoatlán, La Ciénaga, Chapalilla, Ejido Jomulco.
        Ahuacatlán, Ixtlán del Río, Nayarit.

UELTZEN, STEFAN

1993   *Como salvadoreña que soy: Entrevistas con mujeres en la lucha.* San
        Salvador: Editorial Sombrero Azul, ASTAC.

VALDÉS, XIMENA

1987a   Los procesos de incorporación y exclusión de las mujeres del mercado de trabajo agrícola. In *Sinopsis de una realidad ocultada (Las trabajadoras del campo)*. Santiago de Chile: Centro de Estudios de la Mujer.

1987b   Hacia la generalización de las demandas de las trabajadoras del agro. In *Agricultura y sociedad* no. 5. Santiago de Chile: Grupo de Investigaciones Agrarias, Academia Humanidades Cristiano.

1988   Feminización del mercado de trabajo agrícola: Las temporeras. In *Mundo de mujer: Continuidad y cambio*. Santiago de Chile: Ediciones CEM.

1991   Entre la crisis de la uva y la esperanza en crisis: Mujeres temporeras en un proceso de sindicalización. Paper presented at the 47th Congress of Americanists, New Orleans, July.

1992   Mujer, trabajo y medio ambiente: Los nudos de la modernización agraria. Santiago de Chile: Centro de Estudios para el Desarrollo de la Mujer.

VÁSQUEZ GARCÍA, VERÓNICA

1995   Native Women and the State: The Politics of Exclusion. Paper presented at the Learned Societies Conference, Montreal, June.

VENEGAS LEIVA, SYLVIA

1992   Una gota al día . . . Un chorro al año . . . El impacto social de la expansión fruticultura. Santiago de Chile: Grupo de Estudios Agro-regionales.

VENEGAS LEIVA, SYLVIA, and CLAUDIA SEPÚLVEDA L.

1991   Bases para una discusión sobre la participación urbana en el trabajo fruticultura. Estudios Agrarios no. 17. Santiago de Chile: Grupo de Estudios Agro-regionales.

VERA, OSCAR

1987   *La economía subterránea en México*. Mexico City: Editorial Diana.

VILLARREAL, MAGDALENA

1994a   Wielding and Yielding: Power, Subordination and Gender Identity in the Context of a Mexican Development Project. Ph.D. thesis, Department of Rural Sociology, University of Wageningen. Koninklijke Bibliotheek, Den Haag.

1994b   Mujeres campesinas, el estado y la construcción social del poder. Paper presented at a conference "Las disputas por el México rural: Transformaciones de prácticas, identidades y proyectos," Colegio de Michoacán, Zamora, Michoacán, November.

WARD, PETER

1994   Social Welfare Policy and Political Opening in Mexico. In Cornelius, Craig, and Fox 1994.

WESTWOOD, SALLIE, and SARAH RADCLIFFE

1993   Gender, Racism, and the Politics of Identities in Latin America. In *"Viva": Women and Popular Protest in Latin America*, ed. Sarah A. Radcliffe and Sallie Westwood. London: Routledge.

Women's Regional Council of the CONAMUP
1991   Centro de Mujeres de la Regional de Mujeres de la Coordinadora
        Nacional del Movimiento Urbano Popular. Grant proposal.

YANAGISAKO, SYLVIA JUNKO, and JANE FISHBURNE COLLIER
1987   Toward a Unified Analysis of Kinship and Gender. In *Gender and
        Kinship: Essays toward a Unified Analysis*, ed. Jane Fishburne Collier
        and Sylvia Junko Yanagisako. Stanford: Stanford University Press.

ZAVALA DE COSÍO, M. E.
1992   *Cambios de fecundidad en México y políticas de población.* Mexico
        City: Colegio de México.

ZAVELLA, PATRICIA
1991   *Mujeres* in Factories: Race and Class Perspectives on Women, Work,
        and Family. In *Gender at the Crossroads of Knowledge: Feminist
        Anthropology in a Postmodern Era*, ed. Micaela di Leonardo. Berke-
        ley: University of California Press.

INDEX